Administration Procedures

for

Higher Secretarial Diplomas

Lesley Jefferson

and

Sue Sealy

Heinemann Educational Publishers
Halley Court, Jordan Hill, Oxford OX2 8EJ
Part of Harcourt Education

Heinemann is a registered trademark of
Harcourt Education Limited

First published 1999
2006 2005 2004 2003
10 9 8 7 6 5 4 3

A catalogue record for this book is available from the British Library on request.

ISBN 0 435 45513 3

Cover and pages designed by Sarah Garbett

Typeset by ⫪ Tek-Art, Croydon, Surrey

Printed and bound in Great Britain by Biddles Ltd, *www.biddles.co.uk*

DEDICATION

This book is dedicated to the memories of Dr Alan Jefferson and Mrs Joan Esworthy.

ACKNOWLEDGEMENTS

I would like to thank colleagues at Coleg Glan Hafren and many other friends, family and neighbours who encouraged me and offered support and help. I would particularly like to thank my father, Morris Preston who helped with the proofreading, and Sue Sealy for her help and support and contributions.

Lesley Jefferson

To Lesley – who heard my frustrated remark, 'I could write a book!' and replied with a challenge – for the opportunity to assist with this book. While teaching me so much about writing, she also ensured my computer skills were upgraded. Many thanks for the lesson.

Sue Sealy

CONTENTS

INTRODUCTION

This book has been written for candidates undertaking the Higher Diploma in Administrative Procedures scheme offered by OCR. The unit and element titles in the book correspond to those in the scheme. The book can also be used to support LCCIEB's Business Administration Level 4 award as part of its Executive Secretary's Diploma.

The book has been designed to give candidates the knowledge and understanding they need for the Higher Diploma in Administrative Procedures as well as the information required to enable them to address the performance criteria and evidence requirements for each element.

- Each unit starts with an introduction giving a brief overview of that unit's contents.

- At the end of each element, **Test yourself** questions enable candidates to verify that they have firm grasp of the knowledge and understanding necessary for that particular element.

- Each unit contains **Portfolio activities** that give candidates an opportunity to collect evidence that can then be used to claim competence. Each activity includes a checklist of the performance criteria, knowledge and understanding and evidence requirements that it meets.

- **In-tray activities** provide task-based examination practice in line with LCCIEB's Business Administration Level 4 award.

This book has been written to cover the requirements of administrative diplomas at a higher level, however, there may be times when an administrator needs more detailed and specialist information on other subjects, such as personnel and finance. This information is available in a wide range of specialist books, journals and other sources, all of which will be available in a college or general library. A list of additional reference materials has not been included in the book because new books and journal articles are constantly being published; legislation changes frequently; the areas covered are very wide-ranging; and it is difficult to anticipate the nature of all specialist enquiries that candidates might be making.

Even after competence has been achieved and accredited, it is hoped that this book will be retained by candidates for its practical guidance and support for practising administrators.

Lesley Jefferson

Sue Sealey

STUDENT GUIDE

The Higher Diploma in Administrative Procedures scheme is a level 4 scheme offered by OCR and aims to assess the application of the knowledge and skills that are needed to perform a wide range of administration, secretarial and organisational skills.

Your course will involve learning the relevant knowledge and understanding; showing you can attain the performance criteria and collecting the evidence that will prove your competence in the areas of administration covered by the scheme.

You will need to:

- meet with your assessor initially to decide on an **overall plan** of assessment and training
- ensure you have the relevant **knowledge and understanding** to undertake the tasks involved
- meet with your assessor regularly to discuss **individual plans** of evidence collection for specific elements
- **collect evidence** of your competence in the relevant areas
- **check** that **your evidence** meets the requirements listed in the standards
- collect together all your evidence into a **portfolio**
- **record where the evidence can be found**, cross-referencing this with the performance criteria, knowledge and understanding and evidence requirements that it demonstrates or fulfils.

Establishing an overall plan

Your assessor

As part of the Higher Diploma in Administrative Procedures, all your work will be marked by your assessor – usually you tutor. Your assessor will evaluate your evidence to ensure it proves your competence in all the areas covered by the award.

Action plan and timetable

Your assessor is the first person you should see to discuss the best way to obtain evidence for the award. During your first meeting with your assessor, you should establish an action plan that carefully details the activities you need to undertake to obtain evidence.

When working through this book – and indeed through the course – it is not necessary to start at the beginning and work your way through the whole book. It is a good idea to read units 1 and 10 when you start your course as evidence for these units is collected throughout all the other activities. It is therefore useful for you to collect and record the evidence for these units in particular on an ongoing basis.

When planning the remaining order in which you intend to undertake the units, it is advisable to read the introduction to each unit and also a copy of the standards. This will give you an overview of the content of each unit. After discussion with your assessor and/or employer, you should then be able to plan a suitable programme.

You can compare the units to your planned work activities over the next 6–18 months (depending on the length of your course). For example, a promotional activity might be planned for the end of the year and you could use this to collect evidence for several units.

Whichever elements are looked at first, you should ensure you consistently record where the evidence of your competence can be found and cross-reference this with the performance criteria, knowledge and understanding and evidence requirements specified for each element.

It is a good idea to also set a timetable for completing units – this should make it easier to plan your work and will also help you check your progress as you go along.

Creating individual plans

You should meet with your assessor on a regular basis to establish smaller plans for specific units and activities. Your assessor can check your progress so far and advise on suitable activities that you can undertake in order to collect the relevant evidence. Figure 0.1 shows an example of an action plan.

Action Plan

Name of candidate	Raymond Watkins
Name of Assessor	Harjit Singh
Date	12 March ----
Qualification	RSA Higher Diploma in Administrative Procedures
Element	6.1 Evaluate an Information Storage and Retrieval System

Discussion

Various projects were discussed for this element, in particular the possibility of developing a computerised database to store staff training records. The following actions were agreed:

1. Arrange meeting with Jane Hammond, Head of Personnel to discuss and agree the project – by 21 March.
2. Arrange a meeting with Phil Yelland, Senior Training Officer to discuss and agree the project – by 21 March.
3. Draft 'Terms of Reference' for the report following meetings.
4. Find out about the Data Protection Act and how it applies to staff records. Look at company procedures and check the Internet for full information on the Data Protection Act. Summarise findings to form an appendix for the report – by 30 March.
5. Research suitable software/hardware to store training records – contact the IT department, check software currently available in the company, discuss with IT lecturer at college – by 30 March.

---

6 Investigate storage of current staff training records – by 30 March.

7 Next meeting 2 April to review progress and prepare further actions.

| Signed | *Harjit Singh* | Assessor | 12 March |
| Signed | *Raymond Watkins* | Candidate | 12 March |

Figure 0.1 An action plan

Assessment

Internal verification

As your assessment and tutoring is an ongoing process, this will be checked by an internal verifier. The internal verifier will be someone from within the college who will check that your assessor is both assessing your portfolio to the correct standard and providing you with adequate support and guidance. The internal verifier may:

- interview candidates to check their progress
- observe assessors carrying out assessment-planning sessions; observing candidates and giving feedback
- review portfolios during the course
- review portfolios at the end of the course, or before the external verifier visits.

External verification

The awarding body (OCR) will also arrange for an external verifier to visit your centre. The external verifier has a similar role to the internal verifier; checking the quality of the assessment and agreeing certification. They may ask to meet candidates and portfolios will need to be available for them to assess.

As both the assessment and verification process run throughout the course, it is important to meet with your assessor, update your action plans and check your evidence on a regular basis.

Collecting evidence

Prior achievement

When you read through the standards, you may find elements and units that you have already covered, perhaps in previous employment. If this is the case, you should discuss it with your assessor.

You will need to think about what evidence you can collect to show your competence. If your experience is with your current employer, then this should not be very difficult – copies of correspondence, documents, diaries and witness testimonies can be collected and given to your assessor for checking. If you covered the activity with a previous employer, you will need to think about how much evidence you will be able to collect and you should discuss this with your assessor.

When collecting evidence from prior achievement it is important to show that your competence is up to date, as the impact of technology and new working practices mean that the working environment is constantly changing. This is usually referred to as 'currency' – the general rule for the timescale of currency is 2 years.

Real work

To achieve accreditation for some of the activities, evidence needs to be generated through real work. If you are attending a college course, then opportunities can be identified within the college such as organising departmental meetings, organising travel arrangement for staff and preparing a budget for a training course.

Simulated activities

Simulated activities may be used as evidence in certain elements and this should be checked against the scheme.

Types of evidence

There are various different types of evidence that you can collect. Many of these are mentioned in the book. Evidence usually falls into the following categories.

Product evidence. This describes the actual documents that you produce as evidence – for example, itineraries, minutes of meetings, letters, telephone messages, e-mail messages, etc. You should sign and date the evidence to show it is your work, and you should also get a supervisor/colleague to date and sign it to confirm that this is the case. When your assessor has assessed it they should also date and sign it.

Observation reports. Your assessor should observe you carrying out relevant activities and should record this on an observation report. This is particularly useful for those activities that are difficult to evidence with products – for example, participating in a meeting; interviewing a job applicant; giving feedback to a trainee.

Witness testimonies. These are statements written by supervisors, colleagues or trainees to support your competence. They are particularly useful to confirm that you have carried out activities over a period of time, following your organisation's procedures and within deadlines. They should be prepared on headed paper, include the author's name and organisational title, and should be dated and signed by the author. It can often be difficult to get busy people to write witness testimonies and it may be helpful to them if you get the agreement to providing a witness testimony and then draft the statement for them. They will then only need the time to check it through and to sign the final version.

Personal statements/case histories. You can write a statement explaining how and why you carried out activities. These form a very useful source of evidence and can be used to reference other evidence. They should, where possible, be prepared on headed paper, signed and dated by yourself, authenticated by witnesses and signed by your assessor. Figure 0.2 shows an example of a personal statement.

Element 4.2

Prepare travel documentation

In my job at Granmere Holdings, I am Personal Assistant to Miss Jane French, Sales Director. Miss French regularly makes trips both in the UK and overseas. I regularly book all the travel for her and prepare the documents and papers she needs (see Witness Testimony 35).

After we returned from our Christmas break, Jane told me that she was planning to go to a sales conference in Los Angeles, USA at Easter. I met regularly with Jane to discuss the arrangements (see Personal Statement 25). I kept Jane informed about all the arrangements and gave her copies of all the confirmation and booking documents. Jane is a vegetarian and I included this in all the appropriate booking documentation (see Evidences 12, 13, 14, 15 and 16).

I prepared a detailed itinerary (see Evidence 17) which included information about all arrangements for the trip from door to door. I also included the information about a visit she was making to see a friend in America while there on business. Jane likes full and detailed briefing notes for her visit. I prepared three separate sheets of briefing notes.

- Evidence 18 shows the general information about visits to America, including information on driving, medical information, etc.
- Evidence 19 shows notes about the sales conference with the names of contacts, companies, information that she needed to follow up and details of appointments that had been made.
- Evidence 20 shows the notes about attractions, restaurants, etc. that Jane might like to visit while there. She is particularly interested in art and I included information on the arrangements to visit the Getty centre in Los Angeles.

About a week before Jane was due to go, I put together a travel pack for her. This included the itinerary, briefing notes, conference details, flight tickets, hire car details, medical insurance documents and a guide book (see Supplementary Evidence).

I also prepared a checklist for Jane to ensure that she packed her appropriate personal items – for example, passport, driving licence, vaccination certificates (see Evidence 21).

I prepared all the documents using a word processor.

Signed _ _ _ _ _ _ _ _ _ _ _ _ _ _ _ _ _ _ (Candidate)   Date _ _ _ _ _ _ _

Signed _ _ _ _ _ _ _ _ _ _ _ _ _ _ _ _ _ _ (Jane French)   Date _ _ _ _ _ _ _

Signed _ _ _ _ _ _ _ _ _ _ _ _ _ _ _ _ _ _ (Assessor)   Date _ _ _ _ _ _ _

Figure 0.2 A personal statement

Answers to questions. You should include either written answers to questions, or your assessor's records of oral questioning sessions.

Videos, tape recordings. These can be included, but you must check that they are carefully labelled and that assessors and verifiers will have access to suitable equipment to check them.

Photographs. These are a useful form of evidence – for example, photographs of presentation stands at conferences or other events. They should include an explanation of what is shown in the picture and your participation in the event.

Accreditation of prior achievement. If you are claiming accreditation for prior achievement you need to check that the evidence will be admissible and that you can get signatures and witness testimonies to confirm your competency. You should also check with your assessor the currency of your prior achievement.

Learning knowledge and understanding

You should use this book and other sources of information – including your assessor – to gain the required knowledge and understanding of each unit. Use the Test Yourself questions at the end of each element to test yourself on how much you know. If there are any weak areas, reread the section in the book and try and find some more information from elsewhere – for example, the college library, your assessor, the Internet.

Checking your evidence

You should check that your evidence meets the requirements set out in the standards, and this checking should be an ongoing basis. When you are collecting evidence, check each piece to see which performance criteria, knowledge and understanding and evidence requirements it meets (remember that many pieces of evidence will meet requirements from a number of different units) and tick these off on a checklist – perhaps writing in the number or code you have given that piece of evidence. Ensure you have included all relevant cross-references.

Putting together a portfolio

A completed portfolio is a file of all the evidence you have collecting and will cover all aspects of the award.

The first section of your portfolio should give some background information about yourself, such as your curriculum vitae and job description (if appropriate).

Each unit and element should then follow, in the order of the scheme and should contain the following documents.

Evidence record sheets. You must make sure that all the evidence you provide is clearly tracked in the evidence record sheet against the specific performance criteria, knowledge and understanding and evidence requirements given in the standards. If you update this record with each new piece of evidence it should be easy to see where you have any gaps.

Evidence. This should be neatly filed and clearly labelled. Evidence may be numbered on a continuous basis – for example, 1–250 – as it is collected, and then referenced. Alternatively, it may be filed in unit/element sections – for example, 6.1.1 would be Unit 6, Element 1, Evidence number 1. Evidence is often filed in a lever-arch file.

Every piece of evidence you include should be relevant to the award: try to avoid collecting large amounts of printed papers, leaflets, booklets, etc. – for example, company leaflets, hotel publicity materials. If these are relevant you can include them in your evidence in two ways. The first is to write a note explaining how and why you used them, attach them to the relevant document and include this in your evidence. The second is to file them in a 'supplementary folder'.

Supplementary evidence folders. These may be used to include items of evidence that may not be directly relevant to your competence, but which show sources of information, learning activities, etc. You may wish, for example, to include company information, timetables, company procedures, etc in this file. You may also have completed learning activities during the course that you would like to include and the may be kept in a supplementary evidence folder.

Note: Although plastic 'poly' pockets to keep evidence clean and tidy and avoid having to hole-punch papers, if you do use these, then you should only include two sheets of paper – one to be viewed from each side. If you include multiple sheets in one pocket, assessors and verifiers will need to take them out to check the evidence, which can be very time consuming.

Golden rules of evidence collection

- Always collect evidence as you are going along. Do not think, 'I will collect that later,' as this can become very time-consuming.
- Always get evidence signed and authenticated as you go along. Do not let supervisors or colleagues say that they will sign it all at the end. People move jobs, leave employment and get sick, all of which can make it very difficult to authenticate evidence at a late stage.
- Always file, reference and cross-reference evidence as you go along: this will give you a clear picture of your progress and make your evidence collection more efficient as you will be able to identify 'gaps' on the evidence grids. Do not leave it until the end of the course as this can be very daunting and you are likely to discover that you have unknowingly missed out a lot.
- Only include one copy of a piece of evidence in your portfolio and then correctly cross-reference. There is no point in including multiple copies of evidence in portfolios as this only makes them bulky and repetitive.
- Set a timetable for completing units – although evidence may be collected that can be cross-referenced across the whole qualification, it is a good idea to have targets for completing units – for example, Unit 4 Organise Business Trips by the end of April. It is very motivating to see units being signed off.

1 Manage Business Communications

Communication is the oil that greases the engine of business. Good communications enable business to operate efficiently and effectively, facilitating the exchange of accurate and meaningful information. The focus of this unit is the management of all aspects of communication that you may carry out in your job role. Element 1.1 covers oral and electronic communication, while Element 1.2 covers a comprehensive range of written communications.

Effective communication

Communication is a two-way process and effective communication has taken place when both the sender and recipient have a clear and common understanding of a message. In oral communication, hearing is not the same as listening. Listening implies that the recipient is concentrating on the message. The ability of the recipient to listen to the message is affected by 'interference'. The greater the interference, the less likely it is that the recipient will clearly understand the message. Interference can be affected by the following.

The clarity of the message being sent. The more confused and ambiguous the message, the less clear the recipient's understanding will be.

The accuracy of the message. Mistakes and inaccuracies in the message can lead to mistaken assumptions or the need for further communication to clarify inaccuracies.

The medium used to send the message. Selecting the most appropriate method of transmission can help both the sender and the recipient to clearly understand the message. For example, if you are sending lists of order numbers, prices, dates and times, etc. it is more appropriate to send them by a written form of communication such as a fax.

The environment of the sender and recipient. Sending or receiving a message in a noisy, busy environment can lead to considerable interference. Think how difficult it can be to carry out a telephone conversation in a room with several photocopiers that are producing copies; or in a busy reception office where a number of people are waiting with urgent enquiries. These problems are increased when the message is complex.

The directness of the message. The more stages a message goes through before being sent and received, the more likely it is that problems in understanding will arise. You may be familiar with the game of 'Chinese Whispers', and the same distorting effect can arise when messages are passed through various different staff in an organisation.

The hidden elements of the message. The 80/20 principle applies to messages. Only twenty per cent of our understanding of a message comes from the actual content of the message. Eighty per cent of our understanding stems from the perception of other signals that come with the message.

This is a complex area of understanding human behaviour. We unconsciously 'read' a range of complex factors like tone of voice, body language, quality of paper, choice of words, method of transmission and use these signals to inform our understanding of a message. Think about the impression you would gain of an organisation if you arrived for an interview in a badly organised reception area where you were met by an untidy receptionist who ignored you while they were on the telephone. Your judgement about any further facts or information you were given about the organisation would be coloured by your first impression.

State of mind of the recipient. Our perception of these hidden messages is further complicated by our personal state of mind at the time we receive the message. If you arrive at reception in a good mood because it is a sunny day and you are generally happy with life you are far more likely to be positive in your thinking than if you arrive after a difficult journey where you were held up in a traffic jam on a wet day and the bus conductor was rude to you.

Communication should be effective and efficient. Fully effective communication is achieved when the recipient has received and understood accurate, relevant, up-to-date and sufficient information to enable business activities to proceed smoothly. Efficient communication has been achieved when this has happened within an appropriate timescale, safely and cost-effectively.

Planning and Management

Careful planning and management of business communications aims to maximise the effectiveness of the message by eliminating the interference. This can be achieved in a number of ways. Firstly, by sending clear messages that contain relevant, current and sufficient information. It is essential to ensure all messages are accurate. Of equal importance is selecting the most appropriate method of transmission and using it correctly. It is vital that you receive and send messages in an appropriate environment – for example, in a quiet office. When taking a message for someone else, you must check that the information you are passing on is accurate and that you send it directly. Aim to control the hidden elements of a message to give a positive image and reduce any negative images that may adversely affect understanding. This can be done, for example, by making sure that the presentation and tone of the message is appropriate.

Communications are more effective if the most appropriate method or type of communication is chosen. Information can be given orally, or in writing. It may be prepared in the form of a report, memorandum or letter. It can be transmitted by fax, post or e-mail. The factors that affect the appropriateness of the choice are as follows.

- *Content* – for example: information exchanged between colleagues may be sent in the form of a memorandum; research findings for a project may be presented in a report; urgent internal messages may be sent by e-mail.
- *Recipient s needs* – for example: urgent information about a product required by a customer may be sent by fax; statistical findings to be shown to a group of people may be presented in the form of a graph on an overhead projector.
- *Security* – for example: internal confidential information may be prepared in the form of a memorandum and sent in a sealed envelope marked confidential; sensitive information may not be given out over the telephone.
- *Urgency and cost* – for example: urgent information may be sent by fax; e-mail is cheaper than fax for sending urgent information long distances; fast parcel and international postal services are more expensive than slower services.

This unit looks at communications and looks at the different ways of preparing and sending information. Its aim is to provide the background information to support the selection of the most appropriate type of communication.

Element 1.1

PLAN AND CARRY OUT ORAL AND ELECTRONIC BUSINESS COMMUNICATIONS

The introduction considered communications in general. The word 'message' was used in its most general sense relating to the information being transferred from the sender to the recipient. The word 'message' in this unit is used more specifically to relate to 'verbal messages' – for example, when you receive a telephone message that you need to pass on to a third person, or when a colleague verbally asks you to pass information on to a third person.

The first part of this element looks at using oral methods of communication; later we look at electronic methods.

Oral communication

Oral communication means the same as verbal communication and is literally the 'spoken word'. It is the main method of communication that we use in our business and private lives. It can be divided into face-to-face communication and telephone communication.

Face-to-face communication

Face-to-face communication is the most common form of communication. It allows for the direct exchange of information between participants and can range from an individual interview to a group meeting. It may occur in both formal and informal situations.

Advantages
Face-to-face communication allows for the exchange of views and checking of understanding: the signals sent out through body language can be used to check understanding or read people's reactions to ideas. Face-to-face communication gives you more control over the environment in which the exchange takes place: meeting rooms and venues for meetings can be booked and used.

A range of audio-visual aids and different materials can be used in face-to-face communication to facilitate understanding.

Disadvantages

In face-to-face communication, it may be necessary to respond quickly to difficult questions. Meetings and discussions may need careful control to allow all participants to make a meaningful contribution. On occasion there may be no written record of the outcome of the communication – for example, minutes of meetings, action plans, and appraisal documents. Geographic location and distance can cause problems: travelling and accommodation costs can make face-to-face communication expensive. There is also a hidden cost in the time participants spend travelling to meetings during which they are unable to carry out their routine work. The time needed to arrange and gather people for a meeting may result in a delay in the exchange of information.

Types

Informal

Informal face-to-face communication includes daily face-to-face contact with an internal line manager; informal meetings with teams, work groups and colleagues; chance meetings in the corridor or in-house restaurant.

Formal

Formal communication includes for example:

- structured meetings – committee meetings, customer/client meetings
- interviews – appraisal interviews, job interviews
- presentations – presenting the findings of a report, presenting information about new procedures to colleagues
- training sessions – demonstrations of new equipment, practical training sessions with new computer software
- teleconferencing – for example, video and audio conferencing meetings.

Purposes

You may be asked by a colleague for the name of a good hotel in a local town; you may give a presentation to a committee meeting on your proposals for a new filing system; you may have a discussion with a colleague about how to deal with the problem of the photocopier regularly breaking down. Whatever the reason, most face-to-face communication falls into one of the following categories: giving and receiving instructions; giving and receiving information; responding to requests for information; requesting information from others; discussing ideas and views; agreeing and allocating actions; resolving difficulties and problems.

Procedures
General rules
Social interaction can be an important part of an organisation's culture if used correctly. Asking after people's health and families can show that you take an interest in staff and can help to build relationships. However, this should always be kept brief and at a professional level. Do not waste time 'gossiping'. You should especially not engage in gossip about other members of staff, either about their private or professional lives. Whatever information you exchange should always be kept confidential.

Be polite. It may seem obvious to say that you should use words like 'please' and 'thank you', but it is surprising how many people take the help of their colleagues for granted. Staff at all levels will respond to requests for help more readily if they feel that their efforts are valued. It is also important to make sure that you mean these words when you say them. If you are not careful your body language may cause staff to read other messages into what you say.

Be professional. Use language of an appropriate style and tone for a business organisation. Swearing, slang and very casual language are not appropriate in the office. Adjust your language to suit your audience – for example, you might be more informal with colleagues, but require a higher level of formality with customers and senior colleagues.

Choose your language carefully. Use correct technical language where appropriate, but avoid overuse of jargon. Judge your audience carefully and decide what level of technical language is appropriate. It is very easy to exclude people from discussions by overuse of technical words, acronyms and abbreviations. Imagine answering the following question before you started your course: 'Are you doing HDAP, HDASP or NVQ Administration Level 4?'

Always be tidy and appropriately dressed. You may need to take special care with your appearance when you are representing your organisation in an external situation – for example, at conferences or sales meetings.

Be aware of body language. Do not adopt stances that are threatening, or too submissive. Look at people when you are talking to them. Confirm orally that the communication has finished, rather than just start doing other activities. Body language can also be used to convey messages – for example, you can make it clear that you are busy concentrating on an activity if a colleague approaches you to gossip.

House style

Forms of address. Follow the in-house protocols for addressing colleagues and customers. There are wide variations in methods of address depending on the type of organisation, the age range of the employees and the business activity. In a software company with young employees, for example, first-name terms for all staff may be standard practice. In other organisations, you may call your immediate colleagues by their first name, but would use more formal methods of address for senior staff and external contacts. If you are attending a meeting with senior colleagues, important guests or visitors, it is important to check the correct form of address in advance with colleagues.

Dress code. Follow the in-house style for formality. Your particular role within the organisation may also determine your dress style. Staff who meet the public would generally follow a more formal dress code. When organising social events – for example, a dinner as part of a conference – it is important to be clear about the dress code required. You may receive requests from guests about suitable dress codes and you need to give clear, accurate information.

Meeting procedures. Each organisation may have its own procedures for conducting meetings. These should cover use of venues, methods of address during the meeting and appropriate recording procedures. These procedures may be established as custom and practice, or may be written in procedure documents. When you start in a new job role, you should check the procedures for different types of meetings. Unit 2 discusses meetings (pages 55–91), and much of your evidence for face-to-face communication can be gained from participating in these meetings.

Cultural differences. Special care should be taken with dress code and other cultural protocols when meeting overseas colleagues, clients and visitors. You should check the following information.

* *Dress* – in some cultures bare arms and legs are not acceptable. The rules for men and women may vary.
* *Physical contact* – handshakes, hugging, etc. may be part of normal greeting procedures.
* *Body language* – the codes for eye contact and the messages given by hand gestures can vary between cultures.
* *Business practice* – accepted business practice may vary between

cultures – for example, it may be standard business practice to exchange business cards at an initial meeting.

You need to research this information if you or colleagues are working with overseas clients and visitors. This is particularly important if you are helping to arrange an overseas visit for a colleague. This is discussed in more detail in Unit 4 (page 204) and Unit 8 (page 406).

Organising information

A good administrator will have a logical and organised method for recording information they collect during the course of their work. It is a good idea to have the following three basic desk books.

Name and address book. This is an alphabet-edged notebook in which you record names and locations of staff you meet and key people you telephone and correspond with. When you look up a telephone number, you should record it in the book. This saves looking up numbers later. Personal organisers usually have an indexed section in which you can store this type of information. Alternatively you can store information on your computer using address book software.

Key word book. This is useful if you work in a technical environment. You should record key technical words and terms that you come across during the course of your work. You can also have a section in it to record words that you look up in the dictionary. If your work is not very technical in nature, the two sections can be combined. Alternatively you can add technical words to the custom dictionary of your word processor's spellchecker.

Log book. When you have asked staff for information about procedures, house styles, etc. you should take notes and check the information back with them to ensure your notes are accurate. It is a good idea to use a 'log book' and write down information you have been given straight away. You can then refer to your log book at a later date. You should not try to remember information and write it down later. In a busy working environment your attention can easily be diverted and you can quickly forget information.

Portfolio activity 1.1 **Number 1**

Think about ways in which you can record your oral communications during the course of your work, to include in your evidence.

Design a log sheet to record communications. This should include:

- date of the communication
- participants in the communication – their names and titles
- whether the communication is face-to-face or telephone
- whether the communication is informal or formal
- details of the type of communication – for example, incoming call, outgoing call, informal discussion with colleague
- purpose of the communication – for example, to exchange information, give instructions
- brief confirmation that you checked the content of messages you received, and that you checked that others understood messages you left
- any difficulties encountered during the communication, and how these were dealt with
- brief explanation of why you chose that form of communication in relation to urgency, cost, content, security and recipient's needs
- signature of any witness to the communication.

Produce copies of this log sheet and complete it to record your oral communications. Attach any copies of relevant notes or other written materials that relate to the communication.

Note
You should collect the evidence for this unit when you are completing the activities for the other units – for example, **Unit 2 Organise and Administer Business Meetings and Appointments.** It should not be necessary to simulate any activities for this unit.

Performance criteria:	1.1.1	1.1.2	1.1.3	1.1.4	1.1.7
	1.1.8				
Knowledge and understanding:	1.1.a	1.1.i	1.1.m		
Evidence requirements:	1.1.1	1.1.13	1.1.14	1.1.15	

Telephone communication

A key feature of business communication is the telephone. For any organisation, the telephone is one of the major links with the outside world. These days, more and more business is being conducted over the telephone – for example, you can carry out banking transactions, buy goods, arrange a loan or mortgage, organise insurance, get legal advice. Telephone technology is rapidly advancing to offer a wide range of facilities – for example, automatic call back, voicemail, call routing, etc.

Advantages
- If the person you are calling is available it is quick; and if they are not available you can leave a message, or arrange a call back as soon as the telephone is free.
- Mobile phone technology also means you can make direct contact with people when they are out of the office. You can get in direct personal contact with people, which means you will be certain they have received the information
- It is relatively cheap providing calls are kept brief. It is also cheaper than travelling to meetings.
- Conference calls can be arranged so that groups of people can take part in conversations.

Disadvantages
- If you are discussing complex details, then errors can occur. You will have no written record of the communication.
- International calls can be expensive at peak times.
- Security can be a problem, as you may not be able to establish accurately the identity of the caller.
- If either person cannot be heard clearly, then messages may be interpreted incorrectly.

Service providers
The privatisation of the telephone network system has increased the number of telephone service providers available – for example, Cabletel, British Telecom (BT), Cable and Wireless.

Tariffs
The tariff charged for telephone calls will depend on:

- your telephone service provider and their charging policies
- the distance and length of your call
- special offers – for example, BT's Friends and Family
- call rates – some organisations provide call services at different rates: Freefone, 0800 and 0500 numbers can be dialled at no cost to the caller; 0345 and 0645 numbers can be dialled at the cost of a local call; premium rate 0891, 0893 and 0881 numbers are charged at higher rates – however, the rates charged for these calls must be clearly displayed with details of the premium service.

Telephone services
Information services

There is a range of telephone information services available. These may be charged at local call rates or premium rates. The following are some examples of information services.

- *Weather and travel information* – these are useful when arranging road travel.
- *Talking pages* – these give details of businesses throughout the country. It is not always feasible to have Yellow Pages for every geographic area, but by phoning Talking Pages it is possible to access lists of businesses in other towns – for example, if you were arranging business travel or a venue for a meeting, you might want the name of a restaurant or hotel in another town.
- *Directory enquiries* – if you know the name and location of a company or individual, directory enquiries (192) can provide you with their telephone number. There is a set charge for a maximum of two enquiries.

Telephone directories

Internal. Using the telephone in an organisation is more efficient when you have up-to-date directories. Internal directories are usually prepared in-house and often provide valuable information about locations and titles of staff as well as their telephone numbers. You should try to keep your directory up-to-date as staff changes are made. If you work in a multi-site organisation, it is useful to have directories for the other sites. Organisations with an intranet may also have a telephone/address directory accessible through the computer. These are referred to as Intranet systems which will be discussed in more detail in the section on the Internet (see page 31).

External. BT provides a comprehensive service of external directory services for residential and business listings.

- *Standard paper local telephone listing* – customers are sent a free copy of the book in which their entry appears. A copy of an adjacent area will also be provided free on request.
- *National telephone books* – these can be purchased from BT individually, in regional sets or as a complete collection. The books may be paperback or hardback (they are the same as the books that people in the region receive free).
- *Phone Book Index* – this lists the phone directories for any location in the UK and can be purchased from BT.
- *Phone Book Companion* – this lists the UK area codes, international

codes and a national code decoder (where you can look up the code and find the area it refers to) and can also be purchased from BT.

- *Electronic directories* – the complete collection of telephone directories can be purchased from BT on CD-ROM for either a stand-alone PC or for use on a Local Area Network (LAN). For organisations that regularly need access to national numbers, this provides a very cost-effective service. A CD-ROM takes up far less space than a set of directories, and can be regularly replaced with up-dated copies.
- *Directory-on-line service* – organisations can search the BT database on-line, using a PC and a modem. This service is very useful for organisations that require occasional access to national numbers. No initial cost outlay is required and the only charge for this service is the cost of the call made to the database.
- *International directories* – overseas phone, fax and telex number directories are also available from BT.

External telephone directories also provide other useful information – for example, BT services, Helpline numbers, international time zones, local MPs and MEPs.

Full information about BT directory services can be found at the back of the telephone directory.

Trade. Trade directories are also available. These classify organisations according to their trade activities – for example, caterers, restaurants, hotels, conference facilities. The listings may be basic names and addresses, or advertisements which include more information about the services offered by an organisation.

Advertisements in trade directories can include information about the trade and professional bodies to which organisations belong. These bodies vary in the services they provide for their members and other customers. They may be formed from a collection of organisations from similar trades. Some bodies regulate and inspect their members to ensure quality standards are maintained. They may also offer arbitration services for complaints from customers. The telephone numbers of the head offices of these bodies are usually provided in the directory and you can call these to find out more information. This information can form part of a decision-making process when choosing suppliers of goods and services.

The following trade directories are the most commonly used.

- *Yellow Pages* – a comprehensive regional trade directory available in paper format or on-line.

- *Thomson local directories* – contains information for a smaller local area – for example, local area guides, maps, entertainment guide, A-Z of businesses, classified directory.
- *Specific trade directories* – these are available for specific trades and are usually provided by the trade organisation.

Telephone systems

Telephone systems will vary depending on the size and type of an organisation, but usually consist of a central unit and a number of lines and handsets.

Central unit

A central unit is usually computerised or automated. In a large organisation this may be linked to a switchboard, but in a small business the central unit may be a key telephone. This receives the incoming and outgoing calls and routes them to the correct location. The following facilities may be available on the central unit.

Monitoring and listing of calls. Every call made can be monitored and listed. Detailed analysis of calls can provide the cost of telephone usage for individual users and/or departments. This information can then be used to allocate project costs and determine budgets. It can also be used to check telephone misuse.

Programming of extension numbers. Direct access to frequently used local, national and international numbers can be programmed for each extension.

Call barring. Restrictions on access to international calls should reduce the misuse of the telephone for such calls, as any long distance connections would have to be made through the switchboard.

Queuing. Incoming calls are answered with a recorded message and placed in a queue. Music is played to the caller while they are waiting. The music is usually interrupted at regular intervals to keep the caller informed of the situation.

Group hunting. Extension numbers can be programmed to divert to another number when the handset remains unanswered.

Interactive voice response (IVR). This service allows incoming callers to select from a series of options. They are asked to dial a further number or numbers for a range of services. You have probably dealt with one of these systems if you have rung a large utility organisation like the electricity board. The response is often something like 'Dial 1 for billing enquiries, Dial 2 for connection and disconnection of supply, Dial 3 for supply problems, Dial 4 for connection to an operator.' This system saves money and the number of switchboard operator calls is reduced. It also provides a more efficient system for callers by routing them direct to their required destination. There is, though, some resistance from customers who feel that they are going through a range of options which take time while they are paying for the call. Some customers also feel that they are losing the personal touch and are just connected to machines and pre-recorded messages. However, there is usually an option for being transferred to an operator if required.

Direct dialling in (DDI). Each extension is allocated a direct line number which callers can ring direct without having to go through the switchboard. This reduces cost as the switchboard operator will deal with a greatly reduced number of incoming calls. It is also more efficient as callers are connected direct to the person they wish to speak to.

Voicemail. A message service is provided for each extension. After a pre-programmed number of unanswered rings the telephone will answer with a pre-recorded outgoing message (OGM). The incoming caller can then leave a message in the mailbox. To receive the messages from the mailbox the extension holder just dials a number. Some handsets have a light that flashes when messages are waiting.

Audio conferencing. Facilities are available that allow more than two people to participate in a call. This saves time – for example, when trying to book a date for a meeting: it saves making further calls and ringing back. It can also be more accurate as all parties are able to deal with the message directly, rather than being transferred back and forth.

Handset
The term 'handset' refers to the telephone available on the desk. Handsets form part of the total telephone system and can be supplied with a variety of facilities. These facilities can include the following.

- *Abbreviated dialling* – frequently used numbers can be programmed into the memory and an abbreviated code or number can then be used to ring these numbers. An efficient administrator will make full use of this facility to save time when ringing regular callers such as suppliers and key customers.
- *Camp on busy* – when a line is engaged, a code can be entered and the engaged line will automatically ring back as soon as it is free.

- *Digital display* – some handsets have a digital liquid crystal display (LCD) which will show numbers dialled, and can give digital messages. For example, a caller to a busy extension may key in a message to ask the other person to ring them back.
- *Distinctive ringing* – handsets can have different ringing tones to differentiate internal and external calls.
- *Interrupt* – the line bleeps when another caller is trying to get through.
- *Light messaging* – a light flashes when a message has been left.
- *Loudspeaker and microphone* – these allow hands-free calling.

These are just some of the common facilities available on a handset. You should make yourself aware of the facilities which are available on any telephone system you use in work.

Mobile phones

Mobile phones form an integral part of a communications network. They allow telephone calls and other data to be received at remote locations. Organisations benefit because they can keep in immediate touch with staff, customers and suppliers. Greater working flexibility and faster response times can be achieved using mobile phones.

The initial cost of a mobile phone may not be high, but there are usually hidden costs in the rental fee to the service network. There are two different types of network available for mobile telephones – analogue and digital. Analogue networks operate using radio waves, while digital networks convert the messages into a coded digital format. For business use the digital network is the most appropriate format for the following reasons.

Security. Analogue messages can be easily tapped, but digital messages are computer-coded for security and are virtually impossible to tap.

Speed. When the mobile phone is linked to a computer, e-mail, faxes and other data can be transmitted much faster over a digital network.

International accessibility. Digital telephones can be used abroad.

Wider range of facilities. Short-messaging service and voicemail can be used to leave messages even when your telephone is switched off. The short message service allows short text messages to be sent and received using the telephone's keypad and digital display.

Linking a mobile telephone to a computer allows data to be sent and received by another computer in remote locations. The link requires a suitable personal computer (PC) fitted with a PC card slot to connect it to the telephone, and appropriate software. Staff can then use the system to connect to a central computer system. E-mail messages can be sent and received and database information can be accessed – for example, customer lists, address lists, up-to-date product information.

Limitations

There are still a few limitations to using mobile phones. While the mobile phone networks cover most of the UK, there are still gaps that prevent their use in some areas – for example, remote geographical areas like the Highlands of Scotland and parts of Northern Ireland. The international coverage is also patchy. The extent of the coverage of the networks is increasing all the time, but this should be checked with the network provider when opening an account.

The length of time that the phone can be left on to receive calls ('standby time') and the amount of outgoing call time ('talk time') can vary depending on the quality of the phone and batteries. Frequent business users will need telephones that can be left on all day.

Use of mobile phones while driving can also present problems. It is dangerous to use a standard mobile phone while driving. Many phones now come with a car kit that allows them to be plugged into the car for battery recharging and hands-free use in the car. However, it is becoming increasingly evident that even hands-free mobile phone use can be dangerous because it can considerably reduce the driver's concentration.

There are cost issues involved in the use of mobile phones. The tariffs charged by the providers of networks vary, depending on the package agreed when the caller opens an account. Whichever package is chosen, the charges still represent an additional cost and make calls more expensive than using a traditional telephone system. Callers using traditional telephone systems pay a premium for connection to a mobile telephone. This may deter some customers from contacting someone on a mobile telephone.

There are also social issues to be considered with the use of mobile phones. The ringing of mobile phones in restaurants, trains and other social areas can be intrusive and can also be disruptive in business meetings. Users of mobile phones should be sensitive to the disruption caused by the ringing and should turn them off when appropriate.

If you have details of staff activities, it is a good idea to check these before contacting them on their mobile phone. You should balance the urgency of the call with the importance and nature of the business activity. For example, you would contact a member of staff travelling to a meeting to inform them that the person they were meeting had been delayed; but you should consider an alternative way of contacting a member of staff who was involved in a sales presentation with information about transport delays for the return journey. You could, for example, leave a message with reception at the organisation being visited.

Safety

Questions have been raised about the safety of using mobile phones. Mobile phones receive and transmit electro-magnetic waves and there are concerns that these may cause physical damage to the user and lead to an increased risk of cancer.

Security

The security of the messages and information being sent over the telephone has already been considered in the use of analogue or digital networks, but the phones themselves are also at risk from thieves and should be insured to cover the replacement cost. However, the following simple precautions can reduce the risk of loss.

- Never leave mobile phones on view in parked cars.
- Do not leave mobile phones in briefcases which are on view in parked cars.
- Do not put mobile phones down in public places – for example, on restaurant tables, station platforms, hotel lobbies.
- Set up security passwords and codes which have to be keyed in before use so as to eliminate the cost of calls made from a stolen phone.
- Do not write the security passwords and codes down in an obvious place. If you do write them down, do not keep them in the briefcase with the phone.

Making a telephone call

You can use the telephone more efficiently and effectively if you plan telephone calls. Efficiency is achieved when you convey your message in the shortest telephone time and by making the least number of calls. Effectiveness is achieved when both parties have a clear understanding of the information, which is correct, current, relevant and sufficient. Steps to planning a telephone call are as follows.

1 Identify whom you wish to call, and locate their name and telephone number. Use a direct dial number where possible: this saves the time it would take to be transferred to an extension from an exchange.
2 Collect together the relevant information: have any relevant correspondence, files and information ready and conveniently available when you make the call.
3 Write down the key issues that you wish to cover in the call: this helps you to keep the telephone call focused. Make a note of any key words or phrases that you plan to use. This can help you to control the call, particularly if it is dealing with a difficult or sensitive issue. If you are ringing an organisation to find out information, make a note of the questions you need to ask.
4 Have pen and paper handy to take notes of the telephone call. Always record key details during the course of the call and read them back to the caller.
5 Follow the organisation's procedures for making calls – for example, if you have call barring, ask for a long distance connection through the switchboard.
International calls may need extra planning. You should check the international dialling code, the engaged and call tones for the country you are dialling, and the time zones – to ensure the call is made during working hours.

Answering machines and voicemail

Answering machines and voicemail provide a useful resource for dealing with incoming calls when staff are unavailable. Answering machines are linked to telephones and have a small tape which records the incoming messages. Voicemail is a telephone answering service linked to a computerised telephone system. Answering machines and voicemail services come with a range of features, depending on the cost and type of system. These features can include the following.

Remote listening to messages. Messages can be checked from a remote location by ringing the answering machine number and entering a code. The messages will then be played back over the telephone.

Forwarding messages. Messages can be forwarded to another extension by entering a code, and then the extension number.

Message override. When an incoming caller is answered by the answering machine, the caller can enter an agreed code that overrides the message and keeps the telephone ringing. This can be useful when a manager is calling to contact an administrator who may regularly leave the answering machine on when he/she is busy. The telephone will keep ringing until it is answered or the caller rings off.

It is a good idea to read the manual that comes with the system to check what facilities are provided by the answering machines and voicemail systems available.

If you are connected to an answering machine when you make a call, it is quite straightforward to leave a message. The message should be brief, but should contain: the name, title and telephone number of the caller; the date and time of the message; a brief indication of the reason for the call and any further action to be taken.

Receiving telephone calls

Follow your organisation's procedures for dealing with incoming calls. This may specify the maximum number of times a phone should ring before it is answered. Use the house style for introducing yourself on the telephone. This varies between organisations, and also depends on whether you are answering an internal or external call. Many organisations would use an informal response to internal calls, and a more formal response to external calls. However, in some organisations the house style for telephone response is fairly informal and first names are used – for example, 'Good morning, XYZ company, Accounts department, Jane speaking. How can I help you?'

If the call is for you, deal with it as appropriate. Take notes and read any information back to the caller to check the content.

If the message is for another member of staff who is unavailable at the time, you have the following options.

- *Ask the caller to ring back later* – give a specific time if possible when you know the recipient will be available.
- *Offer to ring back the caller* – this gives a better customer image, if the call is returned promptly. In this case check when the caller will be available to receive a return call.
- *Offer to deal with the matter* – if the matter is a departmental issue, you may be able to deal with it. You may also have responsibility within the relevant work area and be able to deal with it once you are clear on the issues involved. This saves time for all parties and the matter is attended to straight away.
- *Offer to take a message to be passed on* – record the details of the message on a pre-printed telephone message form and read them

back to the caller to check that the information is correct.

- *Transfer the caller to another extension or member of staff who will be able to help the caller* – this gives an efficient image and a good customer impression if connection is made and the matter dealt with. However, care has to be taken that callers do not feel they are being passed from pillar to post when making calls.

It is important to maintain the security of information dealt with over the telephone. If you receive an incoming request for information which is confidential or commercially sensitive, you need to ensure you have the authority to pass on the information. Where there is any uncertainty about your authority to pass on information, offer to ring back or transfer the caller to a colleague with direct authority. If you are unsure about the authenticity of the caller, ask for details of their name, title, company, address and telephone number. The details can then be cross-checked by looking up the name and number and ringing the company direct to check the identity of the caller.

Recording telephone messages

When you receive a telephone message, whether on voicemail or one you have taken from a call, you should record it accurately and neatly (see Figure 1.1.1). It is good practice to record messages on a telephone message form, rather than on random scraps of paper. Telephone message books are available which allow two copies to be taken. The top copy is completed and delivered to the recipient of the message, the second copy is automatically made with No Carbon Required (NCR) paper. This copy can be left in the book for future reference.

Pagers

Pagers are a cheap and useful way of contacting people and passing on messages. A pager is a very small handheld telecommunications device which is bought for an approximate cost of £50. The cost usually includes the allocation of a 'pager' number. The pager has a small display area where digital messages can be displayed. It can also be programmed to give an audible signal when a message is received. Alternatively, if an audible signal would be intrusive – for example, in a meeting – it can be programmed to vibrate when a message is received. The display area will usually display the message – for example, 'Contact John Hancombe urgently.' or 'Ring the office before 1.00 pm.' or 'Ring 01345 784321.'

To leave a message on a pager, the caller dials the pager number, which is answered by the paging service. A spoken message is left which is then transmitted by the paging service. The sender of the message pays the cost of the call to the paging service, which is usually a premium rate call or a fixed charge – for example, 50p per call. The geographic reach of the pager will vary depending on the initial service purchased, however, they usually operate over the whole of the country except for some very remote locations where their use may be limited.

Pagers have the advantage that they are cheap to buy and incur no ongoing costs while still allowing people to be contacted very quickly. Their disadvantage is that no outgoing communications can be made from the pager, so users will still need access to a telephone to respond to the paged message.

Message	**For**	Jonathan Mickelberg
	Taken by	Jennifer Witchell
Phoned you		**Please call**		**Will call again**	✓	
Returned your call		**URGENT**			
Date	2 January		**Time**	3.30pm
From	Harry Yelland, KB Associate			
Message				
The appointment for Tuesday 2 February at 10.00am has been cancelled				
Phone	0132 63478 (direct line)		**Fax**	- - -

Figure 1.1.1 A telephone message

Portfolio activity 1.1 **Number 2**

Look at your telephone system at college or work and make a list of the facilities that are available. Try to make use of these facilities when you are making calls. Record the facilities that you used in your communications log (see Portfolio Activity 1.1 Number 1, pages 8–9).

As you complete the relevant evidence requirements throughout the course, make sure you use the telephone to receive and make calls. Use an answering machine/voicemail to leave or check messages. The following evidence should be collected:

- completed communications log, detailing facilities you have used, messages left, etc.
- list of facilities available on your telephone system
- telephone messages you have taken
- witness testimony to say that you have taken and given messages correctly
- personal statement explaining how and why you have made telephone calls, left messages, etc. including information on preparing for the message and confidentiality.

Performance criteria:	1.1.1	1.1.2	1.1.3	1.1.4	1.1.5
	1.1.6	1.1.7	1.1.8	1.1.9	1.1.10
	1.1.	111.1.	1.1.12	1.1.13	
Knowledge and understanding:	1.1.a	1.1.c	1.1.d	1.1.j	1.1.m
	1.1.n	1.1.o	1.1.p	1.1.q	1.1.r
Evidence requirements:	1.1.1	1.1.3	1.1.4	1.1.7	1.1.10
	1.1.13	1.1.14	1.1.15	1.1.16	

Electronic communication

Fax

A fax machine sends a copy of a document from the sender's fax machine to the destination fax machine. It does this by scanning the document and converting it into coded signals which are then sent over the telecommunications link. The receiving fax then converts these signals and creates a copy of the original image. A wide range of documents, including text, graphics, maps and pictures, can be sent by fax. The cost of sending a fax is the cost of the telephone call for the time the fax is being sent.

Advantages
- The fax is a very fast method of communication: transmission is almost instant to anywhere in the world.
- Messages can be sent and received at all times, which is useful for sending international messages.
- Fax machines are easy to use.
- Many fax machines have advanced facilities which allow faxes to

be saved and then sent out during cheap rate periods or when a number in no longer engaged.

- A fax can be sent to multiple numbers.
- Faxing is a cheap way of sending information, particularly for long distance messages.

Disadvantages

- Fax messages are not best legal evidence of a message being sent as there is usually no guarantee that the message has been received by the correct person – it is best practice to send confirmation by letter.
- Not everybody has a fax machine.
- Fax machines only recognise black and white, not colour.
- There may be problems sending fax messages to some countries – for example, where the telecommunications infrastructure is not of a sufficiently good quality to carry the signals.

Types of fax machine

There are three different types of fax machine: thermal fax; plain paper fax; fax-modem linked to a computer.

Thermal fax machines are usually linked to a telephone handset and answering machine. The copies are produced using a heat process on paper, which is stored on a roll. These fax machines are usually cheaper to buy, but the consumables are more expensive and produce poor quality copies. They are suitable for small offices and home use.

Plain paper fax machines use similar technology to photocopiers and laser printers to produce copies on standard copier paper. They are more expensive to buy, but the consumables are cheaper. They often have more advanced features and are suitable for business and large volume use.

Each fax machine is operated in a slightly different way and you will need to familiarise yourself with the machine in your office. However, all thermal and plain-paper fax machines work on the same basic principle. The document is placed in the machine and the recipient's number is dialled. The fax is sent by pressing the Send/Start button.

Fax messages can also be sent direct from a computer which has a fax-modem link. Instead of printing the fax message to the printer, it can be sent as a fax. This is very fast, saves time and eliminates paper copies. If a fax-modem link is used the computer must be left on at all times to be able to receive faxes.

Sending fax messages

Each organisation will have its own procedures for sending faxes. There is usually a standard format for sending the fax, usually a fax front sheet or fax message sheet (see Figure 1.1.2). This states the name and fax number of the person being sent the fax, the name and fax number of the sender and the number of pages being transmitted. Each page of a fax is numbered – for example, 'Page 1 of 4' – so that the receiver can check that all the pages have been received.

Most fax machines confirm the sending of a message, by printing a code on the sheet or issuing a fax confirmation slip. The fax confirmation slip should be attached to the original message which should then be filed.

Brief messages may be handwritten or typed on the front sheet for speed. For longer messages the front sheet should be used to precede other printed documents.

Receiving fax messages

When a fax message is received, it should be removed from the machine and promptly passed to the appropriate person. The advantages of speed are lost if fax messages are not quickly delivered to recipients. Special action may be required for fax messages marked 'Urgent'. If the appropriate person is not available, the fax message should be delivered to another person in the department who can deal with it.

Security

It is important to retain the security and confidentiality of information. Care should be taken when using the telephone and fax machine not to disclose any confidential organisational information. When sending a confidential fax, the recipient should be contacted to ensure they are available by the machine to receive the fax. Some fax machines have user 'codes' and the fax is stored in the machine until the code is entered. This increases the confidentiality of fax messages.

Electronic mail

Electronic mail (e-mail) is a system where messages prepared on a computer are sent via a modem over the telecommunications network to a central computer. The recipient can then use their computer and modem to collect the message from the central computer.

HTR Heating

16 Hardcastle Drive
Greathampton
GR6 2TL
heating@htr.co.uk
Tel 01234 73344
Fax 01234 73355

FAX MESSAGE FRONT SHEET

To   J K Williams
                            Good Living Exhibitions
Fax Number   01773 373451
From   Tony Smith, Sales Department
No of Pages(including this one)   1

Message

**Good Living Exhibition
Manchester, 13 March, Stand 43**

Can you please confirm that you have arranged for the 4 exhibition
panels to be available for the above exhibition at an agreed cost of
£35.00 per panel.

Sent by Jane Seward
Date   10 January ----

Figure 1.1.2 A fax front sheet

Many organisations have an internal e-mail system. This is used for
sending messages to colleagues within the company and works
through the local area network (LAN) – a group of computers in a
building or group of buildings that are linked together. Once an
internal system has been set up it does not cost anything to send
internal e-mails. This makes it more cost-effective than sending
paper memos. Each e-mail system will have a post office, and each

individual will have their own mail box within this post office. All messages are sent to the post office where they are sorted and put into mail boxes, people then pick up their mail from the mail box – this is all done electronically.

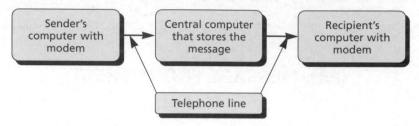

Figure 1.1.3 Sending e-mail messages

Many organisations can also send e-mail externally – to other companies and individuals all over the world. The process is almost exactly the same, except that, in order to send e-mail externally a modem is required. External e-mail uses wide area networks (WANs) – networks that cover much wider areas. The biggest WAN is the Internet and it is becoming increasingly common for people to use the Internet for sending and receiving e-mail – particularly in the case of individuals rather than companies.

To use the Internet – whether for sending and receiving e-mails or surfing the World Wide Web – it is necessary to have a modem and to subscribe to an internet service provider (ISP). The ISP will provide Internet access – it will connect to web sites for you, so that you only have to phone the ISP's local number, rather than phoning New York, for example. Most ISPs also provide one or more e-mail addresses (so that people can send you e-mails) and some will even provide you with space for your own website – this is located on the ISPs central computer, but you can access it and edit it from your own PC. There has been a large growth in ISPs recently, with more and more of them offering free access. Using the Internet as a research topic is covered in more detail in Unit 5 (pages 219–20).

Advantages

* E-mail is a very cheap and quick method of communication: messages are sent very quickly at local call cost to anywhere in the world.
* It is also flexible: complex documents and information prepared in other applications such as spreadsheets and databases can be sent as attachments; computer graphics can also be attached.
* Messages can be sent and received at any time, whatever the local time. The message will be stored by the central computer until the recipient picks up the message.

Disadvantages

- There are confidentiality issues with e-mail: messages and information transmitted on computer networks may be 'hacked' or accessed without proper authority. This risk can be reduced by using encryption procedures – using a code to ensure unauthorised people cannot read the message (see page 29).
- Although messages can be sent immediately, this does not guarantee that they will be received immediately as recipients may not check their mail boxes regularly. However, some messaging systems have the facility to notify senders when messages have been opened.
- There are also problems of overloading systems: it is so easy to send messages that the system is often overused and irrelevant information sent to a large number of users. This can waste the recipient's time – some busy executives may receive over 50 messages a day and these can take a considerable time to deal with – and also clog up and therefore slow down the main computer that stores the messages.
- The legal status of e-mail is still uncertain – it is acceptable as evidence but is not best legal evidence. It is therefore advisable to send important documents by post or at least to confirm them by post.

Sending an e-mail message

To send a message, you need to have the correct e-mail address – for example, John_c@livex.co.uk. This is broken up as follows:

Name	Organisation	Suffix	Country code
John_c	livex	co.	uk

The suffixes have specific meanings, for example:

co – a UK-based company

com – an American-based company (this will not have a country code following it)

gov – government departments

ac – academic institution in the UK – for example, college or university

edu – academic institution in the US (this will not have a country code following it).

The address must be entered correctly. It is generally not case sensitive, which is why most e-mail addresses are shown in lower case, but care must be taken to distinguish between underscore and hyphen and to include any full-stops, commas, etc., otherwise the message will be returned as 'undeliverable'.

The message or information can either be composed directly using the e-mail software in the computer, or prepared in another application – for example, a word processing software application – and then attached to the e-mail message. When sending messages over the Internet, it is more cost-effective to prepare the message 'off-line' – i.e. while you are not connected to the Internet – and only 'dial-up' when the message is ready to send. If the message has been prepared in another application, the file can be attached to the e-mail message. When the message is ready to be sent the 'Send' option can be selected. A message can also be saved as a draft document which can be updated as required before sending it.

Using the 'address-book' can also make e-mail more efficient. E-mail addresses can be stored with the names of the people they belong to. When you need to send an e-mail, this name can be selected from the address book and the full address will then automatically be used to send the message.

E-mail messages are more informal and simpler in format than traditional business communications. Note that it is courteous not to write in capitals as this is considered to be 'shouting' and may annoy recipients. Messages can be signed if required by adding a computer 'signature'.

Receiving an e-mail message

Incoming messages will be stored in an 'inbox'. Messages can be checked in the inbox when you connect to the e-mail system and go 'on-line'. Some internal systems are set up to indicate to recipients that a message has been delivered to the inbox. A 'message delivered' message will appear on the screen. Messages should be checked regularly during the day. Attachments should be opened and read. Attachments are usually saved and then opened in the relevant application – for example, a word processing application. They can then be dealt with as standard word processing files, so that for example they can be edited, printed, etc. Some messaging software allows you to view and print attachments within the e-mail application, but if you want to edit them you will need to use the appropriate software.

Storing and printing e-mail messages

E-mail incoming and outgoing mail boxes can become full, just like paper in-trays. The messages should be regularly sorted to ensure

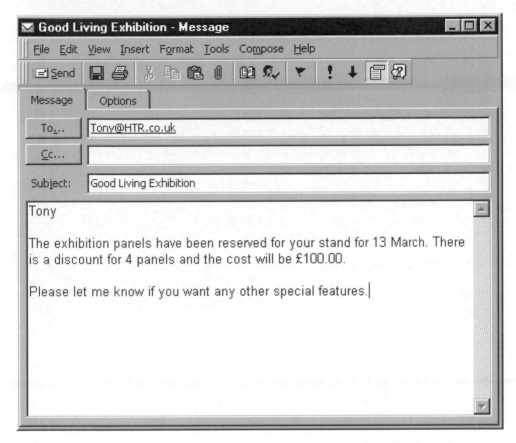

Figure 1.1.4 An e-mail message

the mailboxes are being used efficiently and effectively: messages that are no longer required can be deleted; a paper copy of a message can be printed if necessary or messages can be stored in 'folders' in your e-mail software. Folders should be set up which will store information logically – for example, subject folders.

Security

Special care must be taken when using computer-based systems to ensure information remains confidential and that the risk from unauthorised access to computer systems is minimised. You should use passwords to enter the system, enter software, etc. The passwords should not be disclosed to unauthorised personnel, and should be changed regularly. You can also use encryption software. This converts the e-mail message into code which the recipient will need to decode before the message can be read.

Planning e-mail communications

Whichever method of transmission is used, it is important to plan the method carefully. The following steps should be followed.

1 Check that you have the accurate e-mail address.
2 Check that you have the correct name, designation, etc. of the recipient.
3 Check that you have all the correct information available – for example, dates, invoice numbers, prices, catalogue numbers.
4 Decide on the exact purpose of the communication – for example, to order goods, to request information, to confirm a booking.
5 Prepare the message, including **all** relevant information – for example, order numbers, dates.

Using the Internet

The Internet is a worldwide network of computers which are permanently linked together. The World Wide Web is the information stored on these computers in the form of web pages. Access to the web is available in many organisations, as well as in many public libraries.

To gain access to the Internet and the World Wide Web the following hardware and software are required.

- *Hardware* – a computer and a modem to connect the computer to a telephone line.
- *Access to the Internet through an ISP* – for example, Compuserve, America On Line (AOL), FreeServe.
- *Suitable software* – a web browser that allows you to navigate the World Wide Web – for example, Netscape, Internet Explorer.

A search engine is required if you wish to carry out searches for specific topics – for example, Yahoo, Alta Vista. The search engine is a large website in the form of an index, which can be automatically searched.

When you are searching the web for a topic, you need to enter key words into the search engine. The search engine will then list the sites containing those words, the first selections being the items which the search engine identifies as being most relevant. If your key words are very general, hundreds of selections will be offered.

Each web site has an individual address known as a Uniform Resource Locator (URL). Internet addresses are similar to e-mail addresses, but are always of the form:

http://www.(organisation).(type).(country code).

For example, **http://www.open.gov.uk** is the British Government's site.

Intranets

Many organisations have an intranet. This is like the Internet in that it uses websites and other Internet tools and software for navigation, however, it is only accessible internally within the company. Examples of information that may be found on intranets include phone directories; bulletin boards; information on social events; catalogues and so on. Some organisations will also have limited access to certain relevant websites on the Internet.

Safe use of equipment

All equipment should be used safely. The following table outlines the safety considerations for communications equipment.

Equipment	Possible hazards	Safety guidelines
Telephones	Trailing wires Infection from head and handsets	• Check wires are fixed and tidy. • Clean head and handsets regularly with telephone wipes.
Fax machines	Trailing wires	• Check wires are fixed and tidy.
Computer equipment	Trailing wires Repetitive strain injury Tiredness and headaches	• Check wires are fixed and tidy. • Use keyboard rests. • Take regular breaks. • Check lighting, etc.

Portfolio activity 1.1 **Number 3**

Use fax and e-mail to send and receive messages when you are completing appropriate activities for the other units such as organising business trips, etc. Record the use of the equipment in your log and collect hard copies of the messages you send and receive. The following evidence should be collected:

• completed log, containing details of e-mails, faxes, etc.
• copies of fax messages you have sent and received
• hard copies of e-mail messages you have sent and received
• witness testimonies confirming that you have used the fax and e-mail systems according to your organisation's procedures and used them safely
• personal statement explaining how and why you used the fax and e-mail systems to send and receive information. Include information on safety and confidentiality.

Performance criteria:	1.1.1	1.1.2	1.1.3	1.1.4	1.1.5
	1.1.6	1.1.9	1.1.10	1.1.11	1.1.12
	1.1.13				
Knowledge and understanding:	1.1.b	1.1.e	1.1.f	1.1.g	1.1.h
	1.1.k	1.1.l	1.1.m	1.1.n	1.1.r
	1.1.s				
Evidence requirements:	1.1.2	1.1.5	1.1.6	1.1.8	1.1.9
	1.1.11	1.1.12	1.1.15	1.1.16	

Test yourself

Knowledge and understanding	Questions
a	Explain the purpose and function of oral communication methods.
b	Explain the purpose and function of electronic communication methods.
c	Describe your organisation's house style and/or procedures for making telephone calls.
d	Describe your organisation's house style and/or procedures for receiving telephone calls.
e	Describe your organisation's house style and/or procedures for sending fax messages.
f	Describe your organisation's house style and/or procedures for receiving fax messages.
g	Describe your organisation's house style and/or procedures for sending e-mail messages.
h	Describe your organisation's house style and/or procedures for receiving e-mail messages.
i	Describe your organisation's house style and/or procedures for conducting face-to-face communications.
j	List three factors involved in the safe and effective use of the telephone.
k	List three factors involved in the safe and effective use of a fax machine.
l	List three factors involved in the safe and effective use of an e-mail system.

m	Explain why it is important to have good communications in organisations.
	Describe how you would maximise the effectiveness and efficiency of communications.
n	Explain how you compose and convey messages effectively and efficiently.
o	Explain why it is important to be prepared when making a telephone call and list three ways in which you could prepare yourself.
p	Explain why good questioning and listening techniques are important in business giving two examples each of how to question and listen effectively.
q	List three types of non-verbal language and describe their characteristics.
r	Describe three ways of maintaining security and confidentiality of information.
s	Explain what the Internet is. Describe how to use it.

Element 1.2
PLAN AND CARRY OUT WRITTEN BUSINESS COMMUNICATIONS

Formal, written communications form a very important part of business communications. They cover a range of documents, many of which have very specialised styles and formats – for example, letters, formal reports, etc. Whenever documents are being prepared the following questions need to be asked.

- What is the purpose of the document – that is, exactly what is to be achieved by the document?
- What information should be included in the document – for example, what level of detail is required?
- What type of document is to be prepared – for example, report, memo, agenda, etc?
- What will be the layout and format of the document – for example, open punctuation, following the organisation's house style?

- What technology will be used to prepare the document – that is, the software and facilities to be used – for example, word processor, presentation package, mailmerge?
- What are the appropriate style and tone for the content of the document – for example, level of formality, language, etc?
- Who should receive copies and how many copies are to be produced?
- How are the documents to be stored for future reference?
- How are the security and confidentiality of the documents to be maintained?

Portfolio Note

The HDAP standards require that a range of written documents be prepared. These should be prepared while you are completing work for other units. This should be real work, wherever this is a requirement of the appropriate unit. If the documents are not produced from real work, simulated activities or assignments can be used, provided these satisfy the requirements of the activity.

The table below lists the documents required for Element 1.2, and identifies possible units/activities where the documents may be prepared.

Think about ways in which you can record your written communications during the course of your work to include in your evidence.

Document	Unit/Element	Examples	Possible activities
Letters			
1 Enquiry	3.1 4.1 5.1 7.1	38, 39, 43–4	• letters enquiring about the cost of services and products e.g. accommodation, venues, equipment
2 Confirmation	2.1 2.3 3.1 4.1 4.2 8.2	104, 106, 131	• letters confirming appointments, bookings for accommodation, meetings, venues, refreshments, travel arrangements • letters confirming arrangements for interviews
3 Invitation	2.1 2.3 3.1 8.2	134, 136	• letters inviting people to speak at an event; inviting people to attend appointments; inviting people to an interview
4 Standard letters with merged details	2.1 2.3 3.1 4.1 5.1 7.1 8.2	39	• standard letters which are individually addressed for business meetings, appointments, events • letters inviting people to attend for interview; or rejecting job applicants • letters written to several suppliers requesting information about products or services – e.g. equipment, accommodation, refreshments

Document	Unit/Element	Examples	Possible activities
5 Rejection	2.3 3.1 8.2	38, 437	• letters rejecting requests for appointments; rejecting applications for tickets, places at an event; rejecting applicants for interview
6 Requesting reference	8.2	419	• letters requesting a reference for a job applicant
7 Complaint	2.1 3.1 4.1	43–4	• letters of complaint about poor service provided by a venue; accommodation, refreshments, event organisers, etc.
Memos			
8 Memo reports	2.2 3.1 3.2 4.1 5.1 7.1 7.3 8.3 9.2	324, 485–6	• results of evaluation of meetings • reports on findings about venues, etc. for meetings, events, travel • reports presenting findings for projects • reports on evaluation of information storage and retrieval; budgets; financial information, health and safety, etc. • training reports • recommendation for inducting new staff
9 Multi-routed	All elements	66, 506	• memos addressed to more than one member of staff should occur in every element, unit
Reports			
10 Formal	3.1 5.2 6.1 7.1 7.3 9.2	239–40, 162	• formal reports presented at meetings; as a result of researching information for a specific project; evaluating an event • reports on training outcomes
11 Informal	3.1 5.2 7.1 7.3 8.3 9.2		• informal reports informing meetings of the results of researching information for a specific project; evaluating an event; presenting a budget, etc. • reports on training outcomes, recommendations for inducting new staff
Copies			
12 Use of blind copies	Any unit where a relevant document has been produced		• copies of documents with circulation marked on the blind copy – e.g. letters of complaint
Documentation for meetings			
13 Agendas	2.1 2.2 2.3 3.1 4.2	63, 64	• agendas prepared for meetings, appointments, business events
14 Chairperson's agendas	2.1 2.2	65	• chairperson's agendas prepared for meetings, appointments, business events
15 Records of attendance	2.1 2.2 3.1	68	• attendance lists, delegate lists, meetings registers

Document	Unit/Element	Examples	Possible activities
16 Minutes	2.1 3.1	75, 76	• minutes prepared by minutes secretary • minutes for meetings arranged to organise events
Miscellaneous documents			
17 Summaries	3.1 5.2 7.3		• summaries of information collected for a project; as a result of analysing company reports, newspaper articles
18 Programmes	2.1 2.3 3.1 4.1 8.2 8.3 9.2	139, 505	• programmes prepared for appointments, meetings, events, business trips, interviews • training and induction programmes
19 Schedules	All units	93, 101, 250, 428	• schedules prepared for particular events, programmes, interviews • schedules prepared as time management plans to organise activities
20 Written procedures/ checklists	3.1 6.2 7.2	79, 102, 117, 123, 173, 191, 289, 299, 376, 451, 453	• procedures for events, filing, petty cash • checklists may occur in all elements, as these are used to manage time and to check off planned activities
21 Itineraries	2.3 4.1 4.2	203	• itineraries for travel and appointments
22 Questionnaires	2.2 3.1 3.2 5.1	224, 158	• questionnaires used to collect information; collect feedback from events; collect feedback from performance at meetings
23 Press releases	3.1	118	• press releases prepared for an event
24 Design and preparation of master forms for completion	2.1 3.1 8.2 9.2	77, 90, 198, 277, 278, 420, 430, 431, 507	• attendance forms, booking forms, questionnaire forms, application forms
25 Completed forms	1.1 2.1 2.3 3.1 4.1 7.2	21, 77, 227, 228, 330, 493, 494, 497, 510	• telephone message forms; room booking forms; refreshment request forms; expenses forms; requests for money, travel; petty cash forms
26 Evaluation documents	2.2 3.1 3.2 6.1 6.2 8.2 8.3 9.2	90, 123, 158, 396, 495, 496, 498, 509	• questionnaires, reports, self-assessment for events and meetings • reports on evaluating an information storage and retrieval system • feedback for an individual using an information storage system • evaluating interviewees at an interview • evaluation of training programmes
27 Advertisements	3.1 8.2	414	• advertisements for events; job advertisements
28 Leaflets/ brochures	3.1		• leaflets and brochures for a business event
29 Notices for impact	2.1 3.1		• signage for meetings
30 Charts/ graphs/ diagrams	3.1 3.2 5.2 7.1 7.3 8.3	148, 149, 244, 245, 246, 247, 367	• break-even charts, costs, results of evaluation, research findings

Preparing letters

Letters are the most common form of written communication used in organisations. They are used for formal internal communications – for example, letters of promotion – and for formal external communications – for example, letters to suppliers, customers, etc. They usually follow a standard format for layout, which is agreed as the organisation's house style. The house style can be found in the organisation's procedures or by following examples of previous letters. All letters must be carefully planned as they are written advertisements for an organisation.

There are certain conventions that should be followed when writing letters. When writing to an organisation, rather than an individual, the salutation **Dear Sirs** is used. When writing to an individual whose name you do not know – for example, the Purchasing Manager – the salutation **Dear Sir/Madam** is used. When writing to a named person, the complimentary close **Yours sincerely** is used – for example, **Dear Mr Jones...Yours sincerely**. The correct close for **Dear Sirs** or **Dear Sir/Madam** is **Yours faithfully**.

Open punctuation

The convention in business letters is to use open punctuation. This means that there is no punctuation used except in the body of the letter. For example, **Ref** instead of **Ref.**; **Dear Mr Jones** instead of **Dear Mr. Jones,**; **Enc** instead of **Enc.** – Figure 1.2.1 on page 38 shows an example of a business letter which uses open punctuation. The convention is also to leave a clear line space between sections of the letter and between paragraphs.

Mailmerge

When an individual letter is to be sent to several people, the mailmerge facility of a word processing package can be used. This allows information contained in a 'data file' (see Figure 1.2.3, page 39) to be merged with a standard document (see Figure 1.2.2, page 39). The data file is a list of key information – for example, names and addresses. The standard document is usually a form letter, which contains the standard text, plus field entries for the merge information.

When the standard letter and the datafile have been prepared, they can be merged using the mailmerge facility in the word processing software and then printed onto headed paper.

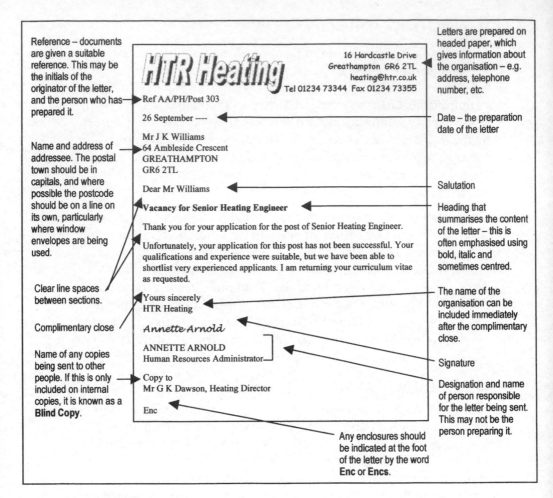

Reference – documents are given a suitable reference. This may be the initials of the originator of the letter, and the person who has prepared it.

Name and address of addressee. The postal town should be in capitals, and where possible the postcode should be on a line on its own, particularly where window envelopes are being used.

Clear line spaces between sections.

Complimentary close

Name of any copies being sent to other people. If this is only included on internal copies, it is known as a **Blind Copy**.

Letters are prepared on headed paper, which gives information about the organisation – e.g. address, telephone number, etc.

Date – the preparation date of the letter

Salutation

Heading that summarises the content of the letter – this is often emphasised using bold, italic and sometimes centred.

The name of the organisation can be included immediately after the complimentary close.

Signature

Designation and name of person responsible for the letter being sent. This may not be the person preparing it.

Any enclosures should be indicated at the foot of the letter by the word **Enc** or **Encs**.

HTR Heating

16 Hardcastle Drive
Greathampton GR6 2TL
heating@htr.co.uk
Tel 01234 73344 Fax 01234 73355

Ref AA/PH/Post 303

26 September ----

Mr J K Williams
64 Ambleside Crescent
GREATHAMPTON
GR6 2TL

Dear Mr Williams

Vacancy for Senior Heating Engineer

Thank you for your application for the post of Senior Heating Engineer.

Unfortunately, your application for this post has not been successful. Your qualifications and experience were suitable, but we have been able to shortlist very experienced applicants. I am returning your curriculum vitae as requested.

Yours sincerely
HTR Heating

Annette Arnold

ANNETTE ARNOLD
Human Resources Administrator

Copy to
Mr G K Dawson, Heating Director

Enc

Figure 1.2.1 A business letter

Composing documentation

When a document is being prepared, the information to be included in the document should be collected. This information should be checked to ensure it is current, correct and valid. One method of doing this is to check that the sources of information are also current, correct and valid. Organisation charts, telephone directories, deskbooks, etc. should be up to date. When situations change, the updates should be accurately recorded in the appropriate record. When updates of telephone directories, etc. are issued, the old documents should be destroyed or archived as appropriate. A regularly maintained, neatly labelled and well organised filing system is a key factor in ensuring accurate information is quickly available.

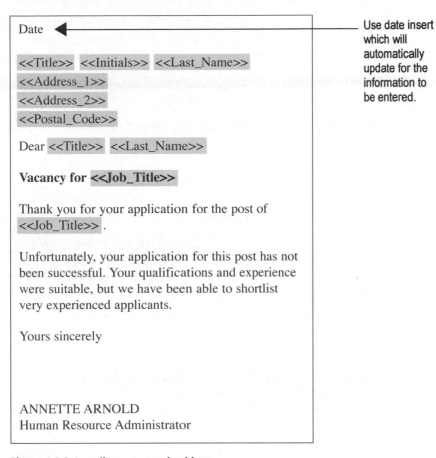

Figure 1.2.2 A mailmerge standard letter

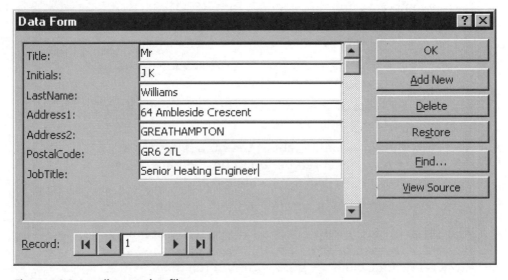

Figure 1.2.3 A mailmerge datafile

Style and tone

Once the information has been collected, the document can be composed. The correct style and tone should be used.

Tone is very difficult to define – it is a combination of the words used and the length of sentences. Compare:

> **You will send me the information. I need it tomorrow.**

with

> **I would be pleased if you could send me the information as soon as possible. I would be grateful if you could fax it to me tomorrow.**

Words like 'must', 'now' and 'will' are different in tone from 'would', 'may' and 'could'. The addition of words such as 'pleased' and 'grateful' also change the tone. Short, very brief sentences can make a message sound curt and sharp. It is also important not to include language which sounds rather bureaucratic and old-fashioned. For example, compare:

> **With reference to your letter of 6th inst, I must regrettably inform you that the request submitted on form ESO199 has been declined on the grounds listed in sub-sections 6 and 7 on the reverse of the form.**

with

> **Thank you for your letter of 6 April containing a completed Training Request form (ESO199). Unfortunately your request has been refused for the following reasons:**
>
> **1 The training requested is not relevant to the current business objectives.**
>
> **2 The cost of the requested course exceeds the current training limit.**
>
> **Further information about the guidelines for a training request can be found on the back of the form – see particularly sections 6 and 7.**

The style and tone will depend on the following factors.

The type of document. For example, letters will have a more formal style than memos. The following table shows the tone/style that might be used with different documents.

E-mails	These are: • brief messages • very informal in style. Internal e-mails may contain standard in-house abbreviations.
Memos	These are: • informal in style • appropriate to the content and recipient of the memo.
Reports	These: • are formal in style • are written in the third person • should be 'neutral' in content. All relevant information about a topic should be included; conclusions and recommendations should be logical. For example: **A suitable colour for decorating the reception area should be chosen. Green is a restful, neutral colour that complements the company's logo and corporate image materials.**
Procedures	These are: • usually fairly brief • written in a straightforward tone • in the third person. It is a good idea to start procedures with 'action words'. For example: **Separate all the Private and Confidential letters and put on one side for departmental sorting later.** **Sort envelopes into batches of standard size.**

The purpose of the document. For example, a letter making a complaint will have a different tone from a letter apologising for a breakdown in services. (See Figure 1.2.4 on pages 43–4.)

The audience. The language used will depend on who is to receive the document. The key factors that affect the language used are as follows.

- *Technical knowledge* – simple rather than technical terms might be used with customers, while more specialised terms would be used when writing to a service engineer or technical expert.
- *Familiarity* – a more informal tone might be used with someone you are familiar with – for example, a letter to a colleague could begin 'Dear Keith'.
- *Educational level* – the choice of vocabulary might be different for people with different levels of educational background – for example, the vocabulary used with teachers/lecturers would be different from that used with young people in secondary education. However, if there is any doubt always choose the simpler language. It is also important to maintain a balance between straightforward plain English and a tone which could be considered patronising.

- *Seniority* – the tone of communications used with higher-level management may be different from that used with colleagues. When requesting information or action from senior management, care must be taken not to 'tell them' what they 'must' do, but rather request information and give them the reason and authority for the request. For example, compare this request made by an administrator for information from the Managing Director:

> **Mr Jones, the Personnel Manager has asked me to contact you for information for suitable dates for the interviews for the Marketing Manager vacancy. Could you please let me have several dates when you will be available at the end of April? I would appreciate this information by the end of tomorrow, so that arrangements for the interviews can be made.**

with

> **Send me dates when you will be available for the interviews for the Marketing Manager. I must have these by the end of tomorrow.**

- *Audience attitude* – it is important to adjust the tone to match the 'mood' of the audience – for example, the tone of the response to a letter of complaint would be very different from the tone of a letter making a complaint.
- *Nature of the audience* – the tone used with customers may vary from the tone used with suppliers. The tone used with the general public may vary from the tone used with a specific group.

The organisation's house style. Some organisations have a very informal house style, while others may maintain one which is far more structured and formal.

Making an impression

The quality of the presentation of documents forms part of the company image. The following factors are some ways to improve this presentation.

- *Select the appropriate paper* – for example, letterhead for external letters; memorandum forms for internal documentation; fax sheets for fax messages.
- *Use appropriate font sizes and styles* to present documents attractively (see Unit 5 pages 241–3).
- *Select the most appropriate form of presentation* of information

in documents – for example, pie charts, tables, etc. (see Unit 5 pages 243–8).

- *Follow the organisation s house style* to ensure consistency of presentation.
- *Ensure documents are accurate* in detail, and also ensure correct grammar, spelling, punctuation and that there are no keying-in errors.

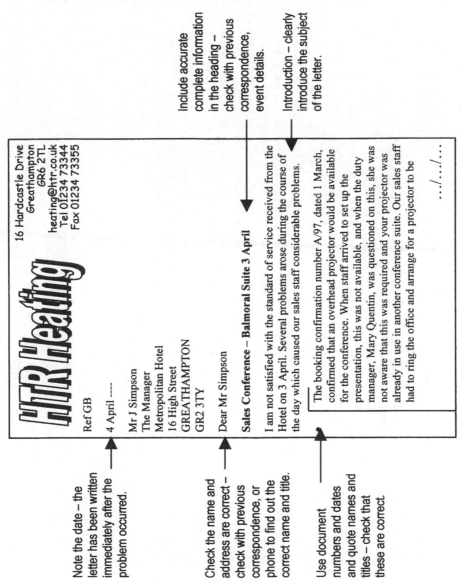

Include accurate complete information in the heading – check with previous correspondence, event details.

Introduction – clearly introduce the subject of the letter.

Note the date – the letter has been written immediately after the problem occurred.

Check the name and address are correct – check with previous correspondence, or phone to find out the correct name and title.

Use document numbers and dates and quote names and titles – check that these are correct.

Figure 1.2.4 A letter of complaint – Page One

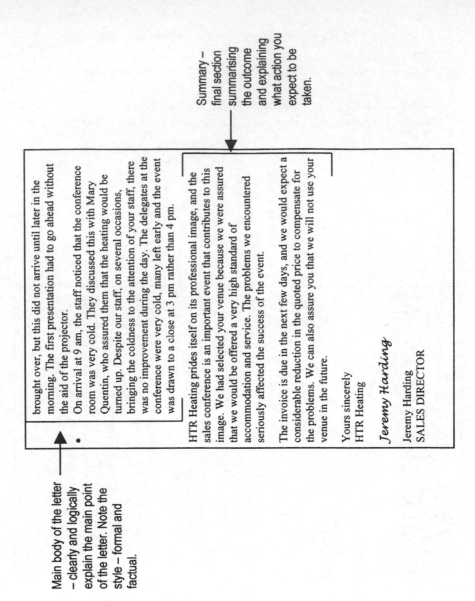

Figure 1.2.4 A letter of complaint – Page Two

Ensuring accuracy

Documents should be accurate. The following are some of the most commonly occurring errors.

- *Incorrect spelling* – use spellcheckers and dictionaries to check spellings.
- *Commonly confused words* – for example, **their/there**, **weather/whether**: the spellchecker will not pick up these errors.

- *Errors of agreement* – for example, plural and singular words being used together – for example, **They was not ready**. **The orders is ready**. Use grammar checkers to eliminate these errors.
- *Punctuation errors* – for example, incorrect use of apostrophes – For example, **companys'** instead of **company's** or **companies'**. The grammar/spellchecker should highlight these errors.
- *Sentence structure* – for example, sentences which are too long, or not sentences at all:

  e.g. According to your letter.

  This is not a complete sentence. This error should be highlighted by the grammar checker.

  e.g. We would like to complain about the poor service which we received when we held a conference at your hotel, it was too cold and the overhead projector was not ready when we arrived and your staff were not very helpful when we asked them to put up the heating.

  This is too long and should be split into smaller sections. This error may be highlighted by the grammar checker.

As well as using the grammar and spell checkers, you should also check the document carefully on the screen, and again when it has been printed out as spelling and grammar checkers do not pick up everything.

Distributing documents

Once the document has been prepared, it should be distributed to the recipient. The method chosen for distribution should take account of the importance, urgency and confidentiality of the document. Some methods of distribution are shown in the following table.

	Internal	External
Important	Send in an envelope in the internal mail system.	Send in an envelope using a suitable mail system – e.g. recorded delivery.
Urgent	Send in the internal mail system if this is quick, otherwise e-mail or fax to the recipient if they are in a different location.	Send via courier, or special delivery systems.
Confidential	Send in a sealed envelope marked 'confidential'.	Send in a sealed envelope marked 'confidential', using special delivery or courier services.

Storing copies

Copies of correspondence should be filed where they can be accessed later for reference. Documents can be filed as paper copies in manual filing systems, or as computer files. Alternatively both forms of storage may be used.

Paper documents may be clipped with other relevant correspondence and filed in a filing cabinet. Other members of staff can remove the file and check information since they are not dependent on access to a computer.

For computer files, it is a good idea to set up different folders (subdirectories) for different topics or authors of documents. If files are stored on floppy disks, different disks could be used for different authors, topics, etc. A logical system should be used for the naming of files – for example, a file might be called **lagcon: 1** – letter, **ag** – Alan Garner, **con** – conference.

A manual log of files may also be kept which lists files prepared each day. This can be useful for reference. Regular back-ups of files should be made so that information is not lost if there are problems with the computer system. The organisation may automatically back up all data held on the computer on a daily or weekly basis. You can always maintain your own back-up by keeping copies of documents on floppy disks, as well as on the hard disk.

Legal requirements

Care should be taken to ensure all information included in documents meets legal requirements. Individual organisations may have to follow specific guidelines and regulations – for example, financial organisations may have to take account of regulations by the Personal Investment Authority. More generally the following legislation may need to be considered.

- *Data Protection Act 1984* – controls the use of information stored on the computer.
- *The Copyright, Designs and Patents Act 1988* – controls information about new processes and products and who owns the right to print and distribute certain materials – for example, books, music recordings.
- *Equal opportunities legislation* – information should not demonstrate discrimination on the grounds of sex or race.

Full information on these can be found in the appendix at the back of this book (pages 539–45).

Maintaining security and confidentiality

The security and confidentiality of information should always be maintained by following these guidelines.

- Use passwords to protect computer systems. Passwords should also be used to protect individual documents if they are particularly confidential.
- Exit computer files, systems and programs when leaving the computer.
- Clearly mark sensitive information as 'confidential'. The printouts should be stored in files, and locked away in filing cabinets when not in use. Floppy disks should also be locked in cabinets when not in use.
- Lock the office and filing cabinets at the end of the day.
- Do not disclose confidential information to unauthorised personnel, either formally or informally.
- Check with senior staff or colleagues if you are unsure about security procedures with regard to information.

Hardware and software

Safe use of hardware and software

The health and safety guidelines for using hardware and software should always be followed. These include:

- taking regular breaks
- ensuring display screen regulations are followed – sit at an appropriate distance from the screen, have adequate light; use anti-glare covers for screens; have regular eye tests
- using wrist pads, ergonomic mice, ergonomic keyboards to minimise problems with repetitive strain injury (RSI)
- ensuring there are no trailing wires.

Effective use of software

Effective use of software means selecting the most appropriate type of software for the particular use and using it correctly and efficiently. Some examples of effective use of software are given in the following table.

Types of software	Uses	Examples
Database *e.g. Access*	To store and sort lists of standardised information	• names and addresses of clients • names and addresses of customers • lists of accommodation • product lists
Spreadsheet *e.g. Excel*	To store and process numerical information To produce presentations of numerical information	• calculating costs and expenses • petty cash • break-even charts • managing budgets
Word processor *e.g. Word,* *WordPerfect, AmiPro*	To store and present text (graphics can be included)	• reports, brochures • memos, letters, faxes • handouts for presentations
Presentation software *e.g. Powerpoint*	To prepare presentations which can include text, graphics, moving and sound images	• sales presentations • product presentations
Desktop publishing *e.g. Pagemaker,* *QuarkXPress, Publisher*	To produce professional, print-standard documents, including graphics, columns	• brochures • leaflets • publicity materials
Communications software *e.g. Outlook Express* *Internet Explorer*	To send e-mails, attach computer files, send information on an intranet and the Internet	• e-mail messages to suppliers • e-mail messages to staff • e-mail messages to customers
Graphics software *e.g. Coreldraw,* *Photoshop, Illustrator*	To draw and manipulate graphic images	• preparing graphic images to be included in presentations, brochures, leaflets, etc.
Diary software *e.g. Outlook*	To store and manage calendar information on the computer	• arranging meetings, booking dates, preparing schedules
File management software *e.g. Windows Explorer*	To manage the storage and sorting of computer files	• setting up and managing 'folders' • sorting and selecting files

Computer software should also be used correctly and efficiently. There is usually more than one way of carrying out an activity on the computer – for example, there may be different methods of printing a document. However, you should be familiar with the different methods and the advantages of each method – for example, using the **Print** command on the **File** menu will allow a selection of pages or multiple copies to be printed, whereas clicking the **Print** icon will just print one copy of the whole document.

The use of 'hotkeys' or 'shortcuts' can be very efficient – for example, **Ctrl + P** for **Print**. The careful selection of the default settings can make the software more efficient to use. For example, setting the spellchecker and grammar checker to be on while documents are being keyed in is a very effective way of reducing errors.

Using the help menus and manuals, and attending training sessions, are helpful ways of ensuring the use of the software and hardware is more effective.

Portfolio activity 1.2

Most of the evidence for this unit should be collected through your real work activities. Design a checklist to include the documentation list (see the example document table on pages 34–6) as listed in the standards. Complete this with an evidence reference for each item.

Write a personal statement explaining how you prepared documents. Include explanations of how you checked sources of information; chose an appropriate format; used the computer; stored copies; routed documents; and maintained security and confidentiality. The following evidence should be collected:

• completed checklist of documents
• personal statement.

Performance criteria:	1.2.1	1.2.2	1.2.3	1.2.4	1.2.5
	1.2.6	1.2.7	1.2.8	1.2.9	
Knowledge and understanding:	1.2.a	1.2.b	1.2.c	1.2.d	1.2.e
	1.2.f	1.2.g	1.2.h	1.2.i	1.2.j
	1.2.k	1.2.l	1.2.m	1.2.n	1.2.o
	1.2.p				
Evidence requirements:	1.2.1	1.2.2	1.2.3	1.2.4	1.2.5
	1.2.6	1.2.7	1.2.8	1.2.9	1.2.10
	1.2.11	1.2.12	1.2.13	1.2.14	1.2.15
	1.2.16	11.2.7	1.2.18	1.2.19	1.2.20
	1.2.21	1.2.22	1.2.23	1.2.24	1.2.25
	1.2.26	1.2.27	1.2.28	1.2.29	1.2.30
	1.2.31	1.2.32	1.2.33	1.2.34	1.2.35
	1.2.36				

Test yourself

Knowledge and understanding	Questions
a	Explain how you would produce documents on a word processing system.
b	Explain how you would produce documents using a graphics or presentation package.

c	Explain how you would produce documents using a mailmerge facility.
d	Explain how you establish the purpose of a document.
e	Explain how you select content, style, format and distribution methods for documents prepared for different audiences and recipients and explain why attention to these factors is important.
f	Describe how you prepare information from a variety of sources.
g	Describe two ways in which you might verify that the source of some information is current, correct and valid.
h	Describe your organisation's procedures for accessing information.
i	Describe the function and structure of three different types of document/business format used in your organisation.
j	Explain how you organise, interpret and present information when you include it in business documents.
k	Describe your organisation's house style and/or procedures for presenting business letters, illustrating your answer with three types of document or business format.
l	Explain why presentation is important to your organisation's image and to its success.
m	Give examples of three different visual techniques that can be used when presenting business documents.
n	Describe how to make sure that you use language and grammar effectively in business communications.
o	Explain the legal requirements that affect the use and provision of information.
p	Describe four ways of ensuring you use hardware and software safely and effectively.

Activity 1.1

Memo

MEMORANDUM

To: Office Administrator
From: Andrew Harland, Director
Date: Monday, -- -- --

Communication procedures

Recent Board meetings have highlighted problems with staff using inappropriate methods of communication; one of our important customers received a memo from a junior member of staff recently. It was decided to carry out some staff training in choosing the correct method of communication – i.e. selecting the most appropriate type of document to use. Internal and external communications should be considered. Please prepare notes for the training session which give the reasons why it is important to choose the correct type of document; and some form of presentation which clearly shows the type of documents and their uses.

Activity 1.2

Desknote

DESKNOTE

rom: *Andrew Harland, Director*
ate: *Tuesday, -- -- --*

Thanks for your help yesterday with the notes for the procedures manual. We now need to look at our procedures for letter layout and presentation. Please draft a section on the company's standard letter layout and presentation.

Andrew

Activity 1.3

E-mail message

HTR

To: Office Administrator
From: Andrew Harland, Director
Date: Wednesday, -- -- --
Subject: Staff contact problems

We need to consider telecommunications systems that would allow us to improve the way we deal with staff contact. We need to be able to contact staff when they are based at head office or working in regional offices; or the sales team when they are out 'on the road'. Please write a brief report outlining a contact system, including information on the type of equipment we could use.

Activity 1.4

Memo

MEMORANDUM

To: Office Administrator
From: Andrew Harland, Director
Date: Thursday, -- -- --

Postage

Our postage costs have risen dramatically over the last year, both for general mail and overseas mail. We have now introduced e-mail and fax facilities on the computer system. Please prepare guidelines to be used by all staff when selecting which method of transmission to be used. These guidelines should take account of cost, speed and security.

Activity 1.5

Memo

MEMORANDUM

To: Office Administrator
From: John Williams, Company Secretary
Date: Friday, -- -- --

Complaints Procedures

Andrew Harland said he had spoken to you about helping with our complaints procedures. Staff are having difficulty with writing responses to letters of complaint. Please prepare some notes for staff on how to write a letter dealing with a complaint, including some standard examples for them to follow.

2 Organise and Administer Business Meetings and Appointments

Meetings are a very important part of an organisation's communication network. They allow for a face-to-face interchange of ideas between a group of people. An important role for administrators is to carry out a range of tasks that ensures all arrangements are made for meetings to take place smoothly, and that accurate notes are made of the meeting. This unit covers the activities required to organise meetings. The words used within the unit are 'organise and administer business meetings', but for simplicity the term 'run meetings' will be used. This will cover all aspects of planning before the meeting, administering the actual meeting, taking notes and follow-up arrangements. The term 'meeting manager' refers to the person you are working with to arrange the meeting – it may be a senior member of staff, or the chairperson/secretary of the meeting.

The chairperson and secretary play key roles in managing meetings. The role of the secretary may be shared between two people – the meeting secretary and the minutes secretary. The meeting secretary is a member of the meeting, the person who officially sends and receives correspondence for the meeting. The meeting secretary may also send agendas and prepare minutes. Where the meeting secretary does not prepare the minutes, a minutes secretary may be appointed for the meeting. The minutes secretary makes no contribution to the business of the meeting and has no voting rights. Their role is to organise the meetings, prepare agendas, attend the meeting to take notes and prepare the minutes. This is the role that forms the basis of this unit.

Element 2.1

ORGANISE AND ADMINISTER BUSINESS MEETINGS

Types of meeting

Formal meetings

Formal meetings are meetings which may form part of the organisation's quality procedures or regulatory or legal framework. They may range from Health and Safety meetings to the very formal occasions of a shareholder's meeting. Some formal meetings may be formal in substance rather than style – that is, the issues and implications of business covered in the meeting may be very important to the running of the business, but the styles of communication used within the meeting may be quite informal.

Many organisations use informal communication styles where, for example, people address one another by their forenames, as this is believed to aid teamwork. However, such meetings require just as careful planning and accurate record keeping.

The formal meeting you run should provide you with opportunities to meet all the performance criteria – for example, providing supplementary documentation and monitoring progress on actions agreed at meetings.

Informal meetings

Informal meetings are usually formed by groups of people who meet together to discuss aspects of their work – for example, course team meetings or departmental meetings. These may require less planning and briefer records may be kept of such meetings. The informal meeting you run may not provide opportunities to meet all the performance criteria and evidence requirements of the HDAP Unit 2 standards.

Annual General Meetings (AGMs)/Extraordinary General Meetings (EGMs)

Annual General Meeting (AGM)

All public limited companies (plc) must hold an AGM, however, they are optional for private limited companies (Ltd). AGMs must be held once in every calendar year and there should be no more than fifteen months in between two AGMs. An AGM usually involves:

- receiving the report and accounts
- declaring a final dividend
- electing directors
- reappointing the auditors and agreeing their remuneration.

All shareholders must be invited and given advance (21 days') notification and information of the AGM. They will usually receive a notice of the meeting, the annual report for that year, the report and financial statement and the agenda. Any shareholders who cannot attend may vote by proxy – allowing someone else attending to vote for them. The rules relating to any specific type of organisation should be checked well in advance of arranging the meeting.

Extraordinary General Meeting (EGM)

EGMs are called in order to discuss urgent business that cannot wait until the AGM. They can be called either by the directors or by certain shareholders. Examples of reasons for calling an EGM are:

- to approve a merger with another company
- to discuss major financial problems – for example, large amounts of debt
- to discuss the future of a director following allegations of malpractice.

Terms of reference

All meetings will have terms of reference. These may be formally agreed and written down in procedures, or they may be informal and accepted as 'custom and practice'. The terms of reference will define the following issues.

- *Title of the meeting* – for example, Health and Safety Meeting, Departmental Meeting.
- *Reporting procedures* – who the meeting is responsible to and reports to, particularly where this is part of a legal or regulatory framework.
- *Scope of the meeting* – guidelines for decision making and level of responsibility of the meeting.
- *Membership* – the minimum and maximum number of members; their roles – for example, chairperson, secretary, treasurer; and their qualification to be members.
- *Voting arrangements* – voting rights and the requirements for voting actions and decisions.
- *Funding arrangements* – where appropriate the arrangements for paying the expenses of the meeting.

- *Frequency of meeting* – for example, monthly, quarterly.
- *Term of the meeting* – the meeting may be an ongoing meeting or may be formed for a particular task and, when this task has been completed, may be disbanded.
- *Notice and record-keeping requirements* – the minimum notice required for a meeting; the records required; and the timescale for the issuing of records.

Note

A group of people appointed to deal with a particular task is called an 'ad hoc' committee.

Portfolio Note

For this unit you are required to produce evidence from organising and administering real meetings. These can be real meetings in your workplace, or if you are in college you need to discuss with your tutor how you can cover this unit. You could arrange to work with a head of department for a period of time to run meetings within their department, or alternatively you could work with a course team and arrange to run course team meetings. The standards require you to run both formal and informal meetings, one of which must be held over a period of time. You need to make sure that you have opportunities to do both.

It may also be a good idea to arrange to work on Element 2.3, 'Arrange and monitor appointments for self and others' at the same time as the meetings. This work has to be carried out over a period of six weeks and should be negotiated with relevant staff. This aspect of the element can be covered by a six-week work placement, or working for a college department one or two days a week over a period of time.

Portfolio activity 2.1 **Number 1**

Arrange a meeting with your tutor or workplace supervisor and agree how you will cover this unit. Agree which formal and informal meetings you will run, and an appropriate timescale. Record notes of this meeting or prepare an action plan. Arrange a meeting with the key person/s with whom you will be working to run meetings. Write and confirm the meetings you arrange. Collect information about the terms of reference for the meetings you are running. The following evidence should be collected:

- copy of entries in your diary for all the relevant meetings
- confirmation of meetings in writing
- notes of your meetings/action plan
- information about the terms of reference for the meetings you are running.

You must include examples of both formal and informal meetings. One of these two types of meeting must be held over a period of time.

Performance criteria:	2.1.1
Knowledge and understanding:	2.1.j
Evidence requirements:	2.1.1 2.1.2 2.1.3

Planning meetings

Careful planning is necessary if meetings are to run smoothly. You need to agree and confirm days, dates and times; book the room and any additional resources; inform staff in writing of meeting arrangements; prepare and issue documents before the meeting; prepare and clear the room for the meeting; prepare and issue the minutes from the last meeting; and monitor the progress of actions.

Before the meeting

Arranging a meeting date

The days, dates and times for meetings may be arranged in different ways. These can include:

- being agreed at a previous meeting – the information would be recorded in the minutes and should also be recorded in staff diaries at the meeting
- being arranged as part of a pre-set programme of meetings – for example, the monthly sales meeting might be held on the last Friday of each month; quality meetings might be scheduled for a year in advance
- being arranged by a senior member of staff – for example, the head of department might call a departmental meeting
- being agreed and negotiated between the members of the committee – for example, you might be asked to contact members of the committee and agree suitable dates for a meeting; several dates might be suggested for the meeting and you might ring members or their secretaries to find out people's availability for those dates

- being set for a specific day – for example, the morning of Wednesday 2 May.

It is possible that while a meeting may be agreed for a specific day – for example, the morning of Wednesday 2 May – the secretary arranging the meeting may set the exact time. The need to allow for travelling time for members must be balanced against the need for time to complete the business of the meeting. A 9.30 am start may be more appropriate than a 9.00 am start. If members are travelling from different locations, it is often a good idea to start with refreshments; this gives members time to recover from journeys and allows for people arriving at different times. The actual start time for the meeting should be clearly stated, and the meeting should start on time – for example, 9.30 am for coffee, meeting starts at 9.45 am.

Many organisations now have electronic diaries and electronic schedulers. Members of staff enter their appointments on the computer in the scheduling program. When a meeting is being arranged, the names of the people can be entered into the program and the computer will give a list of dates and times when all the staff are available. A suitable date can then be selected and booked in the diaries. An e-mail can then be sent confirming the meeting with the members.

When the date has been agreed, it should be entered into both your diary and the diary of the meeting manager with whom you are working.

Booking resources

When the date has been agreed, the physical resources required for the meeting need to be arranged. The availability of meeting rooms and board rooms should be checked, and the organisation's procedures for booking rooms should be followed. Arrangements for booking and confirming facilities for the date, duration, and purpose of the meeting should be confirmed in writing (see Figure 2.1.1) and could involve contacting reception, porters/security, caretakers, etc. When considering the duration of the meeting, allow time for preparing the room and for clearing it up after the meeting.

Other physical resources should also be booked. Refreshments may be required and these should be booked following the organisation's procedures. As well as coffee, tea, etc., water, soft drinks, glasses and mints may be provided for some meetings. Equipment such as overhead projectors, videos and flip charts may be required and arrangements for these should be made.

MEMORANDUM

To   Receptionist

From   Sadia Saleem, Administrator

Copy to   Henry James, Audio-visual technician
Alex Ferguson, Catering supervisor
Cherry Kitson, Chairperson staff
development committee

Date   25 April ----

Staff Development Committee Meeting – 2 May

I confirm the booking for Meeting Room 2 for
Wednesday 2 May from 9.00 am until 12.00 for a
meeting of the Staff Development Committee. I have
arranged for the technician to place an overhead
projector in the room at 8.30 am that morning. Coffee
and biscuits have been arranged for 9.00 am and will
be delivered by the Catering department.

Figure 2.1.1 A booking confirmation memo

Portfolio activity 2.1 **Number 2**

Arrange a suitable date and time for the meetings you are
running. Confirm the date and time by telephone or by
meeting with the appropriate people and/or make
appropriate entries in diaries.

Book the room and other resources required in writing.
The following evidence should be collected:

• copies of telephone messages, diary entries
• copies of written confirmation of room booking
• copies of written confirmation of other bookings –
  for example, refreshments, audio-visual aids.

You must include examples of both formal and informal
meetings. One of these two types of meetings must be held
over a period of time.

Performance criteria:	2.1.1	2.1.4	2.1.5		
Knowledge and understanding:	2.1.b	2.1.c	2.1.m	2.1.n	
Evidence requirements:	2.1.1	2.1.2	2.1.3	2.1.4	2.1.15
	2.1.16	2.1.17	2.1.19	2.1.20	2.1.21

Meeting documentation

Notice

Written notification of meetings should be sent to those attending the meeting as soon as dates have been agreed and the room booked. This is usually done in the form of a notice of meeting, which includes the meeting title, the date, details of venue, etc. The notice may include a list of items to be discussed at the meeting – this is called an 'agenda'. In some situations, the notice may ask staff to notify the meeting arranger of issues they would like discussed at the meeting. An agenda is made up from this list and sent to members at a later date.

Staff Development Committee

Staff Development Committee Meeting – 2 May

A meeting of the Staff Development Committee Meeting has been arranged for Wednesday 2 May from 9.30 until 11.30 in Meeting Room 2. If you have any items to be included on the agenda, please send them by 1 April.

Cherry Kitson, Chairperson Staff Development Committee

Circulation List
(List of members of the Staff Development Committee)

Figure 2.1.2 A notice of a meeting

Agenda

An agenda is a list of items to be discussed at a meeting. Most agendas follow a fairly standard format and include the following items.

- *Title, date, time and venue of meeting.*
- *Apologies for absence* – apologies are received and recorded for people who could not attend the meeting.
- *Minutes of the last meeting* – the minutes of the previous meeting are discussed to ensure they are an accurate record of the meeting. Any alterations are agreed, and the master copy is signed by the chairperson/secretary.
- *Matters arising from the minutes* – issues arising out of the minutes are then discussed. If there are ongoing issues that have been included as later agenda items, these are covered later.
- *Correspondence* – letters or correspondence received by the committee may be dealt with at this point. This item is not always included on agendas.
- *Business items* – the key issues to be discussed at the meeting will then be listed – for example, information technology training.

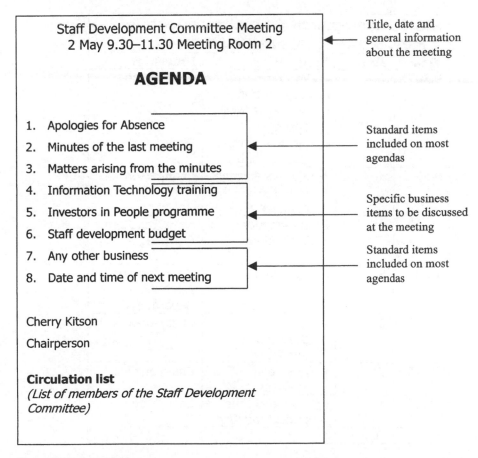

Figure 2.1.3 An agenda

- *Any other business* – this item is included so that members of the committee can bring up any issues that have not been covered in the main items.
- *Date and time of next meeting* – the members discuss and agree an appropriate date for the next meeting.

Timed agenda

Some meetings may use timed agendas, where specific time allocations are given to items on the agenda. These agendas have the advantage that: they give more control of the meeting to ensure all the business is covered; they give an indication to participants of the priority of an item, by the amount of time allocated to it on the agenda; if presentations or talks are given to (or by) people who are not members of the meeting they will have an indication of when they should attend; people who are very busy may attend for the discussion of just one particular item.

Staff Development Committee Meeting 2 May, 9.30–11.30 Meeting Room 2			
Time	**Item**	**Subject**	**Presenter**
9.30	1	• Welcome • Introduction • Apologies for absence	Chairperson
9.40	2	• Minutes of the last meeting	Chairperson
9.50	3	• Matters arising from the minutes	Chairperson
10.00	4	• Information Technology training	Kelly Trenchard, IT Manager
10.30	5	• Investors in People programme	Henry Yarwood, Personnel Department
11.00	6	• Staff development budget	Chairperson
11.15	7	• Any other business	Chairperson
11.25	8	• Date and time of next meeting	Chairperson
11.30	Finish		

Figure 2.1.4 A timed agenda

Chairperson's agenda

The chairperson manages the meeting to ensure it successfully completes its business. This person usually has a special agenda prepared which includes more detailed information for use during the meeting.

***CHAIRPERSON'S AGENDA**\				
***Staff Development Committee Meeting**\ ***2 May, 9.30–11.30 Meeting Room 2**\				
Time	**Item**	**Subject**	**Presenter**	**Comments**
09.30	1	• Welcome • Introduction • Apologies for absence – received from Tony Graham	Chairperson	
09.40	2	• Minutes of the last meeting – check item 4.2	Chairperson	
09.50	3	• Matters arising from the minutes • 3.1 – training targets achieved • 4.1 – any further discussion to be deferred to next meeting	Chairperson	
10.00	4	• Information Technology training – review of targets	Kelly Trenchard, IT Manager	
10.30	5	• Investors in People programme – presentation plus initial discussion	Henry Yarwood, Personnel Department	
11.00	6	• Staff development budget – copy of new budget available for discussion	Chairperson	
11.15	7	• Any other business	Chairperson	
11.25	8	• Date and time of next meeting	Chairperson	
11.30	Finish			

Figure 2.1.5 A chairperson's agenda

Sending out agendas

There are several factors that must be considered when preparing and sending out agendas. If members are travelling to the meeting, a location map and parking arrangements need to be included with the agenda. Some form of confirmation of attendance may be included with the agenda – that is, in the form of a reply slip. This allows final numbers for refreshments to be agreed. If lunches and other substantial refreshment arrangements are being made, confirmation of any special requirements can also be included on the reply slip (see Element 3.1 on pages 124–5 for further information).

For informal meetings, the notice and agenda may be sent in the form of a memorandum, with notice of the meeting and a general outline of topics to be discussed.

MEMORANDUM

From   Cherry Kitson, Head of Marketing
To   Section Leaders
Date   27 April ----

Publicity Materials

It is time for our annual review of publicity materials. I have arranged a meeting for Friday 4 May at 2.00 pm in my office to discuss the proposed formats to be used in the coming year. Please bring with you examples of your current publicity materials. Arrangements have been made for tea to be served during the meeting, but it should finish at 4.30 pm prompt.

If you are unable to attend the meeting, please nominate an appropriate member of staff to represent your section.

Figure 2.1.6 An informal meeting memo

Portfolio activity 2.1 **Number 3**

Prepare the notice of meeting and agenda for the meetings you are running. This should include both a formal meeting and an informal meeting and a further one of these two types of meeting which must be held over a period of time. There should therefore be a minimum of three notices and agendas, one of which should be timed. The following evidence should be collected:

- notice for three meetings
- agendas for three meetings
- witness testimony to confirm that you have sent the notices and agendas as required in sufficient time.

Performance criteria:	2.1.1	2.1.2	2.1.3	2.1.4	
Knowledge and understanding:	2.1.b	2.1.c	2.1.e	2.1.k	
Evidence requirements:	2.1.1	2.1.2	2.1.3	2.1.4	2.1.5
	2.1.6	2.1.18	2.1.19	2.1.20	2.1.21

Supplementary documents

Sets of documents need to be prepared and issued to members in good time for the meeting. This gives them time to read the information and prepare their responses. The following documents may be prepared.

- *Minutes of the previous meeting* – these should be prepared and sent to members.
- *Discussion documents and information* – any documents that are going to be discussed at the meeting should be prepared and sent to members – for example, Investors in People policy document.
- *Copies of correspondence* – these may be copied and sent to members for their information.

Sufficient copies of these documents need to be prepared for issue to members, and spares should be available for the meeting. For large meetings this may require a considerable amount of photocopying, collating and binding. The organisation's procedures for preparing multiple copies of documents need to be followed. Careful planning should allow sufficient time for the originals to be prepared and arrangements made for photocopying and printing. If copies are to be sent in the external post system, arrangements will also need to be made for labels, envelopes and sufficient postage to be available.

Attendance list

A list of members attending the meeting should be prepared. This usually contains space for the members to sign in, either at the beginning of the meeting or when the list is passed round during the meeting. Some organisations may have an attendance book that is signed at every meeting; if this is used it should be available at every meeting, and checked to ensure all members present have signed it.

```
┌─────────────────────────────────────────────────────┐
│                                                       │
│               ATTENDANCE LIST                         │
│                                                       │
│        Staff Development Committee Meeting            │
│         2 May, 9.30–11.30 Meeting Room 2              │
│                                                       │
│                                                       │
│   Cherry Kitson                                       │
│   Chairperson      .................................  │
│                                                       │
│   Tony Graham      .................................  │
│                                                       │
│   Kelly Trenchard  .................................  │
│                                                       │
│   Henry Yarwood    .................................  │
│                                                       │
│   Jennifer Yang    .................................  │
│                                                       │
│   William Hopwood .................................   │
│                                                       │
│   Howard Jones     .................................  │
│                                                       │
│                                                       │
│                                                       │
│   Member's Identification                             │
│                                                       │
└─────────────────────────────────────────────────────┘
```

Figure 2.1.7 An attendance list

Name badges

Name badges should be prepared for meetings, particularly if the members do not know each other. Blank badges can be ordered from any stationery catalogue, or the organisation may have standard badges that are issued at reception. The name badges should be prepared on a word processor in a large, clear, bold font. The style of presentation should be consistent – for example, use of titles and forenames should be the same on every badge. The organisation name and/or organisation role may also be included if this is appropriate.

Spare blank badges should be available at the meeting. These can be completed by hand if any members have substituted other members of staff to attend the meeting on their behalf.

Figure 2.1.8 Name badges

If members are sitting round a large table, it may also be appropriate to prepare name labels to be placed on the table. These are usually prepared on card, which is then folded and placed on the table. The name details should be prepared on a word processor in a large, clear, bold font. Spare cards should be available at the meeting for any substitute members.

Cherry Kitson
CHAIRPERSON

Figure 2.1.9 Name card

Members' contact details
A list of members and their contact details may be provided at a meeting. This is useful if members need to contact other members to carry out actions after the meeting. The list may contain names, organisation names and roles, addresses and telephone numbers.

Signs
A range of signs may need to be prepared for the meeting. These can include: signs at reception to direct members to the meeting room; signs to indicate locations of cloakroom facilities; 'Do not Disturb' signs to be placed on the door; 'Meeting in Progress' signs to be placed as appropriate – some of these signs may already exist in the organisation, and these can be used when required.

Informing staff members
Other people within the organisation may need to be informed of the meeting. These can include the following.

- *Heads of department and senior managers* may need to keep track of meetings taking place within their department.
- *Reception* should be informed of members visiting the organisation. A list of names, together with the date and time of the meeting should be sent to reception in advance.

- *Switchboard/telephone operator* may also require a list of people visiting the organisation so that any messages can be taken and passed on.

Whatever documentation is being prepared for a meeting, it is always a good idea to take spare sets to the meeting. This should include spare agendas, past minutes and other documentation. Packs of documents should be prepared at least the day before the meeting and should be labelled and placed in a folder ready to take to the meeting. Stationery required for the meeting should also be prepared and placed in the pack – for example, pencils and notepaper.

Portfolio activity 2.1 **Number 4**

Prepare the documentation for the meetings you are running. The following evidence should be collected:

- copies of the agenda
- past minutes
- attendance list
- member identification
- member contact details
- appropriate signs
- any other documentation
- witness testimony to confirm that you prepared sets of documents in suitable time.

You must include examples of both formal and informal meetings. One of these two types of meeting must be held over a period of time.

Performance criteria:	2.1.1	2.1.2	2.1.3	2.1.4	2.1.7
Knowledge and understanding:	2.1.b 2.1.o	2.1.c	2.1.g	2.1.i	2.1.l
Evidence requirements:	2.1.1 2.1.7 2.1.14	2.1.2 2.1.10 2.1.18	2.1.3 2.1.11 2.1.19	2.1.4 2.1.12 2.1.20	2.1.5 2.1.13 2.1.21

The day of the meeting

Before the meeting

Time should be allowed before the meeting in order to get the room ready. This may be an hour or half an hour depending on the type of meeting, the number of members, etc. The following preparations should be made.

- *Post signs* – put up any signs you have prepared for the meeting.
- *Check seating and tables* – the layout of tables and chairs should be suitable for the purpose of the meeting. Make sure there are enough chairs and get one or two spare chairs if required from nearby rooms.
- *Check equipment* – where overhead projectors, videos, etc. are required, check that they have been supplied and are working.
- *Check refreshments* – check there are water and glasses on the table. Some meetings also have mints on the table. If coffee or other refreshments have been ordered, check that they have arrived or that space is available for them if they have been ordered for later during the meeting.
- *Check any health and safety arrangements* you may be required to make – for example, check fire exits, trailing wires, etc.
- *Organise stationery* – place notepaper, pens, pencils, place names, etc. in each place on the table.
- *Organise a suitable reception area to greet members* – place name badges and the attendance list in an appropriate area for members as they arrive.

As the members start arriving they should be greeted. The members should be issued with name badges and asked to sign the attendance list. This may also provide a good opportunity to check contact details with members.

During the meeting

The meeting should start on time. If key members have been delayed and are late arriving, the chairperson can make a decision to alter the order of the items on the agenda if this is appropriate. The chairperson should begin with welcome and introductions if these are required.

Before the formal business of the meeting takes place, it is usual to have a small introduction explaining the health and safety requirements for the meeting. This is often called the 'domestics', and should include briefing delegates on:

- the type of fire alarm, including mention of any routine alarm testing that may take place during the meeting
- the location of fire exits and reporting procedures following evacuation
- the location of cloakroom/toilet facilities

- any arrangements for smoking
- arrangements for refreshments, meals, breaks, etc.

Once the meeting is under way, notes should be taken to record the business of the meeting. In some situations a member of the meeting may be appointed to take the minutes of the meeting. This member may still participate in the business, but will take the notes and prepare the draft minutes to be agreed with the chairperson.

A knowledge of shorthand or speedwriting is very useful for taking notes during meetings. It is not usually necessary to write down everything that is said. (If it is necessary to write down everything, then the notes you take are known as 'verbatim' notes.)

Notes are quite easy to take if you remember the following tips.

- Only record the key issues and decisions.
- Use abbreviations for names of members.
- Try to summarise the business in the notes you write, rather than trying to write down everything that is said. For example, write:

> **Reasons for the low uptake were discussed. It was felt that staff did not take up current options because the fixed times clashed with other timetabled activities. Further, staff were not aware of all the provisions.**

rather than:

> **A said that staff were too busy. B said that people in his department did not have much idea of what was available and kept asking him for more information. A said that many of the staff had meetings on the training afternoon. C said that staff did not read the notices placed on the noticeboards. D asked if part-time staff could attend the sessions and chairperson said all staff could attend the sessions and this had been agreed at a previous meeting. C said why wasn't there more publicity...etc.**

- Motions (page 74) or proposals should be recorded verbatim for the minutes. Take these down carefully and read them back to the meeting to check that they are correct. Motions are usually proposed by a member of the meeting and seconded by another member. Their names must both be accurately recorded in the minutes.
- Key in your notes on a word processor immediately after the meeting, if possible, while the business of the meeting is still fresh in your mind. If necessary, just key in a quick draft immediately and tidy it up the next day.

- Have a good understanding of meeting terms. These are listed later in this unit (page 74).

Good note-taking comes with experience both of note-taking in general and also of the working of a particular meeting. With experience, you will get better at summarising the business of the meeting, as well as assessing the quantity and quality of each member's contribution.

After the meeting

When the meeting has finished, the room should be cleared. The following actions may need to be taken.

- Collect up and remove spare papers, pencils, etc.
- Tidy up refreshments and place them ready for collection, where appropriate.
- Leave tables and chairs tidy.
- Check equipment is ready for removal.
- Remove signs.
- Check that no personal belongings have been left. If any items have been left, either take them to reception or remove them and arrange for their collection.

There may be other actions that need to be carried out after the meeting – for example, payment of expenses for members, payment for refreshments, writing thank-you letters to speakers, etc. These actions should be carried out as soon as possible after the event.

Portfolio activity 2.1 **Number 5**

Prepare a checklist to be used when preparing and clearing a room for a meeting. Include the activities to be carried out when greeting members. Use the list on page 71 when you prepare the rooms for the meetings you are running. The following evidence should be collected:

- blank checklist form
- completed checklists for three meetings – that is, one formal, one informal and one held over a period of time – signed by a witness to show that you completed the activities correctly
- photographs and/or videos of the room and of you greeting members.

Note
Make arrangements to take photographs – a Polaroid or digital camera can be very useful.

Performance criteria:	2.1.1	2.1.8	2.1.13	2.1.14	2.1.15
	2.1.16				
Knowledge and understanding:					
Evidence requirements:	2.1.1	2.1.2	2.1.3	2.1.4	

Minutes of the meeting

The notes that are recorded at a meeting are usually presented in the form of minutes. Minutes are an accurate written record of the business of a meeting. They usually contain: the title of the meeting; the date of the meeting; a list of those present at the meeting; a record of key issues and actions agreed; the signature of the chairperson to confirm they are an accurate record.

The main terms used in meetings and when writing minutes are explained in the following table.

Meeting terms

Term	Explanation
Adjourned	an item or discussion not completed at a meeting which is postponed until a further meeting
Ballot	a written vote, which retains the anonymity of the voters
Casting vote	a vote usually held by the chairperson which can be used to settle a split vote
Motion	a formal proposal to be discussed and voted on by members of the committee
Nem con.	'with no-one dissenting' – refers to a resolution passed without opposition, though possibly with some members abstaining from voting
Point of order	discussion about the correctness of the procedures or terms of reference of the meeting
Proposer	the person who formally proposes a motion to a meeting
Quorum	the minimum number of members required for the business of the meeting to be conducted
Resolution	a motion which becomes a firm decision as it has been proposed, seconded, voted on and agreed by a majority of the members
Seconder	the person who formally seconds a motion proposed by the proposer
Split vote	a vote in which equal numbers of the committee are for and against the motion
Unanimous	a resolution passed with the full agreement of the meeting
Verbatim	'word-for-word' – a motion should be recorded verbatim for the minutes
Vote	a decision settled by a show of hands

There are various styles for presenting minutes. The most usual are narrative minutes, resolution minutes and action minutes, though there are some other styles which we will mention briefly.

Narrative minutes

This is the standard style for presenting minutes. A set of minutes prepared in this style will contain the items listed above. The record of the meeting is presented under the agenda headings and includes a summary of the key issues discussed and lists any actions. Any documents presented at the meeting are included in an appendix. They are written in the third person, past tense and in a formal style.

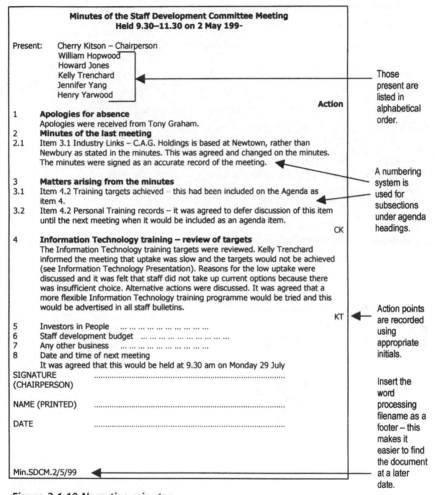

Minutes of the Staff Development Committee Meeting
Held 9.30–11.30 on 2 May 199-

Present: Cherry Kitson – Chairperson
           William Hopwood
           Howard Jones
           Kelly Trenchard
           Jennifer Yang
           Henry Yarwood

Those present are listed in alphabetical order.

Action

1   **Apologies for absence**
     Apologies were received from Tony Graham.
2   **Minutes of the last meeting**
2.1 Item 3.1 Industry Links – C.A.G. Holdings is based at Newtown, rather than Newbury as stated in the minutes. This was agreed and changed on the minutes. The minutes were signed as an accurate record of the meeting.

3   **Matters arising from the minutes**
3.1 Item 4.2 Training targets achieved – this had been included on the Agenda as item 4.
3.2 Item 4.2 Personal Training records – it was agreed to defer discussion of this item until the next meeting when it would be included as an agenda item.
                                                                                    CK

A numbering system is used for subsections under agenda headings.

4   **Information Technology training – review of targets**
     The Information Technology training targets were reviewed. Kelly Trenchard informed the meeting that uptake was slow and the targets would not be achieved (see Information Technology Presentation). Reasons for the low uptake were discussed and it was felt that staff did not take up current options because there was insufficient choice. Alternative actions were discussed. It was agreed that a more flexible Information Technology training programme would be tried and this would be advertised in all staff bulletins.
                                                                                    KT

Action points are recorded using appropriate initials.

5   Investors in People   ... ...
6   Staff development budget ... ...
7   Any other business   ... ...
8   Date and time of next meeting
     It was agreed that this would be held at 9.30 am on Monday 29 July
SIGNATURE   ....
(CHAIRPERSON)

NAME (PRINTED)   ....

DATE   ....

Insert the word processing filename as a footer – this makes it easier to find the document at a later date.

Min.SDCM.2/5/99

Figure 2.1.10 Narrative minutes

Resolution minutes

The minutes should record resolutions which are proposed, seconded and voted on in the course of the meeting. When narrative minutes are being used, this should be included in the relevant section; however, to save time, a briefer style of minutes can be used which just records the resolutions passed at the meeting.

6   Staff Development Budget

Kelly Trenchard proposed that:
'the Committee write to the Principal to request a ten-per-cent increase in the Staff Development Budget for the next financial year.'

This was seconded by Jennifer Yang and passed unanimously.

Figure 2.1.11 A section from resolution minutes

Action minutes

This is a briefer style of minutes that just includes the actions agreed at the meeting. Action minutes are used when it is not necessary to record discussion, and are quicker and cheaper to produce.

Staff Development Committee Meeting – 2 May			
Present	Cherry Kitson – Chairperson, William Hopwood, Howard Jones, Kelly Trenchard, Jennifer Yang, Henry Yarwood		
Absent	Tony Graham		
Agenda Item	**Action Agreed**	**Responsibility**	**Timescale**
Matters arising from the minutes	Include Personal Training records as an agenda item for the next meeting	Cherry Kitson	July 4 ----
Information Technology training	Devise a more flexible Information Technology training programme to be advertised in all staff bulletins.	Kelly Trenchard	End July ----
Investors in People	All members to inform their departments at departmental meetings of current developments in Investors in People	All members of the meeting	July 4 ----
Any other business	Collect further information of training courses advertised in the ASWT Professional Magazine, and circulate to all members of the team	Jennifer Yang	End June ----

Figure 2.1.12 Action minutes

Alternative minute styles
Record of meeting form
Organisations may have developed their own method of recording the business of meetings. The requirements of quality procedures for all meetings to be recorded have put pressure on many staff so

quick, simple methods of recording meetings have often been developed. These methods meet the requirements for recording meetings, but reduce staff pressures. One such method is to use a record of meeting form (see Figure 2.1.13). This form is completed by hand by the secretary or nominated person during the course of the meeting. It is signed by the members at the end of the meeting and is then filed in the relevant file.

Title of meeting	Administrators' weekly meeting		
Date of Meeting	2 June ----		
Members present	June Carew, Andrew Wilkinson, Hamish McEwen, Wendy Robinson		
Items and discussion		Actions	Responsibility and timescale
Weekly management notes were read. Progress was being made on the arrangements for the Annual Sales Meeting. More coloured photocopying paper was required to produce the Sales leaflets. This will be ordered.		Order coloured photo-copying paper	Andrew Wilkinson End of week
Problems with the telephone system and conference calls were discussed and the telephone company would be contacted to see if the correct procedures were being used.		Contact telephone company	Hamish McEwen For next meeting
Signed by members present June Carew Hamish McEwen		Andrew Wilkinson Wendy Robinson	

Figure 2.1.13 A record of meeting form

Minute book

Another alternative method of recording minutes is through the use of a minute book, in which the minutes are recorded by hand by the secretary or nominated person. Copies of the minutes may be photocopied and sent to members, or the book may be kept by the secretary and members can ask to see the book prior to the meeting.

Circulating minutes

The minutes should initially be prepared as a draft, and this draft should then be shown to the chairperson for checking. This checking should be for the accuracy of the record. Every effort should be made to ensure the draft minutes are correct in grammar, spelling, punctuation and keying in. When the minutes of the record have been agreed, sufficient copies should be prepared and circulated to relevant staff. Multiple copies of the document may be printed and collated in the following ways.

- Multiple copies are prepared on a word processor and collated by hand – this is appropriate for a small number of copies of a relatively short document.
- Copies are photocopied and collated by hand or using automatic collating facilities – this is the method most commonly used.
- Copies are printed and collated by a printing company – this method is used when a large number of high quality copies are required – for example, for circulation to shareholders after an AGM.

The circulation list should be agreed with the chairperson. It will usually consist of all members of the meeting, plus any relevant members of management. It is important that the correct address is used when sending copies to members, so the updated list prepared at the meeting should be checked to ensure all addresses are up to date. It is useful to set up a database or mailmerge list of members and produce labels using this file. Where large numbers are to be sent out in the post, the post-room should be informed in advance, so that sufficient postage and staff resources are available.

Copy minutes should be circulated as soon as possible after the meeting. The timescale for this may be agreed within the organisation's procedures, or the terms of reference of the meeting. With certain regulatory or legal meetings the circulation of minutes within a set timescale may be a legal requirement. You need to plan carefully to ensure resources are available and contingencies are allowed for.

Monitoring progress of actions

The minutes will list the actions to be taken by members of the committee. These may or may not include target dates for completion of the activities. The progress of these actions should be monitored in accordance with an agreed timescale. These dates should be listed in a diary or follow-up system, and the chairperson of the meeting or other agreed manager informed of the progress.

Follow-up actions can also be monitored using electronic schedulers on a computer, with entries made in the schedulers of the relevant staff to remind them when to report actions. E-mails can also be sent requesting an update on the progress of actions.

Wall planners may also be used for monitoring actions. The dates for checking and actions should be noted, together with any response, so that progress can be checked by the appropriate people.

Action agreed	Responsibility	Timescale	Monitor date	Progress
Include Personal Training records as an agenda item for the next meeting	Cherry Kitson	4 July ----	16 May – Agenda Issue date	16 May – completed
Devise a more flexible Information Technology training programme to be advertised in all staff bulletins.	Kelly Trenchard	End July ----	Week ending June 22nd	21 June – programme agreed – see attached Advertised in June Staff Bulletin – see attached
All members to inform their departments at departmental meetings of current developments in Investors in People	All members of the meeting	4 July ----	Week ending 22 June	21 June – WH, HJ, CK completed KT – agenda for 24 June JY – agenda for 26 June HY – June meeting cancelled, on agenda for 6 July TG – no progress – still sick
Collect further information of training courses advertised in the ASWT Professional Magazine, and circulate to all members of the team	Jennifer Yang	End of June ----	Week ending 22 June	21 June – collected and sent to all staff on 31 May – see attached notes

Figure 2.1.14 An action follow-up checklist

Portfolio activity 2.1 Number 6

1 Attend a minimum of three meetings – one formal, one informal and one held over a period of time – and record the key issues and decisions made at that meeting. The following evidence should be collected:

• the notes you made at the meeting

- the initial draft and final agreed minutes – at least one set of minutes must be narrative minutes and another set must be in a suitable other style
- the set of finally collated minutes, including any printing or photocopying requests
- distribution lists/memos/labels used for distributing minutes
- witness testimony to confirm that minutes were distributed within agreed deadlines.

2 Arrange to monitor the progress of actions agreed at meetings and report this to the appropriate person. Use a diary, wall planner, action checklist, or scheduler. The following evidence should be collected:

- any notes you made with the appropriate person about monitoring dates, including diary notes
- copy of checklist, wall planner or printout of electronic scheduler notes
- records of any memos, e-mails or telephone conversations you made in order to monitor actions
- copies of the report presented to the appropriate person – for example, copies of the completed checklist, memos or e-mails.

3 Write a personal statement explaining how you have kept all information about the meeting confidential. This should include information on the use of passwords, manual handling of documents, and how you kept information about all meetings confidential.

Performance criteria:	2.1.3	2.1.4	2.1.6	2.1.9	2.1.10
	2.1.11	2.1.12	2.1.15		
Knowledge and understanding:	2.1.a	2.1.b	2.1.c	2.1.d	2.1.h
	2.1.l	2.1.p			
Evidence requirements:	2.1.1	2.1.2	2.1.3	2.1.4	2.1.8
	2.1.9	2.1.18	2.1.19	2.1.20	2.1.21

Test yourself

Knowledge and understanding	Questions
a	Give three examples of legal and regulatory documents relating to business meetings.

b, c	Explain the difference between formal and informal meetings.
d	Explain what an AGM is. Explain what an EGM is.
e	Describe the function and format of notices and agendas for meetings.
f	Describe the function and format of a timed agenda.
g	Describe the function and format of a chairperson's agenda.
h	Explain the function of minutes of a meeting. Explain the difference between narrative, resolution and action minutes.
i	Describe why and how attendance lists may be used.
j	What is meant by 'terms of reference' for a meeting?
k	Describe your organisation's procedures for notice of meetings.
l	Describe your organisation's procedures for the production of multiple copies of documentation for meetings.
m	Describe your organisation's procedures for booking rooms for meetings.
n	Describe your organisation's procedures for booking resources for meetings.
o	Describe the role of the chairperson and the contribution they make in running a meeting.
p	Describe the role of the minute-taker at a meeting.

Element 2.2
CHAIR AN INFORMAL MEETING

Element 2.2 looks in more detail at the role of the chairperson in meetings. The essential function of the chairperson is to manage the meeting to ensure it successfully completes its business. This includes ensuring: the meeting has a clear purpose; all members make a useful contribution; the meeting achieves its objectives within the agreed time. The chairperson's activities can be separated into three sections – before the meeting, during the meeting and after the meeting. Some of these activities are very similar to those described in Element 2.1, the major difference being a higher level of responsibility for:

- making decisions about the purpose and objectives of the meeting
- managing the discussion and business of the meeting
- ensuring accurate records of the meeting have been made.

Establishing the objectives of meetings

It is important to have a clear idea of why the meeting is being held. The meeting may be established to meet a particular need – for example, a meeting of a group of people organising a particular activity. Alternatively it may be an ongoing meeting – for example, a regular weekly administrator's meeting. It may be established by senior management – for example, a senior management meeting deciding to have a regular quality circle meeting – or it may be established by a group of people – for example, the administrators deciding among themselves it would be a good idea to have a meeting to exchange ideas.

The organisation's procedures should be checked to make sure that the meeting fits into the organisation's meeting structure. Care has to be taken to ensure the meeting is not repeating or interfering with an established meeting. Organisations with audited quality procedures may need all meetings to be recorded or checked against the quality procedures.

The objectives of the meeting should be clearly defined in terms of its area of responsibility, reporting lines, frequency and composition of members. For example, it might be an administrative meeting to manage the practical arrangements for the *Annual Toy Fair*, reporting to the sales director:

Toy Fair Administrative Meeting

A meeting to manage the practical arrangements for the Annual Toy Fair, reporting to the sales director. The meetings to be held fortnightly August to November and weekly from the beginning of December (excluding Christmas week) until the fair takes place at the end of January. The membership of the meeting to include a nominated representative of the sales team and the sales department administrators. A chairperson should be nominated who will liaise directly with the sales director about the progress of arrangements for the event. Action minutes should be taken and a copy sent to the sales director. Staff representatives from other departments – for example, Accounts, may be called to meetings as appropriate.

As well as defining the overall objectives of the meeting, it is important to have a clear idea of the purpose of a particular meeting – for example, to discuss the venue to be booked for the *Annual Toy Fair*. This will determine the items to be included in the agenda. Items for the agenda may arise in the following ways.

They may be referred from a previous meeting. For example, it might be agreed that final discussion for the venue of the event will be held at the first meeting in September. Members might have to undertake various actions by that date and have their reports ready for the meeting.

They may arise during the course of normal business. For example, an exhibitor might cancel a stand and this might then be referred to in the next meeting as an agenda item. The chairperson should note these items and include them on the agenda.

They may be referred from other members of the meeting. For example, a member might be having problems with the printing of publicity materials and might request the chairperson to include this on the agenda for the meeting. The chairperson might have to make a decision about the urgency and importance of this item and where it would fit into the business of the next meeting. They might suggest that this be brought up at a later meeting if appropriate. A member might also raise issues during *Any Other Business*, but time is usually limited for consideration of these items and it might be necessary to defer their discussion until the next meeting.

They may be referred from senior management. For example, the sales director might ask the chairperson to include discussion on the budget at the next meeting

Chairperson's role

Before the meeting

At this stage, the chairperson has responsibility for making the decisions about the purpose and objectives of the meeting. This can include deciding on whether a meeting is necessary and, if so, defining its objectives and then deciding on suitable members, agenda items, etc. The chairperson has to: decide on a suitable date, time and location for the meeting; decide on the agenda for the meeting; ensure suitable practical arrangements have been made – for example, the meeting room has been booked; ensure suitable documentation has been prepared – for example, agenda, minutes; monitor the arrangements for the meeting and ensure they are being carried out satisfactorily – for example, the agendas have been sent out so that members have sufficient notice of the meeting.

Portfolio activity 2.2 **Number 1**

Agree with your tutor a meeting that you will chair. This may be a meeting that is part of your normal work, or a meeting that is linked to another of the units in the scheme – for example, Element 3.1, Work Within a Team to Organise and Administer Business Events, is particularly useful for this purpose. It may be a good idea to rotate the role of chairperson for a series of meetings used to organise an event. This will give every member an opportunity to complete this element. Ensure the meeting involves a minimum of five people, including the chairperson and someone to take the minutes of the meeting. The meeting must last at least half an hour.

Make the necessary pre-meeting arrangements. The following evidence should be collected:

- statement of the objectives of the meeting
- diary to show dates agreed for the meeting
- documentation confirming practical arrangements – for example, booking rooms
- correspondence and notes used to confirm and agree dates with members
- notice of meeting and agenda, including a statement saying how you arrived at the items of the agenda
- chairperson's agenda.

It is a good idea to arrange for the meeting to be recorded on video or audio-cassette and this should be organised at this time.

Performance criteria:	2.2.1	2.2.2	2.2.3
Knowledge and understanding:	2.2.c		
Evidence requirements:	2.2.1	2.2.2	

Chairing a meeting

The chairperson has the key role of managing the discussion and business of the meeting. This is very different from the note-taking role of the minutes secretary, who does not participate in the business of the meeting. However, the chairperson will liaise with the minutes secretary to make sure that the key issues and decisions of the meeting are recorded. This may mean the chairperson keeping their own notes of the meeting.

The other members of the meeting also have a role to play – they should: bring with them all the meeting documentation, i.e. agendas, minutes and any other documentation; make contributions to items on the agenda; be ready to make reports to the meeting on any actions which were required of them in the minutes of the previous meeting; listen to and understand the views of others presented at the meeting; make decisions about issues that are in the best interests of the organisation; agree to take on actions as a result of discussions at the meeting.

The most difficult role for the chairperson is the management of the personalities of the members while conducting the business of the meeting. It is important to keep the discussion focused on the business of the meeting, and to manage the pace of the meeting so that its work is achieved within the allotted time. Meetings can become 'hijacked' by personalities with their own agendas, or become an opportunity for negative criticism.

Time allocation

Careful planning of the time allocation for topics during the meeting can help the chairperson to keep the business focused. The chairperson's agenda (see page 65) should include an allocation of time for each item on the agenda. The time allocation may be included in the circulated agenda to members if appropriate. This is particularly useful if someone from outside the meeting has to attend for a particular item – for example, if a member of the Accounts department has been asked to attend the discussion on the budget.

The time allocation should take account of the importance, urgency and complexity of the item. Important and urgent items should be placed near the beginning of the agenda as members are fresher for the earlier items and may be more inclined to listen and promote discussion. Less important or non-urgent items may be put later on the agenda so that they can be discussed in a shorter time, or left until another meeting.

Managing the meeting

When an agenda item is being discussed, the chairperson has a number of tasks.

Introduce the topic for discussion to the meeting. This should be done impartially and in a way that promotes discussion. The notes for this should be prepared in advance and may be included in the chairperson's agenda, for example:

> **Agenda Item 3 – Cancellation of Exhibition Stand**
>
> **XYZ has cancelled its exhibition stand 4A. This is a key stand to the left of the entrance exhibition. We need to discuss the various options open to us to fill this exhibition space.**

Encourage the members to make useful contributions. It is useful to know the members of the meeting – some people may talk a lot but not have a lot to say, while others may be quieter and still have very valuable contributions to make. Consider using the following strategies.

- When you introduce a topic, directly ask someone to make a contribution – for example, following the introduction above you could add:

> **Tony, I believe you have some ideas on this.**

- Stress the time allocation and offer the item for discussion 'round the table'. Start with someone who will make a good contribution:

> **We are short of time and only have twenty minutes to discuss this item. Let's go round the table and spend just a few moments getting everyone's ideas. Jenny, could you start?**

- Keep people to the point and interrupt the discussion if necessary to ask someone to make a contribution:

> **We've heard a range of views. Tony, what do you think?**

Encourage discussion by including your own ideas, or providing other useful options for discussion, for example:

> **We've discussed offering the exhibition space to another exhibitor, or trying to find a new exhibitor to fill the space. Has anyone considered moving the stands along and offering increased space at a reduced price to the exhibitors in this row?**

Discourage unhelpful digressions or time-wasting. Some members may not be focused in their discussion and contributions and may start introducing ideas, or recounting incidents which are not helpful:

> **KTL are always complaining they don't have enough space, yet they're not prepared to pay for it. Their sales director was really difficult last week and went on about how much we charge...**

You need to stop these people politely, in order that the real business of the meeting can proceed. Try to interrupt with:

> **Thank you for that. We need to move on and make a decision about this exhibition space.**

or

> **Thank you for that. Jenny, I believe you dealt with a similar cancellation last year.**

If an issue arises which is not within the scope of the meeting's authority, it should be noted and an action recorded in the minutes to check with a more senior member of staff and report back to everyone concerned.

If the discussion has digressed too far, you need to bring the members back to the business in hand. It may be that there is nothing useful left to discuss and you can begin to draw the item to a close:

> **Let's get back to the exhibition cancellation. If no-one has any further comments on this, we need to agree our future action...**

and then summarise the discussion and move to an action.

Summarise the discussion and agree actions. When the useful discussion is coming to an end, you need to summarise the outcome of the discussion and agree appropriate actions:

> **We've looked at the various options to cover the cancellation of stand 4a and I think we're all agreed that, in the first instance, we offer the space to our biggest customer Make-Actac Ltd, at no extra cost and then consider selling their exhibition space. Jenny deals with Make-Actac Ltd and she has agreed to contact them tomorrow. Jenny will report progress next week and we will review the situation then.**

Close the meeting formally so that everyone is clear that the meeting has ended.

Non-verbal communication

If a chairperson is to manage the meeting effectively, they need to read the non-verbal language of the participants and respond to these. There are a number of signals to look out for.

Voice tones. These can indicate whether people are angry, bored, upset, worried, etc. The chairperson then needs to take appropriate action to deal with any problems, for example:

> **Tony, we know that you feel strongly about this, but overall the meeting has agreed that in the best interests of the company action ... should be taken.**

Other voice sounds: sighs, laughter, etc. These can often be expressed by members other than the one speaking – for example, members might be sighing because another member has just started off on their favourite 'moan'. The chairperson needs to cut this short and move on with the business.

Facial expressions. The eyes raised in the 'here we go again' look, glazed expressions when people are confused, staring-out-of-the-window-bored expressions – all of these need to be carefully watched, and appropriate action taken. For example:

> **I think you have expressed these views clearly before. Can we now move on...**

Body actions. Fidgeting and doodling are usually signs of boredom or lack of interest. Banging the table and clenching fists may be signs of aggression.

Body positions. Be aware, for example, of the laid-back-in-the-chair-bored position and of the attentive listening position.

As well as being aware of the non-verbal communication of the members, the chairperson also has to be aware of their own body language and the message this is giving to members. It is important for the chairperson to remain neutral and this must be reflected in their body language. They should not get heated about a point of debate, or show any preference for particular members of the committee. It is also important to retain control of the meeting and this may mean being assertive with people. This does not mean shouting or being rude to members, but it does mean using a tone of voice and body language that gives the message of control.

Handling disagreement and conflict

There are occasions in meetings when very strongly held views become a source of disagreement and this needs careful handling. The chairperson should remain impartial. Careful management of the discussion by the chairperson can help to reduce conflict.

However, where disagreement does arise the following actions can be taken.

- The chairperson can put the disagreement to the meeting and ask for suggestions as to what action the meeting wants to take. For example:

  There is a range of strongly held views around the table. What do you feel is the best way forward for us to progress on this item?

- The issue can be put to a formal vote and the majority vote carried forward as actions.
- Members can ask for their views to be recorded and minuted.
- The meeting can agree to take the issue to a higher authority for advice. The higher authority is usually the person or meeting to which the meeting reports.

Whatever conflict or disagreements may arise, members should still accept the decisions made by the meeting and work positively to complete the work of the meeting.

After the meeting

The meetings should end on time. Any outstanding issues should be adjourned to be discussed at the next meeting. However, this should not be a regular practice as it can result in a backlog of items building up. It may also be an indication that the meetings are ineffective and that more careful management is required.

Once the meeting has finished, the chairperson should ensure all follow-up actions are completed: meeting records (minutes) are completed and circulated as appropriate; any other actions are completed – for example, letters of thanks; actions are monitored. These items are considered in detail in Element 2.1.

Self-assessment of performance

After the meeting the chairperson needs to carry out an assessment of their own performance. This is part of a process of continual improvement. Most people learn from their experience: they reflect on their actions, think about what they did well and what they could improve. More benefit can be gained from self-assessment if it is planned and clearly structured. Another viewpoint can also be helpful and you could discuss your self-assessment with someone else present at the meeting – perhaps an assessor or just an ordinary member of the meeting.

The assessment should include a reflection on whether the objectives you set for the meeting were achieved. This means that you should clearly identify the objectives for the meeting in advance, as discussed earlier, but you could also include other matters such as resolving issues or checking the response of the members of the meeting to new ideas.

A checklist can be used to structure self-assessment to ensure all aspects of the meeting are reviewed; however, it is not practical to complete the checklist during the meeting, as the chairperson should be focused on the business of the meeting. Notes on your performance should be made immediately after the meeting when it is still fresh in your mind. It is also very useful to have the meeting recorded on video or audio-cassette. You can play this back and analyse your performance more carefully. The checklist can then be completed and discussed with an assessor.

Name		
Date of Meeting		
Title of Meeting		
Item for assessment	What went well?	What could have been improved?
Opening of discussion points		
Skills in encouraging participation		
Ability to summarise and clarify discussions and decisions		
Time management of the meeting		
Were the objectives achieved?		
Third Person/Assessor comment		
Actions for next meeting		

Figure 2.2.1 A self-assessment checklist

Portfolio activity 2.2 **Number 2**

Discuss with your assessor how your performance at the meeting will be assessed. Your assessor may attend the meeting, or you could record it on video or audio-cassette.

Prepare an assessment checklist before the meeting. Chair the meeting and complete the necessary activities. The following evidence should be collected:

- video or audio-cassette recording of the meeting
- assessor's report on your performance
- completed chairperson's agenda and any notes you have made
- completed record of the meeting – for example, minutes and action notes prepared by the secretary of the meeting
- completed assessment checklist on how you introduced discussion points, encouraged participation, clarified and summarised issues, managed the timing, etc. – include your assessor's comments.

Performance criteria:	2.2.3	2.2.4	2.2.5	2.2.6	2.2.7
	2.2.8	2.2.10	2.2.11		
Knowledge and understanding:	2.2.a	2.2.b	2.2.c	2.2.d	2.2.e
	2.2.f	2.2.g	2.2h	2.2.i	2.2.j
	2.2.k				
Evidence requirements:	2.2.1	2.2.2	2.2.3	2.2.4	2.2.5
	2.2.6	2.2.7			

Test yourself

Knowledge and understanding	Questions
a	Describe the role of the chairperson and the contribution they make to the running of a meeting.
b	Describe the roles and responsibilities of participants in a meeting.
c	Explain how you establish the objectives of meetings.
d	Give three examples of rules and procedures for meetings you have chaired.

e	Describe how you organise, analyse and present information in order to promote debate and decision-making in a meeting.
f	List three types of non-verbal language and describe their characteristics.
g	Describe three ways of promoting and encouraging debate in a meeting.
h	Explain how you summarise and clarify discussions and decisions in a meeting.
i	Describe three ways of dealing with disagreements and conflict in a meeting.
j	How do you ensure key issues, decisions and actions are recorded in a meeting?
k	Explain how you would assess and evaluate your own performance as chairperson of a meeting.

Element 2.3

ARRANGE AND MONITOR APPOINTMENTS FOR SELF AND OTHERS

Managing appointments, diaries and other planning aids is an important part of the administrator's role. The administrator ensures appointments and other commitments are met and all arrangements proceed smoothly. Element 2.3 covers the activities required to manage the administrator's personal diary and that of a manager. The word 'appointments' is used throughout the element and refers to an agreed time commitment. This can be a formal/informal meeting, a group meeting or a one-to-one meeting. It may cover appointments with internal or external individuals or groups.

Appointment management systems

Appointments can be managed in diaries or by using appointment schedules (see Figure 2.3.1). Diaries are used by all management and administrative staff to organise their activities over a period of time. Appointment schedules are used where a list of appointments is being booked for a specific activity – for example, for interviews, careers interviews, parents' evenings. A blank sheet with timed intervals is prepared and entries are made as the appointments are booked.

Diary systems

Diary systems can be divided into two types of system – manual and electronic. Organisations may use only one type of system or a combination of the two.

Manual

Manual systems are basically paper-based systems and use a range of diaries or organisers to record appointments. Diaries come in a range of styles and sizes – for example, page a day, week on a page. Diaries are replaced annually and any general information written in them has to be transferred to the new diary at the end of the year.

Organisers differ from diaries in that they contain information in a ring binder. The information can be organised into sections – for example, calendar, contact information, etc. The advantage of using an organiser is that the calendar pages can be replaced without needing to transfer all the additional information. Organisers contain sections which can include a diary, forward calendars, emergency numbers, daily schedules, address lists, project information, financial information, yellow pages. Use of an organiser means that all essential information is clearly organised within one format, rather than keeping information in separate diaries, address books, notebooks, expenses books, etc.

The advantages of paper-based organisers are that: they are simple and easy to use; they are inexpensive; they can be used anywhere independently of the availability of electricity or equipment. The disadvantages are that: they can only be accessed by one user at a time; it is not as easy to find or sort additional information as it is in electronic systems; there is a limited amount of information and storage space; information cannot be kept confidential.

Interview schedule		Vacancy	Trainee administrator
Date	22.08.--	Interviewees	Corinne Aspel Terry Shaw
Venue	Interview Room 2		
Time		Name	
09.30		Derek Coombes	
10.00		Angela Hampton	
10.30		Aneela Khan	
11.00		Barry Utting	
11.30		Siobhan Murphy	

Figure 2.3.1 An appointment schedule

Electronic

Electronic diary systems use computerised technology to record appointments. There are three main types of electronic diary system.

Hand-held electronic organisers. These small organisers can be programmed to contain diary dates and other useful information such as contact details. They can be used on their own, or can be connected to computers to form part of a larger system. They may contain additional facilities – for example, it may be possible to connect them to telephone systems to send e-mails, faxes. They have the advantage that they are small and can easily be carried in a briefcase.

Portable/laptop computers. Diary management software, contact information and standard facilities such as spreadsheet and word processing applications can all be stored within a small portable computer. The computer can be connected to a larger system to give access to a network, send faxes, e-mails, etc. The advantage of using a portable computer is that it can be taken to appointments, and work can also be completed on the journey to and from appointments. Information to be discussed at the appointment can also be stored in the computer – for example, a spreadsheet of budgets under discussion.

Desktop computers. These are usually linked to a network system which allows information to be accessed via the network by a range of users. Passwords can be used to ensure information is only accessed by authorised users. The diaries of a range of users can be accessed, checked and updated. The diary management software also allows a staff list to be entered and a list of suitable available dates and times obtained. A date can be chosen, and this will then be booked into the diary. The staff can also be e-mailed to inform them of the date of the meeting.

Internet diaries. Some ISPs provide diary facilities that can synchronise with your other electronic diaries – for example, the diary on your desktop computer. This means that a manager could access the diary from anywhere in the world and check any new appointments that the administrator had added.

The advantages of electronic diary systems are that: there is a wide range of additional facilities available; diaries on network systems can be accessed by a range of users; large amounts of information can be stored, sorted and accessed easily; information can be backed up in case of loss; passwords can protect the confidentiality of information. The disadvantages of electronic systems are that: they need specialist knowledge to operate them efficiently; they require access to equipment and electricity to access the information; the equipment can be expensive; portable computers and personal organisers require additional security measures as they are easily stolen.

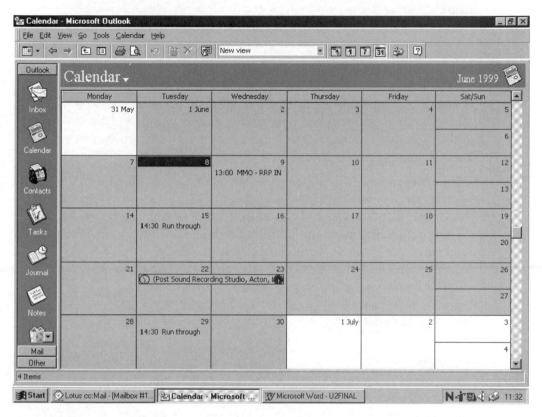

Figure 2.3.2 An electronic calendar

Maintaining a diary

Many organisations run both manual and electronic systems in parallel. The manager may take a manual diary out to meetings, and enter information on the electronic system on return to the office. If both methods are being used, it is important to keep them both up-to-date on a daily basis.

There are some simple rules to follow when maintaining a diary. All regular meetings should be entered in the diary – for example, the sales meeting held on the last Friday of the month. A meeting schedule of regular meetings may be circulated to all relevant staff, and these should also be entered in the diary straight away. Minutes usually include the date and time of next meeting, and this should be noted in the diary. When provisional meetings are being arranged, these should be entered in pencil and rewritten in ink when they have been confirmed. Make sure your writing is clear. Your diary should have sufficient space for all the entries – a 'page a day' diary is useful if you know there will be many entries for each day. Use the diary to record reminder items – for example, a reminder to check replies, confirm bookings. Towards the end of the year, a diary for the next year will need to be started and entries made.

The way that information is exchanged between the administrator and the manager is an important part of the operation of the diary system. The diary maintained by the administrator should match that of the manager. A set of procedures should be agreed by the administrator and manager to ensure the system works efficiently. The procedures should include:

- how appointments are to be recorded – for example, in which diaries, electronic aids, etc.
- how often the record should be updated – for example, daily, weekly
- how often the manager and administrator should meet to check and agree the records – for example, daily, weekly
- agreed guidelines for the administrator to negotiate and agree appointments on the manager's behalf
- agreed guidelines about the priority of appointments and activities to reflect the organisation's objectives and targets.

Recording entries

When recording entries in diaries, it is important to include all the relevant information. The start time and end time of appointments should be entered. When booking an appointment, ask for clarification of the estimated length of the meeting. If it is not clear how long the appointment will take, check this with the manager and enter the information in all diaries. The nature and location of the appointment should also be recorded. This information is important, as it affects other appointments that could be made on the day.

Time should be allowed for travel between appointments if they are in different locations. Time may also be built into the day to allow for catch-up time if appointments over-run, or if there are travel hold-ups. This built-in flexibility also allows the manager to catch up with routine work if the catch-up time is not needed. The way appointments are scheduled and allowance for travelling and breaks should be agreed with the manager at the outset. Travelling time has to be estimated when any journey is being made. A generous allowance for travelling times and weather conditions may need to be built into the estimate.

If managers are held up, they may telephone through to the office to inform you. You should contact the meeting and explain the circumstances. If there is a severe hold-up, the meeting may have to be rescheduled – you should try to agree some alternative dates for the future. If a meeting runs on, or hold-ups occur, it may be necessary to look at the appointments for the rest of the day. Discuss with the manager what action they would like you to take. When an appropriate strategy has been agreed, contact the other appointments and inform them of the situation. If a manager cannot make a meeting, it may be possible to arrange for an alternative member of staff to attend on their behalf. There may also be situations when you are contacted about a problem with a meeting the manager is due to attend that day – for example, you are informed that a meeting is cancelled or will be late starting. Contact the manager as soon as possible by pager or mobile phone. Look at their commitments for the rest of the day and how the change will affect other meetings. You may need to contact later appointments and see if they can be brought forward to save the manager from waiting around in an off-site location for some time.

Practical management of multiple diaries

Managing several diaries needs care. It can be useful for the administrator and the manager to have their own diaries, and for a master diary to be kept in the office. The administrator will have their own diary in which all appointments and targets are recorded. The diary should have sufficient space on each day for all the appointments to be noted. It is a good idea to record information in different colours – for example, the administrator's appointments in blue and the manager's in red. If more than one manager's appointments are noted each manager should have their own colour. If you manage the diary for several managers, rule the diary into columns, and allow a column for each manager. The manager will maintain their own personal diary. The master diary (see Figure 2.3.3, page 98) is usually maintained by agreement between the manager and the administrator and is left in a convenient place in the office. The master diary usually records the manager's business appointments and any other important information.

Long-term planning aids

Long-term planning aids can be maintained in manual or electronic form. In electronic form they may be found on computers and computerised personal organisers. Electronic scheduling aids allow

Monday 24 May ----		
Administrator	JW	JHS
		8.00–9.00 Breakfast meeting, Bakeware product launch, Granary Room, Dingles Hotel, Park Lane, Bristol
9.00 Remind Jenny her mother's birthday is tomorrow – order flowers		
	9.30–10.30 Appraisal with Gordon White	
10.00 Ring the Weston Hotel – 34567 and check they have the OHP for Wednesday's meeting		10.00–1.00 Interviewing for Accountant – Interview Room 6
11.00		
12.00		
1.00	Lunch appointment with Alan Sayers, Sales Director Gingells Ltd. at The Gallery, High Street	
2.00 Prepare Governors' meeting file for JW's meeting and put on her desk		
3.00		
4.00		
5.00		
	7.30–9.30 Board of Governors' Meeting, High School	

Figure 2.3.3 Master diary for Dr Henry Smith, Mrs Jenny Wong and Administrator

dates and targets to be entered into the schedule. The schedule can then be set up to notify the user of outstanding dates, deadlines, etc. on a daily or weekly basis.

Manual planning aids are usually managed in the form of wall charts. These are often yearly calendar charts but may also be three-month planners, monthly planners, multi-purpose planners, 16-month annual planners, academic year planners or European year planners. There should be sufficient space for information to be clearly and neatly added. It may be necessary to use several different charts to allow information to be clearly entered – for example, a holiday planner for staff holidays and a three-month planner for current projects. Choose a suitable chart format – two common ones are wipe-clean and magnetic boards. Highlight information effectively – use coloured pens, self-adhesive coloured shapes and tapes, 'today' symbols, etc. to show information clearly. Locate them in a convenient place, where they can easily be reached to be updated, and where relevant staff can see them. Make sure that they are securely mounted. Keep them up-to-date and check regularly – for example, weekly – that entries are correct.

Many offices also use whiteboards to record shorter-term deadlines, with deadlines or information being transferred from the wall chart to the whiteboard when outstanding work becomes urgent.

Alternative long-term planning aids can be year-at-a-glance pages in diaries. Specific schedules may also be prepared for a particular project – for example, a schedule detailing information and deadlines for booking and organising an event.

Portfolio Note

This element requires you to maintain a diary in a real situation for a minimum of six weeks. Where this is not part of your normal work activities, arrange with a specific manager to manage appointments and complete their diary over this timescale. If you are in college, or on placement in college, arrange with a member of staff to manage their appointments and diary.

You should also keep your own diary in which you record all relevant activities. This activity can be cross-referenced with many of the other elements – for example, Element 3.1, Work Within a Team to Organise and Administer Business Events. The appointments made to meet with assessors, visit libraries, carry out training, etc. should all be recorded in your own diary.

Portfolio activity 2.3 **Number 1**

1 Arrange a meeting with your assessor and agree how you are going to cover this element. Start or continue maintaining a diary in which you record your business appointments, events and target dates. These may be appointments you agree at work. If you are in college, include appointments you agree for meetings with your assessor, team meetings, course events and deadlines for completing work and assignments. Get some form of long-term planner – for example, an annual wall planner, and start entering key dates such as holidays and targets.

2 Meet with the manager whose diary you are maintaining, and agree a set of procedures. Write up the notes of this meeting.

The following evidence should be collected:

- diary with relevant entries (or electronic diary system)
- year planner
- notes/set of procedures for maintaining a manager's appointments.

Performance criteria:	2.3.1	2.3.2
Knowledge and understanding:	2.3.b	2.3.c
Evidence requirements:	2.3.2	

Purpose of planning aids

The information recorded on the planning aid can provide information in three timescales – historical, current and future. On any one day there will be information which relates to what happened in the past, what is happening today and what is planned for the future. The historical information is important as a record of activities – for example, staff holidays, targets achieved, events completed. The current information is used to prioritise the current activities.

Future information is valuable as a forecasting aid. The requirements for resources can be anticipated and organised. These resources may be:

- *people* – staffing needs to be anticipated and planned
- *time* – work to be scheduled in advance and sufficient time allocated to complete tasks and meet deadlines
- *equipment* – the use of equipment to be planned, and any additional requirements to be hired or purchased
- *stationery* – stock levels to be checked to ensure there is sufficient stationery for planned work; any additional requirements to be ordered.

Work planning and scheduling activities

Careful planning of work is one of the key factors in working efficiently and effectively. It greatly reduces the incidence of last-minute crises and panic activities. Routine work can be planned and prioritised using a routine work plan. This lists the routine activities that need to be completed on a daily, weekly and monthly basis.

Job Role – Office Manager		
Daily tasks	**Weekly tasks**	**Monthly tasks**
• Open and distribute mail • Deal with general enquiries • Book training courses • Prepare training materials • Prepare outgoing mail • Check voicemail	• Summarise weekly staff returns • Complete • Check and issue office stationery • Organise weekly staff meeting • Complete weekly training returns • Monitor previous week's evaluation questionnaires • Check and record staff expenses claims • Update expenses spreadsheet	• Prepare sickness and holiday returns and send to Head Office • Complete office health and safety schedule • Complete petty cash record and submit to Accounts • Submit monthly expenses returns to Head Office

Figure 2.3.4 A routine work plan

Lists of actions to be carried out are also useful. These should be recorded in a desk notebook or in the diary. The tasks should be prioritised and ticked off as they are completed.

Activity	Priority	Completed
Ring Mr Jones 01677 432879 re reference	**	
Confirm booking for Excelsior Hotel	***	
Prepare delegate packs for Silex Seminar	***	
Speak to Gerry about e-mail problems	*	
Organise photocopy maintenance – Mike 764233	*	
* – routine ** – priority *** – urgent		

Figure 2.3.5 A daily work list

Specific projects or activities can be planned and monitored using a schedule. These can be prepared using the following guidelines.

- *Start by listing all the activities that need to be completed*, then place them in the time frame.
- *Establish the time frame* – set the end date and then schedule the activities into the identified block of time.
- *Logically schedule the activities* – some activities have to be completed in sequence – for example, enquiries about caterers have to be made before they can be booked.
- *Set schedule milestones* – ongoing deadlines that can be checked to ensure the project is on target.

- *Be realistic* – allow time for the receipt of replies to enquiries.
- *Identify task responsibilities* – allocate names/departments responsible for specific activities.
- *Allow for contingencies* – build in time to allow for things going wrong – for example, photocopiers breaking down.
- *List resources where appropriate* – time, staff, equipment and stationery required.
- *Include some form of monitoring* – build in quality checks and some form of 'ticking' to allow for completed activities to be ticked off. Regular meetings should be included in the schedule where appropriate.

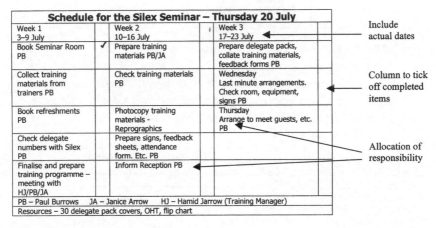

Figure 2.3.6 A project schedule

Arranging appointments

Appointments can be initiated by yourself or your manager, or be organised in response to a request.

Initiating appointments

The first steps to be taken when initiating an appointment are to decide on the purpose, duration, personnel and possible location of the appointment. Some of these issues may need to be negotiated between the personnel involved. It is a good idea to decide on a timescale or suitable dates before making contact – for example, early next week, the first week in March. The appropriate person can then be contacted to negotiate the details of the appointment. The contact can be made using the following communication methods.

Telephone. This is direct and quick, but can be time consuming if the person is not available. The details can be negotiated and agreed when contact is made. The appointment will need to be confirmed in writing.

E-mail. This is direct, quick and information is written. Give full details in the message, together with possible dates. The recipient can use the 'Reply to sender' option to reply to your message.

Fax. This is direct, quick and information is written. A fax is also very useful for confirmation of appointments once the details have been agreed on the telephone (see Figure 2.3.7 on page 104).

Letter. This is a slow, impersonal but more formal method of requesting an appointment. A letter may be used when formality is important – for example, when requesting appointments with important or senior people. Linking letters with mailmerge is an efficient way of requesting appointments with a large number of people – for example, mailshots for salesmen to make appointments to promote products.

Where electronic scheduling aids are available within the organisation, the availability of staff can be checked and suitable free dates identified. It may be possible for appointments to be booked direct or, if not, the person should be contacted to agree the appointment on one of the available dates. The correct way of going about this will depend on the company's procedures together with other factors such as the nature of the meeting and the level and roles of staff concerned. Confirmation and further contact can be made using e-mail.

If you are negotiating an appointment on behalf of a manager, the manager will have briefed you. Make your identity clear when contacting the person concerned. If the contact is straightforward, then the appointment may be booked at that time and confirmed later in writing. If more complex negotiations take place, then a provisional appointment may be agreed. This should then be discussed with the manager and confirmed in writing or renegotiated as appropriate. Complex negotiations may arise when three or more people are involved, or when additional factors such as overnight stays are involved. The appointment may also be negotiated with an administrator acting on behalf of the other participant.

4TH Floor Imperial Building
LEEDS, LD1 3DR
Email ltimp@or.co.uk
Tel 01346 773469
Fax 01346 773470

FAX MESSAGE

To   Mr Jeremy Harding, Purchasing
                Manager, Whycroft Trading
Fax Number 01334 78356
From   Miss Brigitte Delore, Administrator,
                Sales Department
Date   3 January ----

CONFIRMATION OF SALES MEETING

Thursday 2 March 9.30 am – 11.30 am
I confirm the meeting arranged for Glenda Pritchard,
Sales Manager, to visit you on Thursday 2 March. Glenda
will be travelling from Leeds by car, but should be with
you by 9.30 am. As agreed, Glenda will demonstrate the
new accounting software and answer any questions you
may have. This should take approximately two hours.
Could you please send a map to show your exact
location.

If you have any queries, please do not hesitate to
contact me.

Figure 2.3.7 A fax confirmation of an appointment

Preparing for appointments

Appropriate documentation and information should be available
for the participants of an appointment. Discuss with the manager
what information will be required. You may need to prepare:

* *a subject file* – for example, a health and safety file for an
  appointment to discuss health and safety
* *organisation information* – for example, brochures, leaflets
* *specific information* – for example, statistics and information
  required for the appointment
* *meeting paperwork* – for example, agendas and minutes
* *personal materials* – for example, security identification, diaries,
  car sticker, train tickets
* *maps and location information.*

These materials should be prepared well in advance of the appointment. They may be placed in a file and labelled with the relevant appointment information.

Changing appointments

There are occasions when appointment arrangements need to be changed. An appointment might need to be rescheduled due to events such as bad weather conditions, a clash of appointments, or the information required for the appointment not being available. Or it might be cancelled – for example, because the appointment was no longer required for some reason. Sometimes problems with travelling arrangements or other commitments require a venue to be changed. On other occasions, if a manager cannot make an appointment, another member of staff is substituted. In such cases the acceptability of the change should be checked with all participants involved in the appointment.

Participants and any other relevant parties should be informed about changes to appointments as soon as possible. Confirmation of changes of appointment must be in writing. See Figure 2.3.8 on page 106.

Receiving requests for appointments

There are occasions when you may deal with requests for appointments on behalf of a manager. Your response to this will depend on the nature of the request and who has requested it. A policy about appropriate appointments should have been agreed between the manager and administrator, for example:

- requests which are never accepted – for example, from certain categories of people such as sales representatives
- requests which are to be discussed with the manager – for example, a request from a junior member of staff requesting an appointment to see a senior manager
- requests which will always be accepted and confirmed – for example, a request for an appointment from an important customer, or from a senior member of staff.

The sifting of requests for a manager is called 'gatekeeping'. You should discuss and agree a clear gatekeeping policy with your manager and then keep them fully informed about all requests and the responses you made. You should always respond politely and courteously to all requests for an appointment, whatever the outcome of the request.

MEMORANDUM

To   Gordon White, Finance Assistant
From Jenny Wong, Head of Finance
Date 14 May ----

Appraisal Interview
Wednesday 19 May ----

Further to our telephone conversation earlier today, I confirm that the appraisal interview agreed for 19 May has now been rescheduled for Monday 24 May at 9.30 am in my office.

I apologise for this last-minute change, but my presence at the original time is required by the Managing Director at a budget presentation. I hope that you have not been inconvenienced by this change, and look forward to our discussions on Monday.

Figure 2.3.8 A memo changing an appointment

Informing people of appointments

The following people may need to be informed of appointments that have been made.

- *Participants* – copies of the confirmation documentation should go to all participants.
- *Venue/room managers* – you may need confirmation of a room booking.
- *Reception* – they need confirmation of expected visitors.
- *Catering* – you may need to request refreshments for appointments.
- *Security* – you may need confirmation of the identity of visitors.
- *Car-parking attendants* – if space for visitors has been booked in the car park, this should be confirmed with the relevant staff.

Security and confidentiality

As with all aspects of administrative work, it is important to maintain security and confidentiality when making appointments.

Security

If security is not correctly maintained, managers may be put at personal risk when attending appointments with unknown participants at unknown venues. Check with the manager for guidelines on security arrangements – for example, acceptable venues for appointments. The security of the organisation may also be compromised if appointments are not appropriately checked. Participants visiting the organisation may cause damage to the organisation, or gain access to confidential information. The identification of participants may need to be checked before the appointment is made. It may be necessary to check telephone numbers, addresses and company information and the identity of participants attending appointments should be checked.

It is also important for the manager attending an appointment to carry appropriate identification. The appointment may not proceed if this identification is not available.

Confidentiality

Personal and organisational information is confidential. Care should be taken not to give out confidential information when arranging appointments. Managers may not wish their holiday arrangements to be public knowledge, for example, as this may put their personal property at risk. Confidential organisational information should not be discussed when arranging appointments. It is also important to be very careful about what organisational information is discussed during appointments.

Confidentiality can be very important when sensitive issues are being dealt with. If an appointment is declined because the manager does not regard it a priority, then a 'diplomatic' reason should be given – for example, a prior appointment. Disclosing that the manager was available may create a difficult situation. If managers have meetings with competing suppliers or customers, good working relationships with these external clients might be compromised if such information is disclosed. The administrator may also have access to other confidential information that should not be disclosed to other staff – for example, a manager might be attending a job interview, or attending hospital for medical treatment.

Portfolio activity 2.3 **Number 2**

Arrange appointments for yourself and manager over a period of at least six weeks. Record the information in appropriate diaries, and confirm appointment arrangements in writing. Inform all the relevant people of the appointments. Make a checklist for materials to be supplied for a meeting. The following evidence should be collected:

- copies of diary pages, highlighting appointments made
- written confirmation of appointments, including changes in appointments
- written confirmation of arrangements for appointments to other relevant parties
- personal statement explaining how you arranged and negotiated appointments, allowed for contingencies, confirmed appointments, renegotiated changed appointments. Include information on how you ensured the security and confidentiality of information
- witness testimony from managers for whom you arrange appointments
- completed checklist of materials supplied for meetings.

Performance criteria:	2.3.1	2.3.3	2.3.4	2.3.5	2.3.6
	2.3.7	2.3.8	2.3.9		
Knowledge and understanding:	2.3.a	2.3.b	2.3.c	2.3.d	2.3.e
	2.3.g	2.3.h	2.3.i	2.3.j	2.3.k
Evidence requirements:	2.3.3	2.3.4	2.3.5	2.3.6	

Test yourself

Knowledge and understanding	Questions
a	Describe four features of time management techniques.
b	Describe three time management techniques.
c	Describe three aids for work planning and scheduling.
d	Describe two ways in which planning aids are important for forecasting and record keeping.
e	Describe the types and uses of appointment management systems.
f	Explain the function and purpose of electronic diaries, e-mail and the Internet.
g	Explain the effect of work roles and relationships in the communication process.
h	Explain what factors you take into account when estimating the running time of appointments. Describe two ways in which you can make contingency plans to allow for the over-running of appointments.
i	Describe how you prepare the appropriate support materials/documentation for individual appointments.
j	Explain what is meant by the term gatekeeping. Describe how you applied this when you were managing appointments.
k	Give two possible consequences of not maintaining security and confidentiality procedures for appointments.

Activity 2.1

Memo

MEMORANDUM

To Office Administrator
From Jane Hywel, Senior Sales Manager
Date Monday, -- -- --
Subject Sales team meetings

Our area sales managers now have to chair their monthly sales team meetings. I will be carrying out some training with them next month. Please prepare a handout to be given to them with guidelines on how to chair these meetings effectively.

Activity 2.2

E-mail

HTR

To: Office Administrator
From: Jane Hywel, Senior Sales Manager
Date: Tuesday, -- -- --
Subject: Meetings – standard documents

We discussed setting up standard documents on the computer to help the area sales managers run meetings. Please make a list of documents that we could prepare, with notes and/or examples of the information we need to include in each standard document.

Activity 2.3
Desknote

DESKNOTE

From   *Jane Hywel*
Date   *Wednesday, -- -- --*

The date for the annual Sales Meeting has now been set. Anthony Wright is going to make the administrative arrangements for the meeting. As this is the first time he has done this, please prepare a list of the arrangements he needs to make. You are very good at organising this information in clear logical formats. Design a list that will help to indicate the priority of activities. If you have time, prepare some brief guidance notes to go with the list.

Jane

Activity 2.4
Memo

MEMORANDUM

To   Office Administrator
From   Jane Hywel, Senior Sales Manager
Date   Thursday, -- -- --
Subject Annual General Meeting

Thank you for offering to help organise our first Annual General Meeting this year, in the absence of the Managing Director's secretary through illness. We are holding it in the Board Room at Head Office. Please make a list of the resources you will need to have available for the day, under the headings of Staff, Information, Equipment/furniture, General Housekeeping.

Activity 2.5

Memo

> It has been agreed to form an Administrative Procedures Committee to meet monthly to prepare and review the organisation's administrative procedures. The members will be the administrator from each department. The Office Administrator for Jane Hywel, Senior Sales Manager, will chair the meetings. The first meeting to be prepared for the end of next month.

Note for Jane Hywel

> *Please prepare appropriate documentation for this first meeting, together with some notes on the topics for discussion.*

3 Organise, Administer and Evaluate Business Events

Organisations may hold or attend a wide range of events as part of their business activities. These events may have originated within the organisation, or may be part of an event originated outside of the organisation. They cover a very wide range of activities, which can include:

- marketing and selling events – for example, exhibitions, publicity events
- information-sharing events – for example, professional conferences, open days, meetings
- industry-led events – for example, conferences, displays, conventions
- training activities – for example, seminars, workshops, training courses.

The funding and costing of these events will vary. Organisations may be charged for a stand at an exhibition, or you may be involved with organising an event for which your organisation is charging the delegates to attend. The venues will vary from in-house to external locations such as hotels, conference centres, and so on.

This unit looks at the arrangements that would need to be made to organise and administer these events, and also to evaluate them after they have taken place.

Certain terms are used generally to cover a wide range of activities.

- Event – any event organised by the organisation.
- Event manager – the person/people responsible for the event, or for whom it is being arranged.
- Participants – the people who are taking part in or conducting the event – for example, trainers, speakers, lecturers.
- Delegates – people who are attending the event, that is, the audience and/or guests.

Element 3.1

WORK WITHIN A TEAM TO ORGANISE AND ADMINISTER BUSINESS EVENTS

Principles of team work

When organising an event with a group of colleagues, the ability to work in a team is a very important attribute. The general principles which should be followed are:

* *good communication* – keep all members of the team regularly informed about progress and actions
* *reliability* – all members should meet their commitments to the team, and keep the team informed of any problems that might affect progress
* *respect* – all members should respect each other and be prepared to listen to other people's views and ideas
* *tackling problems* – problems within the team should be dealt with openly but tactfully; they should not be the subject of gossip.

Procedures for events

All organisations have procedures for the administrative activities that take place within the organisation, including planning. These procedures may be established as 'custom and practice' – the way things have always been done. Alternatively they may be written procedures.

The advantages of written procedures are that: they ensure consistency; they define acceptable standards; they act as a guide and support for staff; they provide guidelines to cover 'contingency' or emergency arrangements; they clearly define decision-making responsibilities and reporting procedures; they form part of an organisation's quality control procedures.

Written procedures can be prepared for specific events that the organisation regularly organises – for example, parents' evenings which are held annually or termly. These procedures will be very specific and will define every stage of the activity – for example, the date on which the event is to be held (last Wednesday of each term; first week in November; monthly, the last Monday in the month) and the standard documentation to be used (standard letter to parents; standard programme).

Where events arise on a 'one-off' basis, a more general set of procedures is required. These are more difficult to write as they need to allow for a range of different activities. They may be written under general headings, to include off-site activities, on-site activities, externally organised events and internally organised events.

They may also include procedures that already exist for certain activities within the organisation – for example: reception arrangements for visitors; parking arrangements for visitors; room booking procedures; health and safety arrangements for visitors; refreshment booking procedures; accounts procedures for ordering goods and services; accounts procedures for the payment of goods and services; staff expenses, travel, accommodation and subsistence arrangements; job descriptions for staff responsible for arranging events; event evaluation procedures.

Procedures/instructions may also be prepared for other people who are making a contribution to the event. This may be information for delegates, speakers, trainers, company representatives, and so on – for example, procedures given to lecturers for the operation of a parents' evening.

Planning events

Before any practical planning can take place certain fundamental information about the event should be agreed. This is usually discussed in an initial meeting with the 'manager' of the event. The 'manager' of the event is the person or persons on whose behalf the event is being organised. The issues that are usually covered are:

- *objectives of the event* – to make a profit, to promote a product, a public relations activity, a communications activity
- *policy in relation to holding an event* – check with appropriate policies, for example, public relations policies, communications policies
- *purpose of the event* – for example, a college stand at local careers conference
- *profile of the event* – for example, is it a 'high profile' event with national organisations being present, or is it a smaller locally focused activity; is it an activity that is a key element of the organisation's development plan?
- *audience* – who are the guests and intended audience – for example, customers, staff, professional experts?
- *dates* – the date of the event may be set by external organisers, or may be agreed with internal staff – when organising events

that have been externally set, it is important to check that
sufficient appropriate staff are available to support the event;
the date for an event may also be determined by the availability
of suitable venues

- *the duration of the event and activities* – the start and end time for
the events – again this may be pre-determined for externally
organised events
- *outline of the activities to be covered* – a general framework of activities
to be covered during the event: for example, speakers, visits
- *publicity for the event* – agree on the method/s of advance publicity
to be used, for example, press releases, magazine notes, mailshots;
agree on possible mailing list and dates for issue of programmes
- *budget* – agree sum of money allocated for the event
- *sponsorship* – the possibility of attracting financial support for an
event; for example, an organisation may make a contribution to
the costs of the event in return for having a publicity stand at the
event; the appropriateness of this, and the method of attracting
sponsors, should be agreed
- *location* – where the event will take place, possible venues,
rooms, etc.
- *staffing* – the requirements for staff to cover the event
- *materials* – outline of publicity and support materials that will
be required
- *practical issues* – accommodation, refreshments, rooms, parking
and other implications for the event

This initial meeting should be recorded and minutes prepared. An
action plan should also be agreed which lists the activities to be
undertaken and agrees a date for an interim meeting. The team
may then arrange meetings to organise the ongoing activities.
These meetings should also be recorded. See flow-chart opposite.

Action plans

Action plans in the form of checklists are a very useful planning
and monitoring aid for events (see Figure 3.1.1). They can be
general checklists used for all events, or they can be prepared
specifically for a particular event. As well as listing actual activities,
they can include information about who is responsible for an
activity and the timescales of when activities must take place or
be completed by. They should include a space for ticking off
activities so that the checklist can be used as a monitoring device.

While you are monitoring the activities, it is essential that you also
monitor all costs to ensure that the event does not go over budget.

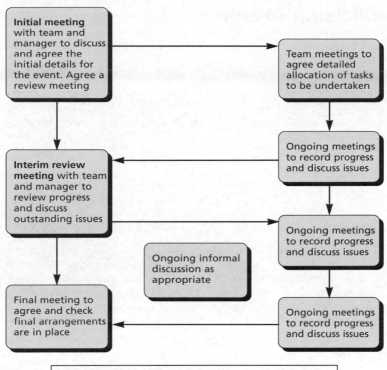

**Checklist for Parents' Evening Planning
2 February ----**

Critical deadlines
Letters to parents to be sent first day of spring term – 4 January
Final confirmation of appointments – 26 January
Final staff appointment lists – 30 January

Resources required
150 C6 envelopes
Training Office support to prepare envelopes
Postage for 150 envelopes

Activity	Responsibility	Timescale	Completed
Arrange initial meeting with Senior Lecturer	LH/JD	31.11.--	
Check appropriate room is free	LH	4.12.--	
Book room	LH	4.12.--	
Draft letter to parents	LH	4.12.--	
Agree parent letter with Senior Lecturer	LH/JD	6.12.--	
Send memo to staff to confirm attendance and appointment times	LH	6.12.--	
Collect student printout	LH/JK	6.12.--	
Prepare appropriate number of parent letters	LH	10.12.--	
Arrange with Training Office for appropriate envelopes to be addressed ready for posting	LH/GL	19.12.--	
Send letters to parents	LH	4.1.--	
Confirm appointments	LH	26.1.--	
Finalise appointment lists	LH	30.1.--	

Figure 3.1.1 An event planning checklist

Publicising events

The information about an event has to be communicated to the possible delegates. The delegates may fall into the following groups.

Type of delegates	Possible methods of publicity
Pre-defined group of people – for example, parents attending a parents' evening, shareholders attending a shareholders' meeting	Individual letters prepared or sent using mailmerge facilities
Interested people who may attend an open event. This event may be free or a minimal entrance fee may be charged. For example, careers evenings, college open days, marketing exhibitions	Publicity arranged using appropriate media – for example, 'fliers' – publicity leaflets sent to local colleges, schools and employment agencies; advertisements in newspapers, on local radio, and so on
Customers who may pay to attend an event – for example, delegates who have paid to attend a training event; exhibitors who have paid for a stand at a trade event	Targeted mailshots; advertisements in appropriate media – for example, professional magazines; previous customers

Press releases

Information about events may also be issued in press releases. The press releases may be in internal newsletters or for inclusion in external publications – for example, local press and trade publications. The organisation's policy and procedures for dealing with the press must be carefully followed. Many organisations will have a member of staff who is responsible for all contacts with the press. A press release may be drafted and submitted to this contact for checking and issue. The accuracy of a press release is extremely important and should be checked very carefully. No information should be given to the press over the telephone, or in informal conversations.

Press releases may also be prepared to accompany large events – for example, national conferences. The event organiser may also invite representatives of the press to attend the conference – for example, trade press representatives, or specialised correspondents for the national press. You may be responsible for inviting these representatives and providing them with suitable support during the course of the event. Press releases publicising an event may also be prepared, particularly for local events. The press release should contain the factual information about the event, its purpose and appropriate information about how further information, bookings, and so on, can be made.

Press release	Chairs rather than shares was the message of Jennifer Baldwin's address at the Annual Antiques Fair. The theme of her talk was that antiques have now become a good alternative investment. Jennifer Baldwin talked about a range of antiques that have proved to be good investments.
Grandstand Promotions	
Annual Antiques Fair	She showed that the increase in value of antiques can be greater than shares. Items can be purchased that can be enjoyed as well as appreciating in value. The level of risk compared well with the risks associated with shares.
Chairs rather than shares	
Antiques as investment	
2 February ----	Speculative buying can also show a profit. Items purchased at car boot sales can occasionally be high value treasures. However, an 'expert eye', knowledge and time are needed to hunt out these bargains.
From	
Mr Andrew Cunningham Press Officer Grandstand Promotions	She suggested that the services of a good antiques' expert would help the serious investor in antiques; just as a good financial adviser can give expert help to the investor in shares. She encouraged all people to look at antiques as investments, as part of their investment portfolio.
Tel 01345 78692	'Buy for today, enjoy for tomorrow and sell in the future' was her advice.

Figure 3.1.2 A press release

Portfolio Note

Element 3.1 looks at the arrangements that would need to be made to organise and administer business events. To complete the evidence requirements for this element you must work with a team to plan, organise and administer three business events. Types of event that must be covered are:

• a one-day event for a minimum of 30 people
• a company-related event
• a trade stand for business/marketing purposes.

The evidence for these should be collected through real work. This can be an event organised in your workplace, or real events in college. College events can include:

• an open day at college
• a parents' evening
• a college stand at a marketing event
• a regional/national conference for college lecturers

- a careers event in college – for example, a one-day careers conference for business studies students which will include speakers from various local organisations
- a senior staff 'away day'.

If it is not possible to cover all the types of event through real work, it is possible to use simulation. However, at least one event must be the result of real work.

Although these activities are team events, your portfolio must include evidence which is your own work and which shows an assessor that you have consistently covered all the performance criteria.

Portfolio activity 3.1 **Number 1**

1 Find out about and collect information about your organisation's objectives, policy, procedures and budget in relation to running an event. Record your findings and collect relevant documentation such as an organisation's standard documents – for example, expense claim forms, event evaluation forms.

2 Find out about and collect information about your organisation's procedures for dealing with media/press regarding conferencing/events. Collect information about the importance of effective advance publicity and the issue of an event programme.

3 Prepare a set of procedures for the event you are organising. Prepare a checklist and a set of procedures for other personnel involved in the event.

Performance criteria:	3.1.3	3.1.4	
Knowledge and understanding:	3.1.a	3.1.b	
Evidence requirements:	3.1.8	3.1.9	3.1.10

Arranging venues

One of the first tasks to be carried out is the selection and booking of a suitable location. Internal and external venues can often be booked up to a year in advance, and you may find that your preferred location is already fully booked. Initial enquiries should be made to determine the availability and cost of suitable locations. The choice and location of a suitable venue will be determined by the following factors.

- *Cost* – the hire charge should be within budget limits.
- *Style of event* – is it a one-day event, overnight event?
- *Purpose of event* – for example, a marketing event may require a different type of venue from a training event.
- *Space* – sufficient space should be available for the number of delegates and type of activity. The event may require a range of large and small rooms for workshop activities.
- *Telecommunication resources* –it should be possible to contact the venue by fax, e-mail.
- *Refreshment requirements* – the venue should have suitable provision of meals and refreshment facilities.
- *Location* – consideration will have to be given to access by car and public transport and also whether the location is suitable for the type of event and the convenience of delegates.
- *Additional facilities* – accommodation, provision of parking, reception facilities, audio-visual aids.

Internal locations such as board rooms, meeting rooms, etc. may be used if appropriate (usually for in-house events). There is usually no charge for the use of these rooms. Checks should be made of their availability and the rooms booked according to the organisation's procedures.

However, most business events are held in an outside location, and there is a wide range of external venues available for hire.

Hotels

There is a very wide choice of hotels. Small hotels, often privately-owned, usually have only small meeting rooms and a limited amount of accommodation. They vary considerably in cost and standards of accommodation. Careful physical inspection is required in order to check the range and standard of the facilities. Larger hotels, particularly those belonging to national chains, usually offer more extensive conference facilities, accommodation and refreshment facilities. The standards offered by these chains is more predictable and so they may be a safer choice when distance and cost makes it difficult to physically inspect the facilities on offer. There are hotels which specialise in conferences and business events and these can be a good choice as they may provide facilities and support not available in general hotels – for example, audio-visual equipment.

Conference/meeting facilities

Conference and meeting facilities vary from hotels in that they do not usually offer overnight accommodation. They range from simple meeting rooms to specialist conference suites. The following list provides a good source of conference and meeting facilities.

- Universities have a range of conference facilities, which may also include accommodation at certain times of the year.
- Leisure centres usually have rooms and other facilities available for hire.
- Sporting venues also offer their facilities for hire – for example, racecourses, football, cricket and golf clubs.
- Heritage venues such as castles and stately homes often offer a range of facilities for hire.
- Local Chambers of Commerce often provide meeting rooms. They can also provide information about facilities available at other Chambers of Commerce.
- Theatres, concert halls and arts centres often have restaurants and conference and meeting rooms available for hire.
- Local Development Agencies and Business Centres provide conference and meeting facilities to encourage businesses to hold events in their area.
- Many large towns have exhibition centres with conference and meeting facilities.

Information about suitable event venues can be found from: Yellow Pages, Talking Pages, Thomson local directories; Internet websites provided by hotel chains, universities and towns; Chambers of Commerce and Regional Business Development Centres; central offices of hotel chains and groups.

Evaluating venues

The careful selection of a venue will make an important contribution to the success of an event. The quality of the venue will form a large part of participants' impressions of an event. Delegates may forget the content of a speaker's talk, but remember that the meeting room was cold! Possible venues should be checked for suitability well in advance of the event. There are various methods for collecting information about the venue.

Reviewing venue information. For example, publicity material and other written information can give details about location, costs, facilities available, parking, etc. It is important to get written details of the facilities offered and the total costs – for example, the provision of audio-visual aids may be charged as an additional cost.

Collecting feedback. Information may be obtained from other users of the venue such as colleagues who have attended events there, or other administrators who have organised events there.

Event title – Managing Change in the Agriculture Industry One-day conference

Estimated number of delegates – 70
Key requirements – one conference room plus three workshop rooms
Refreshment requirements – coffee, buffet lunch, afternoon tea
Audio-visual requirements – OHT, video recorder

Selection criteria	Venue A	Venue B	Venue C
Cost of hiring the venue, including conference room, workshop rooms			
Availability, list available dates in June ----			
Provision of OHT, video recorder – include details of additional cost if charged			
Seating capacity for conference room			
No./size of workshop rooms			
Accessibility by car – for example, distance from nearest motorway junction – for example, 3 miles off J17 M5			
Parking provision, number of free places available			
Provision for disabled delegates – for example, disabled access, loop hearing system			
Cost per head of provision of coffee, lunch and afternoon tea			
Cost per head of provision of overnight accommodation for speakers			
General overall impression of venue. Give rating 1–4: 1 very good, 2 good, 3 acceptable, 4 unacceptable			
Comments on any additional facilities – for example, leisure facilities			
Total estimated cost of venue			

Figure 3.1.3 An observation venue checklist

Visiting the venue and carrying out a physical check of the facilities offered. An observation checklist can be used to record the findings. The checklist should include information about the cleanliness, general décor, health and safety, space, parking, etc. (see Figure 3.1.3)

When collecting detailed information about a venue, consideration should be given to special requirements. This should include special facilities for the disabled: specially allocated parking spaces; ramps, wheelchair access, lifts; toilet facilities; the provision of a 'loop' facility for the hearing-impaired (a loop facility is linked to the microphone and speaker system, and enhances the sound received by wearers of hearing aids); evacuation arrangements.

Several venues may be checked before a final selection is made and it is a good idea to prepare a venue evaluation checklist (see Figure 3.1.3). This should list selection criteria in some sort of order – for example, if delegates are arriving by car it will be important that there is sufficient parking.

Portfolio activity 3.1 **Number 2**

Research several suitable event venues for the events you are arranging. Using a word processor, prepare an informal written report evaluating and comparing the venues, to be presented to the manager of the event. Include recommendations in your report based on the results of your research.

Performance criteria:	3.1.5			
Knowledge and understanding:	3.1.c	3.1.g	3.1.o	3.1.q
Evidence requirements:	3.1.1	3.1.11	3.1.12	3.1.13
	3.1.36	3.1.38		

Catering provision for events

Suitable refreshments may need to be provided for the event. The refreshments may be for visitors, for staff participants or for all delegates, depending on the type of event. The outline of appropriate provision should be agreed with the manager at the initial meeting – for example, coffee, buffet lunch and afternoon tea. A budget should also be agreed to give an indication of the appropriate price levels. Catering can be provided from the following sources.

- *In-house caterers*, the organisation's catering staff, can provide refreshments for in-house events. They should charge reasonable prices, be easy to book and the standard of catering should be a known quantity.

- *External caterers* may be used to provide refreshments for in-house events, or for external events where facilities have been hired but no catering is provided – for example, rooms in a leisure centre. The organisation may have a regular supplier of catering and this should be checked. Alternatively, quotations and menus should be requested from several local caterers. Check the quality of the service through personal recommendations or from references.
- *Venue caterers* can also provide refreshments; this possibility should be checked with the venue. Hotels will have restaurants that can be used, or they may provide buffet meals and refreshments in the meeting rooms.

Whichever source of catering is used, consideration should be given to special requirements. These may be general requirements such as the provision of a vegetarian selection of food. They may also be specific and take account of particular medical conditions, allergies, and religious requirements. For example, it may be necessary to provide diabetic foods, or food free of wheat flour or nuts. The provision of these special requirements may not be known until delegates return booking forms. The booking forms should be monitored and the caterers should be informed of any special requirements as soon as possible. The caterers should be asked to clearly label or indicate food that meets special requirements.

Catering can also include providing water for speakers and delegates. Bottled water is often provided at events. It is usually placed on the tables, together with mints and other soft drinks. Check with the venue to see if these are provided, or whether they need to be supplied at additional cost.

Equipment provision for events

The equipment required for events is generally to support audio-visual presentations. When planning the event, contact should be made with all the presenters/speakers to check their equipment requirements. The following equipment may need to be provided.

Overhead projector. This is used to display presentation transparencies. At both internal venues and external venues the availability of an overhead projector should be checked. If there is one available, follow the standard booking procedures, and confirm the booking in writing. If an overhead projector is not available they can be hired. This is an expensive way of providing frequent access to a projector, but is appropriate for occasional use when other projectors are not available. Some organisations that regularly hold events in external venues may have a portable overhead projector. Check to see what overhead projector facilities are available in your organisation. Suitable transport will have to be arranged for any in-house equipment being taken to an external venue.

Additional overhead equipment. A screen should be available so that the presentation can be seen clearly. Light/laser pointers can be used to highlight the presentation on the screen. Projector trolleys move the projector quickly and easily into place. An acetate autofeeder with a remote control allows fast, automatic presentations, including 'reveal' feature (the reveal feature moves each OHT sheet forward, to highlight particular areas). All of this equipment helps to present a very high level professional image.

Slide projector. This is used for showing 35 mm photographic slides. Advanced models have 'carousels' for the pre-packing of the slides and remote controls which allow the presenter to change the slides quickly and easily. A projector may be available in-house, provided by the venue, or hired. To be effective, slides do need to be shown in a darkened room, and this should be checked with the venue.

Video player and suitable monitors. This is used to show video presentations. The suitability of the equipment should be checked to ensure that it is suitable for the size of the anticipated audience. Large wall-mounted screens may need to be used for a large audience. Standard equipment is only suitable for smaller audiences of approximately 20 people. Suitable equipment may be available in-house, provided by the venue, or hired.

Whiteboards, flipcharts and easels. These are used to record notes and ideas during the presentation. Combination whiteboard/easels are usually available in most venues. Alternatively they may be available in-house, and suitable transport arrangements can be made if required for external venues. If they are not available, they are relatively cheap to buy. However, the flipchart pads and pens are not usually provided. These should be ordered in advance of the event.

Sound presentation equipment. Speakers may need microphone and amplification facilities, usually referred to as a public address system. Check that this is available in the venue. Portable public address systems that can be plugged in at a venue can be used. A cassette or CD player may be needed for audio presentations. This equipment may be purchased or hired if required.

Computer. Computer presentations are now being widely used. Presentation software such as PowerPoint is used to prepare a sequenced presentation which can include text, graphics, sound and moving images. Suitable equipment is required to run the presentation and display it to an audience. Care needs to be taken with supplying equipment to run computer presentations, as specific hardware and software will be required. This is not necessarily a problem for internal venues, where arrangements can be made for a computer to be available in the room. However, electrical sockets and possible access to the network still need to be checked. Any presenter wishing to use a computer presentation at an external venue is advised to provide a portable computer. This eliminates problems with incompatibility of hardware and software.

An overhead projection panel or tablet can be used to show computer presentations on a large screen, via an overhead projector. The panel is connected to the computer and then placed over the glass area of the overhead projector. What is seen on the computer is then projected on to the large screen for all the audience to see. Care needs to be taken to check that the panel is compatible with the hardware and software being used.

Display equipment. This is used to show posters, photographs and literature. This equipment is not usually available at most conference venues. However, many organisations have portable display systems for use at events. Check the availability of this equipment, and book it using the standard procedures. Although it is portable, it is often quite bulky and suitable transport arrangements will need to be made.

Provision of trade stands

A trade stand is an area set aside to display information about an organisation's services or products. There are two elements to the trade stand – the allocation of a suitable physical space for the stand, and the actual stand presentation. The space may be allocated at the following types of event.

- Trade events where organisations are charged for the exhibition space – the event area may be split into blocks of space, which are then booked by the exhibiting organisations. Large or small blocks may be booked, or possibly multiple adjacent blocks. The price for the space may vary depending on size and location in the event. Blocks near the entrance or the refreshment facilities may be more expensive than blocks in remote corners of the venue.
- Trade events where trade stands are allocated free of charge – for example, careers exhibitions where employers, training agents

and colleges may all have the opportunity to set up stands free of charge. The allocation of the stand will still need to be agreed with the organisers.

- Trade stands at other events, where trade exhibitors can set up stands to complement an event – for example, publisher stands at educational conferences, bank stands at college open days.

The stand presentation is important as it gives visitors an impression of the organisation. Many organisations have their own display equipment, or showboards, as mentioned on page 127. The stands usually comprise fabric-covered screens that link together to form a screened area. Posters and professionally prepared panels can be attached to the screens with Velcro or pins. Chairs and tables may be needed for the presentation area, and provision for these should be agreed with the event organisers. Showboards will need to be booked using the organisation's usual procedures.

Additional facilities

Other specialist facilities may need to be booked, and these should be checked and agreed with the manager of the event.

Translation services

Individual translators can be used to support a small group of foreign visitors. The translator may be a member of staff with appropriate language skills, or employed through a specialist agency.

Special venues may provide headphone equipment with simultaneous translators. The delegate can select an appropriate language and use the headphones to listen to the speakers. The language services to be provided have to be agreed in advance. It may be necessary to obtain the translators from a specialist agency.

Written materials can be translated and prepared in advance. The materials may be translated in-house by a member of staff with appropriate language skills, or they may be translated using a specialist agency.

Signers can be used to support deaf delegates with a 'signed' version of the spoken word. There may be a member of staff with sign skills, or one may be employed through a specialist agency.

Transport facilities

Transport for delegates to and from venues may need to be booked. This may be on public transport, in hire cars or using coaches.

Courier services

Documents, materials, display stands, samples, etc. may all need to be transported to an event. Staff may take them in their cars, or they may be sent by courier. Everything should be clearly marked so that it can be identified on arrival at the event. The staff at the event should also be notified that the courier delivery has been arranged, so that they know how to deal with the delivery. Any arrangements for short-term storage will need to be agreed with the event organisers. The use of a courier will incur expense which should be allowed for in the event budget.

Booking arrangements

When the selection of the venue, catering and equipment requirements have been agreed with the manager of the event, they can be booked. Bookings must be confirmed in writing. The confirmation should contain full and clear details – for example, date, duration of time, expected number of delegates, cost. The need for any special requirements – for example, special menus, facilities for the disabled – should be indicated and can be confirmed once exact requirements are known.

Internal bookings

The organisation's booking procedures should be followed when booking catering, equipment and accommodation. The appropriate forms should be completed and bookings recorded in the appropriate diaries. Authorising signatures should be collected where required. Bookings should be made in good time, and any telephone bookings should be confirmed in writing.

External bookings

When quotations are received for external services, the conditions in the 'small print' should be carefully checked. The quotations should be discussed with the manager before a final decision is made and a firm booking made. A deposit may be required, and accounting procedures for paying a deposit will have to be followed. This deposit is usually lost if a cancellation is made.

Penalty charges may also be incurred if cancellations are made after booking. A penalty clause is a clause in a contract that allows an organisation to charge for services they have been contracted to provide, even if the service has been cancelled. Penalty clauses sometimes state the length and timing of notice of cancellation. The principle behind penalty clauses is that they recognise the fact that, for example, once a hotel has booked its accommodation for a particular user for a particular date, it will not be able to book that accommodation to another customer. Similarly, a caterer may have purchased and prepared food which will be wasted if the booking is cancelled at the last minute.

A careful balance has to be maintained between the availability of services, and the booking of services that might need to be cancelled and therefore incur a penalty. Certain services may be critical to the event and bookings should be made as early as possible. Other services may be more easily booked, and these can often be left until later. For example, the booking of a venue may need to be made before any publicity or event information is distributed, but the catering may be able to be booked later.

There are events which are advertised but only take place if enough participants apply to take part. These may be training sessions or workshops which the delegates pay to attend. They are only cost effective if enough delegates book and pay for a place. In these situations the event may be advertised at a general location – for example, Coventry or Oxford, and a specific venue booked only when the bookings have been received and the event confirmed. Where delegates pay to attend a course, penalty charges may also be imposed for late cancellation of the place.

When the services to be booked have been agreed with the manager, a booking can be made. The initial booking may be made on the telephone, but must always be followed by confirmation in writing either by fax (see Figure 3.1.4) or sent in the post. The booking should clearly state what services have been booked, the dates and payment details.

Portfolio activity 3.1 **Number 3**

Collect copies of faxes and letters sent to confirm arrangements for booking venue, catering, equipment and other facilities required for the events. Write a personal statement explaining how you made sure these were carried out in sufficient time. Highlight any special requirements you covered in making these bookings.

Performance criteria:	3.1.7	3.1.8	3.1.9		
Knowledge and understanding:	3.1.j	3.1.o	3.1.p		
Evidence requirements:	3.1.1 3.1.20	3.1.2	3.1.3	3.1.15	3.1.16

**4TH Floor Imperial Building
LEEDS, LD1 3DR
Email ltimp@co.or.uk
Tel 01346 773469
Fax 01346 773470**

FAX MESSAGE

To	The Manager, Angel Hotel, High Street, BIRMINGHAM
Fax number	09334 876235
From	Ruksanna Mohammed, Administrator Training Services
Subject	Training for Success – Team Leadership Seminar – 4 April ----
Date	10 March -----

Further to our telephone conversation today, I wish to confirm booking of the Wedgwood Room on Thursday 4 April from 9.00 am to 5.00 pm at a price of £150.00 for the day. Refreshments to be provided for 30 delegates as detailed below:

Coffee/tea at 9.30 am @ 50p per head
Coffee/tea at 11.00 am @ 50p per head
Lunch in the restaurant at 1.00 pm – £14.00 per head, the menu to include vegetarian selection
Coffee/tea at 3.30 pm @ 50p per head

Water and glasses for speakers and delegates to be provided in the room included in the cost.

The following equipment will be available in the room at no extra cost:

Overhead Projector – with suitable sockets
Overhead Projector screen
Flip-chart easel

Please arrange for the room layout to be in 'theatre' style with the chairs in rows.

Materials for the Conference will be delivered the previous day by courier. Please store in the hotel office as agreed on the telephone. There will be no additional charge for this storage.

Ms Tania Underwood the Seminar Tutor will be arriving at 9.00 am on the day.

Please do not hesitate to contact me if you require any further information.

Figure 3.1.4 A booking fax

Planning the event programme

The event programme needs careful planning and organising. The sequence of planning and organising can vary. With some events the programme may be arranged before the venue is organised – for example, an annual general meeting or a workshop. In other situations, the venue may be arranged first and the programme planned as responses are received – for example, organising a business exhibition or arranging an annual conference. In most situations the practical and programme arrangements are organised in parallel, provisional bookings being made and confirmed as arrangements progress.

Arranging speakers

At some events the main content of the programme will be talks or presentations given by speakers. These speakers may be:

- internal – senior staff, technical experts, lecturers from the organisation. Even where the main content of the programme may be provided by external speakers, internal speakers will be used to act as chairpersons, group leaders, hosts, etc.
- external – recognised experts, people who have submitted papers, or public personalities.

Sources of reference for finding speakers

The background of speakers must be considered in order to check their suitability before an invitation is issued. It will also be necessary to obtain information about a speaker for inclusion in publicity materials and so that an appropriate introduction can be prepared by the chairperson for the event.

The following sources of reference may be used to provide background information on speakers.

- Internal staff information – the speaker may already be known to internal staff or organisers of the event.
- Professional organisations – speakers may be members of professional organisations – for example, the General Medical Council, the Institute of Mechanical Engineers.
- Speaker sources – autobiographical notes may be available about speakers from their secretaries, agents, publicity offices, inside the flyleaf of authors' books, etc.
- Reference books:
  Who's Who – famous people
  Debrett's Peerage – people with titles
  Army, Airforce and Navy lists – officers in the services
  Vacher's Parliamentary Companion – members of parliament, government ministers
  Crockford's Clerical Directory – Anglican clergy.
  Check with the reference section at a good library for suitable reference sources for a particular speaker.

If information about a speaker is to be published in some way – in a speech, or printed in publicity material – it is a good idea to check the accuracy of the information with the speaker in advance.

A draft of the speech or autobiographical note should be sent to the speaker, with a request that it is checked. Sufficient time should be allowed for the speaker to respond.

Inviting speakers

The procedures for inviting guest speakers will vary depending on the organisation, the event and the speaker. The initial approach may be made informally if the manager of the event knows the speaker. This may be in the form of a personal approach or telephone call. Once the initial approach has been made, a formal letter of invitation must then follow it. Check with the organisation's procedures before issuing any invitations, but the guidelines which follow may be useful.

Someone of suitable rank within the organisation should issue the invitation. This may be the 'host' or 'hostess' of the event on whose behalf the arrangements for the event are being made. Alternatively, a senior person in the organisation who personally knows the speaker may make the initial contact. This can then be followed by a formal invitation from the manager of the event, in which the name of the contact is then mentioned, for example:

> **Hazel Jones, our Marketing Director, has mentioned that you would be happy to give the after-dinner speech at our Annual Dinner. It gives us great pleasure to formally invite you to do so at the 32nd Annual Dinner on Thursday 7 May at the Adelphi Hotel. The dinner will take place at 7.30 pm, but the President of the Association would like to invite you to a pre-dinner reception at 6.00 pm in the Windsor Suite.**

It is generally not appropriate for the administrator to issue invitations, and details about inviting guests should be agreed with the manager of the event. However, later negotiations about any special requirements – for example, equipment, photocopies of the speaker's notes, dietary requirements – may be made by the administrator, possibly with the speaker's secretary.

Use the correct form of address when writing to or speaking to the guest speaker. For example, a letter to a Lord Mayor should be addressed to: 'The Right Hon. the Lord Mayor of York' and should begin with 'My Lord'; the correct form of spoken address would be 'Your Lordship'. Information about these forms of address can be found in the reference books listed above.

Use the appropriate level of formality for the event, the speaker and the organisation. An invitation to present the prizes at a school sports day may not be as formal in tone (see Figure 3.1.5) as an invitation to give a keynote speech at an international conference.

Greenstone Primary School
Greenstone, WINCHESTER, Hants, GR2 9BA

Date

Rev. J Schofield
Greenstone Vicarage
Greenstone
WINCHESTER
Hants
GR3 8TQ

Dear Reverend Schofield

Sports Day – Tuesday 26 June 2.00 pm

I would like to invite you to present the prizes at our Sports Day on Tuesday 26 June. The children greatly enjoyed your Easter Talk, and I know they would enjoy meeting you again.

Sports day is a very informal, family event. It starts at 2.00 pm and races take place during the afternoon, with prizes being presented at approximately 4.00 pm. This is usually followed by tea and cakes organised by the Parent–Teachers Association, and they warmly invite you to join them for tea.

We are hoping that the weather will be fine, but in the event of bad weather I will inform you of any alternative arrangements on the morning.

I look forward to hearing from you and do hope that you will be able to join us.

Yours sincerely

J M Khan
Headteacher

Figure 3.1.5 A less formal invitation letter

Finally, invitations should indicate clearly any other arrangements – for example, dress requirements, arrangements for transport and accommodation.

Inviting delegates

Delegates are people who have been chosen to attend an event. They may have been chosen in the following ways.

- *They may have been invited to attend by the organisers of the event* – for example, a professional conference. At professional conferences, delegates may be invited to write papers for presentation at the conference. The conference organisers may then select papers for presentation at the conference.
- *They may have been appointed to represent an organisation at an event* – for example, as a representative on a trade stand hired by an organisation at an event. An organisation may have been invited to host a stand at an event and staff will be selected to staff the stand – for example, a college stand at a careers conference. An organisation may have purchased space at an exhibition, and staff representatives appointed to staff the stand – for example, a kitchen designer booking space at an 'Ideal Homes' exhibition.
- *They may have applied to attend an event* – for example, a conference or training activity. A reply slip or booking form may have been completed on publicity materials.

Composing invitations

Once you know the programme and venue and you are in a position to invite delegates to your event, you should ensure that the following information is included in the invitation.

- Full details of the day, date, time and duration of the event.
- Clear information about the purpose of the event.
- Full information about the venue. A map of the venue and travel details may also be included, or may be sent after the invitation has been accepted.
- Information about any meals or accommodation included in the event.
- Information about arrangements for special requirements – for example, dietary requirements, disabled access.
- Details of any dress requirements – for example, an indication of the formality of the event, or specific dress requirements such as black tie.
- Cost of delegate attendance and methods of payment with details of discounts for early bookings or party bookings if appropriate.
- Arrangements for replying to the invitation – for example, RSVP, tear-off slip, booking form. Final date for receipt of replies may also be included.

The style, tone and method of presentation of the invitation should reflect the profile of the event. Prestigious events such as dinners, banquets and presentations may have invitations printed on card (see Figure 3.1.6). Alternatively formal letters of invitation should be written on top quality letter-head printed paper. A word processor may be used to prepare the letter, but each one should be individually addressed to delegates using the mailmerge facility. Publicity materials with tear-off slips and order forms may be printed, or prepared using word processing or desktop publishing facilities.

Where appropriate, confirmation of attendance at an event should be sent to the delegate. The confirmation may contain more detail than the initial invitation. For example, it may include the travel details, accommodation and catering arrangements that have been made for the delegate. Full details of the programme may also be included with the confirmation letter.

The National Building Institute

The Director of the National Building Institute requests the pleasure of the company of

Dr William Fletcher

on Wednesday 3 April ----

at the 50th Annual Dinner. This will be held at the

Royal Grand Hotel, Park Lane, London at 8.00 pm

Drinks will be served in the Lounge from 7.00 pm

Cost of dinner £50

Keynote address to be given by
Professor H. Thomson, Director of the American Building Institute

RSVP to

50th Annual Dinner Office
National Building Institute
64 Haymarket Lane, LONDON EX2 3PT   Dress Black Tie

Figure 3.1.6 An invitation to a delegate

Monitoring responses to invitations

Once the invitations have been issued, the response needs to be monitored. This is to give the organiser a clear idea of the numbers expected at the event. Such information may be needed before final arrangements are made – for example, confirming numbers for refreshments – and could determine whether or not the event takes place at all. There may be a minimum number of delegates required to make an event viable. If insufficient responses are received the event may be cancelled. In these situations the delegates may be offered an alternative event, or their booking cancelled and any deposits returned.

Checking the responses from speakers is a priority. If speakers are unable to attend, it may be necessary to invite back-up speakers, or rearrange the programme.

Letters, mailshots and advertisements for events should contain a mechanism for delegates to record their response. This may be done using a tear-off slip, or booking form and should include space for the following details:

- name of delegate(s)
- their organisation (with address and telephone number)
- number of days/workshops attending
- type of accommodation required
- any special dietary or other requirements
- invoice/payment request.

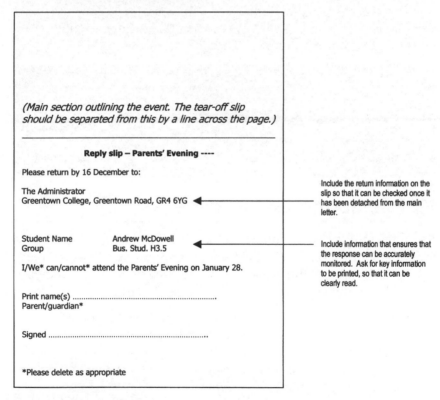

(Main section outlining the event. The tear-off slip should be separated from this by a line across the page.)

Reply slip – Parents' Evening ----

Please return by 16 December to:

The Administrator
Greentown College, Greentown Road, GR4 6YG ◄

Include the return information on the slip so that it can be checked once it has been detached from the main letter.

Student Name   Andrew McDowell
Group   Bus. Stud. H3.5 ◄

I/We* can/cannot* attend the Parents' Evening on January 28.

Include information that ensures that the response can be accurately monitored. Ask for key information to be printed, so that it can be clearly read.

Print name(s) ....
Parent/guardian*

Signed ....

*Please delete as appropriate

Figure 3.1.7 A tear-off slip

A spreadsheet or database can be used to monitor responses. A spreadsheet is particularly useful where delegates are paying to attend and a minimum number is required to cover the costs. See Estimating and Monitoring Costs for further information (pages 146–51).

Portfolio activity 3.1 **Number 4**

Prepare and agree appropriate invitations for the events.
These can be invitations for speakers, those leading activities
and delegates attending the event. You should also monitor the
responses to the invitations as they are received. Use a
spreadsheet or database to record and monitor the responses.
The following evidence should be collected:

- notes of any meetings to agree invitations and possible
  speakers, participants and delegates, and to discuss responses
- copies of the relevant invitations
- a personal statement explaining how you investigated the
  background of possible chosen speakers
- copies of any replies received (where there are a large number
  of replies a small selection will be appropriate)
- diary entries where replies to responses have been logged
- copies of confirmation of arrangements.

Performance criteria:	3.1.1	3.1.6	3.1.9	3.1.10	
Knowledge and understanding:	3.1.c	3.1.e	3.1.f	3.1.g	3.1.i
	3.1.j	3.1.o	3.1.p	3.1.q	
Evidence requirements:	3.1.5	3.1.6	3.1.13	3.1.15	3.1.16
	3.1.17	3.1.18	3.1.19	3.1.20	3.1.34

Finalising the programme

As all the arrangements come together, it is possible for the
programme to be finalised. The final programme will be confirmed
with the manager of the event, and it can then be printed. One or
more of the following programmes may be prepared:

- a detailed programme for the organisers and staff involved
  in the event – for example, detailed arrangements for a dinner
  or presentation
- an outline programme sent to delegates who have been invited to,
  or have applied to attend, the event
- a final programme included in delegate packs issued to delegates.

The final programme will usually contain the following information:

- title of the event and name of the organiser
- day and date of the event
- location of the venue with maps and plans to facilitate delegate
  movement around the event

- details of activities taking place during the event with times and places of activity
- arrangements for refreshments
- any additional information such as arrangements for parking, special requirements for the disabled.

| GRANDSTAND PROMOTIONS

Annual
Antiques Fair

Thursday 2 February –
Sunday 5 February

Cheltenham Race Course

(Location map and exhibition plan on reverse of the programme) | **Thursday 2 February**
Trade Day

10.00 am Opening by Gerald Lucerne, Chief Auctioneer, Melksham Auctions Gold Cup Room

10.30 am – Stands open for business

6.30 pm – Exhibition closes for the day

7.00 pm – Exhibition dinner, admission by ticket only, black tie only
Guest Speaker, Jennifer Baldwin, Fine Art expert, as seen on TV
Gold Cup Room

Friday 3 February
9.00 am – 6.00 pm Public Day
Porcelain and Ceramics day

Saturday 4 February
9.00 am – 6.00 pm Public Day
Furniture and Fine Art

Sunday 5 February
8.30 am – 4.00 pm
Collectors' Day
Racecourse Antiques Car Boot Sale

Refreshments
The Racecourse Restaurant is open for the sale of refreshments during all the Exhibition sessions. Refreshment facilities are also available from a range of stands and locations in the exhibition. |

Figure 3.1.8 A final programme

Portfolio activity 3.1 Number 5

Agree and prepare a programme for the events you are arranging. The programme can be the one used for the manager of the event to show the planned programme for the event, or it can be the programme being provided to all delegates. The following evidence should be collected:

- notes of meetings to discuss and agree the programme
- copy of the completed programme.

Performance criteria:	3.1.1	3.1.6	3.1.7	3.1.9	3.1.11
	3.1.14				
Knowledge and understanding:	3.1.m	3.1.o	3.1.q		
Evidence requirements:	3.1.4	3.1.5	3.1.13	3.1.21	3.1.25
	3.1.26				

Delegate packs

A pack of information is often distributed to delegates. This is usually given as they arrive, but in some situations may be sent in advance. Delegate packs are usually distributed in special presentation folders.

Many organisations have their own pre-printed presentation folders, usually displaying the company logo as part of the organisation's corporate image. The stocks of these should be checked well in advance and sufficient copies should be ordered ready for the event. If the organisation has no pre-printed format, a selection of presentation folders is available from most office stationery suppliers.

Materials may also be presented in bags. The bags may be small briefcases printed with a corporate logo or event information; these are quite popular with international professional conferences. Exhibition-style events may have plastic carrier bags, pre-printed with an exhibitor logo for the presentation of exhibition materials.

Other pre-printed materials may also be provided – for example, pencils, pens, notepads. All pre-printed materials should be ordered well in advance and their cost has to be included in the budget for the event. They may sometimes, however, be supplied free of charge by companies wishing to promote their goods to the audience at the event.

There is no standard list of materials and information to be included in a delegate pack. It may contain any of the following:

- an identification badge for the delegate to wear
- delegate information – the programme, workshop lists, delegate lists, and other event information
- room location details for workshops running throughout the day
- venue information – information on room accommodation, meals, parking

- copies of handouts and printed support materials – for example, biographical information about the speakers and summary notes
- advertising and publicity materials – materials and literature supplied by organisations who may be sponsoring the event
- attendance forms – delegates who are being supported by their organisations may need some proof of attendance
- feedback forms – these should be included for delegates to complete and return before they leave the conference
- list of tourist attractions and services in the area
- paper and pen (possibly sponsored by a local organisation).

A list of delegate documents and the number of packs required should be agreed with the programme manager at an early stage in the planning. A checklist of documents can be prepared, and sets of each document can be ticked off as they are collected. When the sets of documents have been collected, they can be collated into individual sets and placed in the delegate pack. It is always a good idea to prepare some spare delegate packs. Arrangements for transporting the packs to the event should have been made, and the complete packs should be ready to be transported to the event.

Portfolio activity 3.1 **Number 6**

Prepare delegate packs for the one-day meeting you are organising. The following evidence should be collected:

- one copy of a delegate pack.

Performance criteria:	3.1.11	3.1.14		
Knowledge and understanding:	3.1.o	3.1.q		
Evidence requirements:	3.1.21	3.1.22	3.1.23	3.1.31	3.1.35

Arrangements for the day of the event

In addition to planning and arranging the programme of events for the day, it is also necessary to plan the practical administrative arrangements for the event. Matters such as reception, health and safety and administrative support during the course of the event need to be organised.

Arrangements for reception should have been made in advance, and reception duties allocated to relevant staff. There should always be at least one member of the administrative staff available to deal with delegate enquiries and provide support for the duration of the event. A staff rota should have been agreed to provide cover for the event.

One of the key factors that influence the success of an event is the comfort factor. It is important to check the physical environment at the beginning of the event and take steps to put right any problems. The venue management should be contacted if the venue is too cold and the heating should be checked. If it is too hot, check for windows that can be opened, and contact the venue management. It is also a good idea to carry out regular checks with participants that they are happy with the physical environment of the venue.

On the day of the event, the administrator should arrive in good time to check that all final details are in place. This can include checking that:

- final arrangements have been made at the venue – for example, direction signs are in place, audio-visual equipment is available
- rooms are suitably organised – for example, chairs and tables are laid out in the appropriate style, audio-visual equipment is in the right position, stationery is in place
- equipment and materials are all available, with suitable electrical sockets where required
- name badges and signing-in lists are available
- refreshments have been arranged for suitable times, and water is on the tables for speakers and delegates
- special requirements have been met – for example, dietary requirements for meals, disabled access
- health and safety arrangements have all been made
- receptionists and other support staff have been suitably briefed.

Some of the speakers and participants may be arriving earlier than the main event, and it is important to check that all arrangements have been made for their arrival. An appropriate member of staff should be briefed to greet important guests. The briefing may include information about how to greet and address the guest.

Reception at the event

There may well be two levels of reception at an event. Firstly, the venue location may have their own reception arrangements and they will need to be informed of the arrival of participants and delegates. The venue may also have a range of rooms, and arrangements for providing signs to direct delegates to appropriate locations should be made. The venue may have display boards, or you may need to prepare the signs and place them appropriately.

The second level of reception will be provided at the actual venue site – for example, the conference room(s) booked for the event. At a small one-day event, the reception role may be carried out by the administrator of the event. At events having a large number of delegates and/or taking place over a number of days, a rota of staff may be prepared to provide various support roles for the event. The receptionists should familiarise themselves with the location of cloakroom and toilet facilities before going on duty. Reception duties can include the following activities:

- greet visitors as they arrive, check their names against the delegate list and issue them with name badges
- inform visitors of cloakroom arrangements
- issue delegate packs
- direct delegates to refreshment facilities and seating arrangements
- provide support and guidance to delegates
- take messages for delegates.

All staff taking part in the event should be suitably dressed to represent the organisation. Information about standards of dress and codes of behaviour should be included in any briefing for staff. Staff should also have name badges that clearly identify them, their role and the organisation.

Health and safety at the event

Evaluation of the health and safety arrangements in place at a venue should have been carried out before bookings were made. On the day of the event they should be checked again and arrangements made to inform delegates of the health and safety procedures. Once the delegates are assembled, they should be informed of the fire evacuation procedures and regulations with regard to smoking. If there are any disabled visitors present, particularly those in wheelchairs, the disabled evacuation procedures should be checked in advance and the visitors should be informed of the procedures on their arrival.

The initial briefing of delegates with the practical arrangements is often called the 'domestics'. Delegates are usually informed of the health and safety issues, location of toilet facilities, arrangements for refreshments, and any other arrangements.

Portfolio activity 3.1 **Number 7**

Prepare notes for the health and safety briefing during the event, and make arrangements for the health and safety briefing. The following evidence should be collected:

- health and safety briefing notes
- witness testimony and a personal statement confirming that the health and safety briefing took place.

Performance criteria:	3.1.6	3.1.14	3.1.15
Knowledge and understanding:	3.1.a	3.1.o	
Evidence requirements:	3.1.5	3.1.6	3.1.13

During the event

Arrangements are usually made for administrative staff to be available during the event to provide support to participants and delegates. This may mean a member of staff always being on duty at the venue. A staff rota should be prepared for this. The manager of the event should also have a copy of this rota. Where the event is held on internal premises, a contact telephone number may be left with the manager of the event. The purpose of the ongoing support is to carry out any last-minute administrative activities and ensure the smooth running of the event. This can include the following activities:

- photocopying of last-minute notes, handouts, etc.
- taking and passing on messages for delegates
- checking and monitoring refreshments and other arrangements
- taking notes
- organising last-minute supplies of stationery, materials, etc.
- dealing with delegate enquiries – for example, late arrivals, cloakroom facilities, parking.

During the event you should always have a list of delegates and programme and workshop details to hand. You should ensure that reception know where you are at any time so that you can take urgent messages. Remember that your task is to assist in hosting the event and in anticipating and solving problems.

Portfolio activity 3.1 Number 8

Make arrangements for staff cover during the event, and ensure they are carried out. The following evidence should be collected:

- personal statement explaining the arrangements you made to cover the event
- examples of staff rotas, notes/messages to relevant participants, reception, etc.
- witness testimony from the event manager to confirm that arrangements were made to cover the event, documents were distributed, and that visitors were greeted correctly and you were available during the event.

Performance criteria:	3.1.1	3.1.6	3.1.7	3.1.11	3.1.13
	3.1.14				
Knowledge and understanding:	3.1.a	3.1.i			
Evidence requirements:	3.1.4	3.1.5	3.1.9	3.1.10	3.1.29

After the event

An important part of administering an event, and one that is often neglected, is making the final arrangements once the main activity of the event has been completed. These usually fall into two categories: immediately after the event and finalising details later.

Immediately the main activities of the event have been completed, the following tasks should be carried out.

- Make sure the evaluation forms have been given out and collected in.
- Say any relevant goodbyes to speakers, participants and delegates, and ensure that they are aware of and have booked suitable transport for their return journey.
- Ensure that all participants and delegates have taken all their personal belongings.
- Collect all spare papers, handouts, packs, paperwork, OHP pens, flip charts, signs, etc.
- Ensure that arrangements for the return of equipment have been completed.
- Check that rooms are tidy and left in a reasonable condition for the next event.

- Inform reception that the event has been completed and delegates have left.

Finalising the details takes place in the weeks following an event and can include the following tasks:

- writing thank-you letters to speakers, delegates, participants, venues, etc.
- submitting invoices for payment
- completing and submitting expenses forms for payment
- completing spreadsheets to record all payments
- analysing evaluation forms and completing an event evaluation report (this is covered in more detail in Element 3.2; see pages 159–61)
- preparing appropriate publicity information/articles and press releases for publication advertising the success of the event.

Portfolio activity 3.1 **Number 9**

Complete the after-event activities. The following evidence should be collected:

- witness testimony from the event manager to state that the immediate post-event activities were carried out correctly
- copies of evaluation forms, attendance lists, signs used during event, delegate identification
- copies of thank-you letters, invoices, expenses claims submitted and claimed
- copies of publicity information, press releases, articles for internal magazine, etc.

Performance criteria:	3.1.2	3.1.6	3.1.13	3.1.14	
Knowledge and understanding:	3.1.b	3.1.h	3.1.i	3.1.o	3.1.q
Evidence requirements:	3.1.13	3.1.24	3.1.27	3.1.28	3.1.29
	3.1.30	3.1.32	3.1.33	3.1.38	

Estimating and monitoring costs

The issue of finance for the event should be discussed during the preliminary meetings. The actual method of financing and level of budget will depend on the type of event, its profile and the type of organisation. The following sources of finance may be used:

- a fixed sum of money allocated from the organisation – this may be set at the beginning of the event, or may be agreed when the costs have been estimated
- income received from delegates or organisations paying to attend the event
- sponsorship from other relevant organisations who will use the event to publicise their products and services.

In many situations a combination of these sources of finance will be used.

An estimate of the costs should be prepared during the initial planning stages. Even where the budget has been fixed, an estimate can show how the budget is to be allocated between the different costs. It is a very useful guide when negotiating prices for venues, refreshments, speakers, etc. The following sources of information can be useful when preparing an estimate:

- records, budgets and reports on previous similar events
- information gathered during initial enquiries
- information gathered from other administrative colleagues
- advice provided by the event manager
- the organisation's policies and procedures on expenses, payments, etc.

There are two types of costs to be considered when preparing an estimate.

- *Fixed costs* – the costs that have to be paid regardless of how many delegates are attending the event. These can include the room hire at the venue, speakers' costs, hire of equipment.
- *Variable costs* –the costs that depend on the number of delegates – for example, refreshments, overnight accommodation for delegates.

For some events it may be appropriate to calculate a 'break-even' point. This is the point at which the sum of the fixed cost and variable costs matches the budget for the event. This will give an indication of the number of delegates required to make the event viable. If there are fewer delegates than this number then the event is likely to make a loss; if there are more delegates a profit will be generated.

After carrying out the calculation (see Figure 3.1.9), it is useful to produce a graph. In Figure 3.1.10, the graph has been prepared to show the break-even point when a charge of £50 per delegate is made. It shows that 15 delegates are required to cover the costs.

Break-even Cost Calculation for Training Event

Fixed Costs

Venue hire	£150
Equipment hire	£45
Lecturer costs	£250
Lecturer expenses	£50
TOTAL fixed costs	**£495**

Variable Costs	Cost 1 delegate	Cost 5 delegates	Cost 10 delegates	Cost 20 delegates
Refreshment	£12	£60	£120	£240
Training materials	£5	£25	£50	£100
Total variable costs	£17	£85	£170	£340
TOTAL EVENT COST	£512	£580	£665	£835
Unit cost per delegate	£512	£116	£66.50	£40.18

Figure 3.1.9 A break-even cost calculation

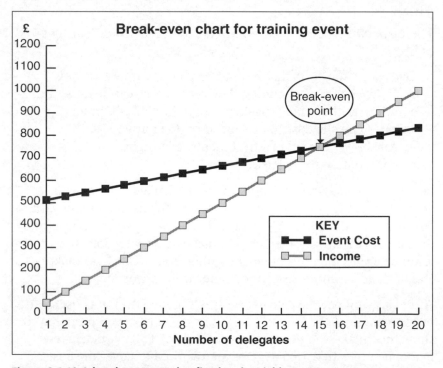

Figure 3.1.10 A break-even graph – fixed and variable costs

An alternative method of preparing a break-even graph is to chart the number of delegates against the budget. The budget would be represented by a straight line, which indicates the maximum number of delegates that would be covered by the budget.

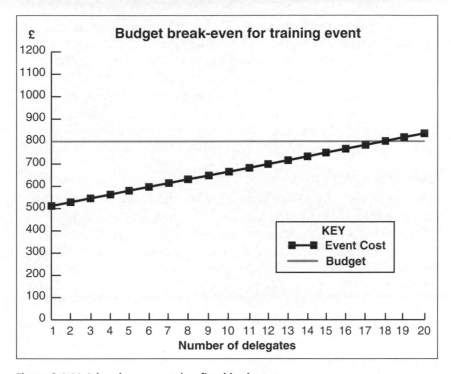

Figure 3.1.11 A break-even graph – fixed budget

This graph shows the break-even point for a fixed budget sum of £800. It shows that 18 delegates can attend the event. Any more delegates would mean going over budget.

Direct/indirect costs

Another way of looking at costs is to divide them into direct and indirect costs. Direct costs are those costs that are incurred and paid for as a direct result of the event – for example, venue, refreshment, speaker costs. However, there are usually also costs that may be incurred which are not paid for directly – for example, postage, stationery, internal staff costs. In some organisations these indirect costs must also be charged to the event. In other organisations it may be acceptable that these costs are not charged directly to the event, and are absorbed within the organisation's general costs. Such costs are then known as 'overhead' costs.

Direct budget method

In the direct budget method of allocating costs, every event is allocated a separate budget number. All costs for the event, including internal costs incurred, will be allocated to the appropriate budget number – for example, staff may have to account for their time against the different budget numbers and this will be recorded on their weekly timesheets. Other costs such as stationery, photocopying and postage will also be recorded against the budget number. The organisation's procedures for costing internal resources should be followed – for example, using the set rate for staff hourly costs. This is a complex method of estimating and paying costs and is only appropriate where it is part of the organisation's procedures.

Overheads method

An alternative method of recognising the indirect costs within an estimate is to allow for overheads within the estimate. Rather than making a direct costing for the organisation's resources, a more approximate method of allowing for internal costs is used. For example, a percentage of the total cost may be allocated as overheads, so that for an event costing £1000, a 10 per cent charge of £100 might be made to cover overheads. Alternatively, a fixed sum may be added to events to cover overheads – for example, £150 per event.

Contingencies

However carefully an estimate is prepared, it is not always possible to predict accurately all the costs that may arise – for example, equipment breaking down and the cost incurred of hiring alternative equipment. An allowance should be made within the estimate for contingencies.

Often a percentage allowance – for example, 10 per cent – is included within the estimate to cover contingencies. An alternative method of allowing for contingencies is to round up estimates to a slightly higher figure. For example, if when making initial enquiries for hire of a venue the figure of £180 is given, the estimated figure could be rounded up to £200 to allow for any contingencies.

Using a spreadsheet

It is a good idea to use a spreadsheet to prepare estimates and monitor ongoing costs. The spreadsheet can be used to monitor the costs as they are incurred and to highlight any costs which are more or less than the expenditure. The difference between the estimated cost and the real cost is called 'variance'. The variance can be negative or positive. When preparing the final analysis for the event, the reasons for variance should be given.

Training Event Spreadsheet					
	Venue hire	Equipment hire	Lecturer Costs	Lecturer Expenses	Total Costs
Estimated Costs	150	45	250	50	495
Actual Costs	183.59	33.5	224	87.54	528.63
Variance	-33.59	11.5	26	-37.54	-33.63

Figure 3.1.11 An event spreadsheet

This spreadsheet shows that overall the event was £33.63 over budget and the main causes of this were the underestimate for venue hire and lecturer expenses. The reasons for this could have been that the usual venue was not available, and an alternative venue was more expensive. The lecturer booked for the event may have travelled by car, rather than rail, and incurred a higher rate of expenses. If a contingency allowance of 10 per cent had been added to the initial event, that is £49.50, the total estimate would have been £544.50 and the event would have been within the budget.

Further information on budgeting can be found in Unit 7 (see pages 311–25).

Portfolio activity 3.1 Number 10

1 Prepare a spreadsheet to show the cost estimates for an event.

The following evidence should be collected:

- printout of the spreadsheet
- a statement to explain how the figures were arrived at, and how contingencies were allowed for. Include or reference examples of information used to include in the spreadsheet – for example, quotations, information from venues.

2 Prepare a graph or chart to show break-even costs, or costs against budget.

The following evidence should be collected:

- printout of the graph or chart.

3 Use the spreadsheet to carry out the ongoing monitoring of the costs.

The following evidence should be collected:

• printouts of the spreadsheet over a period of time.

  Make sure that the versions of the spreadsheet are dated.

4 Prepare a final spreadsheet when the event has been completed.

The following evidence should be collected:

• printout of the final spreadsheet.

Performance criteria:	3.1.1	3.1.5	3.1.12
Knowledge and understanding:	3.1.a	3.1.o	3.1.q
Evidence requirements:	3.1.7	3.1.14	3.1.37

Test yourself

Knowledge and understanding	Questions
a	Explain how you determine the organisation's objectives, policy, procedures and budget for running an event.
b	Describe your organisation's policy for dealing with the media/press regarding conferencing/events.
	Explain why effective advance publicity and prompt issue of an event programme is important when organising a conference/event.
c	Describe three time management techniques. Explain why it is important to have a clear timescale when planning events.
d	Give reasons why you would use courier and translator services for an event.
e	State three principles you should remember when working in a team.
f	Give three different sources of reference you could use to investigate the background of potential or chosen speakers.

g	Explain why the choice of speakers, programme content and location of venue is important to the success of a conference/event.
h	Describe the correct procedures and etiquette for inviting guest speakers and delegates.
i	Describe the points of etiquette you should remember when communicating with speakers and guests.
j	Give examples of how you would book the following: a) hotel/conference centre accommodation b) catering c) equipment d) trade stands.
k	Explain what a penalty clause is. When might it be applied by a venue and to delegates?
l	Explain the effect of work roles and relationships on the communication process.
m	Describe how you would prepare written procedures – for example, for organising events.
n	Explain how you would produce documents using a mailmerge facility.
o	Describe how you would compose and format four of the following types of document: • Informal reports • Letters • Memos • Invitations • Programmes • Booking forms • Press releases.
p	Explain how you can communicate effectively using the telephone, fax, e-mail and the Internet.
q	Explain how you would use information technology to analyse, monitor and present information.

EVALUATE A BUSINESS EVENT

When an event is over, its organisation and content should be assessed to decide whether it has been successful. This can often be separated into two clear areas. Did the event achieve its objectives; and was it well organised? Feedback should be collected on the event content, programme, speakers, etc. as well as the venue, refreshments and practical arrangements. (Further information on evaluating and analysing information can be found in Element 5.1 – see pages 230–3.)

Evaluating an event is about measuring whether it has achieved the objectives. These objectives should be clearly defined at the outset. They should be agreed at the initial meeting with the event manager. This can include both the practical objectives, and the purpose of the event. Evidence or measurements can then be collected during the following stages of the event.

- *While the arrangements are being made* – feedback from people organising the event can be collected about practical arrangements – for example, was enough time allowed for venues or speakers to respond, was sufficient information collected about equipment requirements?
- *While the event is in progress* – feedback from event managers, participants and delegates can be collected while the event is in progress. Notes may be made of the number of visitors who make enquiries at an exhibition stand.
- *At the end of the event* – feedback from event managers, participants, delegates should be collected at the end of the event.
- *After the event* – a meeting may be held by the event manager and the organisers to discuss feedback about the event.

Collecting feedback about an event

There are various methods of collecting feedback that can be used to provide the information to form the basis of analysing and evaluating the event. These can include the following.

- *Self-evaluation* – you can analyse and record information about the way you organised the event. You may think about this as: 'What did I get right, what did not work, and what would I do differently next time?' When assessing yourself you should be objective. It is an opportunity for you to identify the positive and negative aspects of your performance. Where you identify negative aspects, you should think about these constructively and identify ways of improving your performance in the future.

- *Team evaluation* – the team can meet together to discuss the outcome of the event. Members can share their perceptions of what went well, what problems were experienced, how problems were solved. Suggestions for improvements for the future can be agreed. Written procedures for organising events can be reviewed and revised.

- *Evaluating others* – when you are working as part of a team, you can also evaluate the performance of others. Again evaluation should be objective, fair and supported by constructive feedback. Remember always to include the positive as well as the negative aspects of their performance. Feedback to other members of the team should be given sensitively, but honestly.

- *Personal observation* – you can record your own notes about feedback. For example, you may note during the event that the venue was cold, or the reception service was not very good.

- *Informal feedback collected from others* – event managers, participants and delegates may make informal comments during the course of the event. For example, they may remark that the venue was difficult to find, there was insufficient parking, the speakers were very good. Make written notes of these comments as you receive them.

- *Formal feedback collected from others* – participants and delegates can be asked to provide formal feedback. This is usually done in the form of a questionnaire.

Portfolio activity 3.2 **Number 1**

1 Prepare a personal statement that is a self-evaluation of your own performance in organising and administering the event. If you organised the event as part of a team, include an evaluation of a colleague's activities.

2 Hold a team meeting after the event to discuss how the team organised the event. Use the self-evaluation and colleague evaluations as part of this activity.

The following evidence should be collected:

- personal statement
- notes of the team meeting.

Performance criteria:	3.2.1	3.2.2	3.2.4	3.2.7	
Knowledge and understanding:	3.2.b				
Evidence requirements:	3.2.1	3.2.2	3.2.3	3.2.13	3.2.15
	3.2.16				

Evaluation questionnaires

A questionnaire is a very effective method of collecting feedback about an event. It is systematic as every delegate is asked the same questions. It is objective as it is usually completed anonymously at the end of the event. It provides data that can easily be analysed. However, questionnaires have two main drawbacks: they need to be carefully designed and they tend to have poor return rates.

Questionnaire design is covered in more detail in Element 5.1 (see pages 222–4). However, the main points to be considered when designing an evaluation questionnaire for an event are as follows:

- administrative and domestic arrangements
- venue for event
- event publicity
- position of stand (where appropriate)
- content of event
- materials/information available
- effectiveness of speakers/workshop groups
- suggestions for future event topics
- provide for structured rather than unstructured responses – these are much easier to analyse. For example, a structured question might be: 'Was the venue easy to find? Yes/No.' An unstructured question might be: 'Have you any comments you wish to make about the venue?' A final unstructured question will provide the opportunity for delegates to make any comments they may wish to make
- ensure that questions are fair and not biased – opportunities should be provided on the questionnaire for both positive and negative feedback about all aspects of the event

- use an appropriate level of language and questions for the delegates completing the questionnaire – the style of questions would be very different for school-leavers attending a careers conference than for professionals at an international conference.

The organisation's house style should also be followed. Some organisations may have standardised evaluation feedback mechanisms and these should be used or incorporated into the questionnaires prepared for the event. Where all the organisation's documents are subject to quality processes, any proposed questionnaire may need to be submitted for approval.

Return rates for questionnaires at events can be maximised by using the following strategies.

- Issue the evaluation form in the delegate pack – delegates can then complete them during the event and leave them behind rather than posting them later.
- Keep the questionnaire short – long questionnaires can be off-putting and may not be completed at all.
- Arrange for the final speaker to remind delegates to complete and return the questionnaire.
- Ensure that event staff are available to collect questionnaires and evaluation forms from delegates as they leave. Have a few spare questionnaires available, in case delegates have lost theirs or packed it away in their luggage.

It is not a good idea to rely on delegates to return their questionnaires by post. The response to the event will not be as 'fresh' and only a very small percentage will be returned in this way. In addition, your analysis will be delayed while you are waiting for responses.

There may be some events where it is more appropriate to use interviews as a means of collecting feedback – for example, feedback from parents about the organisation of a parents' evening or feedback about an exhibition stand from visitors to the stand. A questionnaire should be designed, and staff assigned to interview delegates and complete the questionnaires. In these situations it may be possible to interview only a random sample.

The design of the questionnaire and the method of issuing and collecting the completed copies should be agreed with the event manager during the meetings to organise the event.

```
┌─────────────────────────────────────────────────────────┐
│                    Top Training Services                  │
│                   Evaluation Questionnaire                │
│                                                           │
│  Course Number  ....................  Course Title .......................... │
│                                                           │
│  Date of Course  ...................  Venue  ..............................  │
│                                                           │
│  We would be grateful if you could complete this questionnaire and leave │
│  it with the trainer at the end of the event.  Please circle your response │
│  to the questions:                                        │
│                                                           │
│  1 very good, 2 good, 3 satisfactory, 4 less than satisfactory, 5 very poor │
│                                                           │
│  1   Did the course meet its stated objectives?  1   2   3   4   5 │
│                                                           │
│  2   Quality of the venue                    1   2   3   4   5 │
│                                                           │
│  3   Location of the venue                   1   2   3   4   5 │
│                                                           │
│  4   Refreshments                            1   2   3   4   5 │
│                                                           │
│  5   Content of the training session         1   2   3   4   5 │
│                                                           │
│  6   Delivery by the trainer                 1   2   3   4   5 │
│                                                           │
│  7   Training materials                      1   2   3   4   5 │
│                                                           │
│  8   Organisation of the event               1   2   3   4   5 │
│                                                           │
│                                                           │
│  Have you any comments you wish to make about the course? │
│                                                           │
│  ......................................................................... │
│  ......................................................................... │
│  ......................................................................... │
│  ......................................................................... │
│  ......................................................................... │
│  ......................................................................... │
└─────────────────────────────────────────────────────────┘
```

Figure 3.2.1 An evaluation questionnaire

Portfolio activity 3.2 Number 2

Working as a team and with the event manager carry out the following activities:

1 Prepare an event evaluation form to be distributed to delegates at an event (see example questionnaire, Figure 3.2.1, page 157).

2 Prepare a procedure for distributing the questionnaires and collecting feedback.

The following evidence should be collected:

- draft and finalised questionnaires; indicate your contribution to the finalised questionnaire
- written procedure for distributing the questionnaires and collecting feedback. This can be in the form of minutes from a meeting where it is discussed and agreed.

Performance criteria:	3.2.3	3.2.4	3.2.5		
Knowledge and understanding:	3.2.d	3.2.e			
Evidence requirements:	3.2.4	3.2.5	3.2.6	3.2.7	3.2.8
	3.2.9	3.2.10	3.2.11	3.2.13	3.2.20
	3.2.21	3.2.22			

Analysing the responses

The responses from the questionnaire are easier to analyse if the majority of the questions have been structured. The results can then be entered into a database or spreadsheet to be sorted and presented in an appropriate form, usually as tables or graphs. (Further information on analysing and interpreting information can be found in Section 5.1; see pages 230–3.) The following guidelines should be used:

The analysis should clearly state the number of responses. For example, '15 forms were received from 20 delegates.' The number of responses must be taken into account when drawing any conclusions.

Conclusions must be supported by the evidence. For example, 'Of the respondents, 50 per cent were very satisfied with the location of the venue, 25 per cent satisfied and 25 per cent not satisfied.' It would not be correct to conclude that most of the delegates were very satisfied with the venue, for two reasons. Firstly, this would be guessing the response of the 25 per cent of the delegates who did not complete forms; and, secondly, the statement is about the location of the venue, not about the venue itself. It would also be incorrect to say that 50 per cent of the delegates were very satisfied with the venue because of its ease of access to the motorway, unless this statement was specifically included on the form.

Conclusions can be supported with other evidence. For example, '50 per cent of respondents were very satisfied with the location of the venue, 25 per cent satisfied and 25 per cent not satisfied. Comments were received from several delegates during the course of the event to say that its ease of access to the motorway made it a good venue. However, one delegate who used public transport said that it was not very convenient for the railway station.'

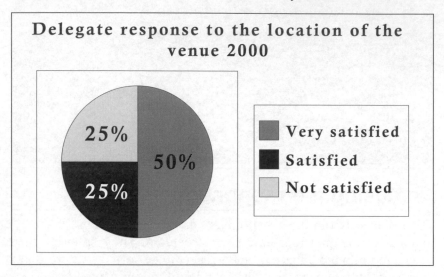

Figure 3.2.2 Pie chart showing delegate response

Comparisons can also be made with other data from previous feedback for similar events. For example, 'A greater proportion of delegates were satisfied with the location of the venue than in the previous year's event.'

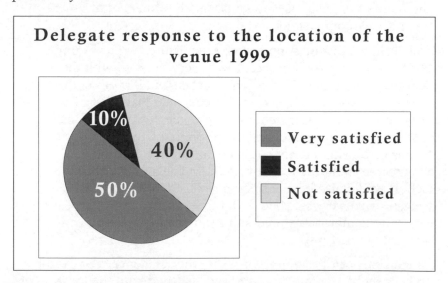

Figure 3.2.3 Pie chart showing delegate response

Evaluating the findings

Once the data has been analysed then it can be evaluated. There may be a large number of responses to the questions and quite a lot of data. The analysis and evaluation is easier if the data is organised into logical groups that relate to the objectives defined for the event – for example, the administrative arrangements, the physical factors of the event, the content and presentation of the event. Success in reaching objectives may be defined quantitatively or qualitatively.

Quantitative measures of success may be, for example, financial or numerical. Was a financial target reached, or a specific budget met? Was a numerical target met – for example, 200 people visited a stand, or all parents of full-time students offered the opportunity of meeting course tutors?

Qualitative measures of success are difficult to assess, but can relate to how many people respond positively to the event. For example: were staff who attended the parents' evening satisfied with the arrangements; did parents find it a useful opportunity to discuss their children's progress with tutors?

An important feature of the evaluation is the recommendations for improvement for future events. These can cover all aspects of organising and administering the event: the arrangements, the venue, the timing, the speakers, etc. Written procedures for organising events should be reviewed and revised to include improvements recommended in these areas.

Presenting the findings

When the all the information has been collected, analysed and evaluated it should be presented in writing to the event manager or other appropriate people. This can be done in the form of an informal report. The format shown in Figure 3.2.4 could be used for the report.

More information on writing and presenting reports can be found in Element 5.2 (see pages 236–49).

Title, date, name of author

1   Introduction

1.1   Introductory paragraph outlining who the report has been prepared for, in response to which event, and the objectives initially defined for the event.

1.2   List the different ways in which feedback was collected.

2   Findings
List under logical headings the findings collected from the feedback. This should include questionnaire feedback and general feedback. Tables, graphs and other detailed findings may be included in the main body of the report, or referenced as appendices to the report. The raw data must be analysed electronically – for example, using a database or spreadsheet.

3   Conclusions and recommendations.

3.1   The conclusions reached as a result of the analysis of the findings. This should cover:
what went well
what problems were experienced
how problems were solved.

3.2   Recommendations for suggestions for improvements for future events.

Figure 3.2.4 Report format

Portfolio activity 3.2 **Number 3**

Prepare an informal report evaluating a business event. This report should include: the original objectives for the event; how feedback was collected; findings from the feedback collected; analysis of the feedback; recommendations for future events. Include any revised written procedures as an appendix within the report. The following evidence should be collected:

• a word processed report including some information presented using a graphics or presentation package.

Performance criteria:	3.2.2	3.2.6	3.2.7	3.2.8	3.2.9
	3.2.10				
Knowledge and understanding:	3.2.a	3.2.b	3.2.c	3.2.e	3.2.f
	3.2.g				
Evidence requirements:	3.2.12	3.2.13	3.2.14	3.2.15	3.2.16
	3.2.17	3.2.18	3.2.19	3.2.20	3.2.21
	3.2.22	3.2.23			

Test yourself

Knowledge and understanding	Questions
a	Give examples of objectives for different types of conference/event.
b	Explain the principles and techniques of evaluation and analysis.
c	Explain how you would assess and evaluate your own performance.
	Explain how you can extract honest, fair and reliable feedback from an audience.
d	Explain how you would compile a questionnaire to elicit required information.
e	Explain how you communicate effectively with colleagues at all levels.
f	Show three different ways of presenting findings to ensure maximum impact.
g	Describe the structure of informal reports.

Activity 3.1

Memorandum

MEMORANDUM

To Office Administrator
From Andrew Willings, Training Manager
Date Monday -- -- --
Subject Evaluation of training courses

We have now several training courses booked for commercial companies. As these are our first courses in this venture, we need to be able to evaluate them carefully to make sure we get them right. Please write some brief notes on how we can carry out this evaluation, and prepare any sample documentation.

Activity 3.2

Memorandum

MEMORANDUM

To: Office Administrator
From: Andrew Willings, Training Manager
Date Tuesday -- -- --
Subject Procedures for booking venues

Administrative staff are involved in booking venues for training sessions, conferences, etc. Please prepare a set of procedures to be followed when booking venues, from the enquiry to booking stage. Include all the relevant checks that need to be made.

Activity 3.3

E-mail

> **HTR**
>
> **To:** Office Administrator
> **From:** Andrew Willings
> **Date** Wednesday -- -- --
> **Subject** Training conferences
>
> We have arranged stands at a series of training conferences. Various staff will be required to attend the conferences to host the stands. Please prepare a set of brief procedures to cover the hosting of publicity stands. You should cover: preparing the stand, greeting potential clients, collecting client information and issuing company information.

Activity 3.4

Memorandum

> **MEMORANDUM**
>
> **To:** Office Administrator
> **From:** Andrew Willings, Training Manager
> **Date** Thursday -- -- --
> **Subject** Guest speakers
>
> We need to build up a list of suitable guest speakers, lecturers, etc. for our training courses. I have several names already. However, we need to check these people carefully before we use them. Please let me have some ideas of how I can check these speakers' experience and capabilities as well as information on suitable sources of reference.

Activity 3.5

Memorandum

MEMORANDUM

To: Office Administrator
From: Andrew Willings, Training Manager
Date Friday -- -- --
Subject Training room equipment

The new training room needs suitable equipment to enable a range of training presentations to be made. Please write a report outlining different uses for equipment that we could purchase to cover all types of presentation. Include recommendations.

---

4 Organise Business Trips at Home and Abroad

The concept of the 'global market' has greatly increased the need for business travel. Although advances in electronic communications have speeded up worldwide communications and reduced their cost, personal contact is still important. Business travellers may make UK and overseas trips for the following reasons:

- *sales* – negotiating the sale of goods and equipment.
- *supply* – purchasing goods and services
- *exchange of information* – national/international conferences, seminars, and training
- *audits* – quality checks on agents, accounts, suppliers, etc.
- *meetings* – exchange of ideas and views about particular issues.

Travelling can be expensive in terms of both money and time, many trips therefore will have multiple purposes. The business traveller may take the opportunity to combine various visits while on a trip, and this can make the planning and organisation of the trip more complex. This unit is about organising business trips and preparing travel documentation.

Element 4.1
ORGANISE BUSINESS TRIPS

Planning

Careful planning is the key to a well-organised business trip. The exact planning required for any trip will depend on the purpose of the trip, the destination and the personal preferences of the traveller. However, factors that will need to be considered for most trips include: the organisation's policies; the personal preferences of the traveller; researching appropriate information; making travel arrangements; booking accommodation; preparing papers and documentation; arranging money and expenses; managing the traveller's absence; informing the traveller of arrangements.

The organisation's travel policy

All travel arrangements must be made in compliance with the organisation's travel policy, so this is the starting point for all planning. The policy will usually cover the following issues.

- *Agreed spending limits* – for accommodation, refreshments, expenses.
- *Preferred suppliers* – the organisation may have negotiated commercial contracts with specific travel organisations, hotel chains, car hire companies, etc. These should always be used where they are available.
- *Standards of accommodation and travel* – the class of travel and hotel-ratings that can be booked will be specified. These can vary depending on the status of the traveller.
- *Use of cars* – company cars, private cars and hire cars.
- *Booking procedures for tickets* – whether direct bookings can be made or travel agents are to be used.
- *Payment arrangements* – the use of company credit cards, claiming of expenses, cash advances.
- *Health and safety policies* – provision of health insurance, arrangements for vaccinations/inoculations, advised driving times and journey lengths.

Initial planning

At the outset of the planning process it is necessary to establish some exact details. Who is going? When are they going? When are they returning? What is the purpose of the trip? Where are they going?

Travellers may have individual preferences for travel arrangements. They may have special requirements for standards of accommodation or types of room – for example, non-smoking/ smoking – and could have special dietary requirements or preferred types of cuisine. Travellers may have views about the use of their own car as opposed to the use of a company or hire car, or about travel by train. If they are driving, they may prefer to use motorways, or alternatively they may prefer direct routes on 'A' roads. They may wish to include an overnight stay with relatives or evening/lunchtime meetings with colleagues, friends and relatives.

The key aspects of the trip that you will need to work on are likely to include:

* *transport* – the agreed modes of transport to get the traveller from the start point to the destination and back again: the start and end points may be home, the office, or a location en route
* *accommodation* – the number of nights, type of accommodation, venues, refreshment arrangements, etc.
* *papers and documentation* – ensuring the traveller has the required travel documents – for example, driving licence, passport, visas, documentation for samples
* *money and expenses* – arranging foreign currency and travellers' cheques for the traveller: expenses claims may need to be completed for cash advances
* *managing the traveller s absence* – arrangements for covering work while the traveller is away, and contact arrangements for getting in touch with the traveller: the traveller may agree guidelines about issues that can be delegated, and those that require their attention; alterations to the schedule of visits, meetings and travel arrangements may also need to be communicated to the traveller
* *informing the traveller of arrangements* – verbal information about progress of arrangements, memos listing arrangements, copies of booking documents, as well as itineraries and briefing details are all ways of keeping travellers informed of travel arrangements.

You will need to research certain information using appropriate reference sources. The information you need to research will vary depending on the exact details of the visit. List the information you need to find out about along with possible sources during the planning stage, for example:

Air travel London–Edinburgh – contact travel agents

Overnight accommodation in Edinburgh – check AA Book.

You can tick off each item of information as it is completed.

Portfolio activity 4.1 **Number 1**

Note

Some of the activities in this unit are designed to allow you to record activities as you carry them out. For example, they may refer to designing logs and checklists that you should complete on an ongoing basis as you research and plan travel and journeys. When completed they will form a valuable part of your evidence.

Prepare a personal preference checklist that can be used to establish general preferences for travellers. Include information on preferred methods of travel, route, times of travel, accommodation, documentation, meals, etc. Complete this checklist with two members of staff for a UK business trip and an overseas business trip. You should collect the following evidence:

• blank personal preference checklists
• two completed checklists.

Performance criteria:	4.1.1 4.1.2 4.1.5 4.1.13 4.2.1
Knowledge and understanding:	4.1. I
Evidence requirements:	4.1.1 4.1.2 4.1.18

Prioritising planning activities

After the initial planning stage of determining the exact details of the trip, the traveller's personal preferences and listing the arrangements to be made, it is important to prioritise the planning activities. It is possible to buy train tickets on the train for some journeys, but airline seats always have to be booked in advance – and remember that flights can be booked up months in advance at peak holiday times and weekends.

Vaccines may need to be ordered by a doctor, and following treatment may take some time to become effective, so inoculations must be organised well in advance. Medical precautions for malaria need to be taken prior to the journey.

While currency for commonly visited foreign countries – for example, USA and Europe – may be readily available at the bank, other currencies may have to be ordered in advance.

If you need to organise replacement or new passports you should allow at least four weeks, although there are special procedures for the issue of passports within shorter timescales.

There are occasions when travellers need to make trips at short notice. In such cases, authority to make arrangements outside the organisation's normal procedures may be required. For example, procedures might require economy seats to be purchased whereas at short notice, it may be that only club-class flight seats are available.

Planning aids, such as checklists, should include an indication of the target deadlines for organising the listed travelling arrangements. An example of a travel checklist is given in Figure 4.1.1 on page 173.

Portfolio activity 4.1 Number 2

Prepare a detailed travel checklist to be used when making travel arrangements. Include space to indicate timescales, deadlines, etc.

Complete the checklist for each of the trips you organise – at least one UK trip and one overseas trip. Include brief information about the bookings, documents, and other arrangements that you have made.

The following evidence should be collected:

- blank checklist
- two completed checklists – one UK and one overseas trip.

Performance criteria:	4.1.1	4.1.2	4.1.5	4.1.6	4.1.7
	4.1.8	4.1.11	4.1.12	4.2.1	
Knowledge and understanding:					
Evidence requirements:	4.1.1	4.1.2	4.1.22		

Establishing suitable routes

A suitable route for the journey can be finalised when you have considered the following factors.

Traveller's personal preference. Some travellers may prefer to drive rather than use public transport. Other travellers may prefer to use a train wherever possible, so that they can complete other work while travelling. A traveller may prefer to travel by a particular airline – especially if they are collecting air miles. It is always a good idea to know the traveller's usual preferences, though for each journey you should check to ensure there are no special considerations – for example, they might be carrying some heavy bags and so would not want to travel by train.

Urgency. The choice of transport may be limited if the trip is urgent and arranged at the last minute. It may not be possible to arrange a flight by the most direct route or in the cheapest seats. Alternatively, if a traveller urgently needs to reach a UK destination, it may be quicker to make the journey immediately by car rather than waiting for public transport to be booked.

Cost. Consideration of cost does not necessarily mean that the cheapest method of travel is chosen – although coach travel may be the cheapest form of travel, it is not often used for business trips as it can be slower and less flexible. It is important to consider the total cost of the journey – for example, at first sight a train fare might seem cheaper than mileage for travel by car, but the cost advantage might not be so great when the cost of taxis at each end of the journey is included.

Company policies can also dictate cost. Some companies may only pay travel expenses up to the cost of second class rail fare. Other companies may allow first class rail fares if this does not represent a greater cost than the mileage for travel by car.

When organising travel for groups, the cost considerations may be different. It can be relatively cheap to hire a chauffeur-driven car if there are three or four occupants, and this could enable the travellers to hold business discussions during the journey. A mini-bus or coach could be hired for a larger group of travellers.

As well as the actual cost of the journey, the work time lost during the journey is also a cost. While it may be more expensive to fly, this method of travel can still be cost-effective – for example, it might mean the traveller was back in the office a day earlier than if travelling by road.

Reason for the trip. The traveller may be required to take display stands, publicity material or trade samples. This may make travel by public transport more difficult. If such items are to be taken on flights, arrangements for additional luggage and the need for suitable packaging should be investigated with the airline. The reason for the trip may also require the traveller to have some flexibility with arrival and departure times, and the ability to travel freely at the destination – for example, taking an important customer on a visit to an organisation's regional offices would require flexibility of timing and a high quality of transport.

Number of travellers. Suitable arrangements for a group of travellers may be different from arrangements for a single traveller. It may be cheaper to hire a car for a group of four travellers to visit a UK destination, rather than buy four train tickets. The driving may also be shared in a hire car, rather than a member of the group taking a private car.

Name/s of traveller/s	Mr James Henderson and Dr Bernard Jackson				
Date/s of travel	Monday 21 January – Thursday 24 January				
Purpose of travel	*International Conference on Railway Systems*				
Destination/s	*Cambridge, UK*				

Item/Preference	Deadlines	Arrangements to be made	Booking	Status	Details
Travel *One hire car for both travellers*	*Friday 19 January*	*Avis hire car – Company depot Collect 2.00 pm Monday and return 9.00 am Friday*	*Direct*	✓	*Ford Escort booked Show driving licence on collection Payment to be made with Company credit card*
Accommodation *Conference accom-modation 2 non-smoking single rooms*	*Friday 8 December*	*Rooms to be booked with conference form*	*Conference Booking*	✓	*Christ College Cambridge, Rooms 37 and 53 Deposit of £150.00 per person paid*
Passport/visas	*Not required*				
Medical arrangements	*Not required*				
Insurance requirements	*Check first week in January*			✓	*UK travel insurance checked and up to date*
Driving requirements	*Check licences first week in January*			✓	*Checked, up to date and no endorsements*
Currency/ money arrangements					*Accommodation to be paid with Company credit card. Arranged £20 from petty cash for parking fees, etc.*
Customs arrangements	*Not required*				
Briefing documents	*Wednesday 17 January*	*Conference programme Paper for presentation Slides for talk Map to show conference and accommodation location Itinerary*		✓ ✓ ✓ ✓ ✓	*Slides to be prepared by publicity department*

Additional notes

Book conference dinner – Tuesday 22 January for one delegate Dr Jackson only – Booked and paid ✓
Book dinner for Wednesday 23 January with Dr Adrian Witchall, American Utilities for Mr James Henderson at a reasonable restaurant.
Booked for 7.00 pm Greengables, High Street, Cambridge - informed Dr Witchall ✓

Figure 4.1.1 A travel checklist

Health and safety. Choosing the method of travel should also take account of the health and safety of the traveller. Driving a long distance, participating in a long day of activity and then driving home can lead to tired travellers being more at risk of an accident. Using public transport can reduce the risk of accidents and eliminate the stresses of difficult driving conditions, parking, etc.

Travel constraints

When planning travel, particularly travel abroad, you need to be aware of the constraints that can affect the traveller.

Border controls. Entry to and exit from all countries is controlled by immigration officials. When travelling by air, checks usually take place at the airport of entry or exit. When travelling by road or rail exit and entry is controlled at border entry points. Travelling within the European Union should not pose any problems for UK residents. However, in other parts of the world, particularly where there are hostilities between neighbouring countries and border disputes, crossing borders can be problematic. There may be queues and time delays as papers are checked. Regulations may be followed fastidiously by local officials and papers, visas and passports may be questioned. Check with the Foreign Office and the embassies of the countries to be visited for information and advice about crossing borders.

Visas/visitor permits. Immigration regulations for countries will specify what documentation is required for entry and exit. The regulations may vary depending on the purpose of the visit – you may be required to state whether the visit is for business purposes or for tourism. Regulations for temporary workers are usually very different from those for permanent workers. Checks should be made with the embassy of the country to be visited to ensure the correct paperwork is completed. Documents may be needed to authenticate the purpose of the visit.

Medical restrictions. Some countries require documentary proof of certain vaccinations/inoculations before entry is permitted. For example, a certificate of immunisation against yellow fever is required when visiting certain countries, particularly if you have travelled from an infected area. Details can be checked in the booklet *Health Advice for Travellers* (available from your local post office or by telephoning the Health Literature Line on 0800 555 777) or MASTA (the Medical Advisory Service for Travellers) 24-hour Travellers' Health Line: 0891 224100.

Political risks. Civil war, terrorist activity and hostile regimes can restrict travel in some countries. Information about these risks can be obtained on the Foreign and Commonwealth Office Advice to Travellers Line 020 7270 4129, or is available on Ceefax.

Holidays and religious festivals. Travel services may be restricted or be very busy at particular times of year depending on bank holidays and religious holidays and festivals. Accommodation may also be more difficult to book – for example, accommodation in Edinburgh is very difficult to book during the weeks of the Edinburgh Festival. Check with travel guides, local tourist offices, etc. for detailed local information.

Driving regulations. If a traveller is planning to drive a hire car abroad, the local regulations for eligibility to drive should be checked. International car hire organisations, travel guides, the AA and the RAC can provide information about driving abroad.

Portfolio activity 4.1 **Number 3**

Write a personal statement explaining how you investigated different methods of travel for travellers' trips and how you established the most suitable route for the trips. You should do this for at least one UK trip and one overseas trip.

Include the information you found out in terms of cost and time and the reasons for your final choice. Attach copies of documents you have used – for example, timetables you used, route printouts from Autoroute or the AA, route maps you prepared, memos you write, travel brochures from travel agents, fax requests for information, telephone information you recorded.

The following evidence should be collected:

- personal statement and attached information for a UK trip
- personal statement and attached information for an overseas trip.

Performance criteria:	4.1.3	4.1.4			
Knowledge and understanding:	4.1.a	4.1.c	4.1.m	4.1.n	4.2.g
Evidence requirements:	4.1.1	4.1.2	4.1.18	4.1.19	4.1.20
	4.1.21				

Reference sources

To organise business trips you will need to research a wide range of information. Useful sources include: travel agents; books and printed information; travel organisations; computer-based information; government and business information services; telephone and Viewdata services.

Travel agents

Travel agents provide a comprehensive source of travel information. However, the range of services offered by travel agents varies. For example, some travel agencies only specialise in selling holiday packages for leisure travellers and do not offer a comprehensive travel service that is suitable for arranging business travel.

It is a good idea to identify an agent in your area that will support arrangements for business travellers. Some organisations have a travel agent that they regularly use and you need to check whether this is the case with your organisation. It is also a good idea to establish how payments for business travel will be made, whether services can be invoiced to the organisation and how tickets will be issued. A very large organisation may have its own travel department and you would work closely with that department when making travel arrangements. As an alternative, a large organisation may 'out-source' its travel arrangements to a travel agent that has an office on site.

Travel agents usually provide the following services and information.

Air travel – the times, costs and availability of flights. The travel agent can book flights and arrange tickets. Remember that business travellers are increasingly using flights within the UK. You should always consider this as a possibility for UK travel. You should be aware of the destinations that are available from your local airport.

Train travel – train timetables, booking information. The travel agent can issue tickets and book seats. If you know which train a traveller is catching it is a good idea to book the seat, particularly on busy routes. Some train companies provide business traveller coaches that include a slightly higher standard of service such as free refreshments. You need to check if this service is available when you book the seats. Train bookings can also be made for European services, particularly services that use the Channel Tunnel. These services provide excellent city-centre to city-centre services – for example, London to Brussels.

Coach travel. The travel agent can book coach travel and issue tickets. Coach travel is cheap and not often used by business travellers. However, there are excellent coach services to the major airports in the UK and this may be a preferred method of travel from home to an airport. Coach travel may also be used when arrangements are being made for a larger group of travellers – for example, a visit of 40 members of staff to Head Office some distance away.

Road travel – car hire service information and booking can be provided. The agent will also be able to arrange taxis, or chauffeur-driven cars. Although chauffeur-driven cars are expensive, they can be cost-effective if there are two or three travellers making a journey. For safety reasons they may be booked to collect an incoming traveller on a long-haul flight – it is inadvisable for jet-lagged travellers to drive.

Currency – currency and up-to-date rates of exchange can be supplied. The agent will be able to provide information about currency restrictions.

Passport and visa requirements. The agent will have up-to-date information on entry and exit requirements, visas, etc.

Customs and excise requirements. The agent should be able to provide general guidelines for customs and excise requirements. They may not, however, be able to give specific information, particularly in relation to commercial goods and supplies.

Medical requirements – general information about inoculation and vaccination requirements for specific countries and details of other health risks. The agent may also have information about countries where there are other personal risks – for example, war or terrorist activities. Specific, up-to-date information and guidelines about this can be obtained from the Foreign Office.

Insurance requirements. A range of policies should be available to cover luggage, health, personal injury, cars, etc.

Accommodation – information, accommodation lists and booking services for accommodation in the UK and overseas. Hotels and accommodation can be booked through the travel agent.

General information. This may include places of interest to visit, cultural information, holiday dates, languages spoken, etc.

Books and printed information

Information about travel can be found in books and other printed information. Some of these may be available within an organisation to use for reference, while others may be borrowed from libraries or purchased for a particular trip.

ABC Travel Guides. This is a list of publications, regularly published, that give travel information – for example, ABC Air/Rail Europe with timetables for all major European services.

Timetables – train, ferry and airline timetables. These should always be up to date. Collect copies of train timetables for regularly-used services from your travel agent or local railway station.

Brochures. Information about hotels, accommodation, ferry services, etc. can be found in brochures. These may be issued by tourist boards and may be linked to a particular area – for example, *Where to stay in London.* Alternatively, they may be produced by travel companies and give comprehensive information about the services available – for example, Brittany Ferries.

Maps. Car travel is the most commonly used method of transport for UK travel. The car traveller will need an up-to-date route atlas. These are available from most high street bookstores, or from travel organisations such as the AA. Other useful maps are:

- an international atlas to show countries and major cities
- town maps and local street maps, to show exact locations
- maps provided by organisations to show location details
- a London Underground map.

Guide books. There is a range of tourist guides to all the major countries in the world – for example, Berlitz, Michelin Blue and Lonely Planet Guides. These give local geographical information, time differences, hotels, restaurants, cultural information, places of local interest, etc. Basic language information and phrases can also be found in most guidebooks. Guidebooks can be purchased from most high street bookstores, or borrowed from a library. Pocket versions of guidebooks are very useful for travellers to carry in briefcases and hand luggage.

Business diaries. World times, maps, atlases, international holidays, road distance charts, useful telephone numbers can all be found in business diaries.

Travel organisations

The two main travel organisations in the UK are the AA and RAC. They produce many publications, offering:

* *maps* – national and major town maps
* *hotel and accommodation information* – classification, facilities, addresses and telephone numbers
* *restaurant information* – listed restaurants
* *garage information* – car repair services
* *local information* – town population, market days, early closing days.

Travel organisations also provide other services, such as insurance, travel advice, and information about weather and driving conditions. This information can usually be obtained by telephoning the services listed in their handbooks.

Computer-based information

There are two major sources of computer-based information: CD-ROMs and the Internet.

A great deal of general information is available on CD-ROM – for example, encyclopaedias such as *Encarta* and the *Encyclopaedia Britannica*. It is also possible to obtain more specific travel information from, for example, Autoroute, AA and RAC guides, and Capital city guides. The advantage of CD-ROM information is that specific information, such as town maps, can be printed and given to the traveller. CD-ROMs also commonly include sound facilities, so that, for example, common phrases can be heard as well as read.

The range of relevant travel information available on the Internet is extensive and includes:

* government information about customs, excise, etc.
* country information about hotels, restaurants, culture, etc.
* timetable information – for example, rail timetables
* individual business sites – for example, many hotels and restaurants have their own sites
* AA and RAC information.

Internet websites may also provide e-mail links, so that further information can be requested or bookings made.

Obtaining information from the Internet is not always straightforward, though an accurate and full definition of the search item can make the search more effective by eliminating irrelevant information. There are no controls over the validity of the information placed on the Internet, so try to use sites produced by recognised, reputable organisations, or cross-check information with another source.

Government and business information services

Government and business information services can be a valuable source of information, for example:

- *the European Commission* – information office at 8 Storey's Gate, London SW1 3AT (020 7222 8122)
- *Department of Trade and Industry* – regulations about importing and exporting goods, trade restrictions, trade agreements (though its website includes a disclaimer that it is for information purposes only and has no force in law!)
- *Foreign Office* – advice about immigration, visas, overseas political issues, where (and where not) to travel
- *chambers of commerce* – advice about trading restrictions, support for exporting and importing of goods, contacts abroad
- *banks* – advice about currency, exchange rates, currency restrictions
- *post offices* – information on passports, travel insurance and government information about travel.

Telephone and Viewdata services

The telephone is a quick source of information, either for telephoning organisations direct or for using information services – for example, National Rail Enquiry Service or Le Shuttle Customer Enquiry Line. Useful numbers can be found in the telephone directory, but should also be noted in your deskbook. Telephone directories also provide useful information about international time zones and international telephone calls.

Viewdata services such as Oracle and Ceefax provide up-to-date information about currency exchange rates, travel conditions, weather and health advice for travellers. Prestel is an interactive source of information which can be used for making and paying for ticket bookings, accommodation, etc.

Portfolio activity 4.1 **Number 4**

Keep a record or log of all the information sources you use when researching information for the business trips you arrange. Use the Internet as a source of information – for example, to research information on Customs and Excise requirements and documents for transporting goods, and information on an overseas country to be visited. Attach printouts of the information you find on the Internet. Get a copy of the free booklet *Health Advice for Travellers* from your local post office or by telephoning the Health Literature Line on 0800 555 777. The booklet contains a copy of the Application Form E111 (see page 189). Complete this form for a member of staff.

The following evidence should be collected:

• completed log or records of information searches
• copy of Health Advice leaflet with form E111 completed.

Performance criteria:	4.1.3	4.1.6	4.2.5	4.2.7	
Knowledge and understanding:	4.1.a	4.1.b	4.1.c	4.1.d	4.1.e
	4.1.f	4.1.g	4.1.h	4.1.i	4.1.j
	4.1.k	4.2.f			
Evidence requirements:	4.1.3	4.1.4	4.1.5	4.1.6	4.1.7
	4.1.8	4.1.9	4.1.10	4.1.11	4.1.12
	4.1.13	4.1.14	4.1.15	4.1.16	

Making reservations

Travel

Reservations for appropriate travel can be made once the traveller's preferences have been discussed and investigations completed. These reservations should be made in line with the organisation's procedures, but may vary depending on the method of travel chosen.

Road

When making reservations for travel by road, a car may need to be hired. This can be done through large national organisations – for example, Hertz, Avis, Eurodollar – or from smaller local organisations. The advantage of using a larger organisation is that arrangements can often be made to pick up and drop off cars at different places – for example, it might be possible to pick up the car locally and drop it off at Heathrow Airport.

Some large companies may have a commercial contract with a large car hire company, and it will be company policy always to use that company. The hire company may even have a depot on site. Some large hire companies will also have international facilities, whereby cars can be hired at destination airports abroad. The car hire company will need to have information about the driver's licence, insurance, etc. When agreeing a car hire price with a company, ensure you get details of the full cost in writing, including any collection and delivery cost. Ask the company to send a fax detailing the costs. Ensure you are clear about any extra costs – for example, there is often an additional charge for collision damage waiver (CDW), which means there is additional insurance cover for any damage caused by a collision.

On certain occasions it may be necessary to book a chauffeur-driven car. This may be booked if there is any chance that the traveller will have been drinking – for example, when attending a dinner or celebration event. Some organisations also have a policy whereby travellers returning on long-haul flights must be driven home in chauffeur-driven cars because it is considered unsafe to drive when suffering from jet-lag. The same policy should be followed for travellers arriving abroad after a long-haul flight.

If the car is to be taken on a ferry or through the Channel Tunnel, you may be required to provide information about the make, size, registration number, etc. It will also be necessary to inform the hire company that the car is being taken abroad, as this may affect the insurance and cost. There may even be restrictions for taking hire cars to some countries – for example, certain Eastern European countries.

Rail

When making reservations for rail travel, it is possible to book seats as well as tickets. Wherever possible, book the rail seats for the traveller. This ensures them a seat on a busy train. Make sure you are aware of the traveller's preference for forward-backward-facing, non-smoking/smoking seats if a choice is available. Check the length of the journey, connections and frequency of the trains. You should always provide a timetable if possible and if this is not possible, give the traveller information on several suitable trains. This is particularly helpful if meetings over-run, or if there are traffic problems. If the traveller will be travelling at night, find out the times of the last trains. The traveller may also want to know what refreshment facilities are available on the train, and whether taxis are available at their destination.

Remember that there may be no facilities available at some rural stations – no buffet facilities, ticket office or taxis. Waiting for a connection at some rural stations can be quite daunting on a cold, wet night. If this is likely to be the case, check with the traveller that they are aware of it.

Ferry

When making ferry reservations, check with the traveller whether a berth is required. This will be essential for an overnight ferry, but can also be useful for some longer daytime journeys. Berths should be booked in advance. The facilities available on the ferry should also be checked – money-changing facilities, refreshments, business lounges, etc.

Air

- The company policy on class of air travel should be checked.
- When making air reservations, it may be possible to book the seat at the time of the ticket booking. Check the traveller's preferences on window/aisle seats, etc.
- Confirm with the airline the baggage allowance that can be taken. This may be particularly important if samples, literature, etc. have to be taken. Check the cost and availability of additional baggage allowances.
- For short journeys, the traveller may want to travel with hand baggage only as this saves time on arrival. Check the size of hand baggage allowed.
- The traveller may need to wait some time in the terminal before the flight leaves, so check the facilities available – for example, the traveller might be able to use a business lounge for a small additional charge if this facility is not included in the ticket price.

The travel agent or airline should provide written confirmation of booking; a typical example is shown in Figure 4.1.2 on page 184.

A summary of reservation methods is given in the following table.

Method of travel	Type of reservation	Methods of reservation
Road	Arranging a hire car	• Booked through travel agent • Booked direct with hire company
	Reserving a company car	• Booked with appropriate department
	Hiring a chauffeur-driven car	• Booked through travel agent • Booked direct with hire company
	Hiring a coach for group travel	• Booked direct with a coach company
	Buying a coach ticket and booking a seat	• Booked through travel agent • Booked direct with coach travel company via telephone
Rail	Buying a train ticket and booking a seat	• Booked through travel agent • Booked direct with rail services via telephone, Prestel

		• Tickets may be purchased by traveller at station on departure or on train while travelling
Air	Buying a plane ticket and booking a seat	• Booked through travel agent • Booked direct with airline agent *Note* Airlines sometimes require confirmation of travel for the outward and return flight
Sea	Buying a ticket and booking a seat	• Booked through travel agent • Booked direct with ferry company
Channel Tunnel	Buying a Eurostar ticket and booking a seat	• Booked through travel agent • Booked direct with rail company
	Buying a Le Shuttle ticket to take a car through	• Booked through travel agent • Booked direct with Eurotunel services

```
BOOKING CONFIRMATION

Stay: Min 7 days:              Max 1 month in country
Check-in time at Heathrow:     05.00 12 June ----

From                    To                          Date     Flight No   Dep     Arr
LHR London Heathrow     FRA: Frankfurt              12Jun--  LH4517      07:00   09:25
FRA Frankfurt Airport   LAX: Los Angeles Internat.  12Jun--  LH456       10:35   13:05
LAX: Los Angeles Internat.  FRA: Frankfurt Airport  19Jun--  LH453       21:40   17:20
FRA: Frankfurt Airport  LHR: London Heathrow        20Jun--  LH4634      18:20   18:55
```

Figure 4.1.2 Confirmation of a flight booking

Accommodation

Overnight stays require accommodation to be booked. The organisation's policy will usually specify in what situations overnight accommodation is authorised and it may be necessary to get authorisation/approval for every overnight stay. There may also be an agreed price limit for accommodation and authority may be needed to exceed the limit if only more expensive accommodation is available. Organisations that have regular business travellers may have negotiated a commercial contract with a large hotel chain, and authority may be required to book accommodation in any other type of hotel.

When booking accommodation

1 Check the traveller's personal preferences – for example, non-smoking/smoking rooms, locations, types of hotel, facilities required.

2 Research and select two or three hotels in the location – in large cities you may need to check the exact location of the hotel in relation to the visit venue.

3 Contact the hotel to check on vacancies, costs, facilities and special arrangements. If the traveller is arriving by car, check parking facilities. Select a suitable hotel and make a booking on the telephone. Some hotel chains have a central booking facility which you may need to contact.

4 Confirm the booking in writing. This may be done by letter or, if the timescale is short, by fax. Include in the confirmation:
  * name and company of the traveller
  * dates of stay
  * number of nights
  * room requirements – for example, single room, non-smoking, with en-suite facilities
  * requirements for food – for example, bed and breakfast, meal required for late arrival
  * special requirements – dietary requirements, late arrival, early departure, transport to/from airport
  * method of payment – cash, credit card, invoice to company.

Currency and funding

There are many expenses involved in business trips so funding will need to be arranged for the traveller. The cost for a visit will have to be paid out of a particular budget – for example, project budget, training budget, sales budget. Before any bookings are made, care should be taken to check that the visit has been authorised and the funding agreed.

In most routine situations there will be a range of trips for which funding has been agreed. However, there may be trips for which authorisation needs to be gained – for example: for visits that are not routine; when the expenses are likely to exceed an agreed limit; when an overnight stay is required.

Methods of payment

There are usually agreed levels for different types of cost, such as mileage, overnight expenses, second class rail fares. However, authorisation may be required for expenses that exceed the agreed limits – for example, hotel charges in London.

Different methods of payment may be used for different expenses. For example, a credit card may be used for accommodation expenses and cash for taxis and refreshments. The methods of payment and levels of cash required should be discussed and agreed with the traveller. Credit cards are a useful way of paying for expenses, and are accepted for most types of payment in the UK. However, their use overseas may be more difficult, particularly in the Far East and third world countries. Where credit cards are used overseas, a small charge may be made for the transaction to cover the cost of currency exchange. It is also difficult to be sure what exchange rate will be used for the transaction.

For overseas travel, currency for the countries to be visited will need to be arranged. This may be done through a bank or travel agent. Notice may be required for certain currencies.

There are methods other than using currency when paying for goods within the European Community. Some banks issue Eurocheques, which allow the traveller to write out cheques in the local currency (or in sterling or dollars in some countries). Banks have also started to issue Eurocards, which are direct debit cards that enable the traveller to pay for goods in euros, the common currency of the European Community. Further information about current cheque and card payment arrangements can be requested from the travel sections of the major banks.

Travellers' cheques are a safe way to carry money – these can be changed for currency as needed once at the destination. A note should be kept of the details of all travellers' cheques, since this information is essential if they are lost or stolen. The traveller should keep the information separate from the travellers' cheques. It is a good idea for this information also to be available back at the office.

However, the traveller should always have sufficient currency on arrival at the destination to make taxi journeys, pay airport taxes, etc. While most major airports have facilities for changing currency, they are not always open 24 hours, and facilities may not be available in smaller local airports. Car travellers moving between countries will need to have sufficient local currency to buy petrol in cash in each country they are visiting. It may be difficult to find money-changing facilities in rural areas, and not all foreign garages will have credit card facilities.

Some countries have restrictions on the amount and type of cash that can be brought in or taken out of the country. There may also be restrictions on the currency credit limits. These restrictions should be checked with travel information sources – for example, embassies and tourist boards.

The organisation's travel policy

Arrangements may need to be made for a cash advance for visits taking place over a longer period of time, for example, more than a fortnight, for visits to overseas destinations or by junior level employees who may not have sufficient funds in hand to cover costs. The organisation's procedures should specify the documentation to be completed for a cash advance. The sum requested should be negotiated with the traveller and be in line with the organisation's spending levels – for example, it could be based on a standard daily rate.

Many organisations now issue staff who travel with a chargecard. It is intended that major expenses should be charged to the card. On return from the trip the traveller claims the expenses in the appropriate way. The money is then used by the traveller to pay the chargecard account. The use of chargecards and credit cards may vary in different countries. This should be checked in advance through travel information sources. Arrangements may need to be made for money to be transferred to an overseas bank by credit transfer. An agent's bank or the organisation's overseas branch, may be used. Arrangements for credit transfer should be checked with the bank.

Security issues

There is always the risk of theft of valuables, so travellers should take the following steps to minimise this risk.

- Insure credit cards, charge cards, etc.
- Record the numbers of travellers cheques and store them in a separate location.
- Only carry sufficient foreign currency in a wallet to pay for taxis, meals, etc. Any additional currency should be stored in a separate place – for example, a money belt.
- Do not leave bags and briefcases on the seats of cars, taxis, etc.
- Do not carry wallets/purses and credit cards in back pockets of trousers or in shoulder bags.
- Do not leave money and valuables in hotel rooms unless in a safe.
- Take care when putting down bags and briefcases in hotels, restaurants and other public places.

Emergency money

If a traveller should lose money, have it stolen or simply not have enough for the trip they may require emergency cash at short notice. If the traveller has a cashcard then cash may be withdrawn from cash machines. However, if cards have also been lost or stolen then arrangements may need to be made for money to be available. Sometimes this can be organised through credit card companies if the traveller has their emergency telephone numbers.

Otherwise money can be arranged using a Moneygram service. This is a telephone service (0800 666 3947) through which money can be telegraphed to a wide range of destinations. They will arrange for money to be available at a suitable location at the destination. There is a charge for this service – for example, it currently costs £33 to transfer £500 from the UK to USA. Further information about Moneygram can be found on the website:

http://www.moneygram.com

Documentation

Regulatory travel documentation

Travellers are required by legal regulations to carry certain documentation with them when travelling abroad. The exact documents will depend on the mode of travel and destination, but could include the following.

Driving licence

A driving licence must be up to date and show the current address of the holder. It should be valid for the country being visited. In some countries an international licence may be required and the legal age for driving in the country being visited should be checked.

Car documentation

The driver should always carry the car's log book, MOT and insurance certificate. Check that these are valid and contain the current address of the holder. If a company car is being used, then company documentation should be carried. The same applies to a hire car. If a private car is being used for business travel, check that the owner's insurance covers use of the car for business purposes.

Passport

Check that the passport is valid, up to date and signed. Some countries have an immigration requirement for a passport to remain valid for a minimum period beyond the date of entry to the country. If the passport is in its final year, you should check with the authorities of the countries to be visited that the passport is still acceptable. It may be necessary for the traveller to apply for a new passport prior to the visit.

Check the stamps on the passport – it may not be possible to enter certain countries if the passport has an unfriendly country's stamp in it. There may also be special medical requirements if the traveller has recently visited a country with a high medical risk. This should be checked carefully when the travel itinerary is being arranged.

Replacements for lost or stolen passports can be obtained from the passport office. Allow at least four weeks for replacement passports. There are arrangements for issuing passports at short notice – contact the passport office for further information (UK Passport Agency, 0990 210410).

Visas and other entry documents

As soon as a visit to a foreign country has been arranged, the relevant embassy should be contacted to check on the entry requirements and documentation. Applications should then be completed and submitted according to the requirements of the embassy. You should do this as early as possible as visas can take quite a long time to obtain. It may also be necessary to send your passport to the embassy with the application.

Medical documentation

Relevant inoculation/vaccination certificates should be carried. Check that the inoculations/vaccinations have been kept up to date and that sufficient time has been allowed for the vaccine to become active. For example, yellow fever vaccine is valid from ten days after vaccination for a period of ten years.

A Form E111 is required for travellers in the European Economic Area who are entitled to reciprocal health treatment. The E111 application form and the E111 can be obtained at most post offices. When the form has been completed it must be stamped and signed at a post office before it can be used. The E111 should be carried by the traveller and kept in a safe place. An E111 remains valid as long as the traveller is ordinarily resident in the UK. A new E111 should be obtained if it has been used to obtain treatment or has been mislaid.

Reciprocal health-care agreements have been reached with a range of countries outside the European Economic Area. Documentary proof of UK residence is required in order to get medical treatment – for example, UK passport and/or NHS medical card.

Travellers suffering from certain conditions – for example, diabetes or asthma, should carry written records. A personal health card or letter from your doctor is useful if you take chemists' or prescription drugs through customs. Always carry drugs in a correctly labelled container, showing both the generic and trade names. There are certain controlled drugs which can be issued on prescription. There are special regulations with regard to these drugs and an Open General Licence is required to export them. Further information about this can be obtained from the Customs and Excise authorities.

Insurance documentation

Travellers are not required by law to have travel insurance, but it is essential for the business traveller to have suitable insurance. The traveller may be covered for business travel in two ways: by the organisation's insurance or by personal travel insurance. Check with the organisation what cover is available for employees travelling on the organisation's business. This may be limited – for example, business goods may be covered, but not the traveller's personal possessions. If the traveller also makes personal visits while on the trip, these may not be covered by the organisation's policy. In the event of an unforeseen incident occurring, the traveller should have information on the organisation's insurance. Ensure the traveller has this information available for the trip.

If there is limited or no organisation cover for travellers, personal travel insurance may be arranged. Many insurance companies provide travel insurance – many of these specialise in holiday cover and it is important to check that business travel is also included. The range of cover is fairly standard and usually includes: personal accident; loss and theft of baggage and possessions; delays; health; and money. When checking the traveller's documentation, ensure insurance information – for example, a cover note – is included. Keep a copy of the policy details in a file in the office.

Where personal travel insurance is arranged, the traveller may be able to claim the cost from the organisation as a valid travel expense. This should be checked with the appropriate people in the organisation.

Documentation checklist

It is useful to prepare a documentation checklist so that you can be sure that all necessary documents have been prepared. An example of a documentation checklist is given in Figure 4.1.3.

Name/s of traveller/s		
Date/s of travel		
Purpose of travel		
Destination/s		
Document	**Items to be checked and included**	**Completed**
Passport	*Current and suitably stamped*	✓
Visas	*Appropriate visas ready*	✓
Medical requirements	*Inoculation documents* *E111 completed*	✓ ✓
Insurance	*Travel insurance up-to-date* *Current cover document* *Driving insurance cover note*	✓ ✓ ✓
Driving requirements	*Current driving licence* *International driving licence*	✓ ✓
Itinerary	*Prepared – full details, plus daily cards*	✓ ✓
Booking documentation	*Copies of booking faxes and letters, accommodation, cars, etc.*	✓
Tickets	*Flight tickets, baggage labels*	✓
Currency	*Local currency* *Sterling travellers' cheques* *Dollar currency*	✓ ✓ ✓
Customs documentation	*Documentation for sales samples*	✓
Briefing notes	*General notes about climate, places of interest, phrases, business hours, etc.*	✓
Information	*Sales files and* *Sales literature*	✓ ✓
Maps	*National and local maps*	✓
Contact list	*Emergency numbers and contact list*	✓
Miscellaneous		
Additional notes *Sales literature has been sent to the hotel by international courier*		

Figure 4.1.3 A documentation checklist

Customs

The regulations with regard to the import and export of goods are complex. Full details can be obtained from Customs (Internet site http://www.hmce.gov.uk/customs), but the regulations are subject to change and you should be sure that you have the most up-to-date information. The regulations cover: duty-free and tax-free items for

personal use; prohibited/restricted goods; commercial goods –
merchandise in baggage.

Duty-free and tax-free items for personal use

When travelling outside the EC there are agreed limits for items
such as tobacco, spirits, wine and gifts that can be imported for
personal use. It is the business traveller's responsibility to ensure
the regulations in this regard are followed. It is a good idea to give
the traveller information about the relevant limits from countries
being visited.

Prohibited/restricted goods

The export and import of the following goods is either prohibited
or restricted:

* *prohibited goods* – unlicensed drugs; offensive weapons; obscene
  material; counterfeit and copied goods.
* *restricted goods for which an import licence may be required* – firearms,
  explosives and ammunition; dogs, cats and other animals; live
  birds; endangered species; meat, poultry; certain plants; radio
  transmitters.

Merchandise in Baggage (MIB)

Merchandise in Baggage (MIB) refers to commercial goods – for
example, samples and display products – being carried by a
business traveller that are: not in free circulation in the European
Community; carried in passengers' accompanied baggage or private
vehicles for trade or business use; not recorded as freight on the
manifest of the ship or aircraft; or are not the personal property of
the passenger.

MIB includes goods acquired for the company, goods for sale,
spare parts and trade samples whether or not they are being
permanently or temporarily imported, in transit or liable to
Customs charges.

If a traveller is carrying MIB, a Form C88 usually needs to be
completed. If the goods exceed £600 in value it may be useful to
use a Customs clearance agent to deal with the formalities.
Evidence of value such as an invoice will also be needed with
the C88.

Where the MIB is temporary importation or re-importation of
professional effects, samples or exhibition goods then a document
called an ATA carnet may be used to accompany it. An ATA
carnet can be obtained from certain chambers of commerce;

further information about this can be obtained from the London Chamber of Commerce, 18 Queen Street, London EC4 1AP (tel. 020 7248 4444).

The import and export of MIB is a complex subject and it will usually be necessary to get further advice about documentation, tariffs, etc. Full up-to-date details can be found on the open government website given above. If you need further help you are advised to contact Customs at the airport/port and ask for MIB enquiries. In view of the complexity of the issues, it is advisable to make enquiries and obtain documentation at the earliest opportunity.

Departure checklist

The traveller will need to carry all the relevant papers that are required for the business to be accomplished while on the visit. These will vary depending on the nature of the business, and the purpose of the visit. The first step in preparing the papers is to discuss with the traveller which documents will be required. Some of the documents may be routine, but the exact requirements should still be discussed. When this has been established the papers can then be prepared.

Sufficient time should be allowed for documents to be word processed, photocopied and collected ready for the visit. The documents should be organised and presented in a suitable format for the visit, such as in labelled manila folders, plastic pockets and ring binders, or company presentation packs or bags/cases.

Portfolio activity 4.1 **Number 5**

1 Collect information about health requirements, driving information, insurance, customs, etc. Visit a travel agent and collect information useful for journeys – for example, timetables, car hire, Channel Tunnel and ferry information, and accommodation details. Put this in a travel reference file. It is not necessary to include all this information in your portfolio, but make a list of the documents you have included and ask your assessor to check the file and sign your list.
2 Prepare a detailed checklist of documentation that should be prepared for a business trip. Include regulatory, customs, insurance and other business papers. Make sure you have indicated dates and times required to prepare the documents. Complete the checklist for two trips – one in the UK and one overseas.

3 Put together copies of the travel documents you have collected and/or checked. Where these are personal or confidential documents, blank out the personal information. Alternatively, ask the traveller to write a personal statement explaining that you have checked these documents. Include copies of forms you have completed – for example, insurance, passport, visa, customs, etc. These documents should cover one UK and one overseas trip.

The following evidence should be collected:

- travel reference file
- two completed documentation checklists
- completed copies of travel documentation.

Performance criteria:	4.1.6	4.1.7	4.1.13	4.2.1	
Knowledge and understanding:	4.1.f	4.1.g	4.1.h	4.1.i	4.1.m
	4.1.n	4.2.a	4.2.b	4.2.e	4.2.f
	4.2.h				
Evidence requirements:	4.1.3	4.1.4	4.1.5	4.1.6	4.1.9
	4.1.22				

Arrangements for the traveller's absence

Prior to the visit, the traveller should have a briefing session with you to discuss arrangements for their absence. This should include arrangements for colleagues to cover their work. Ongoing issues should be discussed, and their priority identified. You should have a list of those issues which are:

- *administrative* and can be dealt with by you in the traveller's absence
- *routine* and can be left for the traveller's return
- *priority* and can be dealt with by a designated colleague
- *urgent* and require the traveller to be contacted while away.

General contact details with the traveller will also need to be agreed. Suitable times for contact should be established, allowing for time differences and appointments. Suitable methods for contact should be agreed – these can include pagers, voicemail, mobile phones, e-mail, fax. Telephone numbers for mobile phones, hotels, etc. should be checked and agreed. The telephone numbers and contact arrangements at different locations should be agreed.

Emergency contact arrangements may also be discussed and agreed. You should make arrangements for contacting the traveller about last minute changes to plans – for example, meetings that are cancelled. You should also make arrangements for contacting appointments if delays occur – for example, severe traffic hold-ups. You should have a list of relatives and/or friends to contact in the event of an emergency – for example, the traveller having an accident. Finally, you should be able to contact the traveller if a personal or domestic emergency arises at home.

Confidential and sensitive issues may be discussed. You should discuss how the business trip is to be described to colleagues – for example, a fact-finding trip, a business visit, or more specific details. You should also discuss how the business trip is to be described to external contacts. It may not be appropriate for a supplier to know that the traveller is visiting a competitor. Alternatively it may be politic for a supplier to be aware that competitors are being visited. It is important to decide upon the exact details that may be divulged to callers – for example, the length of the trip. The absence may have implications for the security of the traveller's home.

When the briefing has been completed the necessary information can be circulated to the appropriate people (see Figure 4.1.4, page 196).

Portfolio activity 4.1 **Number 6**

Make notes of briefing meetings you have had with a traveller about contact arrangements. Include a copy of these notes in your evidence. Include notes for one UK trip and one overseas trip. Collect copies of messages and memos you have sent to other staff informing them of contact arrangements.

The following evidence should be collected:

- notes of briefing meetings
- copies of memos, messages, notes of contact arrangements.

Performance criteria:	4.1.11	4.1.12	4.1.13	4.2.1
Knowledge and understanding:	4.1.l	4.1.m	4.2.h	
Evidence requirements:	4.1.17			

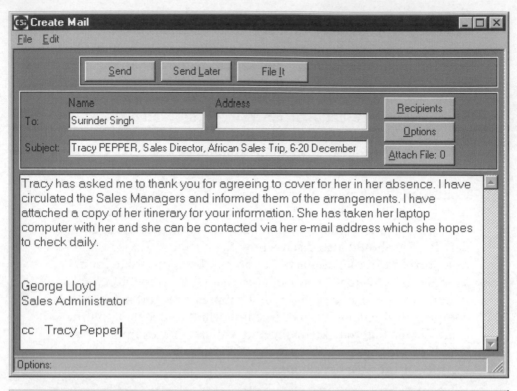

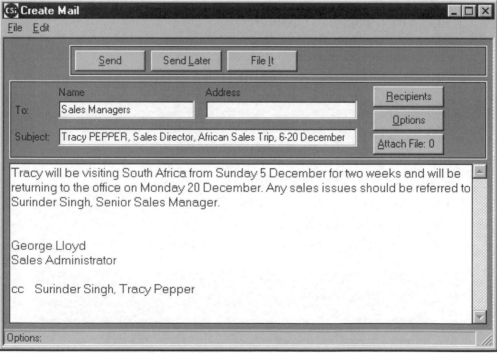

Figure 4.1.4 Examples of circulated information

Claims for travel expenses

On return from the trip the traveller will need to claim for expenses incurred. This should be done promptly if the traveller is not to be left out of pocket or have insufficient funds to settle outstanding chargecard accounts. Travel expenses usually fall into the following categories.

Travel costs. For example, rail, road, taxi travel. Ticketed services will be paid for 'as incurred' upon production of a valid receipt. Road travel by private car is usually paid as mileage according to a fixed rate – for example, 40 pence per mile for the first 50 miles, 25 pence per mile for every mile thereafter. You need to know the exact mileage to calculate the sum owed. Parking and road toll fees can be claimed with a valid receipt.

Accommodation costs. For example, hotel bills. These are paid for as incurred within an agreed rate.

Refreshments/subsistence. For example, lunch, dinner, coffee. These expenses can be claimed in the following ways:

- *as incurred* – expenses refunded up to a specified limit upon production of a valid receipt
- *agreed allowance* – a fixed sum is claimed for each specified period away from home. This method is more often used for travel abroad, as it can be difficult to produce receipts for minor expenses.

Out-of-pocket expenses. For example, telephone calls, photocopying, faxing. These will be paid for as incurred. They should be listed in detail on the expenses claim form.

When all the expenses information and receipts have been collected an Expenses Claim Form should be completed. Correct details of the trip, the purpose of the trip, the name of the traveller, etc. should be completed on the form, together with full details of the expenses being claimed. Any returns on advances should be included on the expenses form. This should be signed by the traveller and submitted to the Accounts department for payment, with a copy kept for the traveller's own files. Expenses can be paid in cash, by cheque or added to the recipient's salary.

An example of a travel expenses claim form is given in Figure 4.1.5 on page 198.

Travel Expenses Claim Form		Claim No	
Name	Department	Pay No	Budget No
Details of Trip			
Date of Visit	Purpose of Visit	Travel to	Travel from

Details	Receipts to be attached where appropriate	£	p
Travel costs Car .... miles @ 25p per mile Fares – rail air Taxi expenses			
Accommodation No of nights Location			
Meals – give details			
Subsistence (state rate daily – UK rate £10.00 per day, overseas £15.00)			
Additional costs, e.g. telephone, postage			
Total claim			
Less advances received			
Total net claim			
Signed Date	Authorised Date	Paid Date	

Figure 4.1.5 A travel expenses claim form

Portfolio activity 4.1 **Number 7**

Write notes about a discussion you have had with a traveller about financial requirements for a trip. Ask the traveller to sign these notes. Include information to show that you have checked credit card requirements with the traveller. Collect copies of documents you have completed to arrange currency and funding for a traveller. Collect information on your organisation's rates and procedures for claiming expenses. Produce a copy of a memorandum sent to an appropriate person in your organisation to ensure funding is available for a traveller's trip. Collect a copy of at least two expenses claim forms – one should be for a UK trip and one for a trip overseas.

The following evidence should be collected:

- discussion notes
- completed currency documents
- organisation's policy on expenses, plus expenses claim form
- memo about funding
- two completed expenses claim forms – one for a UK trip and one for a trip overseas.

Performance criteria	4.1.8	4.1.9	4.1.10	4.2.1
Knowledge and understanding:	4.1.k	4.2.f		
Evidence requirements:	4.1.1	4.1.2	4.1.8	4.1.10 4.1.12

Test yourself

Knowledge and understanding	Questions
a	Give two sources of reference for travel by each of the following methods: • air • road • rail • sea • Channel Tunnel.
b	Give three sources of information about a country being visited.

c	Give two examples of information and/or services provided by each of the following: • travel agents • tourist offices • travel centres • embassies • Internet.
d	Give examples of travel constraints laid down by a specific country.
e	Describe the effect of time differences in different countries.
f	Describe the procedures for obtaining passports and visas.
g	Give examples of medical requirements for various countries.
	Give examples of conditions of personal/company health care for travellers while travelling overseas on business.
h	Explain the purpose of arranging personal, travel and business insurance cover for travellers.
i	Describe the steps you would take to book hotel accommodation both in the UK and overseas.
j	Explain banking, credit card and credit transfer procedures both for the UK and overseas.
	Explain what is meant by currency credit restrictions.
k	Describe the steps you would take to provide for the handling of the duties/responsibilities of a traveller in his/her absence.
l	Explain how you communicate effectively with colleagues at all levels.
	Explain how you communicate effectively with outside agencies and clients.
m	Explain how you interpret information from a variety of sources, including maps and timetables.

PREPARE TRAVEL DOCUMENTATION

In Element 4.1 we looked at the information that needs to be researched when planning a business trip. This element looks at the documentation that needs to be prepared for the traveller when undertaking the trip – in particular, itineraries and briefing notes. These documents help the traveller to meet their commitments while away.

Itineraries

An itinerary is a document that clearly lists the plan for a journey or trip. An itinerary should contain the following information.

- *Heading* – name of the traveller, date, time and purpose of trip.

- *Precise times* – exact times for transport where this is appropriate. Use the 24-hour clock. For example:

    09.47 Manchester–Birmingham train

    and approximate times for car travel.

    For overseas travel any time differences should be clearly indicated.

- *Details of business meetings* – title of meeting, nature of appointment, date, time and place of meeting. For example:

    **XYZ Company, Annual Sales Meeting, 14 October 20--
    13.30, Board Room, Headquarters Building, 63
    Highway Street, Holloway, London.**

- *Names and designations of people involved in meetings* – for example:

    All Sales Executives and the Board of Directors.

    Attendance lists may be included on the agenda which can be attached to the itinerary.

- *Details of arrival/reception arrangements* – name and designation of person(s) meeting the traveller at the destination, location, time, arrangements for recognition. For example:

    **Call at Main Reception and ask for Herr Hans
    Friedman; driver will collect in the Airport Arrival
    Lounge with an XYZ Company sign; meet Madame
    Cloubert in the Lounge, she will be carrying a red XYZ
    Company umbrella.**

- *Exact travel information* – for air journeys this includes exact flight details, airline, flight number, name of airport, terminal number if appropriate, flight times, check-in times. For example:

  British Airways flight BA 2945 London Heathrow Terminal 1 to Paris Charles De Gaulle Airport; depart 0800, arrive 1030 local time; check in 0600.

- Train journeys should include the times, station, service and train company. For example:

  16.35 Birmingham New Street, Central Lines Hi-Speed service to London Paddington.

- *Accommodation details* – the name, address and telephone number of hotels. Additional information about special requirements and payment details may also be included.

- *Special arrangements for travelling companion(s)* – colleagues, customers, visitors or personal relations of the traveller; include relevant, appropriate information. For example:

  Visit to Leeds Factory with Mr Harry Chan, Purchasing Director, Singapore Airlines. Collect from Hilton Hotel, Heathrow. Ask Reception to call him when you arrive. Mr Chan is a vegetarian.

- *Details of attachments and other documents provided* – for example, agendas, notes for the meeting.

An example of an itinerary is shown in Figure 4.2.1.

If the length of a visit runs into more than one day, it is useful to prepare a separate agenda for each day. You should also ensure you have a copy of the itinerary so that you are fully aware of the traveller's movements.

The length of time a journey takes often has to be estimated. Road journey times in particular can vary depending on the time of day, the route chosen, weather conditions and local activities. Guidance about the likely travel times can be gained from: the traveller's or other colleagues' experience of travelling on a similar journey; travel software – for example, Autoroute; or travel organisations such as the AA.

Delays can occur on journeys or at meetings and it can be useful to include information for travellers that will allow them to make appropriate changes to the plan. Maps showing alternative routes and timetables showing full services can be provided.

Dr George Kelly
Wednesday 22 November ----
UK Child Health Research Association Annual Meeting
Embankment Conference Centre, 143 Embankment Road, Vauxhall

06.45 Car – Home to Bradley Stoke

07.15 Collect Dr Wendy Sangster, 17 The Hollows, Bradley Stoke
(Tel 01443 874532 – map attached)

07.35 Bristol Parkway (*Note*: prepaid parking before departure saves time on return)

07.40 Great Western service to London Paddington – Seats C12, C13 booked, tickets attached
(Retain ticket for use on Underground)

09.04 Arrive London Paddington, Underground to Vauxhall
(Bakerloo line: Paddington–Oxford Circus
Victoria line: Oxford Circus–Vauxhall
Rail ticket includes Zone 1 Underground travel)

09.30 (approx.) Arrive at Conference Centre (location map attached)

0945–3.30 Meeting
(Agenda, attendance list, minutes and location map in folder
10.30 presentation on Bristol Project Research Findings
Handouts and OHTs in folder.)

15.30 Vauxhall–Paddington Underground

16.00 Great Western Service to Bristol Parkway*
(*Later trains at 16.30 and 17.00 – current timetable in folder)

17.15 Bristol Parkway – car return home, approx. arrival time 18.00

(Dr Sangster is staying in London for a further day to visit London Children's Hospital)

Figure 4.2.1 An itinerary

Briefing notes

Briefing notes are prepared to give the traveller background information for the trip. They should be comprehensive and accurate but concise. Briefing notes can be prepared for both UK and overseas trips.

For overseas trips, many of the items that must be included in the briefing notes have already been covered in Element 4.1:

- passport/visa requirements, including the travel restrictions between countries
- medical requirements/recommendations
- insurance requirements
- driving requirements
- time differences
- currency and current exchange rate

- customs requirements
- banking and credit card procedures.

Other important areas to cover in briefing notes

Business hours. Information can be found in country guides, obtained from embassies, etc. It is also a good idea to include information on national holidays, religious festivals and celebrations where these influence business hours.

Cost of living. Information can be found in guides and gained from colleagues who may have visited the country. It affects the amount of spending money needed for general subsistence and gives some idea of what would be a fair price for taxis, etc. A list of restaurants and suitable eating places is also very useful for travellers staying away for a number of days.

Climate. Information can be found in country guides. Some large countries have a wide range of climatic conditions and information should be provided for all the areas being visited. This will enable the traveller to pack appropriate clothes and health and safety items.

Cultural/social observations. Accurate information about cultural and social rules can save the traveller from embarrassment and prevent any offence being caused. Business and social protocols should be covered. In some countries it is standard business practice to exchange business cards; even in very hot weather, lightweight suits, shirts and ties may be worn for business; women may cause offence by wearing sleeveless dresses. As well as travel guides, business colleagues who may have already visited the country can provide very helpful information about local customs.

Places of interest. The traveller may have free time in the evenings and weekends and information on places of interest to visit will be appreciated. Again, this can be found in country guides.

Basic phrases and numbers in local languages. These can be provided in the briefing notes or in a separate phrase book. Pocket-size phrase books are very useful.

Emergency contacts. A list of emergency telephone numbers that the traveller can contact if there are any problems while travelling should be included – for example, the UK embassy. They may also include normal and out-of-hours contact numbers for the organisation at home. The traveller may wish to add contact numbers for friends and relatives both at home and abroad.

An example of a set of briefing not.es is shown in Figure 4.2.2.

Briefing Notes for Dr Graham Powell
International Symposium on Airborne Weapon Systems
12–20 June ----

Attendees
Dr Graham Powell to be accompanied by wife (Mrs Frances Powell) and son (Darren Powell aged 7)

Details of flights
See itinerary

Passport requirements
Current UK passports required for all travellers – ensure son has his own passport. Visas not required for stays of less than one month

Medical requirements
There are no special requirements for vaccinations or inoculations. Check that standard vaccinations – e.g. polio and tetanus, are up to date for all travellers.

Insurance requirements
Standard travel insurance required. Current insurance: annual family policy Cornhill Policy POD 93153   10 January ---- to January ----.

Driving requirements
Current UK driving licence required for all drivers

Time difference
9 hours behind UK, i.e. 9 am Los Angeles local time = 6 pm the same day British time.

Accommodation
Family room booked at the Westlake Village Inn, booking reference GH2356 for 12–19 June (confirmation attached). Map and hotel information attached.

Currency
US dollars current exchange rate $1.59 to £1.00 sterling.

Customs requirements
Standard non-EC customs regulations apply. The maximum value of tax-free goods/gifts that can be imported into the UK from the USA is £145 per person.

Banking and credit cards
Visa and American Express are widely accepted.

Business hours
Standard business hours are 9.00–5.00.

Cost of living
Eating out in America is relatively cheap. Meals are available at the hotel, or there are numerous eateries within a short walking distance of the Westlake Village Inn. Many items are available in USA at cheaper prices than UK.

Climate
Mostly sunny and warm with gentle ocean breezes in the summer. The humidity is low with little rain. Average temperatures in June are 71°F/22°C during the day and 53°F/12°C at night. Dress comfortably and use sunglasses and sunscreen lotion.

Cultural/social observations
Business dress generally formal, general social activities informal. Formal dress required for the Conference Dinner.

Places of interest
Local maps attached.
Malibu beach – 20 miles
Ronald Reagan Library – 15 miles
Santa Barbara – 50 miles

Other attractions within driving distance of the Inn
Disneyland, Magic Mountain, Universal Studios and City Walk, Venice Beach, Hollywood and the Hollywood Bowl, The Rose Bowl, the Queen Mary, Dodger Stadium, The Getty Center, The J Paul Getty Museum (Malibu), Beverly Hills Rodeo Drive, LA Convention Center and the Music Center, Long Beach Aquarium of the Pacific.
Specific information requested on Disneyland and the Getty Center attached.

Basic phrases and numbers
Not required

Emergency contacts
In the event you require emergency medical assistance while overseas contact Telephone Mondial Assistance on +44 (0) 20 8645 1666, Fax +44 (0) 20 8645 1700.

Insurance helplines
Medical emergencies 01738 635566
Travel assistance 0113 390 5023
Travel assistance Helpline +(44) 113 390 5023

Additional documentation
The Conference papers, programme, presentation and slides for your talk entitled 'Defence Procurement Analysis'.

Figure 4.2.2 Briefing notes

Preparing and presenting additional material

Depending on the purpose of the trip, additional material may be required, such as: agendas and minutes; sales and publicity literature; standard visit paperwork – for example, interview forms; presentation materials – for example, handouts and OHTs.

Agendas, minutes, handouts and other information that have to be prepared from manuscript, notes or audio tapes should be produced using a word processor following the organisation's house style.

House styles can usually be followed from other similar documents, templates, and procedures manuals. The documents should be prepared on headed paper, or on paper prominently displaying the organisation's logo.

All materials should be presented to the traveller in a professional format. This may be a manila folder, ring binder, plastic pocket or the organisation's presentation folder. It should be clearly labelled and ready for the traveller in good time for the visit.

Portfolio activity 4.2

Using a word processor, prepare the following documents.

1 Itineraries for two trips – one overseas and one UK trip. Attach copies of booking and confirmation documents.
2 Briefing notes for two trips – one overseas and one UK trip. Include the sources of information used.
3 Travel documents checklists – one overseas and one UK trip.

Obtain a witness testimony from the travellers confirming that you discussed their travel needs with them, and prepared and presented the appropriate documents in an appropriate format.

Performance criteria:	4.2.1	4.2.2	4.2.3	4.2.4	4.2.5
	4.2.6	4.2.7	4.2.8	4.2.9	
Knowledge and understanding:	4.2.a	4.2.b	4.2.c	4.2.d	4.2.e
	4.2.f	4.2.g	4.2.h		
Evidence requirements:	4.2.1–4.2.28				

Test yourself

Knowledge and Understanding	Questions
a	Describe two different ways of preparing information from a variety of sources.
b	Describe two ways in which you might verify that the source of some information is current, correct and valid.
c	Give three different ways of organising, interpreting and presenting information.
d	Describe your organisation's house style and/or procedures for presenting business documents.
e	Explain how you construct itineraries.
f	Give two examples of how you completed travel requirements for a business trip.
g	Explain how you interpret information from a variety of sources, including maps and timetables.
h	Explain how you communicate effectively with colleagues at all levels.
	Explain how you communicate effectively with outside agencies and clients.

Activity 4.1

Memo

MEMORANDUM

To: Office Administrator
From: Sarah Reynolds, Director
Date: Monday, -- -- --

Guidelines for travellers

Many of our staff now travel to meetings here in the UK and abroad. Please write a set of guidelines for them to follow to ensure their personal safety and security of their possessions while they are travelling.

Activity 4.2

Desknote

DESKNOTE

From: Sarah Reynolds, Director
Date: Tuesday, -- -- --

Our export drive has meant that some administrators are now arranging for staff to visit clients abroad. I am arranging a training session for these administrators to cover the arrangements they need to make. Please prepare some headings for an OHT to be shown at the training session, together with some brief notes of the essential points to be covered under each heading.

Sarah

Activity 4.3

E-mail message

E-mail

To: Office Administrator
From: Sarah Reynolds, Director
Date: Wednesday, -- -- --
Subject: Documentation for business trips

The procedures manual is making progress and we are now dealing with the section on travel. Please prepare a set of procedures which outlines the standard documentation that needs to be prepared for business trips.

Activity 4.4

Memo

MEMORANDUM

To: Office Administrator
From: Sarah Reynolds, Director
Date: Thursday, -- -- --

Portable computers

We are considering getting portable computers for staff to use when travelling. Please prepare an information report which explains the functions of portable computers, and the benefits for staff when they are travelling on business.

Activity 4.5
Desknote

DESKNOTE

From: Sarah Reynolds, Director
Date: Friday, -- -- --

People keep telling me that a link with the Internet would prove to be very useful, particularly for travel arrangements. I have been asked to give some ideas on this at the next management meeting. I know that you have used it with some success when you organised my recent trips. Please write some briefing notes for me outlining different types of information that can be found on the Internet in relation to travel. I may have to answer questions on issues like security, cost, etc. Please provide some notes on these.

Sarah

5 Research and Present Information for a Specific Purpose

All aspects of our life require information. We need to know which bus to catch, the address for sending a letter to a friend, where to go for an interview for a job, etc. Researching information is also common practice in organisations and there are many types of research you may be asked to undertake.

Information underpins all the activities that go on in organisations – for example, the cost of replacing the photocopier, the telephone extension number of the sales director, the date and time for a meeting. It is essential to the efficient running of the organisation that accurate information is supplied on time.

Routine information is researched and used as a part of daily activities – for example, looking up the address of a customer. Administrators may also be required to undertake more complex research activities to support specific projects or organisational activities – for example, research on venues for a conference or the cost and feasibility of resiting the reception area.

Information can exist in many forms. It may be verbal – the response to a telephone enquiry. It can be in a written form – information in letters, price lists, catalogues. It may also be available electronically – via information sources such as the Internet. (*Note*: Strictly speaking, electronic information is still written – the word 'electronic' describes only the means by which it is presented. When discussing written information you should talk about whether it is paper-based or in electronic form.)

The word information is often used in this unit to mean either 'data' or 'information'. To be precise, raw facts and lists of measurements and figures are usually referred to as data, while information refers to a collection of data which has been selected and analysed to give it meaning – see Figure 5.1. However, in general for our purposes we do not need to make a distinction between the two terms.

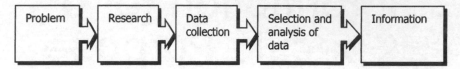

Figure 5.1 'Data' and 'information'

Element 5.1
RESEARCH INFORMATION FOR A SPECIFIC PURPOSE

Planning research

The first step in planning research is to list all the information required to prepare the findings. It should then be possible to list suitable sources of reference against each item. The items on the list should be ranked in terms of 'essential' and 'desirable' information. Clearly ranking these items can help focus research activities when deadlines are tight, or workloads are heavy. Timescales for the collection of evidence should also be considered. Time should be allowed for the following.

- *The receipt of replies to letters, telephone calls, questionnaires, etc. requesting information.* Allow sufficient time for responses. Remember that other people are very busy and your request for information may not be their top priority. You should have a contingency plan to ensure you have sufficient information if you do not receive a reply. For example, you could contact several suppliers for information; arrange to collect questionnaires from non-returners, or contact them by telephone.
- *Arranging meetings with relevant people.* Contacting people and booking appointments should be one of your first tasks.
- *Obtaining books/information from libraries.* Most libraries will have standard reference material which is always available. However, you may want to consult other books, articles, etc. and these may need to be borrowed on a library loan or requested from another

borrower. Ask the librarian for an approximate time for the availability of requested items.

All of this information can be summarised within a checklist. An example of such a checklist is given in Figure 5.1.1 on page 214.

Portfolio activity 5.1 **Number 1**

Note

This unit looks at researching and presenting information for a specific business project or business proposal which you will undertake. This project should be a real work activity and substantial enough to enable you to produce a comprehensive formal report and make an oral presentation. It is important to think carefully about the project you choose. There may be a project at work which will naturally present itself as a suitable topic, such as looking at the intake of students for a particular course and the feasibility of running the course. Alternatively you should discuss this unit with your line manager and discuss the possible projects that you could carry out for this unit. Remember, your research findings and recommendations will form the basis of a formal report and an oral presentation.

Arrange a meeting with your assessor and work colleagues to discuss and agree a suitable project to research. Discuss possible sources of information and set target dates for the oral presentation, review meetings and preparation of a draft report. Keep the notes of the meeting. The following evidence should be collected:

• notes of meeting.

Performance criteria: **5.1.1**

Research techniques

There are two types of research technique: desk research and primary research. Desk research is searching for data from secondary sources – for example, books, files and existing reference sources. Primary research is the collection of data from the primary (that is, first, original) source – for example, questionnaires and interviews. Desk research is useful as part of the initial research as it helps to determine the information that is already available and identify the primary data that needs to be collected.

Research topic – current use and provision of the staff canteen
Draft report available – four weeks

Information item	Possible sources*	Ranking	Timescale	Action taken
List/describe all facilities currently available in the canteen	Observation – visit to the canteen Interview with canteen staff Photograph of canteen facilities	Essential	Week 1 – visit canteen Week 1 – arrange meeting with canteen manager	
Feedback from all staff about their use of the canteen facilities	Questionnaire to all staff Interview with all staff Review of canteen customer log	Essential	Week 1 – prepare and send out questionnaire Week 3 – check responses	
Review Company policy on welfare and canteen facilities	Company policy documents obtained from Human Resources Department	Essential	Week 1 – contact Human Resources Department and check relevant company policies	
Feedback from canteen staff about their views on the current use of the canteen	Questionnaire to canteen staff Individual interviews with canteen staff Meeting with canteen staff	Essential	Week 1 – design questionnaire Week 2 – arrange meetings/ interviews Week 3 – monitor response to questionnaires	
Financial information about the use of the canteen for the last two years	Accounts Department – last two years of audited accounts for the canteen Canteen manager – last two years of financial records for the canteen	Essential	Week 1 – contact accounts and request information Week 1 – contact canteen manager	
Collect information on other similar organisations' canteen provision and use	Collect information from other administrators, network meeting, informal contact Arrange visits to other company canteens Interview canteen managers of other company canteens	Desirable	Week 1 – contact colleagues in similar organisations Week 1 – arrange visits to canteens	
Information on the current trends in canteen provision	Welfare/human resource publications and research projects Check any canteen or catering managers' publications	Desirable	Week 1 – contact library and conduct library search	
Identify and list other food provision available in the immediate location	Observation and recording of other facilities available	Desirable	Week 2/3 – carry out and record observation	

*These represent a range of sources, one or two of which would be selected as appropriate.

Figure 5.1.1 A research planning checklist

Sources of reference

The nature of the research project will determine the appropriate sources of reference. However, the sources should include people both within and outside your organisation, internal information systems and published media.

People within your organisation

The organisation's structure and company's policies and procedures can give an indication of appropriate people who can provide information – for example:

- *financial information* – staff in the finance and purchasing department may have information on prices, costs, records of previous expenditure, etc.
- *legal information* – the company secretary or legal department can usually provide support and advice on legal issues that may arise
- *health and safety information* – the health and safety officer can give advice about current best practice and legal requirements for health and safety
- *product information* – the sales department can provide sales figures and information about new product development
- *personnel information* – the human resources personnel department can provide lists of staff, job descriptions, etc.
- *technical information* – the Information Technology department can provide advice on computer hardware and software
- *library information* – some larger, technical organisations may have an in-house library and library assistants who can provide help with information searches; the library may also have a cuttings service which will locate relevant articles.

Information from people within the organisation can be collected in a variety of ways. Information contained in reports, policies, etc. can be located in filing systems, or requested by telephone, e-mail or memo from the relevant department. A telephone request for information is quick, but it relies on the recipient accurately recording your request. E-mails provide the opportunity for the respondent to 'reply to author' and attach computerised information. A memorandum requesting information is more formal and may prompt a written response.

Where the collection of information needs to be discussed with a colleague, personal meetings can be arranged. This gives you more control over the collection of the information and also allows for the discussion and interchange of ideas. The outcome of the meeting should be recorded and agreed with the participants, particularly if it is to be referenced in the report.

People outside your organisation

Information can be collected from people outside the organisation. This information can be categorised as expert advice/information, parallel experience or third party observation.

Expert advice/information

The administrator cannot be expected to have expert knowledge of all aspects of an organisation's business. There may be situations when it is necessary to consult experts – for example: you might need to consult a solicitor regarding legal issues; an accountant could provide information on financial issues; or an architect might be required to give information on planning issues or building problems.

Experts usually charge for their time and advice and it will be necessary to gain approval for the expenditure.

Technical advice may be provided free of charge by technical sales representatives, but the information needs to be carefully analysed to differentiate between fact and opinion. For example, a photocopier salesperson can provide factual information such as the number of copies per minute a particular machine can photocopy, but information they provide about the reliability of the equipment may not be impartial.

Public and academic libraries have librarians who are information search experts and they can be very helpful.

Parallel experience

Information can be collected from other people who have been in similar situations. If you are considering purchasing a large item of equipment you could ask to speak to other companies who have used the equipment. Talking to relevant people who have successfully completed procedures in their organisation can be helpful – for example, staff who have completed ISO 9000; more information on this can be found in Unit 6 (see pages 286–8).

Contact with people in organisations who have been recognised for 'best practice' can also be used as a source of reference – for example, if they work for organisations that have received awards or been highly graded by inspectors.

Third party observation

Third party observation is information collected from third parties – for example, customers or external clients. Surveys, questionnaires and other organisational data collection methods can be used – for example, customer comment logs. The value of this information can be affected by the size of sample, the questions asked and the method of data collection.

Internal information systems

The organisation should have information and records which can be accessed – for example, the sales department will have details of customers, the purchasing department will have information on suppliers and their products. These may be computerised and/or paper-based sources of information.

Computerised spreadsheets, databases, word-processed reports, stock lists and Management Information Systems (MIS) can be accessed to provide information. Some information may be confidential and password protected. You may need to gain authorisation to access appropriate information.

Paper-based in-house catalogues, leaflets, reports, accounts, policies and procedures can all be accessed to provide information. Confidentiality is again important, and you may need to gain authorisation to access particular files and information.

Published media

Published media represent a vast source of information. If your information search is to be effective, you need to carefully select the information source you use for any particular project. Consider the following issues.

Accessibility. The information source should be easily accessible – for example, available in the local library.

Relevance. Is the information you require really relevant to your report, and is it really necessary?

Reliability/validity. The information should be reliable and valid. Not everything published on the Internet and in newspapers can be trusted to be reliable or valid. Information can be checked by looking at its source – for example, information on the government information site should be reliable. If there is any doubt about the reliability or validity of information it should be checked with independent sources such as books or other reference material.

Paper-based published media

The following sources of information can be used to collect information.

Newspapers. These contain a wide range of useful information including current political and financial debates, currency exchange rates, share prices, etc. They are issued daily or weekly and therefore contain the latest information and analysis.

Official statistics documents. These may be published by the government or other official bodies. For example, the Office for National Statistics publishes the *Annual Abstract of Statistics and the Monthly Digest of Statistics*. These documents are usually available in the reference sections of a library or on the official website http://www.ons.gov.uk. Some information is available from the Office for National Statistics on CD-ROM – for example, the *UK Directory of Manufacturing Business 1997* and Travelpac information on travel patterns to and from UK.

Books. Technical, procedural, legal information and much more can be gained from books. Library catalogues and searches can provide titles on particular topics. A search on the Internet can also give book titles. Good reference sources can include: *Who s Who* – information on famous people; *Willings Press Guide* – information on the press; and AA and RAC guides – maps, accommodation lists, populations of towns, etc.

Journals. Many professions and industries have journals that contain articles about current practice. A library search can provide titles on current articles of interest.

Trade papers. Weekly or monthly papers and magazines are published for all different sorts of trade. The depth and quality of this information can vary depending on whether it is supported by advertising or by subscription.

Suppliers' catalogues. These are always a useful source of information on equipment and materials available. They often contain technical information, as well as prices. Check that you are using up-to-date information.

Other publishing media

Information can be published in a wide range of media including the following.

Television. The quantity and choice of broadcast television is rapidly increasing, as public network broadcasting, commercial television, subscription and pay-per-view television facilities are expanded. Many of the new services offer specialist choices that can make it easier to select relevant information – for example, Discovery Channel shows science, geography and history documentaries. Some libraries may also offer a recording service. Care needs to be taken with the recording of television programmes, as they are covered by copyright in the same way as published written materials (see the appendix, pages 539–45). Ceefax and Oracle services also give useful information – for example, share prices, exchange rates, and weather and travel information. This information is cheap to access and is always up to date.

Video. Training, trade and information videos are now widely available. Video clips are also available on CD-ROMs and on Internet information sources.

CD-ROM. These have a large storage capacity, and can store information such as encyclopaedias, reference books and newspapers. For example, *Websters Dictionary*, *Encyclopaedia Britannica* and UK addresses and post codes can all be found on CD-ROM.

Internet. A vast range of information is available on the Internet, ranging from daily news to the latest computer games. This is now such an important source of information that it is discussed separately in more detail below.

Using the Internet

The Internet is a worldwide network of computers which are permanently linked together. The World Wide Web is the information stored on these computers in the form of web pages. Access to the web is available in many organisations, as well as in many public libraries.

When you are searching the web for a topic, you need to enter the key words into the search engine. The search engine will then list the sites containing those words, the first selections being the items that the search engine identifies as being most relevant. If your key words are very general, hundreds of selections will be offered.

Each website has an individual address known as a Uniform Resource Locator (URL). Internet addresses are similar to e-mail addresses, but are always of the form:

http://www.(organisation). (type).(country code)

For example:

http://www.open.gov.uk

is the British Government's site.

Information available on the web is not subject to any controls or regulation. Anyone can set up a website, so it is important to check and use the information carefully. If you have any doubts about the validity of the information, you should check it against other sources.

Referencing techniques

When information is referred to in a report, the source of that information should be clearly referenced. This allows any reader to check the validity of that information. There are standard protocols for referencing printed works, and references should include the reference number, author's surname, first name and/or initials, the title of the work, edition number where appropriate, date of publication, publisher's name and page numbers referred to. For example:

> **Carysforth, Carol and Rawlinson, Maureen (1992)** *Administration, Student Handbook*. **Oxford: Heinemann, pp. 75–80.**

> **Chambers, L. and Woodward, S. (1994) 'Grading systems for administrative staff'**, *Administrative Management*, **38, 6.**

The referenced items should be numbered sequentially in the text throughout the report. The references should then be listed at the end of the report.

Where publications have been used as background reading for a report but have not been referred to directly, it is appropriate to list them in the form of a bibliography at the end of the report. The same referencing techniques can be used, but it is not necessary to list the exact pages.

Portfolio activity 5.1 **Number 2**

Use the Internet to find information relevant to your research project. Print out the information and include it in your portfolio. The following evidence should be collected:

• printout of Internet information for your research project.

Performance criteria:	5.1.3
Knowledge and understanding:	5.1.f
Evidence requirements:	5.1.6

Using questionnaires

Questionnaires are a useful method of capturing data. A questionnaire has two components – a list of questions and spaces to record the responses. Careful thought needs to be given to the use and design of questionnaires, as they can be overused and can collect information that is of little value. However, they do give an individual's response in a structured format. The information collected may be quantitative – for example, their age, the number of times the respondent used a canteen in a week; or it may be qualitative – for example, giving a quality rating for the food served in the canteen. Questionnaires can be structured or unstructured.

Structured questionnaires

These list all the questions in a logical order. There are two sorts of question – closed and open. Closed questions provide a choice of responses from which the respondent must make a selection (see sections 1–8 of Figure 5.1.3 – on page 224).

Closed questions provide data that is easier to analyse than oepn-ended questions. The questions may require single answers, where only one response to a question can be selected, or may allow respondents to select more than one answer. Most questionnaires are structured with a majority of closed questions.

Open questions allow the respondents to create their own response to a question. These responses are difficult to analyse as they can be so varied. Open questions are used when:

- there may not be an obvious response – for example:
  Where do you eat your lunch?

- the responses may be too many to list – for example:
  At which shop do you buy the food you eat at lunchtime?

- it is the views of the respondent that are required – for example:
  What changes would you like to see made to the canteen?

Unstructured questionnaires

These usually take the form of interviews, where the interviewer determines the questions. They allow for a deeper exploration and exchange of ideas. They may be conducted on a one-to-one basis or in small groups – for example, at a meeting with canteen staff to gain their views on the current use of the canteen. Care needs to be taken that the interviewer remains neutral and accurately records the response to questions.

Designing a questionnaire

The stages involved in the design of a questionnaire are shown in the flow diagram in figure 5.1.2.

Identifying a suitable population to complete the questionnaire – that is, defining the exact group of people to be questioned – is very important as it determines the style and design of the questionnaire. However, defining populations is a very complex activity. In a small organisation it may be possible to study all of the population – for example, all staff. However, with much larger populations – for example, all the residents of Wales – it would be very expensive and time-consuming to conduct a full survey. If this is the case, then it is appropriate to select a sample – a smaller group that represents the total.

Guidelines for designing a questionnaire

- *Keep it short* – it should have as few questions as possible.
- *Keep it simple* – the language should be straightforward and non-technical – for example, write 'shop' rather than 'retail outlet'.
- *Use clear questions and avoid ambiguity* – for example, 'Where do you go for your coffee and lunch break?' is two questions and is ambiguous. It is also unclear in which situation the coffee break occurs. The question should be worded: 'When you are at work, where do you go for your mid-morning break?'
- *Ask relevant questions* – for example, an irrelevant question in the case of the canteen questionnaire on page 224 could be, 'Do you like sandwiches?' A relevant question

Define the purpose of the questionnaire and the information to be collected

↓

Define the population – this will define the level of English and the type of responses

↓

Decide the appropriate method of distributing and collecting the information
Ensure that the questionnaire design is appropriate for the method of distribution

↓

Pilot the questionnaire with a small group to check for ambiguities and misunderstandings

↓

Approve the final questionnaire

Figure 5.1.2 Stages of questionnaire design

might relate to the sandwiches that are served in the canteen.

- *Avoid questions which are too personal* – 'Why are you a vegetarian?' is both irrelevant and personal.
- *List the questions in a logical order* – group linked topics together, rather than jumping around between topics.
- *Avoid leading questions* – for example, don't ask: 'Do you think the canteen should be closed?'
- *Avoid making cultural assumptions* – for example, using the words 'coffee' and 'lunch' breaks makes cultural assumptions about the type of food and eating patterns. It is better to use neutral words such as 'mid-morning' and 'midday' break.
- *Clearly differentiate between the questions and the information/ instructions* – this can be done by printing all instructions in block capitals, or by using a different style of text for the questions.

The canteen questionnaire (Figure 5.1.3, page 224), though not intended to be comprehensive, has been designed to demonstrate different types of question.

Completing questionnaires

There are two different methods of completing questionnaires – self-completed and interviewer-completed.

Self-completed questionnaires are usually delivered by post for the respondent to complete and return – these are often called postal questionnaires. There is usually a low rate of return for these questionnaires – for example, less than 10 per cent return rate. The respondents who do return them may also have a biased view.

Interviewer-completed questionnaires are completed by the interviewer in a face-to-face interview with the respondents. The completion rates of interviewer-completed questionnaires are much higher than for postal questionnaires, but the selected sample may not be representative. For example, completing the canteen questionnaire in the canteen will only elicit responses from staff who are using the canteen at that particular time.

An alternative to the face-to-face interviewer-completed questionnaire is completing the questionnaire by telephone interview. This saves time as interviewers do not have to travel, and reaches a wider sample as distance is not a problem. There is therefore a higher completion rate. However, the sample may not be representative, as it represents only those who have a telephone and are available and willing to answer questions when the call is made.

CANTEEN QUESTIONNAIRE

QUESTION	ANSWER	RESPONSE		
1 Sex of respondent	Male	[ ]		
	Female	[ ]		
2 In which of these age categories do you belong?	16–24	[ ]	1	(these are coded
	25–34	[ ]	2	answers that help with
	35–44	[ ]	3	analysing the data at a
	45–54	[ ]	4	later stage)
	55–64	[ ]	5	
	65+	[ ]	6	
3 Which department are you employed by?	Purchasing	[ ]		
	Sales	[ ]		
	Human Resources	[ ]		
	Administration	[ ]		
	Manufacturing	[ ]		
	Accounts	[ ]		
4 How often do you use the staff canteen?	Every day	[ ]	TICK ONE ANSWER WHICH	
	Two/three times a week	[ ]	MOST APPLIES	
	Once a week	[ ]		
	Never	[ ] Skip to Q8		

5 HERE ARE A NUMBER OF STATEMENTS MADE ABOUT THE STAFF CANTEEN. PLEASE INDICATE HOW MUCH YOU AGREE OR DISAGREE WITH EACH STATEMENT BY PUTTING A CIRCLE AROUND THE APPROPRIATE NUMBER		Strongly agree	Agree	Disagree	Strongly disagree
	The canteen provides good quality food	1	2	3	4
	The canteen represents good value for money	1	2	3	4
	The canteen provides a good choice of food	1	2	3	4
	The canteen provides a pleasant environment for eating food	1	2	3	4

6 During a typical working week, in which of the following breaks do you use services provided by the canteen? TICK WHICHEVER BOX(ES) APPLY		Mid-morning	Mid-day	Afternoon
	Once a week	[ ]	[ ]	[ ]
	Twice a week	[ ]	[ ]	[ ]
	Once a day	[ ]	[ ]	[ ]
	Twice a day	[ ]	[ ]	[ ]

7 What do you think of the services offered by the canteen? CIRCLE ONE RESPONSE	☺	☹	☹

IF YOU ANSWERED NEVER TO Q4, ANSWER THE FOLLOWING QUESTION

8 During a typical working week, where do you most often eat your midday food?	In your office	[ ]
	In a colleague's office	[ ]
	Outside the company's premises in a variety of locations	[ ]
	Outside the company's premises at home	[ ]
	I do not stop to eat food in the midday break	[ ]

9 What changes would you like to see made to the staff canteen?

Figure 5.1.3 An example of a questionnaire

Portfolio activity 5.1 Number 3

Prepare a questionnaire to collect information relevant to the research for the report you have agreed with your assessor/line manager. Test the questionnaire, redesign it if necessary and then organise its completion. You should monitor the return of the questionnaire and take steps to ensure you collect as many as possible. The following evidence should be collected:

- draft questionnaire
- completed test/sample questionnaires
- final questionnaire, plus any instructions in an accompanying memo
- completed questionnaires
- record of steps taken to collect outstanding questionnaires
- personal statement explaining what information you wanted to collect, the different stages of the process you went through in distributing the questionnaire, etc. Highlight any problems you encountered and the strategies you used to overcome them.

Performance criteria:	5.1.1	5.1.2	5.1.3	5.1.4	
Knowledge and understanding:	5.1.a	5.1.b	5.1.c	5.1.e	5.1.g
	5.1.i				
Evidence requirements:	5.1.1	5.1.2	5.1.3	5.1.4	
	depending on the source of completion of the questionnaires				

Questioning techniques

Interviewer-completed questionnaires tend to have a higher response rate as the interviewer can encourage respondents to answer the questions. However, it is important to ensure data collected using questioning techniques is reliable and accurate. The following guidelines should be used when conducting interviews.

- At the outset of the interview interviewers should identify themselves and clearly explain the purpose of the interview. It is helpful to have a prepared 'script'. The script should be neutral and should not contain any information which would bias the responses. For example, the question, 'Can you help me by answering a few questions to find out how the canteen can be improved?' implies that there is something wrong with the current canteen and might prejudice the respondent towards negative answers. A better question would be, 'Can you help me by answering a few questions about the canteen?'

- Have pre-set questions ready, as discussed in the section on designing a questionnaire (see pages 222–3). Have any follow-up or probing questions agreed in advance.
- Do not deviate from the set questions.
- Have a clearly structured format for recording responses. This may require ticking or circling a box. In the case of open questions, the method of recording the response should be agreed with the person managing the research programme – for example, writing down the response word-for-word. This is to ensure consistency when different interviewers are completing the questionnaires.
- Take care to remain neutral throughout the interview. Respondents may want to feel that they are giving the 'right' answers, and any body language or responses you make may give them clues about what you want them to say. For example, if a member of staff comments that the food is awful, you should not indicate in any way whether you agree or disagree with this comment as this might affect the subsequent answers.
- Respect any commitment to the confidentiality of responses. The anonymity and confidentiality of the responses should be clearly identified at the outset of the interview.
- Do not prejudge the responses by stereotyping the respondents. For example, do not assume that the young female office staff are likely to be vegetarians, while the male transport drivers are hearty meat eaters.
- Where a team of interviewers is being used, a questioning strategy should be agreed in advance to ensure consistency. Written instructions for the interviewer should also accompany the questionnaire. The instructions should detail how the questionnaire should be introduced and how the answers should be recorded – for example, whether the exact words are to be recorded, a summary made, or boxes ticked or circled.

Observation

Observation is a valid form of collecting information – for example, if carrying out job analysis the job holder could be observed carrying out their activities. Before observation is used, care should be taken to prepare an appropriate method of collecting the information – for example, using an open format to record relevant activities as they occur. This is a flexible, easy-to-use format, but the observer is making the judgements about relevant activities and it is possible that a key issue may not be recorded. Alternatively a checklist could be prepared which could be completed during the observation. This would ensure information was collected more consistently.

Meetings

As part of your research you may arrange to meet with relevant personnel – for example, you might talk to the network manager to discuss issues about confidentiality arising from the use of computer systems. You should take notes at these meetings. A summary of these notes may be attached to your report.

The organisation's values and legal requirements

When you have identified the sources of information and decided upon your research methods, you will need to carry out the research. The methods of research you use should conform to two fundamental principles: the organisation's values and policies; and legal requirements.

The organisation's values

Most organisations have a mission statement which embodies the organisation's purpose and objectives. The mission statement may then be extended to include the values that underpin the organisation's purpose. The values are used as a measure to evaluate all of the policies and procedures implemented by the organisation to achieve its objectives.

Values may be expressed in a number of ways – for example:

- they may be clearly written in a values statement
- they may be implied by the very nature of the organisation's activities – for example, hospitals and schools
- they may be accepted and owned by the people working in that organisation – for example, a children's charity
- they may be written in charters and codes of practice – for example, patients' charters at hospitals.

A combination of these will exist in most organisations. The values may relate to various aspects and parts of the organisation.

Staff. All staff employed in the organisation are valued and their views, opinions, and welfare are regarded by the organisation – for example, a commitment to Investors In People (IIP) would demonstrate a value commitment to staff training. (IIP is a nationally recognised quality system that relates to training and developing the staff in an organisation.)

Customers. There is a recognition that the customer is of prime importance, and all steps must be taken to satisfy customers' needs.

Public image of the organisation. Values involving quality, performance and professionalism give the organisation a particular public image.

Other organisations. This involves placing a value on building partnerships with other organisations – for example, colleges in a geographical area might have a commitment to work together, rather than see themselves as being in competition for students.

Local community. There may be recognition of the organisation's responsibility to the local community – for example, a commitment to use local labour and services, or sponsorship of activities within local organisations such as schools and hospitals.

Wider community. This is recognition of the organisation's place in a national and international dimension – for example, awareness of environmental issues. Questions about efficiency of energy use or recycling of materials can be asked when buying equipment.

Ethical issues. Awareness of ethical issues has been increasing over the past few years – for example, ethical investment or ethical political policies. This does not mean that other organisations are unethical, but rather that some organisations have a commitment to values which take particular account of human rights, religious belief, the consequences of the sale of addictive products, the non-exploitation of third world countries, etc.

Political values. Some organisations may expressly support a particular political view. For example, many trade unions support the Labour party, while some large industries support the Conservative party.

Legally imposed values. Governments have legislated to impose some values on individuals and organisations – for example, equal opportunities legislation and disability discrimination legislation.

Values can often seem very vague, but can be understood as 'sensitivities' – research should take account of this. If the topic of a report impinges on other staff, it is important to show that you have consulted them and taken account of their views. Where research involves customers, it is important that the customer is presented with a positive image of the company.

The organisation's policies

How the organisation achieves its mission and implements its values will be covered by its policies. The organisation may have written policies that relate to major areas of its operation – for example: a health and safety policy (required by law); an equal opportunity policy (required by law); a staff recruitment policy; a customer service policy; a supply of goods and services policy.

Legal requirements

Legal issues such as health and safety and equal opportunities have been covered already in the above discussion of values. However, there are other areas of information collection, storage and dissemination which are also controlled by legislation – for example, copyright laws and the Data Protection Act. Information on relevant legislation is contained in the appendix, pages 539–45. The information in newspapers and books is available for use by anyone, but copyright laws must be adhered to when reproducing this information in any manner.

Confidentiality

Some information may be confidential and should not be disclosed in documents which might be widely available in the organisation, or issued to outside parties. This could be financial information – for example, sales figures or employee salaries. Employee and staffing policies may also be sensitive – for example, recruitment/redundancy plans. Reports containing confidential information should be labelled 'CONFIDENTIAL' and should be circulated only in specially-labelled envelopes. The access list should be agreed with the person who has commissioned the report or information. Computer information should be protected with passwords, and disks locked away when not in use.

Selecting information

Information can be collected from a range of sources, but when you select information you should check that it is both relevant and current.

Relevant

The concept of relevance is fairly easy to understand – the information collected should relate to the issue being investigated. However, in practice when collecting information it can be tempting to include all the information collected, not all of which will be relevant. Too much information can be confusing – judgement is required to decide what should be included and what should be left out.

Current

The concept of currency is also easy to understand – information quoted should be taken from up-to-date sources. Check railway timetables and price lists to ensure they are current. Statistics should be collected from the most current sources available – for example, you should check that the annual population statistics are the most recent available.

Assessing information

When you have selected information, you need to carefully assess it before you use it as the basis of your analysis. The information should be assessed for its accuracy, validity and reliability.

Accuracy

Accuracy refers to the correctness of the information. The most common source of inaccurate information is the incorrect transfer of figures from an original source. Care should always be taken to cross-check data carefully with the original.

Accuracy does not always refer to precision. The exchange rate of the pound to the dollar may vary between different sources – for example, the Post Office, a bank, a bureau de change, a national newspaper. It may also vary during the day and from one day to another. It would be easy to give a precise figure – for example, 1.6 dollars to the pound, but this may not be totally accurate. In these situations it is not always possible to give a figure that is totally accurate. The information has to be clearly defined, for example, 'On 6 May XYZ Bank quoted the exchange rate from dollars to pounds as 1.6.' Alternatively, 'On 6 May the exchange rate for dollars to pounds was approximately 1.6, depending on the exchange rate source.'

Validity

Validity and reliability are more difficult concepts to understand. Validity relates to making a judgement as to whether the information truly reflects the situation being measured. Reliability relates to making a judgement about the consistency of the information – that is, whether the results can be repeated on further testing. One of the basic judgements you can make about information is to distinguish between fact and opinion. The statement, 'The canteen is not very popular with staff' would be fact if it was backed up by information based on canteen usage and a questionnaire completed by staff. Without any supporting information, the statement is opinion.

Checking validity

The validity of information can be checked according to the following criteria.

Method of measurement. The choice of method of measurement should give information which will be true for the situation. For example, a company questionnaire might not be the best method of collecting information about sensitive company issues – people might feel it is not truly confidential and they might not want to commit their views to paper. A more valid method would be to have a questionnaire prepared, distributed and evaluated by a neutral, independent organisation which would guarantee a higher level of anonymity.

Quality of method of measurement. A questionnaire may be a valid way of collecting staff views on the canteen, but a badly-prepared questionnaire with poor questions may not collect information that truly reflects staff usage and views on the canteen.

Source. Information is not always 'neutral' so the method and purpose of collection of the information should be checked to ensure it represents a 'true' picture. For example, the canteen staff might have provided figures about the use of the canteen over the last three years; however, they would have an interest in ensuring the canteen stays open. They might have collected figures when they had 'special offers' or popular dishes on the menu. Government annual statistics may be a more reliable source of information than information in newspapers and a colleague's verbal comment may not be as reliable as written statements in company reports.

Bias. Information may be biased – that is, it may contain a consistent error. For example, the previous three years' figures for profit/loss made by the staff canteen might contain figures for catering for management events. If you were using them as a measure of costs of canteen provision for staff, they might not represent a valid or true picture.

The reliability of information can be checked by asking whether, if the information collection was repeated under identical conditions, a consistent result would be obtained. For example, if the return for the questionnaire was only 10 per cent, if a further issue of the questionnaire also gained a 10 per cent return would the results be similar?

Reliability

Reliability and validity are interlinked ideas. If information has been collected in a valid way, from a valid source and has no bias then it should be reliable. The reliability of the source needs to be particularly carefully checked – for example, as discussed earlier, information on the Internet may not always be reliable.

Interpreting information

At the beginning of this unit, data was referred to as facts, lists of measurements, figures, etc. It only becomes information when it has been given meaning. The data collected as a result of an information search has to be interpreted and analysed – you need to answer the question, 'What does it mean?' This interpretation and analysis forms the basis of your conclusions.

You must take great care when interpreting data and you need to justify your conclusions and explain your reasoning. You need to show that you have based your conclusions on the evidence as a whole. There should be no ambiguities in the data.

For example, an increase in canteen turnover might lead to the conclusion that there had been an increased use of the canteen. However, increased turnover could be the result of increased prices, or provision of more expensive services. It would only be justified to draw this conclusion if it were supported by other evidence, or any ambiguities were eliminated. It would be necessary to check the level of prices over the same period, and check any statistics about the use of the canteen over that period.

Alternatively, there might be a fall in the turnover for the canteen, and statistics might show that fewer people were using the canteen. However, if the size of the workforce had decreased over that period the percentage of staff using the canteen might actually have increased.

It is important to approach the interpretation with an open mind. Errors in interpretation may be made if you are trying to find evidence for a pre-set idea. It is also important to make sure that the data is not used to support a 'hidden agenda' – for example, the management wanting to shut the canteen.

Interpretations may be based on certain assumptions, and these should be clearly stated. For example, the interpretation of figures showing a particular trend in staff use of the canteen might be based on the assumption that staff levels had remained the same.

Guidelines for interpreting statistical data
- Check the accuracy of the statistics and state the source.
- Look for overall trends and explain problems/causes of inconsistencies – for example, changes in turnover or use of the canteen when special offers are operating.
- Compare different sets of data – for example, comparing staffing levels with turnover.
- Use diagrams and charts to present the information and give a clearer picture of the statistics.
- Use accurate statistics, rather than approximations. For example, 59 per cent and 43 per cent could both be said to be 'approximately half', but they are very different figures and so the approximation might be misleading.

Non-statistical information can consist of facts and qualitative judgements. Facts are easier to interpret than qualitative judgements, and can be used to back up the reasons for qualitative judgements. Stating that the canteen décor is shabby would be merely a qualitative judgement, so should be supported by factual observations such as 'torn curtains' and 'peeling paint'. Interpreting staff comments is easier if they are grouped or categorised in some way. Random complaints in a customer log could be more clearly interpreted if they were listed under headings – for example, general canteen environment, quality and choice of food. Alternatively, 'key words' or themes could be used – for example, cleanliness, temperature of meals – and all complaints containing these words or ideas could be grouped together.

Researching information is not always a linear process – it is often necessary to go through the identifying, planning, collecting and assessing activities several times before there is sufficient accurate, valid and reliable information to justify analysis. When the process has been completed, information is ready to be presented in report form and by way of oral presentation.

Portfolio activity 5.1 **Number 4**

The activities for Elements 5.1 and 5.2 are linked together. Here, you should carry out the research which will then be included in the report and presentation for Element 5.2. You should ensure you cover and record searches from: people within your organisation; people outside your organisation; internal information systems; published media.

Plan and carry out the research for the report you have agreed with your assessor/line manager. The following evidence should be collected:

- research planning checklist that you completed as you carried out the research
- diary or log which records the different actions you took as you carried out the research – telephone calls, visits to libraries, file searches and any other activities you undertook
- collection of the information you found – this may be presented in the form of appendices included with the report: remember to include the result of the searches that provided information you may not have used in the report
- personal statement explaining how you ensured you met with your organisation's values and policies and satisfied all legal requirements.

Performance criteria:	5.1.1	5.1.2	5.1.3	5.1.4	
Knowledge and understanding:	5.1.a	5.1.b	5.1.e	5.1.f	5.1.i
Evidence requirements:	5.1.1 5.1.6	5.1.2	5.1.3	5.1.4	5.1.5

Note

Some of the activities required for coverage of Element 5.1 are covered in Element 5.2.

Test yourself

Knowledge and understanding	Questions
a	Describe the legislation that governs the collection, storage and dissemination of information – for example, copyright and data protection legislation.
b	Describe the techniques you can use to research information for a report or oral presentation.
c	Describe the questioning techniques you can use to obtain information for a report or oral presentation.
d	Explain how you can interpret statistical and non-statistical information for a report or oral presentation.
e	Describe methods of obtaining data for a report or oral presentation.
	Describe how you would reference a printed source of information.
f	Describe how you have used the Internet and other electronic storage systems to select and extract relevant information.
g	Explain how you would compile a questionnaire to elicit required information for a report or oral presentation.
h	Explain how you would analyse and extract data for a report or oral presentation.
i	Explain how you would plan and organise your time effectively when preparing a report or oral presentation.

Element 5.2
PRESENT INFORMATION FOR A SPECIFIC PURPOSE

Reports

Reports allow information to be presented in a structured format. They should contain facts and arguments that can be supported with clearly researched and referenced information. They should not contain opinions. Reports are usually written in the third person, and should not contain the word 'I'. For example, write 'questionnaires were issued to all staff' rather than 'I sent all staff a questionnaire'. Statistical and numerical information should be presented so that it can be easily understood by the reader – for example, in the form of charts, graphs and tables. Where a large amount of information has been collected, it may be easier to include the detailed information in appendices, which can be referenced in the main body of the report. The information should be presented in a logical order. Clearly numbering sections and subsections can make the report easier to follow.

There are three types of report – extended formal report, short formal report and informal report. The table opposite summarises the structure and purpose of each type of report.

Formal reports

Formal reports have standard headings and layout. The style and tone of the writing and presentation of the report are formal. The main elements of a short formal report are described below, followed by an example report (see Figure 5.2.1 on pages 239–40).

Title page
A report should have a title on the front page. The title page should also include the author's name and the date.

Terms of reference
This is the introductory section of the report and should clearly state:

- *who the report is being prepared for* – e.g. the Staff Welfare Committee
- *the purpose of the report* – e.g. to present the current use and provision of the staff canteen
- *deadlines for preparation of the report* – e.g. to be presented at the Staff Welfare Committee meeting on 12 June ----

Type of report	Structure	Purpose
Extended formal report	Title page Contents Synopsis Terms of reference Procedure Detailed findings Conclusions Recommendations Appendices Bibliography	Formal reports for external publication, particularly government, local authority, public corporations
Short formal report	Title page Terms of reference Procedure Findings Conclusions Recommendations Appendices	Formal reports for internal use, particularly for management decision making and non-routine issues Memorandum format is often used for these reports, although a more formal presentation style may be used where appropriate
Informal report	Introduction – purpose of report and actions taken to complete the report Main section – findings Final section – conclusions and recommendations if required	Informal reports for internal use, particularly within departments and for dealing with routine issues Memorandum format is often used for these reports

Procedure

The steps taken to collect the information contained within the report should be outlined in this section. This is where information sources are referenced. The steps should be numbered and set out in a logical order.

Findings

The findings section of the report should contain a summary of the information that you found out as a result of your procedure. More detailed information may be included in appendices. In this section of the report the facts and figures that have been collected should be listed. Any interpretation of the information should be included in the conclusions.

The findings may be listed in numbered format, and these numbers should reflect the sections listed in the procedure section. Information, facts and figures can be presented in a variety of ways, and it is important to select the most appropriate method for the information contained in the findings. This is covered in more detail in the section on presentation of information (see pages 241–248).

Conclusions

This section of the report contains the conclusions that you have been able to draw from the information shown in the findings. This is where you show how you have interpreted the information. You need to clearly show how you came to your conclusions and that they are based on the findings.

Recommendations

The final section should include your recommendations, and should list the actions that need to be taken as a result of your conclusions. They should be practical steps that can be carried out. The recommendations could be that no changes need to be made or that further investigations should be carried out. Care needs to be taken to ensure the recommendations fall within the terms of reference of the report.

Appendices

The appendices listed in the report should be included. Take care to number the appendices carefully and to include them all in the report.

Bibliography

A list of reference sources used as a basis for preparing the report should be listed at the end of the report.

Additional literature

You may also include copies of leaflets and other literature that you have referenced in the report – for example, price lists or photocopies of specific information.

Note

Each page of the report should be numbered. It is also a good idea to include a footer which identifies the report, for example:

Canrep/PW/June--

Informal reports

Informal reports are often produced in a memo format and comprise an introduction, findings and a conclusion. The style and tone of the writing and presentation are usually informal.

Staff Canteen Report
by Peter Worrall

Prepared for the Staff Welfare Committee

Date of Issue 6 June ----

1. **Terms of Reference**
   At the Meeting of the Staff Welfare Committee on 2 April, it was
   agreed that Peter Worrall would prepare a report on the current use
   and provision of the staff canteen. This report would be discussed at
   the next meeting of the Committee on 12 June.

2. **Procedure**
   The following activities were carried out to collect the information
   contained within this report.

   2.1 A questionnaire about current use of the canteen was sent to
   all staff (Questionnaire, Appendix A). One hundred and fifty
   questionnaires were distributed in all. Non-returned questionnaires
   were followed up by a telephone request for completion, and
   by e-mail. The eventual response rate was 36 per cent.

   2.2 Interviews about the current use of the canteen were conducted
   with each of the canteen staff (Question Sheet, Appendix B).

   2.3 The statistics on the weekly takings of the canteen for the last
   six months were requested from the Accounts Department.

   2.4 The comments contained in the Canteen Customer Log
   were summarised.

3. **Findings**
   The canteen is currently based on the third floor of the administration
   building. It is open from 8.30 am to 4.30 pm. It serves a range of
   meals and beverages (see Appendix C).

   3.1 *Staff feedback*
   The response to the questionnaire is detailed in Appendix D. The
   key findings show an interesting pattern of usage, which is shown
   on Graph 1.

   3.2 *Canteen Staff*
   The canteen staff reported that the number of staff using the
   canteen had declined. They commented that they received regular
   comments about the lack of choice, and the poor choice of snacks
   and sandwiches. (Full details in Appendix C).

   3.3 *Canteen takings*
   The Accounts Department provided statistics about the takings and
   costs of the Canteen for the last three years (see Graph 2). These
   show that while the costs have risen slightly in line with inflation,
   the takings have declined by approximately 10 per cent per year.

3.4 Canteen Customer Log

The comments on the Customer Log have been listed in Appendix D and are summarised in a pie chart (Chart 3). They show that 50 per cent of the comments relate to the lack of choice and the non-availability of snacks and sandwiches; 23 per cent of the comments relate to the décor, furniture and atmosphere in the canteen. Twelve per cent of the feedback was positive, and usually related to the helpful attitude of the staff in the canteen.

4. Conclusions

While the staff who currently use the canteen were happy with the value for money, the following major problems were identified by the staff questionnaire:

- The poor standard of the general appearance, décor and atmosphere of the canteen.
- The increasing level of loss being made by the canteen in its present form, in line with the falling demand for its services.
- The lack of choice and variety on the menu, particularly of snacks and sandwiches.
- If canteen usage remains at the present level, the losses being incurred will continue unless steps are taken to upgrade the physical environment and update the range of snacks available.

5. Recommendations

5.1 In the short term the following actions can be taken to update the range of snacks available.

5.1.1 Canteen staff carry out a survey of snacks and sandwiches available at the local shops, cafés and restaurants.

5.1.2 A range of new snacks and sandwiches are made available in the canteen.

5.1.3 The changes in the snacks and sandwiches are communicated to staff.

5.1.4 'Special offers' and other incentives are offered to staff to encourage them to try the new range.

5.1.5 The Staff Welfare Committee carries out a further investigation to look at low-cost ways in which the canteen environment can be upgraded.

5.2 In the long term the Staff Welfare Committee should approach the management to look at carrying out a feasibility study for having the canteen's physical environment redecorated and upgraded.

Figure 5.2.1 A short formal report

Summarising techniques

When the research information has been collected, it needs to be summarised in the report. Summarising information is a skill, and it is important to kccp a balance between conciseness and brevity. Quality of presentation rather than quantity is the key.

Summarising is about 'How can I convey the key points in the most concise and precise way?' rather than 'What can I leave out?' The following techniques can be useful when summarising information.

- Collect all the relevant information together.
- Read through the information completely once to get the sense of it.
- Read it again carefully, highlighting the key points.
- Organise the information into a logical structure and prepare a list of headings. Similar ideas should be grouped together.
- Draft statements that summarise the key points under these headings. It is useful to do this on a word processor so that it can be easily amended.
- Read the material again and read your summaries, checking that they really do convey the meaning clearly.
- Prepare final statements.
- Take care to summarise the information objectively. Do not bias the summary to include your personal views.

Presentation of information

There are many different ways of presenting information, with the choice of method depending on:

- *the nature of the information* – for example, lists of information, statistical information
- *the anticipated audience* – for example, senior colleagues, customers, adults, children
- *the format of the presentation* – for example, formal report, oral presentation
- *the medium for the presentation* – for example, overhead projector, handouts, reports.

The main methods of presentation are narrative text, tables, graphs, diagrams and pictures/illustrations.

The inclusion of a range of different methods of presentation will give reports and presentations maximum impact. They assist clarity, provide variety and break up text. However, care needs to be taken with the selection of the methods of presentation in order to balance variety against confusion.

Narrative text

Narrative text is the commonest form of presenting information. However, the presentation of narrative text can be varied for impact and clarity by using the following techniques.

- *Enhancing text* – for example, emboldening, underlining. These techniques can be used to highlight headings and key points.
- *Listing information* – for example, numbered points, bullet points.
- *Varying font style and size* – for example, using larger size text. Twelve point is easier for the reader than ten point; presentations using an overhead projector should be capable of being read by all the audience and so 26–30 point size may be more appropriate. Different styles of font can be used to make text easier to read – Times Roman and Arial fonts are easier to read than script styles. No more than two different styles should be used in a document.

Staff Canteen – Arial size 10

Staff Canteen – Arial size 20, bold print

Staff Canteen – Times New Roman size 12

Staff Canteen – Comic Sans MS size 14

Figure 5.2.2 Different fonts and sizes

- *Using Word Art* – many word processing and presentation packages have facilities that allow text to be very attractively displayed, in colour, at different angles and in different shapes. This is especially effective on title pages.

Figure 5.2.3 Text displayed using Word Art

- *Putting text in boxes* – discrete sections of information can be separated from the main text by the use of a box around the text. This is very effective on highlighting text:

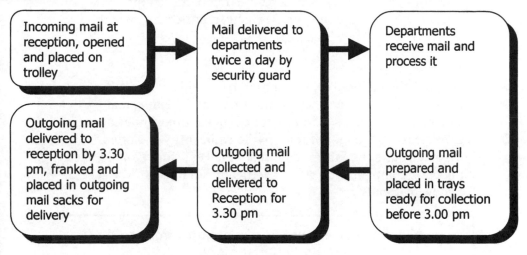

Figure 5.2.4 Some boxed/text

Tables

Table format allows information to be displayed in rows and columns. It is very useful for numerical information. Tables are easy to produce on word processing and spreadsheet packages, but careful thought needs to be given to the selection of information if the table is to be effective.

Table to show the level of complaints about the staff canteen*

Type of complaint	Jan–Jun 1997	Jul–Dec 1997	Total 1997	Jan–Jun 1998	Jul–Dec 1998	Total 1998
Cold food	10	8	18	11	6	17
Poor quality food	23	15	38	8	9	17
Lack of choice	33	28	61	35	31	66
Miscellaneous	11	6	17	8	7	15
Total	77	57	134	62	53	115

*Figures taken from the canteen customer log

Figure 5.2.5 A table

Guidelines for preparing tables
- Always include a full title.
- Keep the information simple.
- Reference the source of information.
- Use distinctive line styles to separate different sections.
- Include units – e.g. hours, metres, percentages, etc. – where appropriate.

Graphs

A graph is the pictorial representation on a grid showing the relationship between two sets of information. The information that is independent of the situation – for example, time (time carries on regardless of the quality of food in the canteen!) – is plotted horizontally and the information that changes – for example, the number of complaints, is plotted vertically. Graphs are very useful for showing trends.

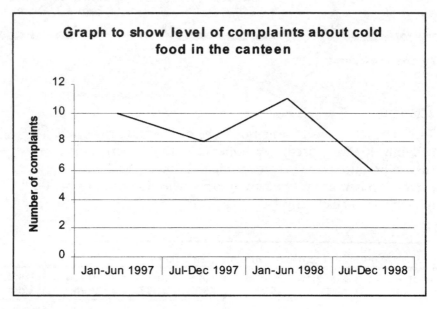

Figure 5.2.6 A graph

Guidelines for preparing graphs
- Always include a full title.
- Include the units – for example, £000s.
- Plot the independent information on the horizontal axis.
- Plot the dependent information on the vertical axis, which should start at zero.
- Reference the source of information.
- Use suitable scales to show the information clearly.

Charts

There are two main types of chart that can be used to present information: pie charts and bar charts.

Pie charts

A pie chart represents information in the form of a circle which has been subdivided into sections. Each section represents the information as a ratio of the whole.

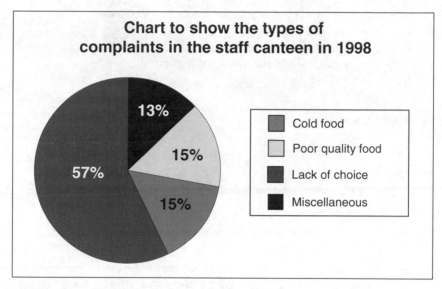

Figure 5.2.7 A pie chart

Guidelines for preparing pie charts

- Always include a full title.
- Use different colours or shading for each of the segments.
- Include any units/percentages.
- Measure each subdivision accurately in the same ratio as the figures.
- Reference the source of information.

Bar charts

Bar charts are very similar to graphs, but the information is represented as a solid bar, rather than as a plotted point. Bar charts follow the same guidelines as graphs.

Stacked or multiple bar charts can be used to show comparative information.

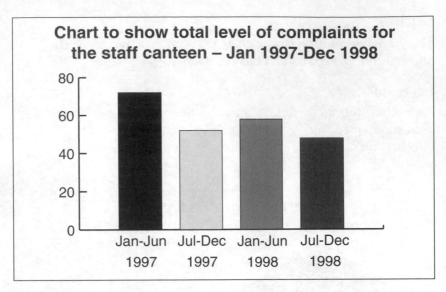

Figure 5.2.8 A bar chart

Diagrams

Diagrams are used to represent information pictorially, and can be presented in a range of formats.

Pictograms represent statistical information in a picture format:

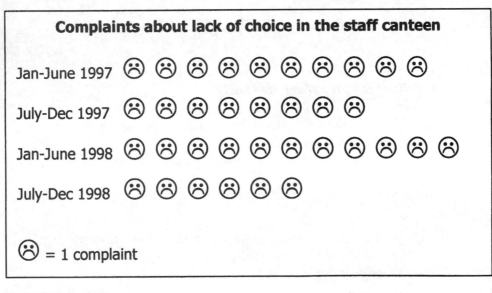

Figure 5.2.9 A pictogram

Organisation charts show linear relationships:

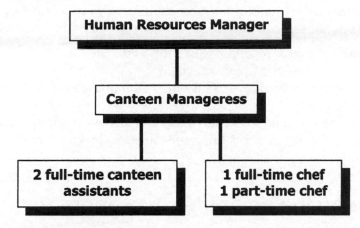

Figure 5.2.10 A simple organisation chart

Flow charts show logical steps to be taken in a procedure or activity:

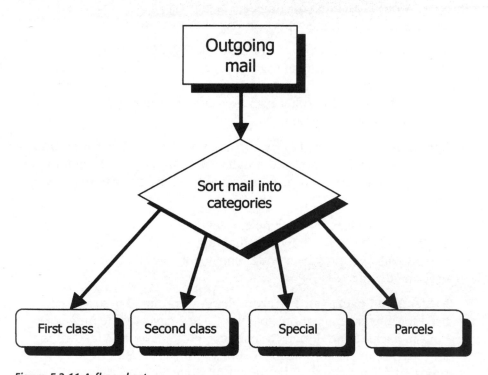

Figure 5.2.11 A flow chart

Pictures/illustrations

Pictures are very useful for showing information, particularly where it would be difficult to describe the idea in words, for example:

- *maps* – to show locations, directions, etc.
- *photographs* – of equipment, etc.
- *cartoons and drawings* – to introduce humour, particularly in oral presentations
- *symbols* – to produce variety into text: arrows, pointing hands, ticks, pencils; symbols can also be used as imaginative bullet points.

Using the computer to prepare presentations

Computers can be used to produce high-quality, professional reports and presentations. Many software applications now have the facility to integrate information prepared in another application – for example, a graph prepared in a spreadsheet can be imported into a word processing document. Various types of software are available for producing reports and oral presentations.

Word processing packages. For example, Word, AmiPro, WordPerfect. These can be used to produce text, lists, handouts, etc. Drawing facilities and clipart are also available. Charts and diagrams produced in other packages can be integrated into a word processing document.

Spreadsheet packages. For example, Excel, Lotus 123. These can be used to prepare charts and graphs from numerical information. Additional facilities may also be available – for example, map templates.

Graphics packages. For example, CorelDraw, Photo Editor. These can be used for drawings, diagrams, editing pictures. Clipart packages provide a wide range of images that can be used in documents.

Presentation packages. For example, PowerPoint. These can be used for drawings, diagrams, pictures. They have a wide range of built-in background designs to enhance presentations. Video clips and music can also be added. A series of pages or 'slides' can be prepared, which can then be shown in sequence – an electronic presentation. These slides can have music, animated images, etc. included to give an interesting and stimulating oral presentation.

Hardware such as scanners and digital cameras can be used to capture pictures and graphic images. Photographs and other pictures can be placed in a scanner, which then converts the image into a digital format. A digital camera takes photographs in a digital format, instead of using film. These pictures and images can then be edited and included in other documents.

Portfolio activity 5.2 **Number 1**

Plan and prepare the formal report for the research project you investigated in Element 5.1. Follow the layout for a formal report, ensuring it includes appendices, a bibliography and any appropriate literature you have found as a result of your searches.

Performance criteria:	5.2.1	5.2.4	5.2.5	5.2.6	5.2.7
	5.2.8	5.2.11			
Knowledge and understanding:	5.2.b	5.2.c	5.2.d		
Evidence requirements:	5.2.1	5.2.2	5.2.3	5.2.4	5.2.5
	5.2.6	5.2.7	5.2.8	5.2.10	5.2.11
	5.2.17	5.2.20	5.2.21	5.2.22	

Preparing an oral presentation

Planning the presentation

When planning an oral presentation the following questions should be considered.

Why is the presentation being made? Is the presentation being made to present information, or to persuade the audience of an argument?

What information is to be presented? The information to be given at the presentation has to be carefully selected. Too much detailed information can present the audience with 'information overload'; too little can leave the audience asking questions.

Who will be in the audience? The following points should be considered:

- status and level of seniority
- level of technical/company knowledge
- age and approximate level of education
- numbers.

Where will the presentation take place? The venue for the presentation can affect the selection of visual aids. For example, there might not be an overhead projector (OHP) and even if there were it might be difficult to project images clearly due to poor lighting conditions.

How long will the presentation last? The length of the presentation will clearly affect the amount of information that can be included.

When will the presentation take place? If the presentation is part of a programme, the audience can be affected by the timing. The slot after lunch is often known as 'the graveyard slot' and it can be difficult to gain people's attention. The last slot of the day is also difficult as people are often keen to get away to catch trains, etc.

Preparing the talk

When you have decided on what you are going to say, and how you are going to say it, you should prepare the talk. The first stage is to put together a logical format for the talk – for example, introduction, main content, summing up and time for questions. List under each heading the information required, and alongside the information any handouts, overhead transparencies (OHTs), etc. that you will need to prepare. An example of a talk format is shown in Figure 5.2.12.

Presentation to the Welfare Committee on the Canteen Report			
Section	**Content**	**Visual aid**	**Handout**
Introduction	Introduction to topic Background to the canteen report	Introductory OHT (1)	Canteen report
Main content	Presentation of findings	OHTs showing questionnaire response (2) Canteen costs (3) Summary of conclusions (4)	
Summary	Review of recommendations Discussion of recommendations	OHT of recommendations (5) Flip chart to brainstorm and record ideas in response to recommendations	

Figure 5.2.12 A talk format

The detailed content of the talk should then be prepared. This should not present too great a problem, as the report should form the basis of the talk. Small prompt cards should be prepared that summarise the talk. The content summary should be in one colour;

the number and title of any OHP should be in another colour. Each card should be numbered in case they get mixed up. It is not a good idea to read a script or a report as this will lead to a very stilted presentation. Any handouts to be used should be prepared at this stage and it is also advisable to anticipate questions and prepare a list of suggested answers.

Use of handouts

There is some discussion about the best use of handouts to accompany talks. If the handout is given at the start of the talk people may start reading the handout and not listen to the talk. They may also not give as much attention to the talk, as they feel they have all the information and can take it away and read it. Alternatively, if the handout is given out at the end of the talk the audience may make notes during the talk, write down the contents of OHTs and not pay full attention to the speaker.

There are several strategies that can be used. You can tell the audience that handouts will be provided at the end of the presentation. In this case you should clearly explain what the nature of the handout will be – for example, full information covering the headings on the OHTs, or a copy of the OHTs themselves. Where the OHTs are summary headings of points to be covered during the talk, provide the audience with handouts of them at the beginning of the talk, and suggest that they may like to take notes during the talk. Your style and speed of presentation should allow for notes to be taken.

Where several handouts are to be given to an audience, it is a good idea to collate them into sets prior to the presentation. The sets of handouts can then be stapled, bound, or placed in a folder to keep them neatly together. Some organisations have company presentation folders for publicity and presentation materials, and these should be used if they are available. Always have a number of spare copies of handouts for unexpected guests or requests for additional copies.

Presentation media

The choice of suitable media for visual presentation will depend on:

- *the type of information to be presented* – for example, technical information, text, figures
- *the audience* – for example, customers, colleagues
- *the facilities available at the presentation site* – for example, OHP,

video projector; always check this information before preparing the presentation; organise the booking of appropriate facilities.

You will need to choose a suitable method of media presentation: OHP, flip chart, video or electronic.

Overhead projector

The OHP projects the information on a transparency onto a wall or screen. OHPs can be difficult to use in rooms with very bright lights. The room and equipment should be checked in advance of the presentation. The OHP should be tested to ensure it can be plugged in, operated and has a functional bulb and the quality and size of the projected image should be checked. Care should also be taken to make sure that the OHP is not obscuring the view of any members of the audience and, if you intend to stand by the projector during the talk, ensure you will not be obscuring their view.

Overhead transparencies are best used to display: charts and diagrams; summaries of headings; and statistical information, numbers, etc.

There are several advantages to using an OHP. The OHTs are easy to prepare in advance, and enable the use of pictures, diagrams, etc. Use of the OHP does not require a blacked-out room, and allows the speaker to face the audience and keep eye contact.

The main disadvantage is that the presentation can be flat, predictable and rather boring, particularly if black-and-white OHTs are used. Another is that special equipment and a suitable power supply is required.

Overhead transparencies can be prepared in a variety of ways:

- on the computer, printed on plain paper and then photocopied onto transparency film
- on the computer and printed directly onto transparency film
- photocopied onto transparency film from other original documents
- by hand directly onto transparency film with coloured pens.

Guidelines for producing OHTs
- Keep the amount of information on a transparency to a minimum.
- Keep the print large – it will need to be clearly seen by the audience at the far end of a room.
- Use colour if possible – colour printers and copiers give good colour transparencies.
- Keep outlines and pictures simple.

- Keep the transparency flat and clean. Special plastic pockets, frames and presentation organisers can be used for storage and protection.

Flip chart

Flip charts are large pads of paper that are usually used with an easel, on which items can be recorded in coloured pen. They are usually used when ideas are being collected from the audience. If you use a flip chart, remember to have an adequate supply of clean sheets and usable coloured pens – they do tend to dry up if they are not used regularly. A spare flip chart and set of pens can be very useful as a back-up if an OHP does not work.

Video

Videos can be shown to an audience with a television and video player. The television should have a suitably-sized screen to enable all the audience to have a clear view. The video may be a commercially-prepared video, or prepared by you using a video camera. If you prepare your own video, make sure that it is of a suitable standard to be shown to an audience.

Advantages
- The use of colour, sound and moving images lends variety to the presentation.
- Real 'live' situations can be captured on video.
- Video equipment is easy to use.

Disadvantages
- Video requires specialist equipment that may not be readily available at some venues.
- It can take a great deal of time to produce a video of a suitable quality to be shown to an audience.
- If the video is too long or irrelevant people may 'switch off'.

Electronic presentation

Presentation packages on the computer allow for a series of slides to be linked together to form a presentation. Video clips, sound, moving images and animation can all be included in the presentation. High quality presentations are relatively easy to prepare on the computer. The biggest problem encountered with electronic presentations is the equipment required to share the presentation with the audience. A computer is required to run the presentation, as well as some means of showing it clearly to the audience. If a screen is unavailable, a laptop or portable computer can be taken to the presentation site and the presentation can be shown to an audience of two or three people.

Advantages

- They are easy to prepare.
- Colour, sound and animation can be included to give variety and interest.
- Information from a variety of sources – for example, sound recordings and pictures – can be incorporated in the presentation.

Disadvantage

- Very specialised equipment is required to share the presentation with an audience.
- Presentations can seem very 'gimmicky' if images, techniques, sound, etc. are not chosen with care.

Whichever presentation medium is chosen, time needs to be allocated to allow for the preparation of the materials. Always allow for contingencies – for example, failure of copier, no copier transparencies in stock, computer facilities not being available, problems printing from specialised software packages, unfamiliarity with hardware and software. Never leave the preparation of materials to the last minute.

Giving the oral presentation

Prior to giving the talk, prepare a checklist of information/items to be taken to the talk. The day before the talk, check that all documentation is available and packed ready for the next day. You should check:

- location information, map of venue if off-site
- prompt cards for the talk
- prepared answers in anticipation of questions
- handouts – sufficient copies of handouts to allow for a few spares, collated in sets and placed in presentation packs
- visual aids – copies of OHTs, videos, computer presentation (disks)
- display equipment required – presentation boards, computer, screens, easels
- contingency supplies – flip chart, fresh pens, plain transparencies, transparency pens
- feedback questionnaires
- supplies of audience notepaper, pencils, etc. – carry spare sets of these, even if they are to be provided by the venue
- any additional paperwork – name badges, participant lists.

Allow plenty of time to travel to the talk venue, to ensure you are not late if there are any hold-ups in the travelling time. On arrival at the venue, check:

- health and safety arrangements, and whether you are required to give house-keeping information prior to your presentation
- room layout – location of OHPs, arrangement of chairs and tables
- equipment – OHP, videos, microphones, etc. are in good working order
- handouts, OHTs – laid out in appropriate locations ready for the talk.

When the room has been checked and papers prepared, give yourself a few minutes to make your own personal preparations. Make a final check of your personal appearance – feeling good about the way you look will give you confidence during the talk. Giving a talk can be stressful and it is not always possible to predict how you will react to 'nerves'. Make sure you have had something to eat to avoid 'rumblings'. The audience may not notice these, but they can be very disconcerting to you! If refreshments are provided by the venue, do not eat too much, or eat unfamiliar items. It may be better to take your own snack with you. **Never** drink alcohol prior to giving a talk. Take a few deep breaths, and practise any relaxation techniques you use. Finally, remember to smile – you should now be ready to greet your audience and give your talk.

Although the talk should be well prepared on the prompt cards, the delivery is as important as the content.

Guidelines for giving a talk
- *Speak clearly* – direct your talk to the people at the back of the audience. If you are concerned that they may have difficulty hearing, or seeing, check with the audience at the beginning of the talk.
- *Speak slowly* – do not rush.
- *Allow space* – when you show a new OHT, allow people time to read it; if you ask questions allow time for people to respond.
- *Maintain eye contact with all the audience.*
- *Be sensitive to the mood of the audience* – watch for the physical body language – for example, fidgeting may be a sign of boredom. Puzzled looks may mean lack of understanding.
- *Be responsive to the audience* – if you feel that you are losing the audience, change the pace. For example, spend less time explaining 'basic' ideas and move quickly on to more complex ideas.
- *Manage your own body language* – try to control nervous habits that can be distracting to the audience – for example, fidgeting with the hands.

Portfolio activity 5.2 **Number 2**

Plan and prepare a presentation that outlines the outcomes of your research project. Ensure you prepare handouts and use at least two visual aids from the following: OHTs, flip chart, video, graphs/charts, electronic presentation. If you are working with colleagues to present your findings, you must make sure that each person speaks for a minimum of fifteen minutes, ten minutes of which must be continuous. A video recording should be made of your presentation if possible. The following evidence should be collected:

- talk format, including the purpose of the presentation
- prompt cards
- master documents for OHTs and other aids
- handouts to be given during the presentation.

Performance criteria:	5.2.2	5.2.3	5.2.5	5.2.9	5.2.10
	5.2.11				
Knowledge and understanding:	5.2.a	5.2.c	5.2.d	5.2.e	5.2.f
Evidence requirements:	5.2.9	5.2.10	5.2.11	(two of: 5.2.12	
	5.2.13	5.2.14	5.2.15	5.2.16)	5.2.18
	5.2.19	5.2.20	5.2.21	5.2.22	

After the presentation

Feedback

When the talk has been completed, feedback should be gained from the audience to allow the effectiveness of the talk to be evaluated. Feedback can be collected in the following ways.

- *Self-assessment* – you will assess and make a judgement about your own presentation. You may feel that you used too many handouts, or the pace may have felt 'wrong'. After the talk, list the areas you were pleased with, and list the areas you felt could have been improved. More benefit can be gained from preparing such a list if it is then discussed with a colleague who attended the presentation. This should be done in an open and honest way.
- *Informal feedback* – the audience may make comments about the presentation – for example, whether they found it helpful, interesting, informative or whether it went on too long. The reliability of this evidence is difficult to judge, as people may not

want to make critical comments face-to-face with the presenter. The presenter may also be biased in responding to comments. Both positive and negative informal feedback should be recorded.

- *Formal feedback* – more reliable feedback can be gained by asking the audience to complete a feedback questionnaire. Designing questionnaires is covered earlier in the chapter (see pages 222–3). Most of the questions should be closed and should ensure respondents can give fair comments, both negative and positive. With a small audience it may be helpful to have one or two open questions which allow for personal comments. These comments may be helpful for quoting in reports or documents later. Honest feedback is encouraged if the questionnaire is anonymous. The most important point is to ensure the questionnaire is kept very short, and the questions are relevant to the presentation. The rate of return can be increased by ensuring: the questionnaire is given to the audience at an appropriate moment – for example, with the handouts; the audience are reminded about completing it at the end of the talk; a member of staff asks for the return of completed questionnaires as the audience is leaving.

A questionnaire can be prepared for the audience at your presentation. You could ask questions on the following.

- *Content* – was the content of the presentation relevant to the title?
- *Handouts* – was the handout on canteen improvements clear?
- *Audio-visual aids* – was the graph on canteen complaints clear?
- *Actual presentation* – were you able to hear the presenter clearly?
- *General comments*:
  – What were the good points of the presentation?
  – What were the poor points of the presentation?
  – How could the presentation have been improved?

Evaluating the effectiveness of a presentation

The aim of the talk should have been clearly identified at the outset – for example, to inform the welfare committee of the findings about the current use of the canteen. The effectiveness of the talk can then be evaluated against this aim. Collecting information about whether people 'enjoyed' the talk may be irrelevant if entertainment was not the aim of the talk. The talk would be effective if all members of the audience went away from the talk with a clear idea of the how the canteen is currently used. It may then be useful to identify which parts of the talk helped them reach this stage – for example, whether the handouts and OHTs were appropriate and helpful.

The feedback and evaluation of the presentation should be summarised and recorded. The format of this summary will depend on the context of the presentation. It is usually presented in a short report or memorandum to a project manager. It may also be recorded as a personal note, to be kept on file for future reference.

Portfolio activity 5.2 **Number 3**

Prepare a questionnaire to collect the audience response for your presentation. Distribute and collect the completed questionnaires at your presentation. Complete your own self-assessment of your presentation. Arrange to meet and discuss this with a colleague. Record this meeting, and ask your colleague to sign and agree the record of the meeting. The following evidence should be collected:

- blank questionnaire
- completed questionnaires
- self-assessment of your presentation
- notes of meeting with a colleague.

Performance criteria:	5.2.12
Knowledge and understanding:	5.2.g 5.2.h 5.2.e
Evidence requirements:	

Test yourself

Knowledge and understanding	Questions
a	Describe three different presentation skills and techniques you could use to present information in a report or oral presentation.
b	Describe the structure of a formal report.
c	Explain how you summarise information for a report or oral presentation.
d	Show three different ways of presenting findings to ensure maximum impact in a report or oral presentation.

e	Explain how you communicate effectively with colleagues at all levels during the course of preparing a report or oral presentation.
f	Give examples of two different styles of oral presentation.
	Describe how you would prepare and use effective visual aids and handouts for an oral presentation.
g	Explain how you would assess and evaluate your own performance following an oral presentation.
h	Explain how you would compile a questionnaire to elicit required information relating to an oral presentation.
i	Describe the legislation that governs the collection, storage and dissemination of information – for example, copyright and data protection legislation.

Activity 5.1

Memo

MEMORANDUM

To: Office Administrator
From: Brenda Underwood, Finance Manager
Date: Monday, -- -- --

Researching information

We have been asked to prepare notes for staff who are researching and including information in reports. Please prepare staff guidelines on checking information that is to be included in company reports to ensure it is accurate, valid and reliable.

Activity 5.2

Desknote

DESKNOTE

From: Brenda Underwood, Finance Manager
Date: Tuesday, -- -- --

Staff found your recent guidelines on checking information very useful. Several staff have asked if you could give them more information on how to carry out an information search. I thought a flow chart would be a good idea. Please prepare a flow chart outlining the different stages involved in making an information search. Include brief notes to explain the flow chart.

Brenda

Activity 5.3

E-mail message

E-mail

To: Office Administrator
From: Brenda Underwood, Finance Manager
Date: Wednesday, -- -- --
Subject: Report writing

Staff are often asked to prepare formal reports. Please prepare a set of staff procedures for these, outlining the structure, information to be included, etc.

Activity 5.4

Memo

MEMORANDUM

To: Office Administrator
From: Brenda Underwood, Finance Manager
Date: Thursday, -- -- --

Presenting information

I have been asked to prepare a training session for staff who have to present information at formal meetings. Please prepare the headings for an overhead projector transparency for the various methods of presenting information, and prepare some notes for me to give under each heading.

Activity 5.5

Desknote

DESKNOTE

From: *Brenda Underwood, Finance Manager*

Date: *Friday, -- -- --*

We are updating our computer systems and need to consider the staff requirements for software to use when preparing presentations. Please prepare a report detailing the software and hardware required for staff to prepare high-quality, interesting presentations.

Brenda

Manage the Storage and Retrieval of Information

Organisations need information in order to carry out their business. This can include:

- product information – plans, drawings, specifications
- financial information – budgets, accounts, banking records, invoices, orders, salaries
- client information – customer lists, records of orders
- sales information – records of sales made, sales projections
- purchasing information – goods ordered, supplier lists
- stores information – item descriptions, stock levels
- administrative information – records of meetings, administrative procedures
- management information – records of board meetings, policies, forward planning
- personnel information – staff records, appraisals, training, welfare information.

The storage and retrieval of information needs to be well organised to ensure the efficient and effective operation of the organisation. The following are the key factors that determine the efficiency and effectiveness of an information storage system.

Accessibility. It should be easily accessible by all authorised users.

Security. The information should be protected from fire, theft, water, vandalism and accidental damage.

Cost. The system should be cost-effective in terms of the importance of the information and the available budget, allowing for both start-up and on-going costs.

Ease of use. Users should find it easy to use with a minimum of training.

Trackability. The system should enable the location and users of information to be monitored and tracked.

Speed. Information should be available within appropriate timescales to allow the work of the organisation to proceed without delays.

Space. The system should make efficient use of space.

Flexibility/expandability. The system should be able to cope with changes within the organisation – for example, expansion to cope with the storage of future information requirements.

Currency. The system should contain information that is up to date, but should also allow for the long-term storage of relevant information.

Suitability for the job. The system should be appropriate for the type of information to be stored. Complex systems may not be required for routine or low-volume information. High-level security requirements are not required for storage of information which is generally open and available to outside organisations.

The titles of the elements in this unit refer to 'an information storage and retrieval system'. However, we shall simply use the term 'information system'. The storage and retrieval of information will be implied within this term. The term 'filing' will also appear within the unit, as many information systems are commonly identified as filing systems.

Element 6.1
EVALUATE AN INFORMATION STORAGE AND RETRIEVAL SYSTEM

Information systems

An information storage and retrieval system, or information system, is a methodical combination of information storage and retrieval activities that enable information to be systematically managed within an organisation. An information system should clearly identify:

- *who is responsible for the different elements of the activity* –
  authority to access, authority to release, responsibility for
  day-to-day activities, responsibility for monitoring and
  supervision of system
- *where the information is to be kept* – geographical/office location,
  on-site/off-site, cabinet location, computer locations, etc.
- *how the information is to be managed* – a clearly defined set of
  procedures that covers the input, storage, tracking and removal
  of information
- *timescales for activities* – the length of time documents should be
  kept, when the system should be updated, when files should be
  archived for long-term storage.

In a small organisation the system may relate to the total
information for the organisation. In a larger organisation the
system may relate to a department or a particular activity – for
example, managing the information relating to staff recruitment.

Portfolio activity 6.1 **Number 1**

You are required to evaluate an existing information system and
present your findings and recommendations for improvement in
a formal, written report.

Arrange and record the following meetings to discuss and agree
an appropriate information system to be evaluated: a discussion
with a work-based colleague to agree an appropriate system;
and a discussion with your assessor to agree an appropriate
system and to prepare an action plan. Draft the terms of
reference to be used in your written report. The following
evidence should be collected:

• records of discussions with colleague and assessor
• terms of reference for the written report.

(See also the suggested activity on page 290 for a possible
information storage and retrieval system project.)

Different types of information system

There are many different ways of managing information systems.
However, fundamentally there are only two types of system: paper-
based and electronic.

Paper-based information systems

As the term implies, this refers to the storage and retrieval of all records and information that are contained on paper – invoices, orders, letters, memos, application forms, copies of minutes, reports, etc. This is often identified as the traditional filing system.

In a paper-based system, the filing of documents is usually dealt with in the following stages:

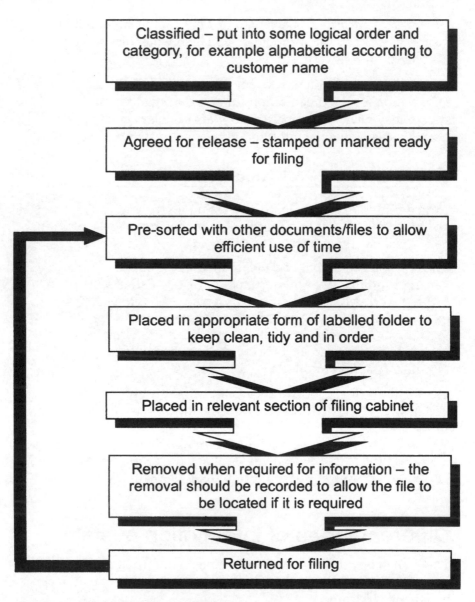

Figure 6.1.1 Paper-based filing procedure

Advantages

- It is easy to use and to follow.
- It does not require high-cost capital equipment to implement.
- Security can be maintained by the use of lockable cabinets.
- It remains independent of equipment, electricity and changes in technology.
- The removal of physical files can be recorded and monitored.
- It is appropriate for original legal documents – for example, contracts, insurance policies.
- The storage of paper-based systems is not covered by the Data Protection Act.

Disadvantages

- There is limited access, as only one person can use the file at any time.
- Information may be duplicated, as documents may be photocopied and stored in different offices or locations in the organisation.
- Information is difficult to sort efficiently – for example, a manual search of all personnel records might be required to identify all female employees, under a certain age, with a certain set of skills.
- Although security of information can be maintained with lockable cabinets, it may be difficult to track a file once it has been removed from the system unless efficient tracking procedures are in place – efficient monitoring and tracking of documents relies on staff completing records accurately.
- Paper-based systems are difficult to access over distances – for example, files might need to be sent through the post or physically delivered to remote locations – this can take time.
- Paper files can be destroyed by fire and flood.
- Searching for information has to be done manually – where the information is difficult to identify, or the indexing and cross-referencing systems are inadequate, retrieving information can take time.
- Paper files take up a lot of space, and it can be difficult to predict how much space will be required in the future – it is difficult to balance the current use of space with the need for availability of space for future expansion.

Electronic information systems

Electronic information systems use electronic equipment to manage the storage and retrieval of information. This usually relates to computer-linked systems. There are various levels of electronic filing system, from the use of a computer to store a simple database to

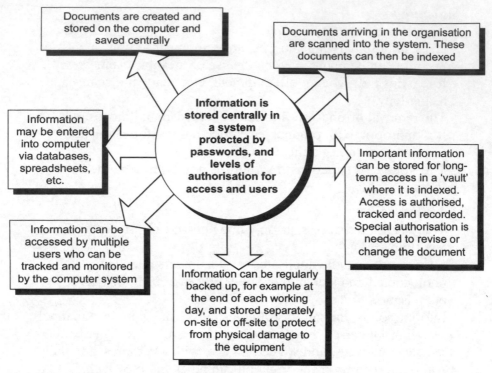

Figure 6.1.2 Electronic filing procedure

organisations that use computers to manage the whole of their information systems. Large electronic information systems are often known as Electronic Document Management (EDM) systems. EDM systems are usually used in organisations where the majority of staff have access to a computer that is linked to a network.

Advantages
- Information is very easy to sort – multiple sorts can be carried out.
- Information can be accessed by a number of users at any one time.
- Access to information is very fast – almost instantaneous.
- Information is easy to access over a distance, whether between computers linked on a Wide Area Network (WAN) or by sending files via electronic mail systems.
- Electronic systems are easily expandable – if hard disks and network space becomes full more storage space can be acquired by upgrading systems, rather than using up more physical space.
- Electronic systems can save space, as large amounts of information can be saved on disks and CD-ROMs.
- The use of information in an electronic system can be tracked and recorded by the computer system.

Disadvantages

- Not all information can be kept only in electronic form – some paper information may still need to be kept.
- Some offices may operate dual systems and this can be wasteful of staff time and space.
- The systems are dependent on electricity, machines and technology – power failures and computer problems can mean serious disruption of the activities of the organisation; this can be frustrating to staff and customers if it happens on a regular basis.
- The systems are expensive to set up and operate – electronic systems require a large capital investment in computer technology; network systems also incur an ongoing cost in network support staff for management and maintenance.
- Computer-based systems may not be user-friendly, and staff may require special training.
- While security can be maintained by the use of passwords and other strategies – for example, encryption of data – there is concern that access may be gained by 'hackers' and other unauthorised people.
- Data stored on computers is subject to the Data Protection Act (see the appendix on pages 539–45), and care must be taken to ensure information systems comply with the act.

Technological change and electronic information systems

While paper-based information systems remain static, electronic systems are subject to rapid changes in technology. Every time organisations upgrade their systems with new hardware and software, they are faced with the problem of transferring their data into the new system. In the past, this meant that some electronic systems were inflexible – they were locked into particular formats and considerable time and expense was incurred in converting data to new formats. The long-term planning of information systems was difficult when technological change could not be predicted. New standards have now been introduced to enable systems to be developed which will produce data in formats that can be accommodated in new systems. These standards are covered by Standard for Exchange of Product model data (STEP), ISO 10303.

Filing classifications

Whichever type of filing system is used, information has to be classified. Information should be grouped into logical categories, and then sorted and filed in logical order. Standard methods of ordering are alphabetical, numerical and chronological.

Alphabetical filing

In alphabetical filing, information is sorted into alphabetical order. Alphabetical filing is easy to understand – it is a direct system and requires no indexing. However, in paper-based systems it is difficult to expand, as the amount of space required in particular alphabetical groupings is difficult to predict – for example, the drawer containing B/C files may fill up much quicker than the X/Y/Z drawer. This can often mean physically reorganising the whole of the filing system.

When filing information alphabetically, there are certain rules that should be followed. These are basically the same as the rules used for storing information in a telephone directory.

1 File by the surname, and then by the initials. Titles are ignored:

> **James, H, Mrs**
>
> **James, H I, Dr**

2 Nothing comes before something:

> **J**
>
> **James Co**
>
> **James, H, Mrs**
>
> **James, H I, Dr**

3 Abbreviations are filed in alphabetical order before full names:

> **JAC**
>
> **JB**
>
> **JBC**
>
> **James**

4 Numbers are filed as if they were written in full:

> **'2–5 Company' is filed under T for 'Two–Five Company'**

5 'The' is ignored:

> **'The James Set' is filed under J for 'James Set, The'**

6 Multiple surnames are treated as one word:

> **'De La Rue' is filed under D as if it was 'Delarue'**

7 Names with St, Saint, are all filed under Saint:

> **St James School**
>
> **Saint John's Church**

8 Government Departments are filed under their key word:

Education, The Department of

Information within alphabetical systems can be grouped in a number of ways, depending on the type of information and the needs of the users. The three most commonly used groupings are by name, by subject and by geographical location.

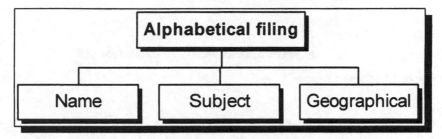

Figure 6.1.3 Information within alphabetical filing systems

Name

This system uses the surname of the person or the name of the organisation to classify the information.

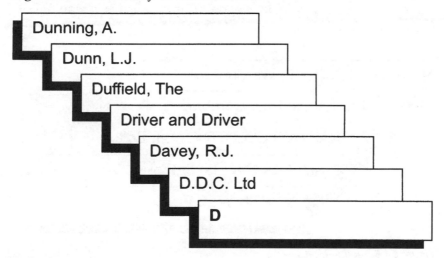

Figure 6.1.4 Name system

Subject

Information may also be sorted according to subject. Items may then be listed in alphabetical order by the information contained within them. Subject filing is useful for projects and topics – for example, health and safety or office redecoration. However, it can cause problems because it is not always easy to identify the subject listing. Cross-referencing systems are often required to make it easier to find information.

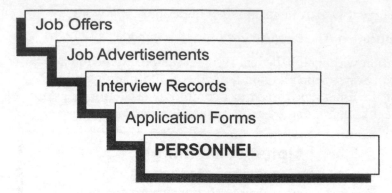

Figure 6.1.5 Subject system

Geographical location

Information may also be sorted in geographical order. This is often used where organisations operate on a regional/national basis – for example, national utilities may file information according to address or postcode. The areas, or information within an area, may still be subdivided and ordered alphabetically. Geographical filing can cause problems as some geographical knowledge is required of the users.

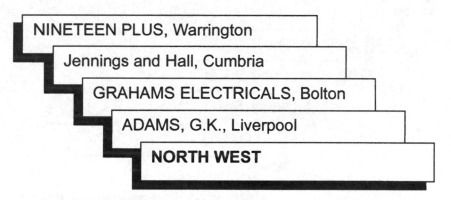

Figure 6.1.6 Geographical system

Numerical filing

In numerical filing systems, information is filed according to a number. Each file or set of information has a unique number. Numerical systems are used where there is a large volume of filing. The major advantage of numerical filing is its ease of expansion. New files are allocated the next number in the system and are then added to the end of the existing system. The disadvantage of numerical filing is that it requires some form of indexing to link the number to the relevant topic or name. The index can be kept on the computer, or may be in the form of index cards. The index cards are usually filed in alphabetical order. Further problems can occur with numerical filing if numbers are incorrectly written down, or files are incorrectly filed, as it is then very difficult to locate these files.

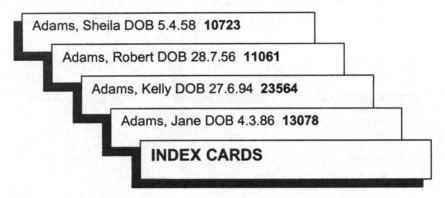

Figure 6.1.7 Numerical filing

There are four common forms of numerical filing: standard numerical, alphanumeric, terminal digit and Dewey Decimal.

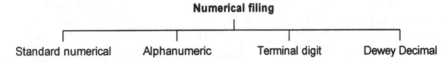

Figure 6.1.8 Numerical filing systems

Standard numerical

Standard numerical filing is the most common form of numerical filing. It is often linked to a reference number – for example, invoice numbers, order numbers. Numbers will run consecutively – for example, 1512, 1513, 1514, …

Alphanumeric

Alphanumeric filing uses a combination of letters and numbers – for example, A106. The letter can indicate a location – for example, a shelf or row, and the number will then indicate the file reference in that location. The letter may refer to a category of work – for example, all Personnel Department files may be preceded by the letter 'P' followed by a file number. The most commonly used form of alphanumeric filing is the use of postcodes to file information. The availability of postcode information on CD-ROM enables many organisations to have a record of all addresses and postcodes, and these can be used to file information about customers.

Terminal digit

Terminal digit filing uses numbers in a sequence that relates to the location in the filing system. Numbers are usually allocated in sets of pairs – for example, 330642. The numbers are usually read from right to left.

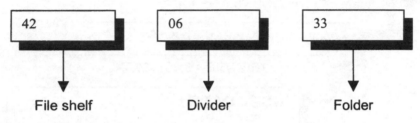

| 42 | 06 | 33 |

| File shelf | Divider | Folder |

Figure 6.1.9 Terminal digit system

This system is used in large filing systems, as it makes numerical filing much easier for filing clerks.

Dewey Decimal

The Dewey Decimal system of classification is a standard system used in libraries. Information is classified into ten major divisions according to subject – for example, '500 Mathematics and Natural Sciences'. This division is then subdivided into further subsections which are numbered to indicate greater detail – for example, '574 Biology'.

Chronological filing

Chronological filing is usually used in conjunction with other methods of classification. Files may be classified alphabetically, but the documents within the file are filed in date order, with the most current document on the top. However, there are situations where the date is particularly important and when information is filed solely chronologically – for example, renewal dates for licences or insurance.

A bring-forward system can be used, where documents are stored in the section relating to the day/month. The current month may be sorted by date, and the following months sorted into month order. Towards the end of the month, the documents for the following month are sorted and filed in daily order.

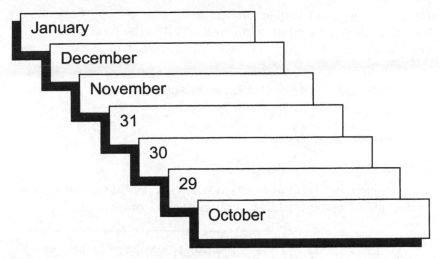

Figure 6.1.10 Chronological filing

Referencing systems

There are two types of referencing system: document referencing systems and cross-referencing systems.

Document referencing systems

Document referencing systems are used by organisations to identify documents accurately. The standards for referencing documents are usually contained in company procedures, and can include reference to the following.

Correspondence. This should contain the initials of the author, the secretary or operator keying in the document and a file reference number. The file reference number may be the insurance policy, customer number, file reference, etc. – for example:

HJ/APL/6723A

Reports. Each report should have a unique reference, which should be included in the footer of each page of the document. This reference may include the following:

Topic category/Type of document/Author's name/Date of issue

For example:

H&S/Rep/JAB/2.4.--

Procedures. It is important that procedural documents are clearly identified with a reference number, to ensure all staff using the procedures are clear they are using the most up-to-date version. Standard forms and other documents listed in the procedures will also be referenced in a similar way. The reference may include the following:

Document type/Subject/Issue number/Date

For example:

Proc/FireEvac/2/Jan--

Cross-referencing systems

Cross-referencing systems are used when confusion may arise due to documents being filed in several locations, for example:

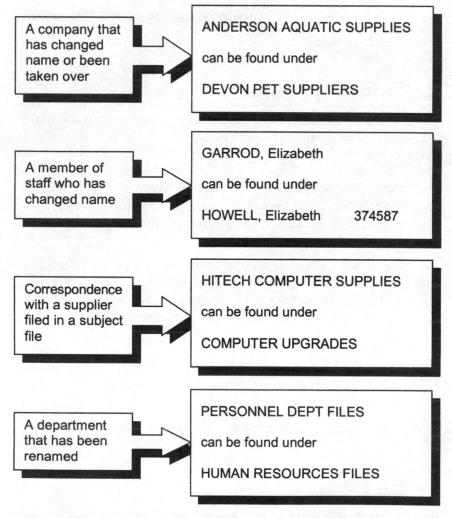

Figure 6.1.11 A cross-referencing system

In a direct filing system, the cross-reference is usually an A4 coloured card with an edge tab, located in the place that would have been occupied by the file. In an indirect system which has an index to reference names to numbered files, the cross-reference card is filed in the index in the appropriate place.

In/out, tracer systems and procedures

A good information system should include procedures that allow the location of a file to be traced. When files are removed from/returned to the system, the following information should be recorded.

- The name of the person removing the file.
- The name of the file being taken.
- The name of the department using the file.
- The date the file was taken.
- The date of return.
- The name of the person returning the file.

This information can be recorded in a file log. This is usually a book which records the above entries (see Figure 6.1.12).

Date of removal	Name of file	Person removing file	Department	Date of return	Person returning file
16.1.--	Mendelsohn v. Briggs	Surindhar Kumar	Matrimonial	24.1.--	Surindhar Kumar
17.1.--	Fletchley v Fletchley	Jane Hopkins	Matrimonial	18.1.--	Peter Jones
17.1.--	Madison and Hinchliffe	Sian Taylor	Conveyancing		
18.1.--	Winchester Holdings	Peter Jones	Corporate		

Figure 6.1.12 A file log

File logs are used in small companies with a relatively small number of files. An alternative system is to use an 'out-card'. The out-card is a coloured card that is placed in the file in the location of the file removed. The card records the same information as the log. When a member of staff looks in the filing system for the file, it is easy to see who has removed the file by looking at the card.

Date of removal	Number of file	Person removing file	Small section that stands out above the files so that the card can be clearly seen			
			Department	Date of return	Person returning file
16.1.--	1735	Keith McIntyre	Household	20.1.--	Keith McIntyre
18.1.--	2350	Bridget O'Hara	Motor Vehicle		

Figure 6.1.13 An out-card

Checking return of files

In some organisations there is a system for checking that files are returned. The procedures may define that files can be removed for a certain period – for example, two weeks. If the file is not returned within this time, a note requesting the return of the file will be sent to the person who had removed it. This system is easier to track if a filing log system is used. In larger systems, where out-cards are used, it would be time-consuming to check them all on a weekly basis. In these systems, a check may be carried out once a month. The out-cards will be removed and a list prepared of files that have been removed from the system for longer than a month. A note requesting the return of the file would then be prepared. The following week, the list could be checked to monitor the return of the outstanding files. Keeping track of files in this way should reduce the problem of lost files.

Problems arise when files are not returned within the specified period of time. Follow-up action has to be taken, including: further requests for the file; contact with heads of department; identification of departments/personnel who regularly do not return files; and circulated reminders of the procedures.

Filing audits

Regular filing audits may be carried out. This will be a check to ensure filing procedures are being correctly carried out. Departments and individuals causing problems with the non-return of files may be informed of 'non-compliance' and action plans agreed to ensure procedures will be complied with in the future.

Archiving systems

Archiving is the long-term storage of files. An archiving system usually consists of:

- a retention policy to define length of storage of documents/files
- a method of classification/indexing of long-term files
- arrangements for the physical storage of files
- arrangements for retrieval and access.

Retention policies define how long files and documents should be kept when they are no longer in current usage. Legal, organisational and practical considerations will determine the retention policy.

By law, certain documents need to be kept for specific periods:

- Balance sheets, Directors' Reports – 30 years
- Accounts and financial documents – 6 years
- Accident and medical records – of identifiable employees, 40 years; otherwise 5 years.

Organisational requirements will vary depending on the type of activity and records that are kept. Typical periods might be: messages and memos, six months; general correspondence, one year; product information, as long as the product remains in use.

Classifying and indexing the archive files has to be agreed once the retention policy has been defined. Many organisations use a chronological system. When files have been released from the current files and are ready for archiving they are given a file number. The name of the file is then recorded in the number register, and an index card is prepared. The index entries can also be maintained on a database.

Physical storage of the files has to be arranged. A small organisation with only a few archive files may use a filing cabinet in a long-term storage area. A medium-sized organisation that has access to sufficient storage space may use archive storage boxes. The boxes are numbered with the relevant index numbers and are stored in numerical order in a long-term storage area. The area selected for the long-term storage of files should be dry, fireproof and secure. Files stored in unsupervised damp basements, unheated rooms and attics may quickly deteriorate in quality and get mislaid.

Retrieval and access – there are occasions when the archive files will be needed, and provision should be made for this. Some record should be kept of who has removed the file, which department is using it and when it was removed. This record may be kept in a register, or an out-card may be used.

Off-site archive storage

Many organisations now use specialist off-site storage facilities for their archive files. The storage companies offer facilities under a range of names such as 'records management', 'document and computer media storage' and 'secure vault storage'. The storage companies usually provide:

- collection and delivery of files
- a dry, dust-free and temperature-controlled storage environment for paper-based, magnetic and computer media
- secure and confidential storage
- a fire-proof environment
- shredding services
- a computerised inventory system, bar-code recording of files, recording of retrieval.

Computerised data can also be stored off-site in the form of physical storage of back-up CD-ROMs, disks, tapes, etc. Alternatively, the data may be sent via a modem to be stored in an off-site computer – this is called 'vaulting'.

Advantages
- It saves space – expensive office space is not tied up storing archive files.
- It gives access to specialist equipment and staff – expensive computer equipment and specialist staff expertise can be accessed without the need to invest in capital equipment.
- Files are kept in good condition – the specialised storage areas maintain files in the best condition possible.
- High levels of security can be provided – the storage areas have specialist security provision.
- It reduces the risk of loss of computerised data from damage to buildings – storing back-ups off-site reduces the risk of important data being lost from fire, flood or bomb damage to buildings.
- Expansion is not a problem – the storage facility provides additional space as required.

Disadvantages
- The cost – the service has to be paid for on an on-going basis.
- The access – files are not immediately available, up to 24 hours may be required for delivery of a file.
- The lack of control – the reliability of the service and the control of the files is subject to the quality of the service provided by the storage company.

Suggested activity

Housekeeping techniques

The purpose of all filing systems is to ensure the efficient and effective storage of information. The information system will define the procedures to be followed. Housekeeping techniques refer to general day-to-day good practice that ensure filing systems are maintained according to the procedures.

Paper-based systems

Papers should be filed daily, and current files returned to the filing cabinets at the end of the day. Filing should not be allowed to build up, as this means that papers and files are then more difficult to find. Use colour coding to make filing easier and quicker – coloured files, and matching coloured labels on the drawer/shelf location, can make filing much more efficient. Different coloured lever arch files can be used for different years.

Papers and files should be pre-sorted before filing – place them in a logical order – for example, in numerical or alphabetical order. This saves moving backwards and forwards between files and drawers.

Fix papers in files so that problems with pages getting out of order, or falling out of the file, are eliminated.

Files should be regularly updated to remove out-of-date material – every three to six months. Replace untidy, well-worn folders with new folders. Every six months remove files that are no longer current to the archive system.

Electronic systems

Files should be labelled with relevant file names: type of document, initials, dates, etc. For example:

letchajDec98

might be a file name representing:

Letter/Charles Hammer (author)/Andrew Jones (keyboard operator)/December 98 (date of origination)

They should be deleted when they are no longer required.

Create directories to store documents – for example, a directory for letters in date order, a directory for files prepared for a certain member of staff. Make daily back-ups. If you store documents on the hard disk, make a back-up on a floppy disk.

Filing equipment

The equipment used in filing systems can be categorised as:

- storage furniture
- filing aids
- computerised/electronic filing equipment
- microfilm/microfiche equipment.

Storage furniture

The basic item of storage furniture is the traditional horizontal drawer filing cabinet with two, three or four drawers. Another important item is card index storage equipment with single or multiple drawers, rotary card index and/or visible card index trays. The most suitable equipment for different types of file is shown in the table opposite.

Filing aids

There is a range of miscellaneous items of equipment designed to help with filing systems. Filing trays and baskets can be used to provide temporary storage of files and documents before they are filed. File sorters with compartments for the pre-sorting of documents prior to filing in the system are very useful. Large filing departments often use mobile filing trolleys. Other specialised items

Type of file	Equipment	Features
Index card storage	Index card boxes Card index drawers – single or multiple drawers Rotary card index Visible card index trays	Index cards can be easily seen Cards can be quickly checked
Document files	Traditional horizontal drawer filing cabinets	Lockable Fireproof Can be used with hanging pockets (suspension files)
	Lateral filing cabinets – cupboard or drawer style Rotary files are also available	Lockable Fireproof Can be used with suspension files Take up less space than traditional style cabinets Suspension files can be fitted More flexible filing provision in cupboard style cabinets
Lever arch and box files	Lateral filing cabinets – cupboard style, shelving units	Can be used with shelf separators/ file retainers to keep files upright and tidy Adjustable shelving, flexible in use and easy to move
Maps, drawings and artwork	Large cabinets with drawers that allow information to be filed flat	Lockable Fireproof
Computer media, disks, CD-ROMs	Disk boxes CD-ROM files Multimedia racks	Lockable

of equipment are available, and information about these can be found in a good office equipment/stationery catalogue.

Computerised/electronic filing equipment

The components of an electronic filing system are shown in Figure 6.1.14.

Organisations that use electronic filing systems usually have their computers linked together in a network. The network can be a local system within one geographical location, known as a Local Area Network (LAN). More complex systems may be based over a range of geographical locations and linked by telephone lines, known as a Wide Area Network (WAN). The advantages of using a network for storing and managing information are: information is available to a range of users over a wide area; information can be entered, transferred and retrieved virtually instantaneously; 'real-time' systems mean that information is always up-to-date – for example,

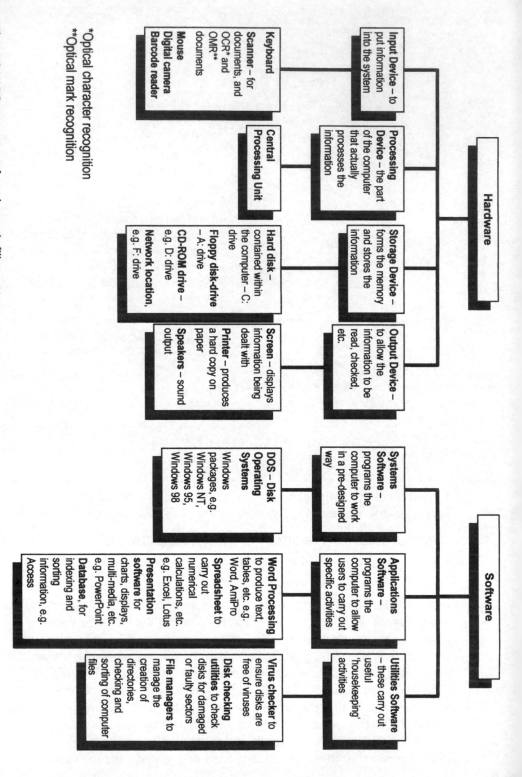

Figure 6.1.14 Components of an electronic filing system

*Optical character recognition
**Optical mark recognition

banking systems, holiday and airline booking systems;
the computer can track and record users of information.

Microfilm/microfiche equipment

Microfilm and microfiche are two variants of a photographic system that stores images of printed papers considerably reduced in size on a negative film. They are usually used for long-term storage of information and archiving of records. The negative image is prepared in two forms: microfilm where the images are stored in a long strip on a reel; or microfiche where groups of images are stored on a sheet about the size of a postcard. Alternatively, single images may be stored on cards, with a cut-out aperture where the image is placed. The microfiche may be mounted in jackets – transparent holders the same size as the microfiche – in which the microfiche images are stored for easy, long-term access.

Microfilm and microfiche systems may use the following equipment:

- *microfilm camera* – to produce the image from the paper files
- *reader* – a screen that displays the reduced image at normal size so that the information can be read
- *printer* – converts the image into a printed image similar to the original
- *reader/printer* – combines the facilities of reading and printing the image.

The reduction in size means a considerable saving of space, and this is the main reason for the use of this system. It is also very useful if the original documents are large and difficult to store – for example, maps, plans and drawings. The major disadvantages with using microfilm/microfiche are:

- *the cost of the equipment* – specialist bureaux can be used to produce the film, but reading and printing facilities are still required to view it
- *indexing problems* – an accurate index is required in order that information can be easily retrieved
- *storage difficulties* – the film and fiche can deteriorate in quality if they are stored in areas that are damp, too hot, etc.
- *poor quality printed documents* – the documents printed from the film/fiche can be of very poor quality and detail can be difficult to see.

One particular reason for using microfilm and microfiche systems for storing information is that they are independent of computer technology. Information may need to be retrieved over a long period of time, perhaps five to ten years, and technological change is so rapid that during this time computer systems may have changed and disks or CD-ROM storage may no longer be compatible with updated hardware and software.

Computer output to microfilm

COM, computer output to microfilm, is a system where the computer information can be output directly to microfilm without being processed on paper. This system includes indexing facilities to reference and store the microfilm. The image can be viewed on the VDU and hard copies produced using a printer. The equipment is expensive and would be used where large volumes of archive data need to be stored. For example, banks would use COM to store archive copies of customer bank statements.

Quality systems – ISO 9000

ISO 9000 is a series of internationally defined quality standards that relate primarily to organisations that design, produce, install and test products. The standards require an organisation to have a quality manual and fully-documented procedures that define the correct operation of the organisation. The standards also require organisations to have a system of quality checks or 'audits' to ensure there is compliance with the procedures. The ISO standards are produced by the International Organisation for Standardisation, a non-governmental organisation based in Geneva, Switzerland.

Adoption and implementation of ISO 9000 standards is voluntary. However, companies who adopt and implement the standards can become ISO 9000 registered companies. The ISO standards process is shown in Figure 6.1.15.

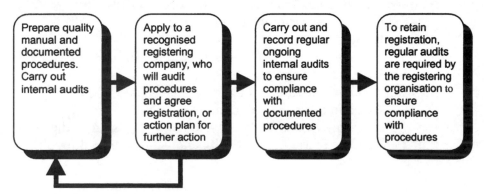

Figure 6.1.15 The ISO standards process

There are many benefits to an organisation in becoming an ISO 9000 registered company:

Quality checks. The use and production of quality manuals and documented procedures form the basis of quality checks and can have further benefits for staff training and staff reference.

Increased market opportunities. Some companies will only deal with ISO registered companies. European community regulations require registration for certain companies. Particular market sectors require ISO registration for suppliers, especially where safety is important.

International recognition. The registration is recognised in over 130 countries in the world.

Cost reductions. Using standard parts can be cheaper and money can be saved through the elimination of costly waste caused by poor-quality operation.

Improved customer service. The improvement in quality and reliability should reduce complaints.

Standardisation. Products have greater compatibility with other goods and services – for example, paper sizes, photographic film speeds, telephones and bankers' cards.

Improved health and safety. ISO standards include health and safety standards. Although many countries will have included these in their health and safety legislation, this may not be the case in some third world and emerging economies.

Quality audits are an integral part of a quality system. This means that there is a system of checking that the procedures are being correctly followed. Internal audits can be carried out by the organisation's staff to ensure standards are being maintained. External audits may be carried out by customers, or by the registering body. All audits should be recorded to provide evidence of compliance and non-compliance and non-compliance should generate corrective actions. These actions should then be checked to ensure they have been implemented.

The following activities are involved in an audit.

Observation. Staff carrying out processes can be observed to ensure they are following procedures correctly. An appropriate checklist should be designed for the observation, and this should be completed with the full details of the observation.

Document check. The documents completed as part of the procedures can be checked to ensure the correct documents are being used and that they are being correctly completed. Any non-compliance should be recorded and corrective action taken.

Computer check. Some processes can be recorded on the computer, and summarised on regular printouts. These printouts can then be checked and any non-compliance dealt with.

Monitoring of customer complaints to identify problem areas and identify corrective action.

The records of an internal audit should be available for the external auditor. Further information about ISO standards can be found on the ISO website:

http://www.iso.ch

Documented procedures

Procedures will exist for all activities carried out within an organisation. They may either be formalised and documented or form part of custom and practice. Even if an organisation does not intend to become registered as an ISO organisation, it is still good practice to formalise and document company procedures because they:

* can be used as part of staff training
* provide support and guidelines for staff, particularly in non-routine situations
* ensure consistency of operation
* provide standards for checking and monitoring staff actions
* can ensure legal and regulatory requirements are correctly followed – for example, health and safety, confidentiality, data protection.

Guidelines for preparing a set of procedures
* Make them 'fit for the purpose' – complicated procedures should not be required for routine, straightforward activities.
* Present them as lists of points, rather than as dense paragraphs of text.
* List them in logical order – for example, pre-sorting documents should come before filing them.
* Make contingency arrangements – for example, where actions are to be taken if files cannot be found.
* Date all procedure documents and record the issue number in the footer of each page.

* Include checks and audit requirements.

Procedures and documentation may need to be submitted for approval to a Quality Committee before they can be adopted. An example of some documented procedures is shown in Figure 6.1.16.

Storage and Retrieval of Copy Invoices

Prepared by Grant Matthews, Office Administrator
Issue 1.1 January ----

ACCOUNTS OFFICE STAFF
A copy of all invoices issued by the company shall be kept in the Accounts Office main filing system.
All invoices printed each day shall be passed to the Administrator by 3.30 pm.

ADMINISTRATOR
Hole-punch copy invoices.
Pre-sort into numerical order.
File according to date of issue in relevant monthly invoice lever arch file stored in Filing Cabinet 2.
File all invoices by the end of the day.
Photocopy invoices for departments that request invoices.
Check there are sufficient blue file markers available in the envelope provided on the door.
At the end of the week, check file for blue file markers and request return of invoices.
Report any problems with missing invoices, or problems with the return of files, to the Office Manager.

STAFF REMOVING AN INVOICE
When removing an invoice, place a blue file marker with your name and the invoice number in the file location. The blue file markers are available in the envelope on the door.
Return all copy invoices to the file by 3.30 pm on Friday afternoon of each week.

STAFF REPLACING AN INVOICE
Replace the file in the correct date file and in the correct numerical order.
Remove the blue file marker and return to the envelope provided.

NOTE: ALL INVOICES SHOULD BE RETURNED TO THE FILE BY 3.30 PM EACH FRIDAY.

Procedure check
The Office Manager will make regular checks of the invoice file (minimum of monthly) between 4.00 and 5.00 pm on a Friday. It should be complete and in correct numerical order. The file check will be noted on the check sheet (CS21) pasted to the inside of the file. Any non-compliance will be noted on the check sheet, together with recommended action. The Administrator must carry out actions by the following Monday lunchtime, and action taken should be initialled on the check sheet.

Proc.copinv/GM/iss1.1/Jan--

Figure 6.1.16 Documented procedures

The investigation of the use of documented procedures could form the basis of a report for Element 6.1. It could include:

- investigation of the organisation's filing practice
- identification of suitable procedures
- investigation into documented procedures used in another organisation
- investigation into the use of equipment in the procedures
- investigation into the inclusion of training, security, safety in the procedures
- comparison of costs of informal and documented procedures
- analysis of the informal and documented procedures for:
  - user-friendliness
  - suitability for the job
  - speed of retrieval
  - cost
  - flexibility (including expansion possibilities)
  - access
  - security.

Health and safety

While the general health and safety rules apply to all storage and retrieval systems, there are specific issues that can be identified.

Filing cabinets

Traditional filing cabinets with drawers can present problems. They can topple over if the top drawers are opened together, though modern cabinets are fitted with safety features that ensure only one drawer can be opened at a time. Similar problems can occur if heavy files are stored in the top drawers while the bottom drawers remain empty. There is a tendency to start a filing system by filling the top drawer, but files should be distributed evenly between the drawers. Drawers that are left open can cause a hazard for staff tripping or bumping into them.

Shelves

The storage of files on shelves can also cause problems when files are lifted from the top shelves. Safety steps should be provided so those files can be removed without staff needing to stretch, or stand on chairs, desks, etc.

Transportation of files

If heavy and bulky files need to be carried between offices, a trolley should be provided to ensure lifting and tripping incidents do not occur.

Legal and regulatory requirements for the storage and retention of information

The main issues that relate to the legal and regulatory requirements for the storage and retention of information are:

- general legal requirements that determine how long information is stored – see the earlier section on archiving (pages 279–280)
- Data Protection Act – refers to the storage of computerised information about individuals (see the appendix on pages 539–45); all activities relating to the storage and retrieval of this information should comply with the law
- employees who have access to confidential information that would materially affect the value of a company's shares are prevented from dealing in the shares, or disclosing the information to others who may also benefit from the sale or purchase of shares; this is controlled under the Company Securities (Insider Dealing) Act 1985
- the storage, retrieval and provision of information in certain organisations – for example, defence organisations and government departments, may be controlled by the Official Secrets Act.

Confidentiality and security

Information needs to be kept confidential for the following reasons.

- *Legal* – there are legal and regulatory requirements relating to information, as listed above.
- *Commercial* – product information, marketing, customer lists, etc. can all be valuable information to competitors.
- *Management* – internal management information may be very confidential – for example, redundancy, promotion, pay, future policies, relocation, restructuring.
- *Technical* – product technical details, product development, processes and research are all very confidential. Patents, inventions, designs and copyright are often referred to as 'intellectual property'. The ownership and use of this information is known as 'intellectual property rights' and is covered by

legislation such as the Patents Act 1977 and the Patents, Designs and Marks Act 1986.

Any information system should include proper provision for confidentiality and security. The following steps can be included in the system.

- *Staff training* – provision for suitable staff training, at induction and on an ongoing basis, to ensure staff are fully aware of confidentiality issues.
- *Comprehensive procedures* – these should take account of confidentiality – for example, listing authority to access files, provision for the separate storage of very sensitive files.
- *Provision of suitable environment and equipment* – lockable cabinets that are kept locked, offices that are locked when unsupervised. General office security should also ensure visitors do not have access to confidential or secure areas.
- *Suitable disposal of confidential information* – provision of shredders with suitable levels of shredding for different security and sensitivity levels. Shreddings should be bagged for removal by a security officer.
- *Provision of adequate password protection* – passwords on computer files, use of screen savers and suitable siting of display screens. Passwords should be changed regularly, and several levels of password may be needed for various levels of information. Very confidential information may be subject to encryption, which is a system for coding information so that it cannot be used without the decoding software.

There are times when staff are asked for information that is stored in the system. Staff should be clear about the procedures and authority for providing information. This can be covered in training and in procedures.

The issues considered so far in confidentiality and security have related to information being kept confidential and only being accessible to authorised users. However, there are also issues of security which relate to information being kept safe. Information is very important to organisations, and if it should become lost or damaged in any way, the organisation may not be able to operate effectively. Information may be subject to the risks shown in the following table.

Risk	Safeguard
Paper-based systems	
Destruction by flood or fire	Fireproof and waterproof cabinets, provision of adequate fire extinguishers, smoke alarms, sprinklers in storage area; no smoking
Deterioration by poor storage conditions – for example, damp, excessive heat	Storage of files in an area with suitable temperature and humidity controls; use of specialist storage facilities
Destruction by vandals, malicious damage or terrorism – for example, terrorist bombs	General security controls – controlled access and exit,security guards, CCTV, general staff awareness
Files being removed and stolen	Lockable cabinets, lockable rooms
Electronic systems	
Destruction of information by physical damage to computer hardware – for example, flood or fire	Provision of adequate fire extinguishers, smoke alarms; no smoking
Deterioration in poor storage conditions – for example, disks being incorrcctly stored near a source of magnetism or heat	Provision of specific disk storage boxes, temperature and humidity controlled environment
Destruction by vandals, malicious damage or terrorism – for example, information being deleted from the system	General security controls – controlled access and exit, security guards, CCTV, general staff awareness, use of passwords, regular back-ups of data
Destruction by viruses	Rigorous virus checking, regular back-ups of data, control of disks that are used in the system, particularly when they are transferred from home or other computer systems. Filters on e-mail and Internet systems
Destruction and damage caused by operator error	Suitable training and monitoring of users, regular back-ups, software that is user-friendly and not sensitive to operator error

Portfolio activity 6.1 **Number 2**

You should already have agreed on an information storage and retrieval system to evaluate and the terms of reference for your report, and have prepared an action plan. Now carry out the following activities.

a) Evaluate the existing information storage and retrieval system you are investigating. Record the activities you carry out as part of your evaluation.

b) Consult with users of the system. Remember to include managers, direct users of the information and the filing staff. Record the arrangements you made for the consultation and record the outcome of the consultation. Discuss the future use of the system with the people who use it.

c) Plan and carry out research to look at alternative systems. The areas of research should include comparisons of equipment, classification methods, cross-referencing, retrieval procedures, tracking procedures, confidentiality and security, space, archiving, expansion, costs, and legal requirements. The sources of research could include: reviews of relevant literature – for example, administration textbooks; information on computerised systems; manufacturers' handbooks; office equipment literature; the Internet; CD-ROMs/computerised data; visits to look at alternative systems.

d) Select and organise the information into a suitable form – for example, using a computer to enter data onto a spreadsheet, word processing package and/or presentation software.

e) Look at the information you have collected and analyse the effectiveness and efficiency of the information storage and retrieval system. Compare this with anticipated future needs. The following criteria should be used for evaluation:
   – user-friendliness
   – suitability for the job
   – speed of retrieval
   – cost
   – flexibility
   – access
   – security.

Make sure you clearly differentiate between your findings – what you actually found out – and the interpretation – what the implications of the findings are in relation to the system you are evaluating.

f) Prepare a formal report for your line manager. Include recommendations for improvement and describe the implications for those affected. The recommendations must be fully justified and supported by evidence of your research.

The following evidence should be collected:

• records of activities carried out as part of the evaluation*
• records of consultation with other users*
• records and findings of research*

- formal report
- personal statement to explain how you carried out the research, evaluated information and prepared the report.

* These should be included in the full report within the procedures, findings, conclusions, recommendations, appendices and bibliography and therefore may not need to be included separately.

Note

Information about questionnaires, interview techniques, carrying out research and preparing reports is covered in Unit 5.

Performance criteria:	6.1.1	6.1.2	6.1.3	6.1.4	6.1.5
	6.1.6	6.1.7	6.1.8	6.1.9	6.1.10
Knowledge and understanding:	6.1.a	6.1.b	6.1.c	6.1.d	6.1.e
	6.1.f	6.1.g	6.1.h	6.1.i	6.1.j
	6.1.k	6.1.l	6.1.m	6.1.n	6.1.o
	6.1.p	6.1.q	6.1.r	6.1.s	
Evidence requirements:	6.1.1	6.1.2	6.1.3	6.1.4	6.1.5
	6.1.6	6.1.7	6.1.8	6.1.9	6.1.10
	6.1.11	6.1.12	6.1.13	6.1.14	6.1.15
	6.1.16	6.1.17	6.1.18	6.1.19	6.1.20
	6.1.21	6.1.22	6.1.23	6.1.24	6.1.25
	6.1.26	6.1.27	6.1.28	6.1.29	6.1.30
	6.1.31	6.1.32	6.1.33	6.1.34	6.1.35
	6.1.36	6.1.37	6.1.38	6.1.39	6.1.40

Test yourself

Knowledge and understanding	Questions
a	Describe the different types of paper-based and electronic information storage and retrieval systems.
b	Give four different methods of classifying information.
c	Explain what is meant by referencing systems.
d	Explain what is meant by archiving systems.
e	Explain what is meant by expansion possibilities, with reference to an information storage system.

f	Explain what is meant by housekeeping techniques, with reference to an information storage system.
g	Give examples of two types of equipment available, with reference to an information storage system.
h	Explain the implications of ISO 9000 on storage and retrieval systems.
i	Explain the implications of health and safety legistlation and legal and regulatory requirements relating to the storage and retention of information.
j	Describe the techniques you can use to learn about information storage and retrieval systems.
k	Describe how you have used the Internet and other electronic storage systems to select and extract relevant information about information storage and retrieval systems.
l	Explain the importance of security and confidentiality in relation to storage, retention and provision of information.
m	Describe the questioning techniques you can use to obtain information about information storage and retrieval systems.
n	Explain how you communicate effectively with colleagues at all levels.
o	Explain how you can interpret statistical and non-statistical information about information storage and retrieval systems.
p	Explain how you analyse and extract data about information storage and retrieval systems.
q	Explain how you plan and organise your time effectively when researching information storage and retrieval systems.
r	Show three different ways of presenting findings about information storage and retrieval systems to ensure maximum impact.
s	Describe the structure of a report that looks at an information storage and retrieval system.

Element 6.2

MONITOR AND SUPERVISE AN INDIVIDUAL IN THE USE OF AN INFORMATION STORAGE AND RETRIEVAL SYSTEM

Supervision and monitoring

Supervision is the direction and overseeing of the performance of another member of staff. The individual carrying out the activity should know what they have to do, how to do it and what standards are expected to ensure they have carried out the task successfully. Overseeing the activity implies an active ongoing check that activities are being carried out correctly. However, just as important is the ability to build up a positive working relationship with the individual you are supervising.

Directing the activity is the first stage of the supervision process. This can include:

- clearly defining and identifying the tasks to be carried out – for example, to file all outstanding copy invoices in the copy invoice file
- providing clear instructions and procedures to be followed, including the quality standards that define acceptable performance – for example, filing procedures (see the procedures earlier in this unit, pages 288–289); quality and quantity guidelines should be included – for example, that all files should be correctly filed by the end of the day
- ensuring suitable resources are available – for example, hole punch, suitable filing stationery, lever arch files, photocopier
- dealing with any queries or problems that may arise – for example, being available to deal with any questions; this is particularly important when the individual has no experience of completing the task
- providing suitable training to enable the individual to carry out the tasks effectively; the training can consist of formalised training sessions, demonstrations, coaching and ongoing advice – remember in any training session to ensure you go at a suitable pace for the trainee, allowing them to ask questions and check with them regularly that they understand each stage of the activity.

When the individual has received the direction and training required, they can then carry out the activity. This is when you need to ensure you monitor their progress. You should explain to the individual that you are going to monitor their activities, and the methods you are going to use. However, your monitoring should be unobtrusive and should be undertaken while the individual is routinely carrying out the activity. Monitoring methods can include the following.

Observation of performance. You can watch the individual carrying out the activity. It is a good idea to record this observation and this can be done using a checklist (an example of a monitoring checklist is given in Figure 6.2.1). The checklist will help you to focus on the key aspects of the performance. It is a good idea to show the individual the checklist before they start the activity – this helps them to be clearer about what is required of them.

Checking the performance outcome, the actual product. For example, files can be checked to ensure invoices have been correctly filed and written records used in filing systems can be checked by looking at whether out-cards have been completed.

Collecting feedback from other users of the system. Checking with other users of the system will indicate how reliably the system is operating and will also identify any problems.

Collecting feedback from the individual. Regular reviews should be carried out with the individual to check on how the system is working. The individual should be given the opportunity to have input into ways in which the system may be improved.

Developing a supervisor relationship

The key factor in supervision is the relationship between the supervisor and the individual. All staff working in an organisation belong to a team working together to achieve the organisation's objectives. The supervisor and individual are part of that team, and good teamwork is essential. The establishment of a good supervisor relationship is part of teambuilding. The relationship should be built on trust, co-operation and achievement of common goals. A careful balance needs to be maintained between support, advice, guidance and criticism. The relationship is a two-way process and there are expectations and responsibilities on both sides that need to be maintained (see Figure 6.2.2).

Name of supervisor	
Name of individual	
Date of activity	

Activity	Yes	No	Comment
Hole-punch copy invoices, ensuring holes are central			
Pre-sort invoices into numerical order			
Select the correct lever arch files from Cabinet 2			
File invoices correctly in the relevant monthly invoice file			
Replace lever arch files correctly in Cabinet 2			
Follow relevant health and safety rules			

Figure 6.2.1 A monitoring checklist

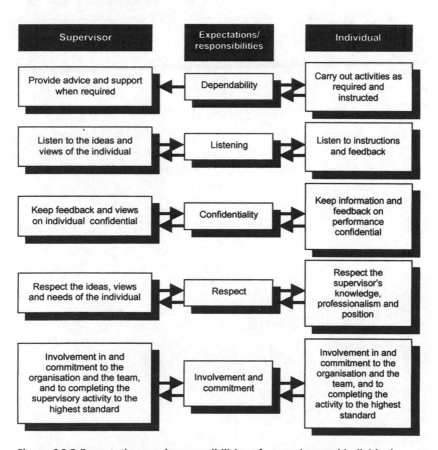

Figure 6.2.2 Expectations and responsibilities of supervisor and individual

Portfolio activity 6.2 **Number 1**

You are required to monitor an individual in the use of an information storage and retrieval system (paper-based and/or electronic).

a) Arrange and record a meeting with your assessor and/or workplace supervisor and agree the individual to be supervised and the filing system to be used. This is best carried out as part of your normal work-based supervisory duties. However, if this is not possible you could arrange to supervise a work-experience trainee or a colleague. Alternatively, your training centre may have a business centre, training office or model office where you could arrange to supervise a suitable trainee. Agree an action plan with your supervisor.

b) Prepare a clearly written set of operating instructions for the information storage retrieval system. These instructions should be easy to follow and understand. They should be written in a style suitable for all levels of staff using the system.

c) Prepare a training session for the individual covering:
   – explanation of the instructions and a practical demonstration
   – your organisation's requirements
   – legal requirements
   – security and confidentiality of information.

d) Design a way of checking that the individual has understood the training – this can be with written questions or oral questions. Whichever method is used, the answers should be recorded.

e) Arrange and carry out the training session with the individual. It is a good idea to get your assessor to observe you carrying out the instruction.

The following evidence should be collected:

• written set of instructions
• set of operating instructions
• plans for a training session
• completed record of checking that the individual has understood the training
• evidence to show you have carried out the training session – for example, observation report, video, personal statement where you explain what you did, how you carried it out, how you gave feedback
• witness testimony from the trainee.

Performance criteria:	6.2.3	6.2.6	6.2.7	6.2.8	
Knowledge and understanding:	6.2.k	6.2.m	6.2.o	6.2.p	6.2.q
Evidence requirements:	6.2.1 6.2.6	6.2.2	6.2.3	6.2.4	6.2.5

Identifying, defining and assessing competence

The purpose of the monitoring and supervisory activity is to ensure an individual is 'competent'. Competence is the ability to consistently carry out a task to the required standards. It is about what an individual 'can do', but implies that the individual also has knowledge and understanding of why an activity is carried out, the associated health and safety legislation, etc.

The process of identifying, defining and assessing competence is very similar to the process already outlined as the stages in the supervisory process.

The key activity needs to be identified – for example, filing. It is then possible to define the key components of that activity in a series of statements – for example, 'ensure security and confidentiality of information'. These statements are the key criteria that make up an activity and they should contain the measures of the activity. It should be possible to identify the actions that would be required to achieve that competence – for example, ensuring the filing cabinet is locked at the end of the day or ensuring passwords are used on the computer.

The individual can then be assessed. The assessor has to make a judgement about whether a candidate has achieved competence in all the criteria listed. This can be done using the methods on page 302.

Standards of achievement

The identification and definition of standards is formalised with National Vocational Qualifications (NVQs). These are sets of standards for an occupational area – for example, administration. They are defined from levels 1–5, level one being basic operator and level five senior management level. Each set of standards is structured in the same way: Units, Elements, Performance Criteria, Range Statements and Knowledge.

Assessment activity	Evidence collected
Observation of the individual completing the activity	Observation report completed by the assessor, listing all the actions seen and the criteria covered
Assessment of products, the finished product of the activity – for example, a copy of a letter, a fax message	Letters, memos, fax messages, reports
Witness testimonies completed by colleagues specifying the activities completed by the individual	Witness testimony statements
Personal statement from the candidate explaining in detail the activities they complete	Personal statement
Questioning to check knowledge. This can be done orally, or with written questions	Written questions and answers, written questions and a record of oral answers, records of any other questions asked

Each unit is made up of elements and performance criteria. In an NVQ, the Performance Criteria are the activities to be carried out, including the quality and quantity standards – for example, effectively supervise and monitor an individual in the operation of

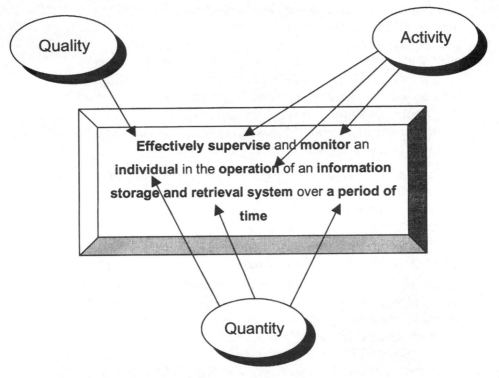

Figure 6.2.3 Key activity statement

an information storage and retrieval system over a period of time (see Figure 6.2.3). The Range refers to a range of situations in which the activity can take place – for example, the range for the storage and retrieval system could include paper-based and electronic storage systems.

The standards used for the Higher Diploma in Administrative Procedures are very similar to those used in an NVQ.

If, as part of your job as supervisor, you are assessing candidates against National Vocational Standards you may want to gain an assessor qualification. The NVQ assessor qualifications are currently:

TDLB D32 – Assess Candidate Performance

TDLB D33 – Assess Candidates using Differing Sources of Evidence

Legislation

The employment legislation that relates to supervisory activities is Equal Opportunities legislation and Disability Discrimination legislation. This legislation is dealt with in the appendix on pages 539–45. The main implications relate to dealing fairly with all the individuals you supervise. The clear definition of activities and the use of checklists, etc. can help to eliminate unfair judgements. As a supervisor you should give the necessary support and ensure appropriate resources to enable any disabled individual to achieve competence.

Organisation's procedures

As a supervisor you should be clear about your role as such, as defined in the job description. You may only have responsibility to supervise within a particular activity – someone else may be the individual's line manager. Care has to be taken that supervision is kept within the defined boundaries – for example, the supervisor may have responsibility for an individual filing copy invoices, but have no authority to comment on the individual's punctuality or attendance. Such issues should be dealt with by the relevant line manager.

Giving feedback

Feedback is the final part of the supervisory and monitoring process. Once the initial training and input has been followed by completion of the activity and the monitoring process, trainees need feedback on their performance. The following factors should be considered when giving feedback.

Consistency. Both the supervisor and the individual being supervised should be clear about what is required from the activity and the standards required. The supervisor should discuss monitoring, checklists, etc. with the individual before monitoring takes place. Individuals can be very demotivated when they feel that the 'goalposts are constantly being moved'.

Timing. Give feedback as soon as possible after the activity has been completed. Sufficient time should also be allowed for the feedback to be carried out thoroughly.

Environment. Choose a suitable environment for giving feedback. A quiet room is better than a busy office where interruptions from telephones, etc. can occur.

Confidentiality. Ensure feedback is confidential.

Be positive. Give praise and positive feedback first and on an ongoing basis. Do not fall into the trap of only giving feedback when it is negative or critical.

Be constructive. Where problems are occurring and standards are not being met, give feedback in a constructive way. Explain the actions that are needed to improve the performance. For example, rather than saying, 'You're not using the correct date when filing the invoice', say, 'Check that you're filing the invoice by the date shown in the top right-hand corner of the invoice. If this date is not clear, check the invoice number on the computer.'

Clearly identify and allocate any follow-up actions. Further training, provision of sufficient resources and information to other staff may all be needed to improve performance. Make sure that you clearly identify to the individual what they need to do and what actions you need to take. For example, as a supervisor you might ask other accounting staff to make sure they put the copy invoices in the filing tray during the course of the day, so that the individual you are supervising is not left with a lot of copy invoices to file at the end of the day.

Portfolio activity 6.2 **Number 2**

Design a checklist to be used to monitor an individual's use of a storage and retrieval system. The checklist must include: speed of retrieval; compliance with the organisation's requirements; compliance with legal requirements; and security and confidentiality of information.

Carry out supervision of an individual using an information storage and retrieval system over a period of time. Complete the checklist each time you carry out the supervision. Use the checklist to give feedback to the individual. Arrange for your assessor to observe you monitoring and giving feedback on at least one occasion. The following evidence should be collected:

- sample checklist
- checklists completed each time an individual has been monitored – a minimum of twice
- witness testimony from the individual being supervised
- observation report from your assessor
- personal statement written by you explaining your checklist design, how you carried out the monitoring and how you gave feedback.

Performance criteria:	6.2.1	6.2.2	6.2.5	6.2.6	6.2.8
Knowledge and understanding:	6.2.m	6.2.n	6.2.o		
Evidence requirements:	6.2.3	6.2.4	6.2.5	6.2.6	6.2.7
	6.2.8	6.2.9	6.2.10	6.2.11	6.2.12
	6.2.13				

Test yourself

Knowledge and understanding	Questions
a	Describe the different types of paper-based and electronic information storage and retrieval systems.
b	Give four different methods of classifying information.
c	Explain what is meant by referencing systems.
d	Explain what is meant by archiving systems.
e	Explain what is meant by expansion possibilities, with reference to an information storage system.
f	Explain what is meant by housekeeping techniques, with reference to an information storage system.

g	Give examples of two types of equipment available, with reference to an information storage system.
h	Explain the importance of controlling a filing system.
	Explain why it is important that a filing system is simple and information can be retrieved quickly.
i	Explain what is meant by booking in/out and tracer systems and procedures.
j	Explain the implications of health and safety legislation and legal and regulatory requirements relating to the storage and retention of information.
k	Explain the importance of security and confidentiality in relation to storage, retention and provision of information.
l	Describe the questioning techniques you can use to obtain information about information storage and retrieval systems.
m	Explain how you communicate effectively with colleagues at all levels.
n	Describe three different methods of identifying, defining and assessing the competence of individuals.
o	Explain how you would coach, advise and instruct individuals in the use of an information storage and retrieval system.
	Describe how you can you provide constructive feedback to an individual you are supervising.
p	Explain the implications of employment legislation and the organisation's procedures in relation to supervisory activities.
q	Explain how you can compose effective written and visual instructions using appropriate tone, style and vocabulary for the use of an information storage and retrieval system.

Activity 6.1

Memo

> # MEMORANDUM
>
> **To:** Office Administrator
> **From:** John Williams, Company Secretary
> **Date:** Monday, -- -- --
>
> **Researching information**
>
> We are starting on our review of systems and procedures. The first system for review is our information storage and retrieval system. Please prepare a set of notes for me for a meeting listing the key factors that determine the efficiency and effectiveness of a storage system.

Activity 6.2

E-mail message

> **E-mail**
>
> **To:**   Office Administrator
> **From:**   Jenny Pollock
> **Date:**   Tuesday, -- -- --
> **Subject:** Electronic storage systems
>
> We are currently putting all our customer records on computer and some members of the sales team are not sure about the benefits of using computerised systems for storing information. I am giving a presentation for them at the next sales meeting. Please prepare a handout outlining the advantages of electronic storage systems. Remember that the sales team all have portable computers that can be linked to the main system. It would be a good idea to give examples of how the electronic storage system would benefit them.

Activity 6.3

Desknote

DESKNOTE

From: John Williams
Date: wednesday, -- -- --

The organisation review outlined the need for a much more systematic approach to our filing systems. All files will be centrally filed, but we need to decide on a standardised method of classifying information that will cope with files from all the different departments. Please write a brief report about methods of classification and give your recommendations for a suitable method to be adopted in a centralised system.

John

Activity 6.4

Memo

MEMORANDUM

To: Office Administrator
From: John Williams
Date: Thursday, -- -- --

Archiving

Our system for storing our archive files has broken down. There seem to be boxes of files in all sorts of cupboards and storage areas. Orders are having to be made for new filing cabinets because the cabinets are filling up with out-of-date information. Important archive files are going missing. At a recent management meeting I agreed that you would research options for archiving and give a presentation at the next meeting. Please prepare a presentation, with your notes, on options for organising our archiving more logically.

Activity 6.5

Memo

MEMORANDUM

To: Office Administrator
From: Henry Yusuf, Personnel Department
Date: Friday, -- -- --

Supervisor training

Many of the administrators now have administrative assistants and need some training on supervisory skills. Please prepare a suitable handout to be given to them at a training meeting.

7 Contribute to Financial Planning and Control Activities

The management of financial resources is a very important feature of an organisation's activities. This unit looks at the financial activities that may be part of the administrator's role in estimating, recording and controlling income and expenditure.

Element 7.1
DRAFT A BUDGET

A budget is an itemised financial statement showing the planned allocation of resources over a specified period. It is a very important management tool for the planning, control and monitoring of spending. A feature of budgeting is forecasting (the prediction of future income and expenditure). The budgets prepared by the various departments and/or activities will all be included in a 'master budget' that will then be used to prepare a forecast set of final accounts. These predicted final accounts can help management to identify the profit- and loss-making activities in the organisation. This information is then used by management to make policy decisions about the future of the business. The careful ongoing control and monitoring of the budget can also alert management to problem areas, and corrective action can then be taken.

There are many reasons why an organisation should prepare budgets. Budgets provide standards for the measurement of performance, and enable greater accountability for the decisions and activities of budget holders and their staff if their budgets are not met. There is consequently a greater understanding by budget holders and staff of the implications of their costs, and their contribution to overall income and spending. Preparation of budgets ensures time is spent on thinking and planning for the future, as well as dealing with current activities. Critical analysis of income and spending can generate changes to working methods and practices – for example, overspending a budget on postal costs could lead staff to look at different methods of sending information, cheaper services or reducing the number of documents sent.

The use of budgetary planning, monitoring and control represents good management practice. However, there are several limitations that can arise from the use of budgets. Careful management of the budget process can help to reduce these limitations. The main limitations are as follows.

- Budgets can be very inflexible and may reinforce poor business practice, or lead to poor business decisions. For example, a college department might have a very limited budget for books, thereby causing staff time and photocopying costs to be incurred on preparing materials. This could easily represent a higher cost than if books had been purchased in the first place.
- The reliance on budgets as a measure of performance can be very restrictive. Managers may spend their time ensuring budget targets are met, rather than developing new business methods or creating new business opportunities. For example, a course manager in college might spend a lot of time ensuring staff did not exceed the photocopying budget, rather than developing innovative courses that will generate increased long-term income.
- Spending can become budget led. Managers may find they have money left in the budget which must be spent by the end of the financial year. In these situations unwise spending decisions may be made.
- Unspent budget may be 'clawed back' by the organisation and lead to a reduced budget in the following year. Efficient departments and managers may feel they are being penalised for their efforts.

There are two types of budget: **capital** and **operational**.

Capital budgets

Capital budgets relate to planned expenditure on *capital items* which are fixed assets, such as machinery and equipment purchased by the organisation. Capital items have a value that could be realised by a later sale, and they are usually represented as *assets* in the company's financial statement – for example, computer equipment. The resale value of the capital item usually reduces with time, and this loss is written off as *depreciation* in annual accounts. Capital budgets are usually planned over a long period – for example, three years – as capital items usually have a long-term use. Capital budgets may also involve relatively large sums of money, as equipment and machinery can represent a high cost.

The organisation may acquire the use of capital items by hiring or leasing them. In this case, the equipment is provided by a leasing company for the payment of an annual cost and the equipment is not an asset as it is not owned by the organisation. When the leasing contract is finished, the equipment is returned to the leasing company. Leasing usually represents a short-term cash saving as the cost of the use of the equipment can be spread over several years. There may be tax advantages to leasing as compared to capital expenditure and leasing equipment also has the advantages that maintenance costs are included in the contract, and items can be easily replaced with more up-to-date equipment. However, leasing equipment can work out more expensive in the long term, as the annual leasing costs add up each year and can represent a higher cost than the capital purchase.

Operational budgets

Operational budgets (also called **revenue budgets**) are used to show the planned income and expenditure of a specific business activity for a period of time – for example, the administrative budget or sales budget. The budget would show the income and then detail the estimated expenditure for all the ongoing costs. An operational budget would include the expenditure on *consumables* and the depreciation on capital items. Consumable items differ from capital items in that they retain no value once they have been used – for example, computer ink cartridges, paper, hotel accommodation, equipment leasing costs.

Sources of income

The budget represents a detailed allocation of how income will be spent. The amount of money available in a budget may be determined in a number of ways, including the following.

- *Allocated historical income* – a sum of money may be allocated to an activity – based on historical usage – for example, an annual departmental administrative budget. It may be increased each year in line with inflation. It may also be decreased in line with the organisation's cutbacks. This is a cost-effective method of allocating budgets and ensures stability. Spending decisions may be made on a long-term basis.
- *Bid for income* – a bid for an allocation of money may have to be prepared and presented to management. This bid may represent

a sum of money for a specific project – for example, a training budget – or it may be required each year for ongoing expenses. This method allows for a more critical look at costs, but it can be time-consuming for staff to prepare bids and can also be unsettling. In addition, only short-term spending decisions tend to be made when income cannot be guaranteed over a long term.

* *Charged income* – a budget may be prepared related to income – for example, a budget for a conference that will generate conference fees. The income is estimated and the budget prepared to allocate the costs. The budget may also be used to determine the cost charged for the activity – for example, the delegate cost.

* *Management allocation* – the management may determine a budget for an activity and relate this to the administrator. The administrator then looks at how the various costs can be allocated against the sum provided – for example, organising a dinner or training activity.

Budget costs

The costs to be calculated for an activity will depend on the activity involved. They can be listed under the following expense headings.

* *Labour expenses* – the labour cost should include both the hourly rate/salary paid and the additional costs to the organisation of employing the labour. These additional costs may be *direct* costs – for example, employer's National Insurance costs or employer's pension contributions – or *indirect* such as the cost of providing welfare and training for staff. See Figure 7.1.1 on page 316 for an example of a salary/wages calculation.

* *Material expenses* – the cost of materials required for the activity – for example, stationery, photocopying, printing.

* *Building/premises expenses* – building maintenance, rent and rates, water, buildings insurance, premise hire.

* *Fuel expenses* – electricity, heating.

* *Finance expenses* – interest to be paid on loans, discounts given for prompt payment.

* *Equipment expenses* – hire or leasing of equipment.

* *Administrative expenses* – telephone, postage, office expenses.

* *General expenses* – office cleaning, security costs.

* *Contingencies* – provision may be made for unforeseen future events such as the cost of repairing or replacing equipment that breaks down. Contingencies may also include a provision for inflation – that is, the general increase in costs and prices. A

contingency may be included in a postage budget, for example, to allow for the fact that the cost of first- and second-class postage might increase in the coming year.

Costs can also be defined as **fixed** or **variable costs**.

Fixed costs remain the same whatever the level of activity. For example, it might cost £150 to advertise a training event – this cost does not depend on the number of delegates attending the event and is therefore fixed.

Variable costs will vary depending on the level of activity. For example, the cost of refreshments for delegates at a training event will depend on the number of delegates attending and is therefore variable. An example of this can be seen in Unit 3 (page 148).

The budget should contain details of the costs to be incurred in carrying out an activity. The costs can usually be divided into **direct costs** and **indirect costs.**

Direct costs are those costs that are only incurred if the activity takes place – for example, salary paid to a trainer for a training course, hire of a hotel for a training course, travel expenses for the trainer, postage costs incurred for a mailshot, advertising for a training course.

Indirect costs are those costs that are incurred in the normal running of the organisation – for example, administrative costs, rent for premises, rates, insurance. These are often referred to as **overheads**. Allocation of a portion of the overheads is usually made for any project or activity. However, it is not possible to work out this apportionment exactly, and different organisations will have different methods of doing it. It is, therefore, important to discuss and agree this with the Accounts department before preparing a budget.

The total cost is calculated by adding the direct costs and the indirect costs:

Total cost = Direct costs + Indirect costs

Some common methods of determining overheads are as follows.

* *Cost ratio* – one simple method of determining overheads is to calculate them in relation to the direct cost – for example, 80% of the direct cost. Thus, if the direct cost of a training course was £500 then an overhead cost of 80% would be added, that is £400, making the total cost £900.

- *Revenue ratio* – an apportionment for overheads may relate to the revenue derived from an activity. For example, if one third of an organisation's revenue is generated from training courses and two thirds from consultancy activities, then overheads may be apportioned between the activities in the same ratio.
- *Salary/wages calculation* – if a major proportion of the direct cost is staff hours it is possible to do a calculation to allow for the additional costs of staff such as National Insurance. A further calculation can then be made to include a sum for other overheads. For example, salary/wages might be calculated as in Figure 7.1.1.

Annual salary for full-time administrative assistant		**£6500.00**
Annual salary	£6500	
Employer NI contribution rate is 12.2%: £6500 x 12.2% = £793.00		£793.00
Total direct staff costs		**£7293.00**
Add an additional amount of 20% of the basic salary to allow for indirect staff costs such as pensions, welfare, training:		
£6500 x 20% = £1300		£1300.00
Subtotal		**£8593.00**
Add a further amount of 20% of the total to allow for overheads:		
£8593 x 20% = £1718.16		£1718.16
TOTAL COSTS		**£10311.60**

Figure 7.1.1 Salary/wages calculations

Note
The National Insurance rates change annually and it is important to check that the figures used are up to date. Current taxation rates are available on the website:

   http://www.inlandrevenue.gov.uk

- *Area ratio* – the buildings overhead such as rent and rates may be apportioned according to the space taken up by an activity. This is usually calculated from the total floor area of the building and the floor area required for an activity. The ratio of the two figures is then used to apportion costs – if an activity uses approximately half of the space then it will carry half of the costs. This can be expressed as:

$$\frac{\text{Activity floor area}}{\text{Total floor area}} \times \frac{\text{Building costs}}{\text{(rent and rates)}} = \text{Activity building overhead}$$

This method can also be used to apportion other overhead costs such as lighting, heating, building insurance.

Researching budget costs

The information needed to prepare a budget has to be researched from various sources. As budgets are only estimates, the figures cannot be exact, but should be reasonably accurate – that is, they should represent a realistic estimate based on all available evidence. The time spent researching the costs represents a cost in itself, and the need for accuracy should be balanced with the cost of preparing the budget. Information can be collected from the following sources.

- Information on costs and expenditure may be included in previous budgets, and can be obtained from files for previous activities.
- The Accounts department will have previous accounts and costs for rent, rates, insurance, etc. The department should also have information on its accounting procedures for allocating overheads and for budget procedures.
- The Purchasing department will have costs for stationery, materials, etc.
- The Personnel department will have personnel costs for different grades of activity.
- Staff with experience of the activity will be able to provide helpful information such as estimates of staff time spent on activities.
- External suppliers will be able to provide information on materials, services, etc.
- Equipment and stationery catalogues are good sources of information on costs.
- Business equipment/trade magazines, journals, etc. have articles that give useful information on suppliers, new developments, costs, etc.

Stages in preparing a budget

The stages in preparing a budget are summarised in the following flow chart:

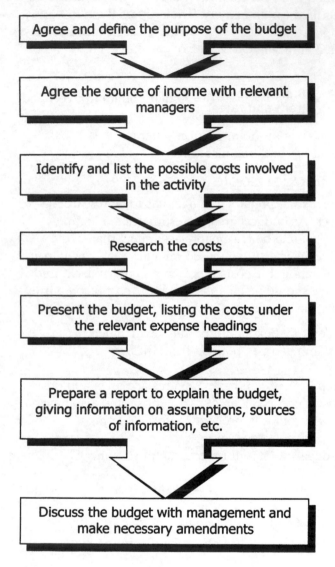

Example budget

You might be asked, for example, to prepare an operational budget for a centralised post room. After research, the findings might look like Figure 7.1.2.

Any budget is only an estimate, and allowance has to be made for any unforeseen rise in costs. This is usually called a 'contingency'. Contingencies can be allowed for in the following ways:

Item	Cost (£)	Estimated/planned cost	Source of information
Staffing	8593	One full-time administrative assistant, £6500 pa plus NI costs and indirect staff costs – see earlier calculation in Figure 7.1.1 (not including the extra overheads)	• Personnel department • Local staffing agency • Government taxation information on the internet www.inlandrevenue.gov.uk
Materials	1200	£1200 pa for stationery and small consumable items	• Stationery list prepared from suppliers' catalogues
Postage	8000	Annual expenditure on postage, based on last year's total postage costs – £7230. This sum was increased by 10% to allow for contingencies	• Historical figures from the Accounts department
Equipment	870	Lease of franking machine £750 pa Lease of plain paper fax £120 pa	• Franking machine supplier and local office equipment supplier
Telephone	150	Annual rent of ISDN line for fax receipt and transmission	• Telephone service supplier
Rent/rates	1650	Room allocated for post room approx. 5% of office space. Allocation of 5% of rent and rates, i.e. 5% of £33 000 total rent and rates	• Accountant and Accounts department
Overheads	1350	Apportionment of other overheads – for example, cleaning, security, insurance, allocated on office space figures of 5% of total overheads – £27 000	• Accountant and Accounts department
Contingency	Add 2% of total costs	Figure based on the Retail Price Index figure quoted in the government's quarterly report for June 1999	• UK Government's Quarterly Reports – available on the UK Government's website

Figure 7.1.2 An operational budget for a centralised post room

- *adding a percentage to the total costs* – when the total cost has been calculated a contingency sum may be added – for example, 3%
- *adding a percentage to variable costs* – fixed costs may not vary a great deal and so a percentage can be added just to the variable costs – for example, 10% to the postage cost as shown in the table
- *making a specific allowance* – if a fixed budget sum is allocated to an activity, a fixed percentage can be allocated for contingencies – for example, 5%. Thus, a total budget allocation may be £12 000 and when the costs are listed, 5% of the budget – that is £600 – is put on one side to cover any additional unforeseen costs.

Preparing the budget

When the initial budget has been prepared, it can be presented using a computer. This is usually done with a spreadsheet application or an organisation's standard accounting or budgeting software. The information can be entered into columns and rows (see Figure 7.1.3) and the budget prepared in such a way that it can then be used to allow ongoing monitoring of costs and also to calculate variances. In addition, the spreadsheet can be used to carry out 'what if' analyses to see the effects of changes in costs – for example, calculation of increases in National Insurance or the cost of postage.

Budget codes

Once a budget for a project or department has been agreed, arrangements have to be made to acquire the necessary resources. These may be available internally or externally, and should be ordered or organised according to the organisation's procedures. In order to monitor the ongoing costs, the expenses will have to be recorded in such a way that they can be clearly identified. This may mean giving each project or department a code or identity that can be used on invoices, orders, photocopying requisitions and staff timesheets. All items bearing this code are then allocated to the project or department. Further information on cost centres can be found in Element 7.2 (pages 336–7).

Methods of payment

When goods or services are ordered for the budget, they have to be paid for. There are various methods that organisations use for paying for goods. You should check your organisation's policy for the payment for goods, including petty cash for small items (see Element 7.2, pages 328–39) and cheques to settle invoices sent for goods and/or services supplied.

Standing orders may be set up to pay regular payments such as monthly leasing costs. A standing order is an authorisation by the payer to the bank to pay a regular fixed sum into another specified bank account. Standing orders are used for paying sums that are fixed.

Direct debits can also be used. In this case, the paying organisation authorises the bank to pay directly a claim for payment made by the receiving organisation. Direct debits tend to be used when sums are likely to vary such as electricity costs. They have the disadvantage that the unpredictability of the amount of the claim

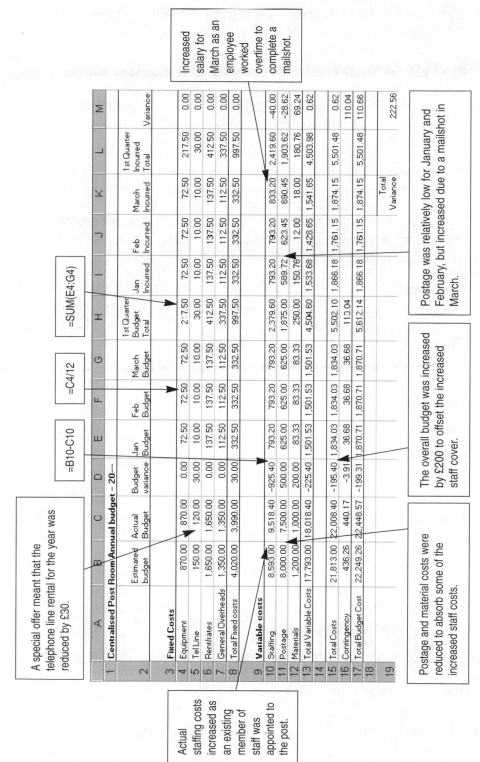

Figure 7.1.3 A budget prepared on a spreadsheet

can make it difficult to control the level of funds in the bank, although the supplier usually notifies the customer in advance of the amount to be taken.

The **bank automated clearing system (BACS)** is used to transfer funds from the organisation's account directly to the account of another person. Salaries and expenses are very often paid in this way. To set up a BACS it is necessary to have full details of the payee's account.

Calculating budget variances

During the course of preparing a budget, differences in budgeted costs may arise. For example, the initial findings in the post-room budget may have to be revised as the actual costs become apparent. The budget needs to be analysed to identify any variance.

Example 1

The estimated salary for staffing was £6500, but a member of staff may be appointed who is already on the payroll and earns £7200. This would then have an unfavourable effect on the budget.

Estimated total staffing costs (direct + indirect) = £8593

Actual total staffing costs:

Annual salary		**£7200.00**
Annual salary	£7200	
Employer NI contribution rate is 12.2%: £7200 x 12.2% = £878.40		£878.40
Total direct staff costs		**£8078.40**
Add an additional amount of 20% of the basic salary to allow for indirect staff costs – for example pensions, welfare, training: £7200 x 20% = £1440		£1440.00
Total direct + indirect costs		**£9418.40**

Figure 7.1.4 New salary calculation

The variance for staffing costs can then be calculated:

Estimated cost – Actual cost = Variance

or

£8593 – £9518.40 = –£925.40: an unfavourable variance of £925.40.

Example 2

Another example of variance could be the telephone line costs. The estimated cost prepared from the initial findings was £150 per annum rental for an ISDN line. However, since producing the initial estimate, the company providing the line have introduced a special offer and reduced the cost to £120 per annum. The variance for the costs can be calculated:

£150 – £120 = £30, a favourable variance of £30.

These two differences between estimated and actual cost can be added together to give the effect on the total budget: an unfavourable variance of £895.40. Steps would have to be taken to ensure that the project does not go 'over budget'. This can usually be done in the following ways:

- *increasing the budget to allow for the unfavourable variance* – this can be difficult as organisations are usually working within tight budget limits
- *reducing expenditure in other areas of the budget* – this may be difficult as the budget may have already been prepared within tight limits
- *using the allowance made for contingencies* – care has to be taken using the contingency fund, as this can mean that any other unforeseen events may cause problems with the project going 'over budget'
- *increasing charges* – where a budget is linked to an event or activity which is being charged to customers, the charge may need to be increased to cover the variance. Care needs to be taken doing this, as increased charges may mean a reduction in customers.

As soon as problems with a budget occur, the relevant staff should be informed in writing. The nature of the variance and any suggested solutions should be included in the information. In some circumstances it may be necessary to revise the forecast to allow for increased costs. Figure 7.1.5 shows an example of a budget variance memorandum.

MEMORANDUM

To: Jane Harding, Administrative Finance Officer
From: Dougal O'Halloran
Date: 3 April ----

Centralised post-room budget

The initial estimated budget for the centralised post room has had to be amended to allow for the appointment of Grant Yardley. The initial estimated staffing cost of £8593 has had to be amended to £9518.40. This has increased the budget by £925.40. A saving of £30 has already been made by taking advantage of a special offer reduction in the telephone rental costs from £150 to £120; however, this leaves an unfavourable variance of £895.40. If the budget for the post room is to be kept in line with the estimated cost, then savings will have to be made.

The fixed costs cannot be changed and any saving can only be made from the variable costs of staffing, postage and materials. The largest of these sums is the postage at £8000. Can I suggest that steps are taken to look for savings in the cost of postage. These could include:

- reducing the number of first-class letters to those marked 'URGENT'
- encouraging staff to use e-mail where possible
- reducing the use of expensive postage services such as next-day courier and parcel services.

The cost of postage needs to be carefully monitored over the next few months to ensure the new lower target is met.

However, I feel that it will be difficult to achieve such a large saving, and I would recommend a small increase in the budget of £200 to meet the increased costs.

There is a contingency cost built into the budget of 2% – that is, £436.26. However, I do not recommend that we use this sum at this stage to cover some of this variance, as it may still be needed to cover possible equipment problems or increases in the cost of postage.

Figure 7.1.5 A budget variance memorandum

Monitoring budgets

When the budget has been agreed, the actual costs incurred need to be monitored. The costs incurred should be entered on the spreadsheet and compared with the budgeted costs (see Figure 7.1.3

on page 321). The information should be collected from relevant forms, accounts, orders, receipts, invoices, etc. Using a code for each type of expenditure makes it easier to identify costs. This monitoring will also indicate variances between the budgeted cost and the costs incurred.

It is important to regularly monitor and check the budget carefully before analysing any variance in incurred costs. The following checks should be made.

- All invoices have been paid, and there are no outstanding invoices which will affect the budget figures.
- All costs have been allocated against the correct invoices, so that no invoices are allocated to the wrong budget.
- All income has been collected. If any outstanding income remains unpaid, it could become a bad debt (an unpaid bill) and represent a cost against the budget – for example, a delegate at a conference who fails to pay the balance of their booking.

Check carefully that there are no outstanding invoices to be paid. The budget could look quite healthy, even though there is still money owing against an item.

When the expenditure has been analysed and the areas where corrective action needs to be taken have been identified, it may be necessary to take steps to reduce costs or to follow up any outstanding costs that might cause problems with the budget. In some circumstances it may be necessary to renegotiate the budget to allow for increased costs.

Analysing the variance

Where a variance has been identified, questions need to be asked to establish why it has occurred. In the budget example in Figure 7.1.3 (page 321) there is an increase in the staffing costs for March. The cause of this increase should be identified. The wages office may identify that it was caused by staff working overtime. However, it should be checked that this overtime is attributable to the post room. For example, the post-room administrative assistant might have worked overtime to reduce a backlog with another project, in which case the overtime costs should be taken out of the post-room budget and allocated to the relevant task. It may also be important to check that the volume of work in the post room has not been underestimated, and that overtime does not become a regular occurrence that could affect the staffing allocation in the budget.

Portfolio activity 7.1

Discuss with your assessor and/or line manager a suitable budget for you to prepare. The budget must be detailed enough to provide evidence that you have fully understood and applied the principles of budgetary control. Preparation must include: salaries, including calculations for tax and National Insurance; overhead items including rent, rates and insurance; contingency funds; other expenditure to include standing orders or direct debits.

Your budget should be prepared on a computer in the form of a spreadsheet or printed report form from an accounting package.

On completion of your budget, you should investigate variances between the actual and budgeted figures and send a memo to your manager outlining these variances and suggesting possible solutions. Alternatively, produce a variance analysis using a spreadsheet or accounting package and suggest solutions in memo form.

The following evidence should be collected:

• detailed budget on a spreadsheet or accounting package report form
• variance analysis
• memo suggesting solutions for resolving the differences between actual and budgeted figures.

Performance criteria:	7.1.1–7
Knowledge and understanding:	7.1.a–m
Evidence requirements:	7.1.1–6

Test yourself

Knowledge and understanding	Questions
a	Explain why forecasts and budgets are important for management purposes.
b	Explain the need for and scope of budgets.
c	List three sources of budget content.
d	Explain the principles behind budgetary control.
e	What procedures should be followed to operate within a budget?
f	What are the current taxation and NI requirements and legislation?
g	Explain the purpose of a budget/variance analysis.
h	Explain how you would calculate the differences between 'actual' and 'estimated' figures. Give the formula you would use.
i	Explain the difference between consumable and capital expenditure.
j	What computer system is used to analyse and present financial information in your organisation and what are its main functions?
k	List three items of accounting terminology; define them and give an instance when you would use them.
l	How would you organise, prepare and present a financial report?
m	Explain the differences between and functions of BACS, standing orders and direct debits.

Element 7.2
CONTROL A PETTY CASH SYSTEM

The majority of costs incurred by an organisation are settled by cheque and direct payment. However, for small items it may be quicker and easier to pay by cash and most organisations will, therefore, have a system for paying for small items in this way. This is called a petty cash system. A petty cash system usually includes:

- identification of a person responsible for dealing with petty cash
- procedures for claiming and recording petty cash payments
- procedures for transferring petty cash payments into the accounting system
- procedures for reimbursement of petty cash funds
- procedures for the safety and security of cash held for petty cash purposes.

Responsibility for petty cash

An appropriate member of staff will be identified to handle the petty cash. This person may be called the petty cashier. The type of organisation, nature of the business, size of the business and costs to be covered by the payment of petty cash will determine who is an appropriate person. In a training organisation, where trainees can claim for bus fares, it may be the receptionist who is responsible for petty cash. In a sales department it may be the administrator who is responsible for settling claims for sales representatives' expenses. In a small organisation, it may be the office manager. In very large organisations there may be several staff who manage petty cash.

Petty cash expenses

The petty cash procedures should specify what items can be covered by petty cash. These will vary between organisations but can include the following:

- *travel* – reimbursement of certain travel expenses such as bus fares for candidates attending interview, taxi fares to deliver an urgent item to a local office, petrol expenses for representatives; parking vouchers, meter payments, etc. may also be included
- *refreshment/entertainment* – payment for tea, coffee, sandwiches, etc. that are agreed business costs
- *postage* – stamps, recorded and registered delivery payments
- *stationery* – small or specialised items of stationery, particularly those that are not often used and not carried in stock, such as wrapping paper for parcels or postal tubes

- *cleaning* – in a small office cleaning materials may be purchased using petty cash; cash may also be used to pay for window cleaning and other cleaning services
- *office expenses* – a general term that may be used to cover small items bought for the office – for example, items such as a first-aid kit or newspapers for reception
- *miscellaneous/sundries* – this term is usually used to cover items of expenditure that cannot be classified under any other title and often includes items similar to those covered by office expenses.

There may also be a limit on the amount of a petty cash item – for example, £20. In that case, items or charges that exceed the limit would need to be claimed through the standard payment system – for example, with an invoice and payment by cheque, or claimed via expenses and paid with the salary.

Managing petty cash

The most commonly-used method of managing petty cash is called the **imprest** method. A sum of money is allocated for petty cash, from which payments are made. This sum is agreed and is called the float. At the end of an agreed period the total sum of money that has been spent is reimbursed to restore the float to the agreed sum. The level of the float and the period of time are agreed between the petty cashier and the finance department – for example, £50 on a monthly basis or £40 on a weekly basis. The level of the float and the period will depend on the type and size of organisation and the items to be paid for. Some large organisations use very little cash because of the problems of security and risk of fraud, whereas some small organisations may use petty cash on a frequent basis, as postage, cleaning items, etc. are purchased as and when they are required. The items covered by petty cash may also vary. Some organisations may not have a franking machine, and may, therefore, buy all their stamps with cash; stationery items may be purchased from local suppliers with cash as and when they are needed.

The petty cash should be monitored regularly to ensure the float is sufficient to cover the claims during a period. If petty cash runs out during the period, the float may be increased. A request for an increase in the float should be made in writing to the cashier or accountant. The account should also be monitored to ensure that petty cash is not being used incorrectly – for example, to purchase stationery items that could be ordered from a stationery supplier and paid for by invoice.

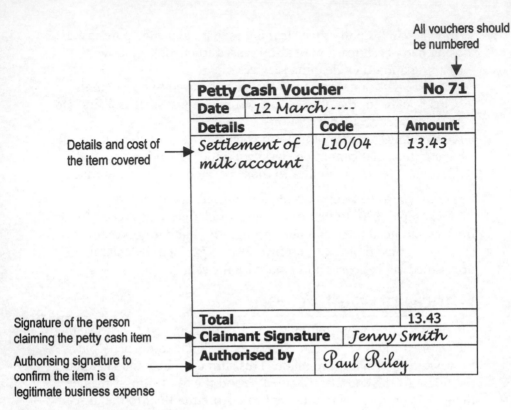

All vouchers should be numbered

Petty Cash Voucher		No 71
Date	12 March ----	
Details	**Code**	**Amount**
Settlement of milk account	L10/04	13.43
Total		13.43
Claimant Signature	Jenny Smith	
Authorised by	Paul Riley	

Details and cost of the item covered

Signature of the person claiming the petty cash item

Authorising signature to confirm the item is a legitimate business expense

Figure 7.2.1 A petty cash voucher

Claiming petty cash

To make a claim, a petty cash voucher should be completed (see Figure 7.2.1). The petty cash voucher should always be accompanied by a suitable receipt. This is to ensure claims are not made fraudulently. The authorising signature should also ensure only approved items are claimed for. Petty cash should only be used for legitimate business expenses, not for personal items. For example, sandwiches might be purchased for a business meeting, but not for an employee's personal routine lunch.

The petty cash account

When the claim has been made, it should be recorded in the petty cash account (see Figure 7.2.2). The petty cash account should record the receipts and payments. Entries should be made as soon as the claim has been settled. The account should be balanced at the end of the period by adding a reimbursement sum to replace the expenditure for the period.

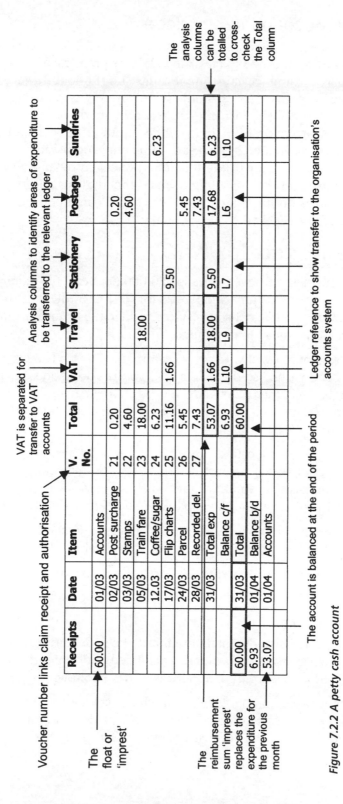

Figure 7.2.2 A petty cash account

Simple accounting practices

The purpose of different accounts and financial documents is covered in Element 7.3 (pages 346–53). For petty cash and expenses recording, certain simple rules should be followed. In manual systems, entries should be accurately and promptly recorded in pen. Any corrections should be made in ink and initialled. Correction fluid and rubbers should not be used to amend accounts. Calculations should be checked using a calculator. Calculations should be cross-checked by adding the total column and then totalling each of the analysis columns. If the answers do not match, the entries and calculations need to be carefully checked.

Value Added Tax (VAT)

When a business turnover exceeds £50 000 per year it is required to register with the Customs and Excise for VAT regardless of the VAT banding of the goods or services supplied. Turnover is goods and services invoiced to customers.

Many items purchased with petty cash may incur VAT and these need to be identified so that when VAT returns are made the tax paid can be reclaimed. Currently VAT is charged at 17.5% for most items and 5% for fuels. Certain other items are zero rated or exempt from VAT:

* *zero-rated items* – foodstuffs, books, children's clothes, prescriptions, postage, construction of new homes, mobile homes/houseboats and transport
* *exempt items* – health services, banks, education services.

These rates can alter with government budgets and should be checked at any time for the current rates applicable.

When receipts are collected to support petty cash claims, they should be VAT receipts.

Calculating VAT

The receipt will give the total amount of the expenditure, and the VAT content of the sum has to be calculated and separated from the total for analysis purposes. This is done as follows.

If you purchased an item for £11.16 which included VAT at 17.5%. That is, the total cost you paid was 117.5% of the net cost excluding VAT. So, the net cost without VAT is given by:

Net cost = £11.16 ÷ 1.175 = £9.50

The amount of VAT is therefore:

VAT amount = £11.16 – £9.50 = £1.66

You could use the following formula:

Total cost ÷ 1.175 = Net cost
Total cost – Net cost = VAT amount

Always use a calculator to do any calculations.

Verifying claims

Any claim must be checked to ensure it is a legitimate business expense. The following checks should be made before a claim is dealt with.

- The items being claimed must be covered by the organisation's procedures as legitimate claims for expenditure.
- The sum being claimed must not exceed any limits for petty cash claims. These limits may relate to individual items or types of item rather than the total on a voucher. For example, a claim for £24.00 might be made up of £14.00 for postage and £10.00 for envelopes. This claim might be acceptable and entered on the account as two different sums. However, a claim for £24.00 for different items of stationery might not be acceptable if it were company policy for items of stationery totalling more than £20.00 to be purchased through a supplier who then invoices for the order.
- The voucher must have been correctly completed and authorised by an appropriate person. A list of authorising signatures should be kept on record.
- The claim must have an accompanying original receipt. This should be checked to ensure it matches the item and sum claimed. The receipt should be stapled to the voucher.
- Calculation of multiple amounts on the voucher must be accurate.

Cash advances

There may be occasions when cash needs to be issued in advance of the purchase such as for the purchase of stamps. The organisation should have a procedure for issuing cash advances, which should include the signature of the recipient to confirm receipt of the money.

Expenses

In some organisations, the petty cash system is used to reimburse claims for business expenses incurred by staff. These expenses may be for travel, subsistence, accommodation and incidental expenses such as postage, stationery, telephone, photocopying.

The organisation will usually have a policy that will specify the:

- legitimate expenses that can be incurred by staff
- level of these expenses – for example, mileage rates, subsistence levels
- method and timing of claims for these expenses
- rules for including receipts
- procedures for authorisation of expenses
- appropriate methods of payment – for example, cash, cheque, BACS.

Methods of payment for expenses

Different methods of payment may be used to settle claims for expenses, depending on the amount, the grade of employee and the type of expense. Claims for sums greater than a certain amount – for example, £20 – may be settled by cheque or may be paid with the employee's salary. When employees are paid by bank transfer, the expenses will be added to the sum paid to the employee through the transfer. Claims for expenses that require a cheque or BACS are usually submitted to the Accounts department for them to settle and process. An example of an expenses claim form is shown in Figure 7.2.3.

Expenses claims need to be checked in the same way as petty cash vouchers. The dates, amounts and details on receipts should be checked to ensure they match the claim. All calculations on the claim should be checked. The authorising signature should be checked. Any unusual items should be queried and checked with the relevant person – for example, inclusion of a claim for a stationery item that is normally carried in stock should be checked with the claimant. A large claim may be checked with the authorising manager, or with the budget manager of the project.

Some organisations now organise the issue of credit cards to staff to enable them to pay for their expenses. Petrol, fares, etc. are paid for with the card. The employee claims for the expenses and the money is paid to the employee with the salary. The employee then settles the card account using the money received with the salary.

Expenses Claim Form	EXP/10/--		Claim No. 127	
Employee Name	**Department**	**Date of claim**		
Paul Chan	Sales	3 October ----		
Employee Pay No.	**Project No.**	**Date expenses incurred**		
62357	201	2 October ----		
DETAILS OF CLAIM			**£**	**p**
Journey From				
Cardiff Branch Office To Avon Holdings, Bristol				
No of miles 72 @ 33p per mile			23	76
Total fares – rail, bus, etc.				
Subsistence				
Lunch			5	95
Other expenses (please specify)				
Parking in Bristol			9	50
Severn Bridge Toll fee			4	20
Total expenses (please attach all receipts/proofs of payment)			43	41
Signature of claimant	Paul Chan			
Authorisation signature	Sarah Malting, Head of Sales			
For Office Use Only				
Payment Code		**Payment made by:**	Cash/Cheque/BACS	

Figure 7.2.3 An expenses claim form

Priority claims

Petty cash or expenses claims may require priority treatment in certain situations.

- *Timing of claim* – a regular time may be set aside for paying claims, etc. – for example, at the end of the week, but situations might arise when claims need to be dealt with immediately. For example, a cash advance might be required for postage stamps because there are no stamps left and mail needs to be despatched.

- *Nature of the item required* – procedures may specify that in normal circumstances all stationery must be ordered through the standard stock procedures. However, an urgent item may be required for a specific situation – for example, a non-standard item requiring a special envelope or wrapping might need to be sent urgently to a customer.
- *Level of claim* – claims may normally be restricted to a certain level – for example, the maximum level of cash claim for expenses might be £20 and any claim in excess of that might need to be settled with a cheque or via BACS. However, if, for example, a junior member of staff has been asked to attend a training course and incurred a rail fare of £35, then waiting for a cheque or BACS transfer might impose an unfair level of hardship. In this situation the payment might be settled immediately in cash.

When dealing with petty cash and expenses claims it is important to establish the level of discretion that is available to the person operating the system. When anticipated problems arise it is better to have discussed them in advance – for example, in the case of the junior member of staff attending a training course it might be agreed in advance that the train fare cost would be settled with cash on return.

Allocating costs

In many organisations costs are attributed to a particular department, function or project. This is carried out so that budgets and costs can be carefully monitored.

In a college, for example, as financial systems become more sophisticated and to meet the requirements of funding councils, it might be necessary to determine the costs for each course. Any photocopying, stationery, staffing, in-service training costs, etc. that relate to a particular course must be calculated. A reference code might be given to each course as in Figure 7.2.4.

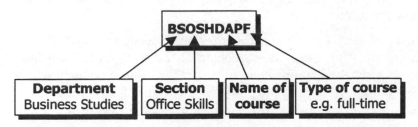

Figure 7.2.4 A reference code system

Alternatively a number code may be allocated as in Figure 7.2.5.

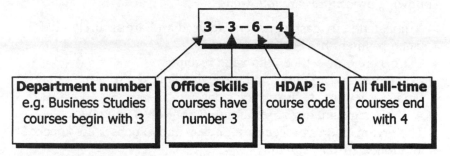

Figure 7.2.5 A number code system

The course code would be entered on all photocopy requests, expenses claims, etc. At the end of each period the total of expenditure for each course would be calculated and the budget holder informed. For example, at the end of each month the Curriculum Manager would receive the total costs for each course from reprographics, the post room, etc.; the ongoing costs of the courses could then be accurately monitored.

Dealing with discrepancies

Money is always a very emotive issue and great care has to be taken when dealing with money issues that affect the financial situation of staff. When discrepancies arise they need to be dealt with tactfully. If a simple discrepancy such as a mistake in a calculation is made, the claim can be returned to the claimant for correction. If staff are making claims without receipts, the claim may be returned with a standard reminder outlining the procedure and requesting the appropriate receipts before payment can be authorised. If staff consistently do not follow procedures, or other serious issues arise, this should be discussed with a senior member of staff who may then take appropriate action.

Security

Security is always an issue when dealing with money. The organisation may incur financial losses through theft and fraud. All cash should be kept in a locked cash tin that should be locked away when not in use. The location of the keys should be known to only two people in the organisation: the person handling the cash and the cashier. If large sums are kept in the petty cash tin, it may be locked away in a safe when not in use or at the end of each day. Many organisations have reduced the risk of theft from petty cash by eliminating or reducing petty cash to an absolute minimum.

Fraud can also be a problem and can be minimised by ensuring the following procedures are followed.

- Numbered petty cash vouchers are used and are securely filed when payment has been made.
- Claims are only settled with valid receipts.
- All claims are carefully and thoroughly checked to ensure they represent legitimate business expenses.
- Authorising signatures are carefully monitored and checked.
- The organisation's procedures for cash and expenses are checked and followed very carefully.
- The levels of petty cash and expenses are monitored regularly and carefully to identify areas of concern – for example, staff with very high levels of expenses claims.

Confidentiality

All issues with regard to finance should be dealt with confidentially. The petty cash and expenses accounts should be carefully and securely filed. The levels of expenses and claims for individual members of staff should not be discussed with unauthorised members of staff. It can create jealousy if some staff are seen to be receiving large sums on expenses, or receive expenses at a higher rate than others.

Concerns about payment of expenses should not be discussed with unauthorised personnel. Any written communications about such concerns should always be dealt with very carefully.

Computer passwords should be used to lock computer files. Written documents should be marked *CONFIDENTIAL* and should be sent in sealed envelopes similarly marked.

Using computers

Petty cash and expenses can be recorded on the computer. If you are creating your own records, it is preferable to use a spreadsheet (see Figure 7.2.6). However, in some organisations there may be a petty cash or expenses option already set up in the computerised accounting system. This should then be used, as it can be linked to the computerised ledgers and other appropriate accounts.

The major advantage of using a spreadsheet to record cash/expenses is the range of functions that can be used to analyse and present the information. As well as the basic calculations, more advanced calculations can be carried out, such as averaging and statistical analysis. The **Sort** function can be used to sort items into categories, or into order of the amount of expenditure. Graphs and charts of the expenditure can also be prepared easily.

Passwords should be used when setting up spreadsheets to ensure confidentiality of files. Files should be backed up regularly using the organisation's back-up procedures to ensure security of the data. The back up should be in a separate location to the main record – for example, on a floppy disk locked in a filing cabinet.

The main disadvantages of using spreadsheets are that some specialist knowledge is required to set up the spreadsheet and access to the computer is required when records need updating.

Formula to calculate mileage: =D4*GS1 (G1 is an absolute cell as it refers to the entry in G1 for mileage allowance which remains the same.)

	A	B	C	D	E	F	G	H	I
1	EXPENSES CLAIM FOR THE MONTH OF OCTOBER					Mileage rate	0.33		
2	Member of staff								
3	Date of claim	Claim No.	Project No.	No. of miles	Mileage	Other travel	Subsistence	Other	Total
4	01/02/00	131.00	210.00	10.00	3.30	7.90	5.96		17.16
5	01/10/00	143.00	208.00	72.00	23.76				23.76
6	01/15/00	156.00	210.00			32.00	2.50		34.50
7	01/24/00	173.00	210.00	50.00	16.50	9.00			25.50
8	01/30/00	182.00	199.00	13.00	4.29	5.00		3.30	12.59
9	TOTAL				47.85	53.90	8.46	3.30	113.51

Other functions such as *sort* can be used to sort information into project numbers, allowing different types of analysis.

Total columns are calculated using formulae, e.g.: =sum (E4:E8)

Total rows can be calculated using formulae, e.g.: =sum (E4:H4) Note: Care must be taken not to include the number of miles in this formula.

Figure 7.2.6 An expenses spreadsheet

Portfolio activity 7.2

Discuss with your assessor and/or line manager how you will control and maintain a petty cash system for at least 30 items of expenditure, across at least 6 headings and balanced at least 3 times. Record your meeting.

The system can be manual or computerised.

Note
The petty cash should be maintained as a result of real work if possible. If not, evidence may be generated through simulated

activities which is relevant to a specific section or department. However, the items must be varied in content and amount. In addition, items on which VAT can be claimed must be identified and the amounts calculated.

The following evidence should be collected:

- your organisation's procedures for dealing with petty cash
- appropriate petty cash records
- personal statement explaining how you prepared the accounts, including information on how you: checked the claims; decided payment priorities; identified and dealt with discrepancies and queries; requested reimbursement; maintained security and confidentiality
- witness testimony from the accountant or cashier to confirm that you correctly dealt with petty cash, requested reimbursement and completed the correct records within the correct timescale
- printout of one set of records prepared on a computer to show the data, calculations and formulae (you will have to prepare a set of records manually if the main records are not on the computer).

Performance criteria:	7.2.1–11
Knowledge and understanding:	7.2.a–o
Evidence requirements:	7.2.1–5

Test yourself

Knowledge and understanding	Questions
a	What is the purpose of petty cash?
b	What are the main principles and procedures involved in maintaining a petty cash system?
c	Explain where petty cash accounts fit into your organisation's budgetary system and accounts.
d	Explain the procedures involved in allocating costs to sections/departments.
e	Explain the procedure for the reimbursement of claims for expenditure using BACS transfer.

f	Explain your organisation's procedures for the operation of its petty cash system; reimbursement of expenses and restoring/increasing funds.
g	What are your organisation's requirements for verifying and authorising expenditure, including priority claims?
h	What are the current VAT rates and exemptions and how would you calculate them?
i	Explain the accounting practices in relation to petty cash.
j	What methods can be used for keeping petty cash secure?
k	What are the possible consequences of not maintaining confidentiality when dealing with expenses?
l	What computerised systems might be used for analysing and presenting petty cash information and what functions would they need to perform?
m	Explain how to create a spreadsheet and enter data and formulae on your organisation's system.
n	Explain the methods for checking and transferring information correctly; balancing accounts; and restoring funds.
o	Explain how you would use tact, discretion and sensitivity in interpersonal communication.

Element 7.3
ANALYSE FINANCIAL INFORMATION

This element looks at the information prepared by organisations to show their financial situation. Financial statements allow the various financial activities of an organisation to be measured and compared. Financial statements also make it possible for your organisation to measure itself against other, similar, organisations. This financial information is used to help organisations make decisions and plans about their future operations. They can identify areas of strength and weakness, identify problems and prepare strategies to ensure future success.

However, organisations do not exist in a vacuum and outside influences will also have an impact on its successful operation. These influences may be political, economic, social and technological. This element will include consideration of the impact of these factors.

Accounting terms

It will be helpful when working through this element to have an understanding of certain accounting terms.

Assets. The property and outstanding debts that can be realised by the organisation. Assets are usually balanced against the liabilities on the balance sheet. *Current assets* are assets that are easily realised and turned into cash – for example, money in the bank, stock, debtors. *Fixed assets* are long-term assets that are used for the profit-making activity of the company – for example, buildings, equipment, machinery.

Liabilities. The financial obligations or money owed by the organisation – for example, creditors. Liabilities are balanced against the assets on the balance sheet.

Capital. The property or resources of the organisation, usually represented by the excess of the assets over the liabilities. Capital can be share capital or loan capital. Share capital is the money provided to the company by shareholders. Loan capital is money provided by banks or other lenders in the form of loans.

Shares. The shareholders 'own' the organisation through providing portions of the capital of the business, known as shares. In return for risking their money, the shareholders receive a share of the profits.

Dividend. The percentage of the profit paid out to each shareholder.

Depreciation. The reduction in value of a fixed asset due to use or obsolescence over time.

Debtors. Companies or individuals that owe the company money, usually customers for services purchased.

Creditors. Companies or individuals that are owed money by the company, usually suppliers of goods and services.

Types of organisation

When analysing financial information it is important to have an understanding of the different types of organisation. This can affect the information that is legally available. It can also affect the financial aims of the organisation – for example, a person running their own company might wish only to earn enough money to maintain a certain standard of living; while a large public company will have a responsibility to earn profit for its shareholders.

There are various methods of classifying organisations. The first relates to the sector of the economy in which they operate – public or private. The public sector relates to organisations that are owned by the state on behalf of the public such as schools and hospitals.

The private sector relates to organisations in which the ownership is with private individuals or large institutions. These organisations are usually classified according to the following types of ownership.

Sole trader

Here, one person owns the organisation. This person may employ people to carry out the activities but all the debts and profits are the responsibility of the sole trader. The sole trader is personally liable for all the debts incurred in the operation of the business. Typical examples of sole traders are a window cleaner, decorator, small builder. Sole traders are not required to publish their accounts, although they are required to keep accurate accounts for tax and VAT purposes.

Partnerships

Here, two or more people join together to run a commercial organisation in order to share in the profits. Again, they may employ people to carry out the activities, but all the debts and profits are the responsibility of the partners. These will be divided between the partners according to ratios agreed in the partnership agreement. The partners are personally liable for all the debts incurred in the operation of the business. Partnerships are not required to publish their accounts, although they are required to keep accurate accounts for tax and VAT purposes. Partnerships are regulated by the Partnership Act 1890 (see the appendix on pages 539–45).

Limited companies

These are trading organisations that are registered under the Companies Act of 1985 (see the appendix). To form a limited company the following documents must be provided to the Registrar of Companies:

• Memorandum of Association – this states the business's main objectives

- Articles of Association – these state the internal management of the company
- statement of nominal capital
- list of directors and company secretary.

There are two types of limited company: **private limited company** and **public limited company**.

Private limited company

A private limited company can be formed by preparing a Memorandum of Association and complying with registration requirements of the Companies Act 1985. The money required for the operation of the company is provided by the members of the company in exchange for shares. There must be a minimum of two shareholders. These shares can only be sold privately and with the agreement of the other shareholders. The minimum share capital (the amount of shares sold to shareholders) is £2. The liability of the shareholders for the debts of the company is limited to their shareholding. This is called 'limited liability'. A private limited company has 'Ltd' as the last word of its name. The publication of its accounts is controlled by the provision of the Companies Act 1985, but as it is a private company the disclosure returns are not as onerous as those for a public limited company.

Public limited company

The main difference between a private and a public limited company is that a public company that wants to be listed invites the public to buy shares in the operation of a public limited company. The prime market for shares is the Stock Exchange although there are also smaller markets such as the Alternative Investment Market (AIM).

The liability of the members is limited to the value of their shareholding. Because the public is invited to buy shares in a public limited company and are at a risk of losing their money, the returns for the publication of accounts and financial information are much more onerous. A public limited company must use the term 'plc' at the end of its name.

Public limited companies must also make suitable arrangements to have their accounts audited. Auditors are appointed by the shareholders to review the stewardship of the funds invested by them and to give an opinion as to the value of the accounts present. The accounts are usually prepared on an on-going basis in accordance with statutory guidelines and accounting standards drawn up by the Stock Exchange and accounting professional bodies.

While the structures described above are the most common forms of structure, there are others:

- *companies limited by guarantee* – members of the organisation provide a 'guarantee' of a financial contribution. The members may then be liable for this sum of money if the organisation folds or closes with outstanding debts. Many charities and educational institutions are limited by guarantee.
- *chartered corporations* – created by royal charter. These tend to be the professional bodies or some of the older universities – for example, the Institute of Chartered Secretaries and Administrators. These are also limited by guarantee.
- *statutory corporations* – created by Act of Parliament – for example, local authorities.

The structures of the different types of organisation are summarised in the following table.

Type of organisation	Ownership	Liability of owners	Main legislation	Financial publication requirements	Audit requirements
Sole trader	One owner	Personally liable for all debts		None	None
Partnerships	At least two	Jointly and personally liable for all debts	Partnership Act 1890	None	None
Private limited companies	At least two	Liability limited to their shareholding	Companies Act 1985	**Profit and loss accounts** and **balance sheet** are made available to shareholders at an annual meeting. **Annual returns** sent to the Registrar of Companies* within 10 months	Recognised auditors should be appointed at the Annual General Meeting**

Type of organisation	Ownership	Liability of owners	Main legislation	Financial publication requirements	Audit requirements
Public limited companies	At least two	Liability limited to their shareholding	Companies Act 1985	**Profit and loss accounts** and **balance sheet** are made available to the shareholders. **Annual Returns** sent to the Registrar of Companies* within 7 months	Recognised auditors should be appointed at the Annual General Meeting**

*Full details should be made available to all shareholders, but certain 'small' and 'medium-sized' companies can file summarised accounts with the Registrar of Companies. A 'small' or 'medium-sized' company is defined in terms of turnover, assets or employees. To be a small company it must meet two out of the following conditions: have turnover less than £2.8 million, have assets of less than £1.4 million and/or fewer than 50 employees. A medium-sized company must meet two out of the following conditions: have turnover less than £11.2 million, have assets of less than £5.6 million and/or fewer than 250 employees.

**Similar exemptions with regard to audit also relate to some small companies.

Financial records

All organisations need to keep financial records. For VAT and tax purposes, records need to be kept to enable accurate VAT and tax returns to be sent to the relevant authorities. For customers and suppliers, it is important to keep an accurate record of money owed and paid. Accurate financial records will give a clear picture of the financial position of the company, and will provide information for the auditors who will check the accounts. They will also provide the necessary information for the financial statements required to be published by law. Last, but not least, they will provide the management with information that will enable them to make strategic decisions about the future activities of the organisation.

Financial records are prepared following standard procedures. These are often referred to as 'double-entry' book-keeping systems. The basic principle for this is that every transaction is entered into the system twice. It is like putting weights on a balance. The weights on both sides of the balance must be the same to keep the scales level. One side of the balance is the 'credit' side and the other side is the 'debit' side. Every entry entered on the credit side must have an entry on the debit side to keep the accounts in balance. A trial balance is prepared to list all credit and debit balances and check that they reach the same total.

Financial records are summarised in Figure 7.3.1 on page 348. The main financial documents that you are required to analyse are the profit and loss account and the balance sheet.

Profit and loss account

The profit and loss account is a financial statement showing the surplus or deficit of income compared with expenditure for the organisation over a particular period. It should list all the income received by the organisation during this period, from which the operating costs are then deducted. If this results in a surplus, it is the net profit. If a negative result is achieved it is a loss:

Total income – Total operating costs = Profit (loss)

It should also show how the profit is to be allocated – for example, how much will be paid out to shareholders as dividends.

Profit and loss accounts may be prepared for internal use or for publication. The accounts prepared for internal use may contain quite detailed information, which it would not be appropriate to publish. The Companies Act 1985 (see the appendix on pages 539–45) lists the minimum information that should be included in the published accounts. These are usually listed in vertical format:

1 Turnover
2 Cost of sales
3 Gross profit or loss
4 Distribution costs
5 Administrative expenses
6 Other operating income
7 Income from investments
8 Other interest receivable
9 Interest payable and similar charges
10 Profit on ordinary activities before taxation
11 Tax on profit or loss
12 Profit on ordinary activities after taxation.

An example of a profit and loss account for a fictitious company is shown in Figure 7.3.2 on page 349.

Initial source information

- Records of goods sold – invoices sent by the organisation
- Records of goods bought – invoices received by the organisation
- Wages slips, expenses claims, repairs, rent records, rate demands
- Records concerning the capital goods, machinery, premises, fixtures, fittings, etc.
- Receipts and records of cash transactions, cheques paid in and out, cash receipts, petty cash

Books of first entry

- Sales ledger Customer accounts
- Purchase ledger Supplier accounts
- Nominal ledger
- Fixed asset ledger
- Cash book

Trial balance

The credit and debit balances of all of these accounts are entered into a 'trial balance'. This acts as a check of the arithmetic accuracy of the ledger accounts. It also forms the basis of the final accounts

Final accounts

Trading Account – this calculates the gross profit or loss over a specific period. After allowing for stocks held at the beginning and end of a period, the value of goods purchased is balanced against the value of goods sold.

Profit and Loss Account – this follows the trading account and calculates the final or net profit (or loss) of the business. All business expenses and any incidental income will be included.

Balance Sheet – a statement of the assets and liabilities of an organisation at a specific time. It is a snapshot of the financial situation of the organisation. The assets and liabilities are listed in order of realisability or priority.

Figure 7.3.1 Summary of financial records

Profit and Loss Account for the year ended 31 March ----		
	£000	£000
1 Turnover		950
2 Cost of sales		400
3 Gross profit		550
4 Distribution costs	240	
5 Administrative expenses	160	
		400
		150
6 Other operating income		20
		170
7 Income from investments	30	
8 Other interest receivable	10	
		40
		210
9 Interest payable and similar charges	40	
		40
10 Profit on ordinary activities before taxation		170
11 Tax on profit		30
12 Profit on ordinary activities after taxation		140
Transfer to Profit and Loss Account	40	
Proposed ordinary dividend	100	
		140

Figure 7.3.2 A profit and loss account

Balance sheet

A balance sheet is a statement of the assets and liabilities of an organisation at a specific time. It is a snapshot of the financial situation of the organisation. The assets and liabilities are listed in order of realisability or priority. The standard format for the layout of balance sheets is given in Figure 7.3.3 on page 350. To be correct, the balance sheet must balance! That is:

Capital + Liabilities = Assets

Analysing the financial statements

The information in the profit and loss account and the balance sheet can be analysed to give a picture of the financial 'health' of the organisation. What you are trying to do when you carry out this analysis is use the information provided to answer the following questions.

- Is the company making a profit?
- Does the company have enough money to pay its debts?
- Is the company earning a suitable return on the money invested?

```
                         ASSETS
A    Called-up share capital not paid
B    Fixed assets
     I    Tangible assets
          1    Land and buildings
          2    Plant and machinery
          3    Fixtures, fittings, tools and equipment
          4    Payments on account and assets in course of construction
     II   Investments made up of shares and long-term loans to companies
C    Current assets
     I    Stocks
          1    Raw materials and consumables
          2    Work in progress
          3    Finished goods and goods for resale
     II   Debtors
          1    Trade debtors
          2    Other debtors
          3    Prepayments and accrued income
     III  Investments
     IV   Cash at bank and in hand
                 CAPITAL & LIABILITIES
A    Capital and reserves
     I    Called-up share capital
     II   Share premium account
     III  Profit and loss account
B    Creditors (including 12 months or less)
     1    Bank loans and overdraft
     2    Payments received on account
     3    Trade creditors
     4    Other creditors including taxation and social security
     5    Accruals and deferred income
```

Figure 7.3.3 A balance sheet format

The results of the analysis will be used by other people and/or organisations to make business decisions such as: whether to buy or sell shares in the company; whether to lend the company money, or sell goods on credit to the company; whether to supply the company with goods; whether to carry out other investment policies – for example, a merger or takeover bid.

The following are certain standard concepts to look at when analysing this information.

- gross profit percentage
- net profit percentage
- liquidity ratios
- gearing ratios
- return on capital

All of these accounting terms are quite complex so they will be explained by using the example of a fictitious greetings card company.

In this example, you decide to go into business selling greetings cards direct to the public on a market stall and to shops, post offices, etc. by offering a delivery and stock service. To start up the business, which you call Card Business, you need a van and an initial stock of cards. To buy these items you need **capital**. You will also need some money to pay for petrol, road tax, replacement stock, interest payments and salaries. This is called **operating capital**.

You then need to consider the various sources of funds to start up your business. You can provide the capital yourself from savings. You can borrow it from a bank – **loan capital**. Friends and relatives can lend you the money in return for a share in the profits – **share capital**. You might use a combination of these.

You sell the cards to shops on credit: they are your **debtors**. You buy the cards on credit from the wholesalers: they are your **creditors**.

At the beginning of business your financial statement could look like that in Figure 7.3.4.

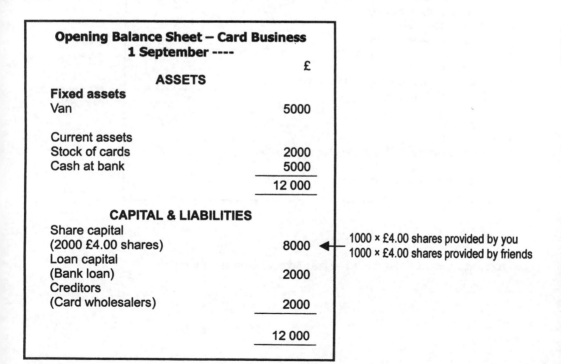

Figure 7.3.4 Card Business Balance Sheet at start of trading

You operate the business for six months and produce a profit and loss account and balance sheet to show the progress of your business:

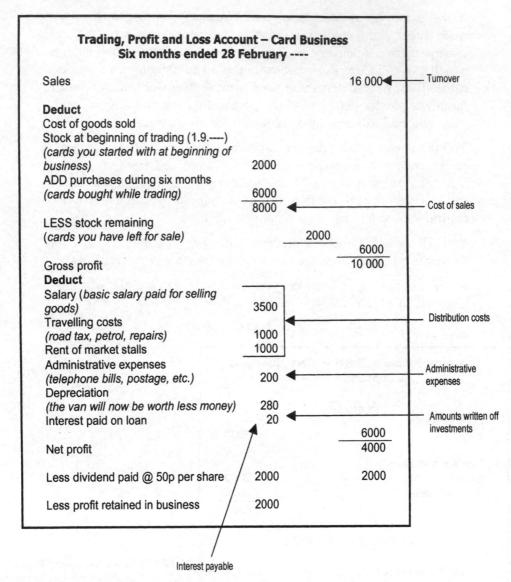

Figure 7.3.5 Card Business Profit and Loss Account after six months

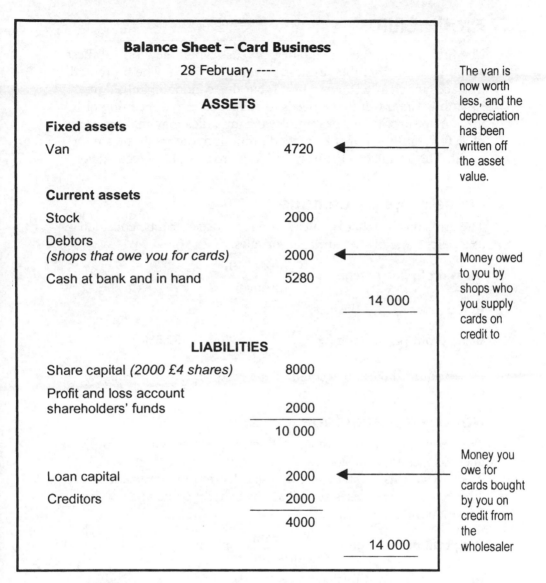

Balance Sheet – Card Business

28 February ----

ASSETS

Fixed assets

Van   4720   ◄────── The van is now worth less, and the depreciation has been written off the asset value.

Current assets

Stock   2000

Debtors
(shops that owe you for cards)   2000   ◄────── Money owed to you by shops who you supply cards on credit to

Cash at bank and in hand   5280

                                                      14 000

LIABILITIES

Share capital *(2000 £4 shares)*   8000

Profit and loss account
shareholders' funds   2000
                                             10 000

Loan capital   2000   ◄────── Money you owe for cards bought by you on credit from the wholesaler

Creditors   2000
                                             4000
                                                      14 000

Figure 7.3.6 Card Business Balance Sheet after six months

This example will now be used to look at the terms and concepts raised earlier.

Profitability

The first question the shareholders will ask when they look at these accounts is whether the business is making a profit. The profit and loss account clearly shows a profit, but this cannot be judged in isolation. The profit figure needs to be turned into a meaningful measure of profit – for example, two companies may make a profit of £6000, but one might be a good profit and one might be a poor profit. The profits can be measured as a gross profit percentage or a net profit percentage.

Gross profit percentage

The gross profit – that is, sales less direct costs – can be considered as a percentage of the 'turnover' or sales:

$$\text{Gross profit percentage} = \frac{\text{Gross profit}}{\text{Turnover}} \times 100$$

In the case of Card Business:

$$\text{Gross profit percentage} = \frac{10000}{16000} \times 100 = 62.5\%$$

However, this takes no account of the costs of actually selling the goods.

Net profit percentage

The net profit – that is, your profit on ordinary activities before taxation – can be considered as a percentage of the 'turnover' or sales, but this *does* take into account distribution costs and administration expenses as well as any other income and interest payable:

$$\text{Net profit percentage} = \frac{\text{Net profit}}{\text{Turnover}} \times 100$$

In the case of Card Business:

$$\text{Net profit percentage} = \frac{4000}{16000} \times 100 = 25\%$$

This level of profitability is quite high. When analysing the results of Card Business you would need to consider why this high percentage has been achieved. In fact it is because the figures are for the six months including Christmas and card sales would therefore be very high for this period. The level of turnover could not be guaranteed for the following six months: this represents a 'seasonal' factor. The figures for operating the business for a whole year would be required to give a fuller picture.

Liquidity

Even though a company is making a profit, it may still have 'cash-flow' problems. This means that it does not have enough money in the bank to pay its ongoing expenses. To take a personal example, you may get a good job, but need a car to travel to work. If you spend all your money on the capital cost of the car, you may find in the first few weeks that you cannot afford to pay the road tax, insurance, petrol, etc. before you get your first pay packet. You now have a 'cash-flow' crisis and unless you borrow some money or sell some of your possessions you cannot get to work.

Companies can suffer with similar problems. Organisations can have money tied up in assets, stocks and debtors and may not have enough money to pay the wages, even though the organisation has a large profitable contract to supply goods. Liquidity is the ability of the company to realise its assets. A company that can no longer meet its financial commitments may have to go into liquidation, which is the process of terminating the affairs of the organisation by selling the assets to settle the debts.

The liquidity of an organisation can be measured by comparing the value of its current assets and its current liabilities using the current ratio or the liquidity (acid-test) ratio.

Current ratio

Here, the current assets are measured against the current liabilities. This shows the relationship between the quickly realisable assets and the current debts:

$$\text{Current ratio} = \frac{\text{Current assets}}{\text{Current liabilities}}$$

In the case of Card Business:

$$\text{Current ratio} = \frac{9280}{2000} = 4.64$$

The current ratio measure includes the stock as a current asset. This ratio appears quite healthy – a healthy ratio occurs if current assets are more than twice current liabilities. However, stock can be valued using a variety of accounting principles. Therefore the value shown in the balance sheet may not represent the realisable value as it can be difficult to realise the full value of the stock if it has to be disposed of quickly. The remaining card stock left in the card business may include Christmas cards and these will have very little value if they have to be sold in January.

Liquidity ratio

This is a measure of liquidity that excludes the value of stock from the current asset figure:

Liquidity ratio = $\dfrac{\textbf{Current assets – stock}}{\textbf{Current liabilities}}$

In the case of Card Business:

Liquidity ratio = $\dfrac{\textbf{7280}}{\textbf{2000}}$ **= 3.64**

This figure is also called the quick or acid-test ratio. It is based on the concept that debtors and cash can be used to settle debts quickly, while stock can take longer to realise. A ratio of one would mean that there was enough cash and money owing to the company to pay off the company debts. An acceptable level is slightly higher than one, as not all people who owe the company money may pay up. A small number of these debts may be represented by 'bad debts'. In the case of Card Business this may be shopkeepers who have had cards on credit and then gone out of business.

The Card Business ratio of 3.64 is quite high and this is represented by the large amount of cash in the bank. As a new business, the bank may have requested a large initial deposit to ensure there were sufficient funds to cover all possible debts and reduce the risk of overdraft facilities being required.

Gearing ratios

Another method of analysing financial statements is to look at the capital structure of the company. This means looking at the relationship between the sources of capital and the effect this has on the profits of the company. In the example of Card Business, the capital comes from two different sources: shares (equity capital) and a bank loan. In the first six months of trading, interest of £20 was paid on the loan and this meant that there was £20 less profit for the shareholders. A higher level of bank borrowing would have meant higher interest payments.

Gearing also looks at the issue of risk. In Card Business the shareholders have all invested money at high risk. If the business has to be wound up, all loans and other outstanding debts have to be settled before the shareholders receive their share. If there is no money left, they will lose their investment. If the company still has outstanding debts remaining after all assets have been realised, however, the shareholders are not liable for any further funds. This is in line with the principle of 'limited liability'. The obligation or liability of the shareholders is limited to their share – for example, the £8000 share capital in Card Business.

Sources of capital funds

Before looking at calculating gearing ratios, it is a good idea to have a look at the different sources of capital funds.

Bank loans. These are funds provided by banks and other financial institutions. They may be for a fixed period and carry interest payments. Different interest rates may be charged, depending on the length of the loan and the security offered against the loan. Loans that are regarded as 'high risk' will usually incur higher interest charges. Banks may also provide money in the form of overdrafts where the bank allows the company to spend more money than is held in their accounts. An overdraft is 'repayable on demand'. When the bank lends money in the form of an overdraft it is usually treated by the borrower as a creditor in the current liabilities, rather than as capital.

Debentures. These are a form of loan capital raised by a company on which interest will be paid. The debentures are usually also secured by a charge against assets. They offer a guaranteed return to investors and are regarded as high security as the income is guaranteed and in a winding-up situation repayment is made before ordinary shares. Debenture holders have no voting rights in the running of the company and are not regarded as 'owners of the company'.

Preference shares. These are a form of share issued by a company on which a fixed rate of dividend is paid after the debenture interest has been paid, and before profits are calculated for the ordinary shareholders. They are also repaid on the winding-up of the company before any repayments are made to ordinary shareholders. Preference shareholders do not usually have voting rights.

Ordinary shares. These are the 'ordinary' form of share issued by a company and the holders are regarded as the owners of the company. The dividend, or share of the profit, is calculated after all other payments have been made. Shareholders also have the last claim on any money left following the winding-up of the company. Shareholders take the highest risk, but if profits are high they will have a larger share of those profits. As the highest risk-bearers they have voting rights in the running of the company at annual general meetings.

Sources of funds are summarised in the following table.

Source of funds	Cost	Voting rights at annual general meetings	Repayment priority	Risk
Bank loans an mortgages secured against fixed assets	Interest charged at relatively low rates	None	Paid as a first priority	Low
Debentures usually secured by a charge on assets	Fixed rate of interest	None	Repaid in priority to other shareholder claims	Low
Bank unsecured loans	Higher rates of interest	None	Loans repaid after secured loans	Low/medium
Preference shares	Dividend paid at a fixed rate though moderate percentage	Not usually	Usually repaid on winding-up of company if sufficient funds	Medium
Ordinary shares	Dividend paid as a share of the profits	Yes	Last claim on repayment after all other claims have been met	High

Calculating gearing ratios

Gearing can be defined as the relationship between ordinary shareholder funds and long-term loans carrying fixed interest charges and dividends. There are various methods of working out gearing ratios, but the most commonly used method is:

$$\text{Gearing ratio} = \frac{\text{Long-term loans} + \text{preference shares}}{\text{Total shareholders' funds}} \times 100$$

Note: Total shareholders' funds also include the retained profits or reserves which represent profits that could have been paid to shareholders but have been kept back by the company. They are in fact a 'loan' made by the shareholders to the company.

In the case of Card Business:

$$\text{Gearing ratio} = \frac{20000}{8000 + 2000} \times 100 = 20\%$$

The higher the gearing ratio the greater the multiplier effect of changes in profit on shareholders. Similarly if profits fall the effect is also multiplied.

It is also important to look at the cost of interest as well. Higher loans mean more of the operating profit is used to pay the cost of interest and/or meet loan repayments.

Return on capital

Another way of looking at a business is to consider the profit made in relation to the money invested in it. The profit figure used is the operating profit or pre-tax profit. The following formula is used:

$$\text{Return on capital} = \frac{\text{Net profit}}{\text{Gross capital employed (total assets)}} \times 100$$

In the case of Card Business:

$$\text{Return on capital} = \frac{4000}{14000} \times 100 = 28.6\%$$

The return on capital can be compared with the return on the capital if it were invested risk free in a building society. This return is currently approximately 5%. The usual rule is that the greater the risk to the capital, the higher the expected return. In the case of Card Business, this means that the friends who have bought shares could lose all the value of their shareholding if the business fails. However, the return on capital in Card Business is currently five times higher than the rate of return from a building society.

Ratios and performance indicators are summarised in the following table.

Measure	Formula	Definition
Gross profit percentage	$\text{Gross profit percentage} = \dfrac{\text{Gross profit}}{\text{Turnover}} \times 100$	Profitability – gross profit considered as a percentage of turnover (sales)
Net profit percentage	$\text{Net profit percentage} = \dfrac{\text{Net profit}}{\text{Turnover}} \times 100$	Profitability – net profit considered as a percentage of turnover (sales)
Current ration	$\text{Current ratio} = \dfrac{\text{Current assets}}{\text{Current liabilities}}$	Liquidity – relationship between quickly realisable assets and current debts
Liquidity ratio	$\text{Liquidity ratio} = \dfrac{\text{Current assets} - \text{stock}}{\text{Current liabilities}}$	Liquidity – relationship between current assets less the stock and current debts
Gearing ratio	$\text{Gearing ration} = \dfrac{\text{Long-term loans} + \text{preference shares}}{\text{Total shareholders' funds}} \times 100$	Relationship between ordinary shareholder funds and long-term loans
Return on capital	$\text{Return on capital} = \dfrac{\text{Net profit}}{\text{Gross capital employed (total assets)}} \times 100$	Relationship between profit made and the money invested in the company

Calculating the ratios

A spreadsheet package can be used to enter the basic information and calculate the ratios. This has the following advantages.

- Once the formulae have been entered correctly, the calculations can be carried out accurately and quickly.
- The basic spreadsheet can be set up as a template and used with different sets of information to produce comparative data.
- The information can then be presented in a variety of formats such as tables, graphs, charts.
- The information can be imported into other software applications – for example, a spreadsheet or graph can be imported into a word-processed document.

Figure 7.3.7 shows a spreadsheet used to calculate ratios.

Obtaining company information

To carry out the analysis of financial information you will need to collect as much information as possible about the organisation you are analysing. This can be collected in the following ways.

- Writing to companies for information. Many large public limited companies will send copies of their annual accounts and reports in response to written enquiries.
- Public/college libraries often have copies of annual accounts for large public limited companies.
- Internet searches can also provide useful information about organisations. The *Financial Times* has an Internet site which can be visited for up-to-date company information. The site **http://www.ukinvest.com** contains information about all companies quoted on the London Stock Exchange, including some of the ratios described earlier.

	A	B	C	D
1	Ratios and Performance Indicators - Card Business			
2	Current stock		2000	
3	Sales		16000	
4	Gross profit		10000	
5	Net profit		4000	
6	Creditors	2000		
7	Loan capital	2000		
8	Current liabilities		2000	
9	Shareholders funds		8000	
10	Fixed assets		4720	
11	Current assets		9280	
12	Retained profit		2000	
13				
14	Gross profit percentage		62.5%	=C4/C3
15	Net profit percentage		25.0%	=C5/C3
16	Current ratio		4.64	=C11/C8
17	Liquid ratio		3.64	
18	Gearing ratio		20.0%	
19	Return on capital		28.6%	

=B7/(C9+C12)   =C5/(C10+C11)   =(C11-C2)/C8

Figure 7.3.7 A spreadsheet used to calculate ratios

Portfolio Note

Certain organisations – for example, public limited companies – are legally required to publish annual accounts, and copies of their annual accounts can be obtained by writing to the company's registered office. Copies of the company accounts may also be available in your college library or learning resource centre. For this reason, it is a good idea to choose such an organisation.

Portfolio activity 7.3 Number 1

Discuss with your assessor an appropriate company on which to conduct an analysis of its financial performance. Collect a copy of the previous accounts for the organisation, including the balance sheets and annual report for the company you have chosen and use a spreadsheet to calculate the gross profit percentage, net profit percentage, liquidity ratios, gearing ratio and return on capital employed for one complete financial year. Prepare this information to be included as an appendix with your final report. The following evidence should be collected:

- copy of the balance sheets
- spreadsheet printouts showing the data and formulae used to calculate the ratios
- appendix detailing the ratios and performance indicators.

Performance criteria:	7.3.1	7.3.2			
Knowledge and understanding:	7.3.a	7.3.b	7.3.c	7.3.d	7.3.h
Evidence requirements:	7.3.1	7.3.2	7.3.3	7.3.4	7.3.5
	7.3.6	7.3.7	7.3.8	7.3.9	
	7.3.16				

Analysing financial information

So far this element has looked at calculating a series of ratios that can be used to analyse financial information. However, these figures do not have any meaning on their own. The next step is to analyse the statistics. You now need to think about the information carefully. What does it mean? Is there an improving or worsening situation?

The Annual General Report accompanying the balance sheet usually contains an analysis of the financial statement. This may include reference to any 'exceptional' situations that may have occurred and that affect the statement such as the costs of a takeover, the costs of shutting a plant, or downsizing and redundancy payments. This analysis may form a useful starting point. However, this statement cannot be totally impartial as it has been prepared with the purpose of presenting it to shareholders to maintain their confidence in the company and the Board of Directors.

Comparing ratios and performance indicators

The ratios and figures you have collected do not have much
meaning unless they can be compared with other similar figures.
It is like asking whether £10 000 is expensive for a second-hand car.
Unless you can compare it with other prices you cannot answer the
question. You need to look at other identical models, at other
similar models and at other cars of the same price. In the same
way, the financial ratios calculated as a result of looking at a
balance sheet need to be compared with other similar information.
The following comparisons can be used:

- *historical comparisons* – comparing the same ratio for the same
  company over a period of time. Previous years' statistics are
  usually published in the balance sheet and previous years'
  balance sheets can be used.
- *industry comparisons* – comparing the same ratios for a similar
  company in the same industrial sector. This is more difficult as
  even though a company may be operating in the same industrial
  sector, it may still have differences such as size, exact range of
  activities, accounting practices.

If industrial comparisons are to be made, it will be necessary to
collect information about similar companies. There is a range of
recognised sources for financial information that should be
available in most libraries. The following table summarises
these sources.

Source of information	Publications	Information
Government statistics published by the Central Statistics Office or Stationery Office	Financial statistics *UK National Accounts* *Economic Trends* *Company Finance*	Information about different industries, balance sheets, lists of companies
Stock Exchange publications	*Stock Exchange Press Company Handbook* *Stock Exchange Official Year Book*	Information about the Stock Exchange and companies listed on the Stock Exchange
The Times	*The Times 1000* *Financial Times –* daily issues	Information on listed companies, daily price of shares and company information

Source of information	Publications	Information
CD-ROMs		Business information, government statistics available on CD Rom
Ceefax/Prestel/Oracle		Current value of shares

The business cycle

Businesses are dynamic organisations that are constantly changing. It can be useful when analysing a business to consider what phase of the business cycle the organisation is in (see Figure 7.3.8).

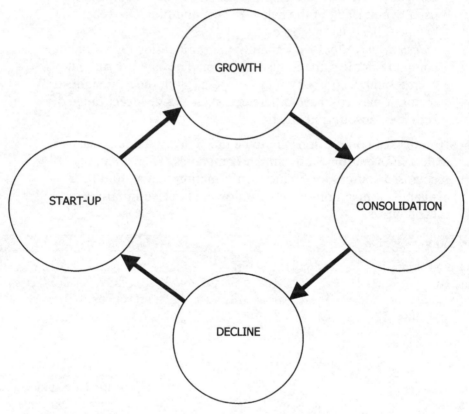

Figure 7.3.8 The business cycle

Start-up is the initial phase. This is the formation of a new business venture – the situation which has been considered in the example of Card Business. Start-up is a high-risk phase as there is no history or prior evidence of activity of the organisation on which to base any investment decisions. New companies will issue information about their activities in a prospectus which outlines the proposed business activities. However, many new public limited companies may not actually be new businesses, but may be small successful private companies which have decided to go public. In these cases they will have a track record on which investment decisions can be based.

Growth is the phase when an organisation seeks to expand its business. It can do this in the following ways.

- *Increase volume* – sell more of the same by increasing the market share or by tapping into other markets – for example, exporting overseas. This gives the advantage of economies of scale. The fixed overheads can be spread over a wider number of products made, which in turn can reduce the price of the goods or increase the profit per item.
- *Expand the range of products/services* – more goods or services can be introduced. Expertise within a particular market area can be used to develop a wider range of associated products – for example, Card Business could sell wrapping paper and small gift items. This has the advantage of building on an existing customer base and organisation expertise.
- *Diversify* – the business can expand by diversifying into different areas. This can be seen by the example of many retail organisations – for example, Marks and Spencer offering financial services. Diversification has the major advantage that organisations are not dependent on one particular type of business, but can spread the risk across a range of activities.

Growth is not always the aim of an organisation, as this may involve risk if a high level of borrowing is required in order to invest in the new activities.

Consolidation is the phase during which businesses consolidate or build on their existing success. This may allow them to accumulate or 'save' profits that can later be invested in expansion.

It can be difficult for organisations to remain static for too long as outside influences such as other competitors and new product development can force them to change. Organisations may change in a number of different ways.

- Internal structures and management methods may be changed – for example, many building societies have recently become banks in order to enable them to expand the range of services and take advantage of different operating regulations.
- Working methods may change as new technologies develop – for example, the growth of call centres to deal with telephone enquiries and selling as a result of new telephone/computerised technologies.

- Products may change as fashions, social patterns, etc. change – for example, the increased sale of diesel and the number of diesel-powered cars rather than petrol-driven ones.
- Ownership may change as businesses are taken over or bought out by other organisations.

Organisations, businesses and activities may also decline and die, or after declining may regenerate or start up again as new businesses – hence the term 'business cycle'.

Decline may be the result of poor profits or bad management. It may also be the result of changing social patterns, technologies, etc. For example, the high street bakery industry was badly hit by the growth in sales of fresh bread in the large supermarket chains. The effects of political, economic, social and technological change are discussed further under PEST analysis (see pages 368–72).

Understanding trends

The figures and ratios discussed earlier are called performance indicators. This means that they are indicators or pointers of how well a company is doing. The figures over a period of time will form part of a trend, and this trend can then be compared with the trends in other similar companies within the industry. The figures collected can be prepared in the form of a table. An example of comparative figures for three fictitious high street shops is shown in Figure 7.3.9.

	Year	Current assets £000	Current liabilities £000	Current liquidity ratio
Shop One	1998	45 000	28 000	1.6
	1999	65 000	50 000	1.3
	2000	73 000	57 000	1.3
Shop Two	1998	90 000	50 000	1.8
	1999	92 000	60 000	1.5
	2000	94 000	63 000	1.5
Shop Three	1998	87 000	73 000	1.2
	1999	70 000	50 000	1.4
	2000	63 000	42 000	1.5

Although in Shop One the liquidity ratio has fallen, the figures show that the current assets have increased by 28 million and the liabilities have increased by 29 million. This could be accounted for by the chain carrying a higher level of unsold stock.

The assets in Shop Two have remained relatively stable, but the level of liabilities has grown.

Figure 7.3.9 Comparative figures for three fictitious high street shops

One of the easiest ways to analyse the trends is to use graphs. Line graphs are usually prepared to show trends. Figure 7.3.10 shows a graph to compare the trend in liquidity ratios for the three fictitious shops.

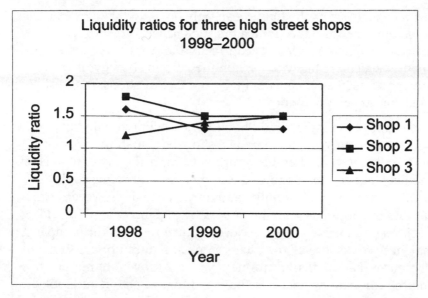

Figure 7.3.10 Trend in liquidity ratios for three fictitious high street shops

Both sets of information have to be carefully analysed and should also be looked at in conjunction with other information. If you look at them on their own, you can only make very general conclusions (see Figure 7.3.11).

Shop One

Assets have increased by £28 million (£45–£73 million) over the three years. This could be because of:
- an increase in stock
- an increase in the number of debtors
- an increase in the cash in the bank
- poor credit control on debtors.

Liabilities have increased over the same period by £29m. This could be because of:
- an increase in creditors
- an increase in short-term loans.

Shop Two has maintained relative stability over three years. Its current liquidity ratio has fallen slightly, but the asset and liability figures have remained stable over the period.

Shop Three has increased its liquidity and reduced both its liabilities and assets. This could be because:
- it is realising its assets and paying off its debts
- it is holding lower stock levels and carrying a lower level of debt.

It could also represent a business going into decline.

Figure 7.3.11 General analysis of the liquidity figures of three fictitious high street shops

Contribute to Financial Planning and Control Activities **367**

Detailed analysis of the figures can only be undertaken by looking at the other performance indicators such as levels of profit and return on capital. You also need to read the Annual General Reports which are likely to explain the current strategy of the companies such as expansion in the number of shops, range of goods or range of activities.

For example, the increase in Shop One's liabilities could be explained by the company taking a short-term loan to increase its stock and that stock then remaining unsold. If the increase in stock had been due to the opening of a number of stores this could indicate that the stock is only temporarily unsold. However, if the number of shops has remained the same, the increase in unsold stock might indicate a reduced level of turnover and the company may need to dispose of the excess stock at reduced prices. It could also mean that predictions for next year's turnover are not positive and the company would therefore need to take action and look at the levels and types of stock held.

PEST analysis

As we have seen, sets of figures cannot be looked at in isolation as companies do not operate in isolation. External events can have an impact on their operation. These events can fall into the following categories:

- Political
- Economic
- Social
- Technological

Consideration of these is often called PEST analysis.

Political influences

Actions taken by government can influence companies and impact on their activities. Governments:

- *pass laws* – for example, Sunday Trading legislation, requirement for health warnings on tobacco products, minimum wage legislation. The passing of the minimum-wage legislation may have increased the costs of some service industries. The disability discrimination laws have an impact on employers and trading organisations and can have financial implications.
- *develop policies to change the way people act and behave* – for example, planning policies that discourage the growth of large out-of-town shopping centres due to concern about the death of town centres.

- *control taxation* – for example, increasing VAT, taxes paid on company profits, duty on petrol, spirits and tobacco. The increase in petrol duty can increase the transport and distribution costs of companies.
- *introduce competition policies* – for example, the introduction of development agencies which may offer incentives for locating businesses in certain areas. Subsidies and tax relief may also be offered to support technological and scientific developments.
- *control foreign policies* – for example, policies that may affect the ability to trade with 'hostile' countries. Trade embargoes may exist for countries with harsh human rights regimes.

Economic influences

There are also financial influences that can affect organisations.

- *Interest rates* – when interest rates are high, companies will have to pay high charges for loans and loan capital. Rising and high interest rates can quickly reduce profits for organisations that depend on high levels of loan capital. High interest rates can also give increased profits to financial investment and banking organisations.
  Falling and low interest rates can mean cheaper mortgages, which can have a positive effect on the housing market and linked industries. When interest rates are low, more people buy shares, as they look to alternative ways of getting a return on their investment. Low interest rates can also mean that companies pay lower interest on capital loans and this will be reflected in larger profits which can lead to an increased share price.
- *Exchange rates* – the value of the pound against other currencies can also have an effect on companies. When the pound is strong so that, for example, it will buy more dollars, goods and raw materials from America are cheaper and English goods sold in America will be more expensive.
- *Overseas economies* – the value of foreign currencies and the level of overseas economies will affect organisations. Goods can be produced at very low costs in 'low-wage' economies. This makes it difficult for goods produced in 'high-wage' economies such as the UK to compete.
- *Salary levels and disposable income* – the amount of money people earn can affect the level and price of goods sold. People with a higher level of disposable income will spend more money on luxury goods such as expensive foreign holidays and top-of-the-range cars.

Social influences

The way people think and behave can change and therefore have an effect on companies.

- *Family patterns* – a falling birth rate and smaller families can lead to a reduction in the volume of childcare goods sold. However, as the average age of mothers rises and more women stay in work the value of the goods sold may rise as higher-priced items are purchased. This tends also to lead to a growth in the numbers of nurseries and childcare activities.
- *Medicine* – advances in medical care together with the falling birth rate have led to an increase in the proportion of older people in the population. There is now a large market for goods and services for older customers – for example, holidays targeted at older people.
- *Fashion* – there are often 'fashion crazes' – for example, skateboards, mountain bikes, YoYos. It would be unwise for a business to build its future on these crazes, but they can affect traditional businesses. However, there are deeper fashion influences – for example, the fashion to be fit and slim has meant an increase in slimming clubs, slimming products and fitness activities.
- *Social awareness* – the growth in the interest of environmentally-friendly products and organic food products has been the result of people's increased interest in the environment. Many organisations now have environmental policies and make commitments about the source of their products.

Technological influences

The rapid growth in technology has been one of the major factors in change in the last twenty years. Technological change can have two major effects. It can affect the way existing organisations work and it can lead to the growth of new businesses which provide the technologies. Technological changes may occur in the following areas.

- *Communications* – the development of fax, e-mail, mobile phones, satellite communications, etc. have all meant that international communications are now cheap, fast, and effective.
- *Computers* – the expansion in the availability and power of computers and the introduction of local and wide area networks have rapidly increased the dependence on computers for the management of organisations. Many organisations now sell hardware, software and consultancy services to support the use

of computers. The number of homes with computers has also rapidly grown.

Internet technologies have also developed rapidly. The number of computers in the home and the access to information internationally is beginning to bring about changes. Goods can be bought and sold using the Internet across geographic boundaries. This has increased competition with cheaper goods available abroad being bought through the Internet. Local tax issues have also become a problem – goods purchased abroad may not have VAT and sales taxes charged at source and so these charges should be paid when the goods are imported into the country. However, this can be difficult to police when goods are purchased through the Internet.

- *Manufacturing processes* – goods can often be produced more cheaply or to a higher standard and organisations need to be aware of changes that occur.
- *Materials* – the growth in the use of plastics and other man-made materials has resulted in a wide range of cheaper products being developed.

Sources of information for PEST analysis

Sources of information for PEST analysis are summarised in the following table.

	Newspapers	Government publications	Books	Internet
Political	The broadsheets – e.g. The *Guardian*, *The Times* – publish articles about the current political situation.	*Hansard* publishes the details of daily government debate. The government produces papers for discussion – e.g. Green Papers.	Books are available on political comment and current political issues.	Government sites give good information on current developments, press releases.
Economic	The *Financial Times*, the *Economist* magazine and other business publications give information on current economic situations.	Government publications give details of economic information – e.g. annual reports published by the Statistics Office and the Stationery Office.	Up-to-date economics books give information on the effects of economics on industry.	Government sites give up-to-date economic information and lists of publications.

	Newspapers	Government publications	Books	Internet
Social	The broadsheets have commentaries, editorials and articles about current social issues.	Government policy documents and Green Papers provide information on 'social' policies. Government publications list information on social trends.	Books on commentaries on modern life, trends, etc.	Government sites give up-to-date information on social trends and lists of publications. Other articles and sites give information on social issues – e.g. environmental issues.
Techno-logical	Trade magazines and publications give information on new processes and materials relevant to a particular industry. Computer information can be found in computer magazines.	Government statistics and social trends information are available.	There is a wide range of books on the effect of the computer, Internet and other technological changes.	Government sites and many sites on computers, etc. can provide technological information.

Forecasting financial performance

When all the information has been collected and analysed a prediction of the future performance of the organisation can be made. This can include a prediction of revenue and profit, values of shares, and the future financial position of the organisation.

Making financial predictions is a complex and specialist activity. You cannot be expected to produce a forecast with the detail and accuracy of a financial specialist. However, you are expected to produce a reasonable, balanced forecast that is based on your research. Your forecast should show that you have a clear understanding of financial statements, ratios and issues that affect organisations. You should show that your forecast can be justified based on the conclusions from your research and analysis. Your forecast should also include reference to your PEST analysis. If you make assumptions, you should state these assumptions, for example: 'If the current sales figures continue then ...' or 'If interest rates remain the same then ...'. You could also explore the effect of change, for example: 'If interest rates rise to a higher level of 8% then ...'.

A very simple forecast for Card Business could look at the effect of inflation and increases in taxation on costs and subsequently on profits.

In the case of Card Business, it would be difficult to increase the costs of goods sold, as there is a high level of unemployment locally, and prices have been kept low to match other outlets. We can assume that increased costs will not be passed on to the customer.

Assuming that sales remain at the same level may be rather optimistic as a large percentage of sales may have included Christmas items and Valentine's Day cards, which are seasonal items. The same level of sales may be difficult to maintain in the next six months. A forecast could be made taking into account a reduced level of sales (see Figure 7.3.12)

Item	Balance Sheet figures	Inflation at 2.5%	Inflation at 5%
Sales	16000	16000	16000
Cost of goods sold	6000	6150	6300
Gross profit	10000	9850	9700
Salary	3500	3587.50	3675
Travelling costs	1000	1025	1050
Rent of market stalls	1000	1025	1050
Administrative expenses	200	205	210
Depreciation	280	287	294
Interest paid on loan	20	20.50	21
Costs	6000	6150	6300
Net profit	4000	3700	3400
Cash at bank	5280	8980	8680

Figure 7.3.12 Forecast for Card Business based on a reduced level of sales

Other factors could also be added to the figures such as:

• increased travelling costs to allow for increased levels of taxation on petrol and vehicle licensing costs as the government increases the costs of travelling on environmental grounds – for example, travelling costs increased by 10% would reduce the profit by £100

- depreciation of stock to allow for cards that are damaged, out-of-season or very poor selling lines could be set at 10% of the stock costs which would reduce the profit by £600.

Even taking into account the increased costs, there would still appear to be a large amount of cash in the bank – that is, the liquidity or acid-test ratio is still much greater than 1.5. The repayment of the bank loan of £2000 could be considered. This would increase the profit and reduce the effect of increases in the bank's lending rates of 10 to 15%. However, as bank rates are still relatively low this does not represent a very good return on capital, compared with the return on capital figure of 25%. A forecast might consider ways in which the capital could be used to increase the revenue and the profits. This could include:

- renting premises to sell cards – this would greatly increase costs as rent, heating, lighting, salaries and a higher stock level would be required
- increasing the number of market stalls and outlets – this would require an additional van, increased market rents, increased travel costs, higher stock level and another salary
- expanding the range of products sold – for example, small stationery items – this would require higher spending on stocks and a larger van to carry the increased range of items.

Technological change may also need to be considered. You may find that you are missing business opportunities because you are busy travelling around delivering cards or running market stalls. It may be a good idea to invest in better communications – for example, a mobile telephone and/or telephone answering machine and fax facilities. The expenditure on these items could be included in the forecast.

Preparing a report

This element requires you to produce a formal written report which should be sufficiently detailed to enable management to use the information with confidence as an aid to strategic planning.

A formal report must include all the relevant information, analysis and forecast. The layout of formal reports is covered in Unit 1. However, you should ensure you include the following details.

- *Terms of reference* – who the report is for, who is writing the report, about which organisation, and any issues to be dealt with in the report.
- *Procedure* – the procedures, methods of research used and sources of information checked.
- *Findings* – a summary of the findings of the research. The detailed research should be included in appendices and the key facts summarised in the findings of the report. You should include your analysis of the findings here. Check that you have included:
  - sales figures
  - profit figures
  - gross profit percentage
  - liquidity ratios
  - gearing ratios
  - return on capital employed.

  Structure your findings carefully. Use headings and/or numbered sections.
- *Conclusions* – the conclusions that can be drawn from the analysis should be included in this section. This should also include the forecast.

The report should be presented using a computer. A word-processing package should be used to key in the main text. Your report should also demonstrate that you have used a spreadsheet to analyse the financial information. Information from the spreadsheet (or financial/accounting package) should be imported and merged into the word-processed report. Some of the information should be presented in graphical form, and this should also be merged into the word-processed report.

For a report of this type the tone should be formal and in the third person.

Remember to reference clearly the sources of information you have used. Where you have copied information from printed sources you should acknowledge the source and should pay attention to copyright legislation.

It may be useful to use the following checklist when you are preparing your report.

Item	Included	Prepared	Completed
Structure of report	Terms of reference		
	Procedures		
	Findings – clearly structured		
	Conclusions including forecast		
	Appendices including information		
Presentation	Word processed and completely accurate		
	Spreadsheet used for financial information		
	Spreadsheet information merged into report		
	Graphs prepared on the computer and merged with the report		
Information	Previous accounts of organisation		
	Information about national and market trends from financial press		
	Sales figures		
	Profit figures		
	Gross profit percentage		
	Liquidity ratios		
	Gearing ratios		
	Return on capital employed		
	Financial forecast		
	Political, economic, social and technological analysis		

Security and confidentiality

Much of the information you will be dealing with is public information. However, if you have been using financial information from your employer, or from a private company, you should treat it as confidential. A password should be used to protect computer information, and printed information should be stored in a confidential file in a locked cabinet.

The finished report may contain other information which is confidential, particularly if you have made forecasts that relate to the activities of your organisation such as forecasts that relate to using companies as key suppliers. If the report is confidential it should be marked as such and all information on the computer should be protected with a password.

Portfolio activity 7.3 **Number 2**

Prepare a report on the financial status of your chosen company using the information collected in Portfolio activity 7.3 Number 1. In addition, you must include a PEST analysis and forecast of the probable performance of your chosen company for the next financial year. Use the report checklist on page 376 to make sure that you have covered all the evidence requirements. The following evidence should be collected:

- full report and appendices
- completed checklist
- personal statement explaining how you carried out the research, organised your time and ensured that you complied with the requirements of confidentiality, the Data Protection Act and copyright.

Performance criteria:	7.3.1–8				
Knowledge and understanding:	7.3.a	7.3.b	7.3.c	7.3.d	7.3.e
	7.3.f	7.3.g	7.3.h	7.3.k	7.3.l
	7.3.m	7.3.n	7.3.o	7.3.p	
Evidence requirements:	7.3.1–20				

Test yourself

Knowledge and understanding	Questions
a	What are the main differences between a public limited and a private limited company and what documents are they both legally required to publish?
b	Explain the different functions of balance sheets and profit and loss accounts.
c	Explain the difference between fixed and current assets, giving examples of both.
	Explain the difference between share and loan capital, giving examples of both.
d	Select two types of statistical material and explain their uses, purposes and functions in reference to business.

Knowledge and understanding	Questions
e	Explain the method(s) you would use for conducting a statistical investigation, giving reasons for your choice of method(s).
f	Give an example of financial information that could usefully be presented in the form of: • a table • a chart • a diagram.
g	Explain the methods you would use for selecting, extracting, interpreting and analysing figures, statistics and non-statistical information accurately.
h	Where would you find information on the finances of a public limited company?
i	Explain the importance of maintaining confidentiality and security about your oganisation's finances, giving an example of a possible consequence of breach of confidentiality.
j	How do the Data Protection Act and copyright legislation affect analysis of financial statistics?
k	What would be the impact of visual presentation of statistics in a report in comparison with verbal presentation?
l	Which software packages would you use for presenting financial information and how would you import information from a spreadsheet/graphics presentation program into a word-processing program?
m	Give two sources of financial information and explain how you would classify and organise this information.
n	Explain how the person/people for whom you are presenting financial information can affect the way in which you present the information.
o	Select one type of written report on financial information and explain its: • purpose • style • format.
p	Explain why time management techniques need to be used when analysing financial information.
	Give two possible consequences of not managing your time efficiently when preparing financial information.

Activity 7.1

Memo

> **To:** Office Administrator
> **From:** Finance Manager
> **Date:** Monday, -- -- --
>
> **Financial Information**
>
> Staff frequently need to research financial information on organisations. Please prepare for them a list of information sources where they can find out:
>
> - the financial situation of public limited companies
> - the financial situation of organisations within an industry
> - the current share values of an organisation
> - information on current social trends
> - information on current economic trends.
>
> Include in the list some helpful guidelines on the information available from each source.

Activity 7.2

Desknote

> # DESKNOTE
>
> **From:** Jill Saunders
> **Date:** Wednesday, -- -- --
>
> Thanks for your help in providing the financial report. Other staff need to provide financial reports. Please prepare guidelines about the structure, presentation and information required in a formal financial report.
>
> Jill

Activity 7.3

E-mail

E-mail

To:	Office Administrator
From:	Jill Saunders
Date:	Friday, -- -- --
Subject:	Computer update

As discussed in your recent appraisal, you will soon be responsible for producing financial reports for the department. It is probable that you will need some additional software to do this. Please produce a report outlining the hardware/software that is necessary for producing financial reports, listing what you already have and what will need to be purchased.

Please include an explanation as to why the relevant hardware and software is necessary.

Activity 7.4

Memorandum

MEMORANDUM

To: Office Administrator, Finance department
From: Karen Yelland, Reorganisation Project Manager
Date: Thursday, -- -- --

Budget procedures

The first stage of the reorganisation is virtually completed and all departmental administrators now have a networked computer with the full range of office software on their desks. The next stage of the project is to prepare a set of procedures on how this hardware and software can be used for preparing and monitoring their departmental budgets.

Please draft a suitable set of procedures that will enable them to monitor their budges and also allow the Finance department to keep track of their spending.

Activity 7.5

E-mail

E-mail

To:	Office Administrator, Finance department
From:	Harry Threader, Account
Date:	Friday, -- -- --
Subject:	Departmental budgeting

From the beginning of the next financial year, all departments will have to prepare full departmental budgets. Draft a memo to all departmental administrators giving them suitable cost headings and information on appropriate methods of determining spending under each heading.

8 Contribute to the Provision of Personnel

This unit looks at the steps that need to be taken to recruit a new employee to an organisation. The three elements follow the process from the analysis of the job role through advertising and interviewing to the induction of a new member of staff, as outlined in the following diagram:

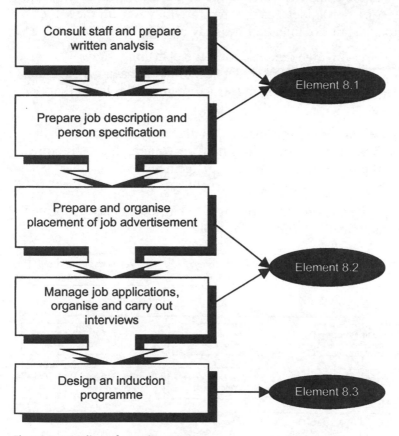

Figure 8.1 Outline of recruitment process

Element 8.1

PREPARE JOB ANALYSIS, JOB DESCRIPTION AND PERSON SPECIFICATION

Organisation charts

Every organisation has a structure to inform employees who they report to and what they have to do. Most organisations define their structures in the form of an organisation chart. Those at the top of the chart are more important and have more responsibility than those lower down. Charts can be used to show the following.

Staffing. This includes the titles of job roles in departments, and the lines of responsibility. The names of the postholders may be included in the chart. However, some organisation charts leave out the names of postholders, as the structure may remain the same even though staff holding the roles may change. (See Figure 8.1.1)

Departments. In large organisations, the chart may show department and function, each department then having a separate, more detailed chart showing the structure and job roles in that department.

Hierarchy. This shows the levels of management within an organisation. Some organisations have very hierarchical structures – that is, there are many levels of management – while other organisations have much 'flatter' structures.

Project groups. People from different departments may be formed into teams to manage a particular project.

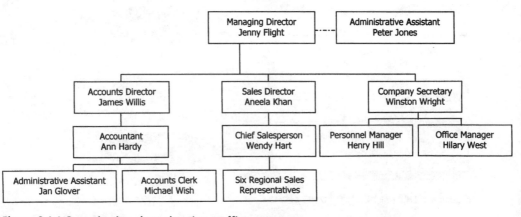

Figure 8.1.1 Organisation chart showing staffing structure

382 Administration Procedures for Higher Secretarial Diplomas

Types of organisational structure

Hierarchical structures

A hierarchical structure is one in which there are many levels of management. Usually, the more hierarchical an organisation, the more 'formal' it is – that is, with more systems and procedures to be followed. Hierarchical structures are often shown in the shape of a pyramid and are called pyramid structures. (See Figure 8.1.2)

The pyramid shape reflects the numbers of people employed at each level. At the top of the pyramid there is usually a senior person who has overall responsibility for the organisation – for example, a college principal or managing director. This senior person is usually supported by a small team of staff – for example, a board of directors or deputy principals. This small group is responsible for the strategic management of the organisation – that is, it has an overview of the whole organisation and plans its future direction. The middle management then prepares tactical plans that detail the activities required to implement the management plan, identifying the resources required and defining targets and milestones in relation to its particular working area – for example, the Sales department. The bottom level of the pyramid usually contains a greater number of staff and contains the operational staff. These are the staff that actually carry out the day-to-day activities detailed in the tactical plans.

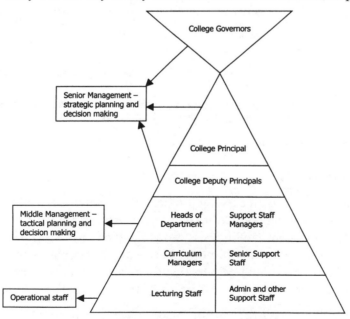

Figure 8.1.2 An organisation chart showing a hierarchical structure of management in the shape of a pyramid

Flat structures

An organisation with only two or three levels of management is known as a flat structure. The business is likely to have an informal style of working as everyone will know everyone else and there will be good communication between bosses and employees.

Matrix structure

In a matrix structure people report to two bosses – one of whom is a line manager and the other a service manager. Figure 8.1.3 shows a college that has related courses and staff grouped into separate departments in a hierarchical format with heads of department and department representatives. However, all these departments are supported by other sections that are concerned with the operation of the organisation such as Finance, Administration and Student Services.

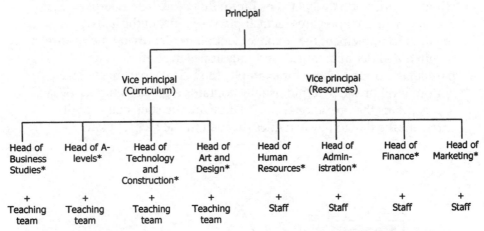

* Lecturers in each department mainly teach on courses in that department – for example, Business Studies staff would teach accounts, law, business studies, etc. to students on business studies courses.

Figure 8.1.3 A matrix chart in a college

Job vacancies

A vacancy may arise when an existing job becomes vacant as a result of staff promotion or resignation. Vacancies may also arise when new posts are created in response to business growth and change. However the vacancy has arisen, it is important to analyse the requirements of the post accurately. This should help to ensure the applicant appointed to the post is able to meet the business needs of the organisation.

Staffing costs are high, and the authority to replace staff and/or create new posts usually has to be gained from senior management. The senior management will work with the Human Resources and

Finance departments to develop a manpower plan and staffing budget. The manpower plan will include estimates of future recruitment requirements for different grades of staff across all departments. Approval for the staffing vacancy should be gained from senior management before any further steps are taken.

Portfolio note

In the college environment you could simulate the activities required for this unit by selecting a real post in the Administration department or by choosing a post from the training office/model office.

Portfolio activity 8.1 **Number 1**

Agree with your assessor and/or line manager which job you will prepare evidence on to cover this unit. Record the notes from this meeting. Obtain written approval from senior management to confirm the post you will be working on. This may be in the form of a memo or notes from a meeting. The following evidence should be collected:

• written confirmation of the job.

Performance criteria:	8.1.1	
Knowledge and understanding:	8.1.a	
Evidence requirements:	8.1.1	8.1.3

Job analysis

Job analysis requires the systematic collection of detailed and objective information about a job role followed by careful analysis. Job analysis is usually carried out in order to:

• design the selection criteria for a job
• identify job gradings and promotion opportunities
• identify training needs
• analyse the extent to which Equal Opportunities requirements are being satisfied.

The first step in carrying out a job analysis is to collect data about the job role. There are various ways of doing this, depending on the type of analysis to be carried out, the cost and the acceptability of the method to employees. Expensive, time-consuming methods of data collection will not be appropriate for routine, straightforward job roles. You need to ask yourself how you are going to analyse the data and what data you need in order to carry out the analysis.

Collecting job data

Observation

The postholders currently carrying out the tasks can be carefully observed for a defined period and records kept of activities undertaken. The record of observation may just be a list of tasks (see Figure 8.1.4). This method of collecting data can be time-consuming, but it does allow all details and information to be collected. Alternatively, some form of activity grid may be prepared and checked off as activities are completed, as in Figure 8.1.5.

Job role	Location	Date
Filing Clerk	Sales Department	22 January ---- 9.30-11.30
Time	**Main activity**	**Interruptions**
20 minutes	Presorting daily filing	Telephone calls (3) - messages taken
30 minutes	Filing papers in filing system	Telephone request for information - provided
20 minutes	Preparing new folders	Request from member of staff for a folder - provided
30 minutes	Entering new information in folders and filing in filing system	
20 minutes	Entering new orders into computer system	

Figure 8.1.4 A record of observation

If a key feature of the job is operating equipment it may also be appropriate to observe the member of staff doing this. An equipment-operation grid may be used for this purpose (see Figure 8.1.6). This is quick to complete and may be completed by different members of staff – for example, a supervisor or colleague. It also makes statistical analysis much easier. However, the grid needs to be carefully constructed so activities are not missed out.

Job Role	Filing Clerk					Date
						22 January ----
Department	Purchasing (Sales) Personnel Manufacturing					
General activity	Specific activities – circle activity carried out					Comments
Manual filing	(Creating new files)	(Filing new material)	(Presorting routine filing)	(Routine filing)		Spent time sorting incorrectly filed folders
Telephone activities	(Answering telephone calls)	(Taking messages)	Providing information	Making telephone calls		
Computer database	Entering data on customer database	Retrieving data from customer database	Printing out data from customer database			

Figure 8.1.5 An activity grid

The problem with observation as a method of collecting data is that the observation activity itself may affect the way the job is being done. The postholder(s) being observed may be trying to impress and therefore may make the tasks seem more complicated, or carry them out with more care than they usually do. Observation also relies on the objectivity of the observer.

Logs and diaries

The postholder may be asked to complete a log or a diary to record activities. The diary may have an 'open' format with spaces to write activities completed, say, every half hour (see Figure 8.1.7), or alternatively the postholder may be asked to make an entry every time they start a new activity.

The diaries and logs can be easily collected over a period of time. The level of detail and information in the logs will depend on the person completing them and may vary considerably. Staff completing the logs may take many parts of the job for granted and so may not include all the activities. They may also miss 'interactions' that take place as part of the job. Logs and diaries do take time to complete and very busy staff may regard completing them as a low priority. If they are completed at the end of the day, or very quickly, they may not be an accurate reflection of the activities actually carried out.

Observation and completion of diaries/logs require relatively little knowledge, and focus on the content of the job. Job analysis interviews, considered next, can probe more deeply.

Name of postholder			Week beginning		
Department					

	Circle average for a week														
Equipment	Frequency of use*					Level of difficulty**					Time spent on task***				
Computer – customer database	1	2	3	4	5	1	2	3	4	5	1	2	3	4	5
Computer – word processing	1	2	3	4	5	1	2	3	4	5	1	2	3	4	5
Computer – spreadsheet	1	2	3	4	5	1	2	3	4	5	1	2	3	4	5
Fax machine	1	2	3	4	5	1	2	3	4	5	1	2	3	4	5
Photocopier	1	2	3	4	5	1	2	3	4	5	1	2	3	4	5

*   1 = infrequently – e.g. maximum of once a day
        5 = frequently – e.g. on at least 10 occasions each day

**   1 = simple use required to complete routine tasks
        5 = complex, expert use required to complete routine tasks

***   1 = maximum of one hour a day
        5 = at least 5 hours per day

All figures should be averages, and should be recorded for routine or normal activities completed as part of the job role.

Figure 8.1.6 An equipment-operation grid

Name		Job title	
Date		Department	

Time	Activity completed	Comments/difficulties, etc.
9.00–9.30	Filing invoices Answering telephone	Telephone kept ringing with calls for other members of staff
9.30–10.00	Making new files	
10.30–11.00	Filing new files	Some files had to be sorted out because someone had misfiled them
11.00–11.30		

Figure 8.1.7 A job analysis diary

Interviews

These can be carried out with postholders, with line managers and/or with service users. Interviews may be structured, with questions that require straightforward factual answers. For example:

What equipment do you use during the day?

They may also be more open, with questions that have no predetermined answers. For example:

Tell me about your job.

Interviews provide more opportunities for exploring the postholder's understanding of why activities are undertaken and how they fit into the organisational/departmental activities as a whole. Interviews can focus on behaviour rather than activities and allow postholders to share their understanding with interviewers. However, interviews take time and require planning and preparation. The quality of the data depends on the quality and objectivity of the interviewer. Interviews can be summarised and recorded in writing by the interviewer, or may be recorded on tape for later analysis.

When there are several people in the organisation carrying out an activity, it can be useful to hold group interviews. These allow postholders to share their different understandings of the job and can highlight aspects of the job that might not be anticipated in a one-to-one interview. These interviews can be recorded on tape or video for later analysis.

Interviews with supervisors or service users can also be helpful in the case of a new job where there is no existing postholder to interview or observe. This allows for staff expectations about the requirements of the new job to be recorded.

Participant observation

Another method of collecting job data is actually to carry out the activities required of the postholder. This can give valuable insight into the interactions and constraints of the job. However, this is time-consuming and not always practical. It may be particularly difficult to carry out specialist activities or activities in situations where not making a mistake is crucial.

Content analysis

The documentation relevant to the job can also be studied. This may include job descriptions, procedures, performance appraisals for postholders, or may involve looking at previous analysis activities and examining the products of the job. Personnel policies, job grading criteria, salary scales, standard contracts and working conditions can all be used to collect relevant information. This method may be useful for a new job, where procedures and other written documentation can be reviewed. However, this is a very 'flat' method of collecting data and will not reflect the human interactions and behaviour required to carry out a job effectively.

Standardised questionnaires

More sophisticated methods of job analysis have been developed using standardised questionnaires. Saville and Holdsworth developed a method called the *Working Profiling System* where three separate job analysis questionnaires cover managerial, service and manual/technical work areas. The questionnaires have two parts: the first establishes the main tasks of the job and the second examines the context in which the job is performed. Another method is Position Analyses Questionnaires (PAS) where standard structured job analysis questionnaires containing 194 job elements are used. Complex computer analysis is then carried out to produce results. These methods would be used by specialist consultants when asked to carry out job analysis and this would carry quite a considerable cost. You would not normally be required to use these methods for analysis.

Critical incident technique

Data may be collected by observing the critical incidents of the work area. This means recording activities that, if not carried out correctly, can make the difference between success and failure – for example, completing invoices incorrectly, not answering telephone calls, not issuing visitors with security passes. The critical incident should be observable, clearly identifiable and leave no doubt about its effects. The critical incidents can be recorded from observations or interviews.

Analysing job data

The job data is usually collected using a combination of the above methods and can then be analysed. The results of this analysis will determine the content of the job description and the person specification. There are various methods of analysing the data.

Activity analysis

Once the activities to be carried out as part of the job role have been identified, they can be analysed in terms of the level of difficulty, the percentage of time spent on them and the frequency with which they occur. The emphasis of job descriptions and person specifications usually reflects the activities that occur most frequently and take up the greater percentage of time. These activities reflect 'essential' skills and knowledge required by the postholder – difficult activities that occur infrequently and take up little time may define skills and knowledge that are 'desirable' rather than essential.

Activity analysis is very helpful in designing job descriptions, as these usually consist of lists of activities to be completed – for example:

Key in customer information on a customer database.

(see the section on job descriptions, pages 398–400). However, for a person specification the activities need to be defined in terms of skills and knowledge that are required – for example, keyboard skills, computer skills, knowledge of computer database systems.

Skills, knowledge and attribute analysis

Another way of analysing the data is to list key features of the activities under headings of skills, knowledge and personal attributes required for those activities. Then each section can be subdivided into essential, desirable and non-essential (see Figure 8.1.8). The information for this may have been collected from interviews with current postholders, line managers and service users. Skills and knowledge are relatively easy to define, but personal attributes are those personal aspects that are required to carry out a job effectively and are much more difficult to define. For example, receptionists may need to have a good standard of personal appearance and a pleasant manner.

Activity: entering data on a computer database		Essential	Desirable	Non-essential
Skills	Keyboard skills	*		
	High-speed touch-typing			*
Knowledge	Computer systems/ computer literacy		*	
Attributes	Accuracy	*		
	Confidentiality	*		
	Ability to work to short deadlines		*	

Figure 8.1.8 A skills, knowledge and attribute analysis table

Outcome analysis

In this method of analysis it is the outcomes, rather than the activities, that are analysed. The outcomes of a job role are identified as operations that fit within the goal of the department/ organisation. For example:

Accurate and up-to-date records of customer information are maintained.

This outcome can then be broken down into task statements.
For example:

**Update customer database daily with accurate
customer details received from the Sales Co-ordinator.**

The factors that affect the outcome can also be identified.
For example, the details have to be received from the Sales
Co-ordinator, otherwise they cannot be entered on the database.
The outcome method of analysis can also provide information on
the skills and qualities required to complete activities – for
example, accuracy and being able to work to deadlines.

As well as listing activities, it is important to consider the
acceptable standards of achievement and proficiency at work.
A postholder may spend all day entering data on the customer
database, but if the data is not accurate customers may be lost,
the data may have to be re-entered and time may be lost in
constantly having to check work. The timescales are also
important – data may be entered accurately, but at such a slow
rate that the database quickly becomes out of date and a backlog
builds up. Care needs to be taken to ensure the workload is
realistic and help may need to be given, particularly to new staff.
One advantage of outcome analysis is that quality standards
about the way a job is done are included – for example, being
accurate and up to date. If problems do arise, these should be
discussed with the postholder and training and action plans
prepared to remedy the situation.

Critical incident analysis

In this method the critical incidents within a job role are identified.
These critical incidents should be observable and the outcome
should leave little doubt concerning its effects. For example, not
entering customer information correctly can result in losing orders,
delayed payments and delivery of incorrect goods. Identifying the
critical activities can identify the skills and knowledge that are
essential for postholders.

Performance analysis

Another method of analysing data is to identify the key features
of good performance and bad performance. Staff may have been
asked to identify their own performance on grids, and may also
have collected feedback from other staff that identifies their areas
of good performance. This information could be gained from
appraisals where staff grade areas of their work. Observation can

also be used to highlight the activities, skills and attributes that are present in good performance. These can then be built into the person specification.

Job grading

Most organisations operate methods of grading for jobs. This usually helps determine levels of payment and promotion opportunities. As part of the job analysis it will be necessary to identify the appropriate grading level. In small organisations the job grading system may be informal, but in larger organisations a formal structure is likely to exist. In a college, for example, there will be grading systems for administrative staff, lecturing staff and management staff. In order to determine the appropriate grade for a job, certain criteria will be applied. These criteria can be used for job analysis to determine the appropriate grading for a new job.

The criteria used for grading jobs will often consist of the following.

Level of supervision. This usually means the number of staff supervised or controlled by the postholder. For example, most junior grades might have no supervisory responsibility at all, while a head of department might be responsible for supervising all the staff within the department.

Level of financial responsibility. Junior staff may have very limited responsibility for financial activities such as budgets.

Level of specialist knowledge. Some job roles require high levels of specialist knowledge and the grading will reflect this – for example, specialist engineers, accountants.

Level of job complexity. Some jobs can be defined as routine, while others may require a high level of complex activities to be carried out. The more complex the activities, the higher the grading.

Level of experience. Grading may reflect the level of experience required to carry out particular jobs – for example, senior personnel may have many years of experience.

Level of qualifications. Grading may reflect relevant qualifications held by postholders or required for particular posts – for example, degrees, professional qualifications.

Length of time with the organisation. Some job roles may be graded as trainee or junior posts depending on the length of time the postholder has served with the company.

Preparing the job analysis

When the data has been collected and analysed it should be presented in a written format using a word processor. The document should contain a summary of the detailed information collected and the analysis carried out, which may be included in appendices.

The analysis should contain discussion about each of the following:

Job title. The title is important and should accurately reflect the activities of the post. For example, administrator, administrative assistant, secretary and personal assistant may all mean slightly different things. The rationale for choosing a title should be included.

Job purpose. The overall purpose of the job should be stated. For example:

Maintain accurate and up-to-date customer records.

The findings of the research and the relevant discussion which led to this description should be included in the analysis.

Level of responsibility, including any supervisory duties. The observation and interviews should have shown whether any supervisory activities were involved as part of the job role. Details of who would be supervised, for which activities and how often should be recorded and reflected in the job analysis. Information should also have been collected about the accountability of the post.

The post in relation to the organisation's structure. This should include likely career progression routes. An organisational and/or departmental structure should be prepared to include the new post.

Location. The actual location of the post should have been agreed as a result of interviews with line managers and service users. A suitable location means one that allows work to be carried out efficiently – for example, near the fax and photocopying machines if their operation is a major part of the job. Sufficient space should also be allocated to allow for all the necessary equipment to be safely operated – for example, space for a computer, telephone and sufficient suitably-placed sockets to eliminate trailing wires. The advantages and disadvantages of several locations may be discussed in the analysis.

Salary and grading. The job analysis should have provided data on suitable grading and salary scales from personnel documentation and policy documents. The rationale for final decisions should be discussed in the analysis.

Hours of work. The hours required to complete the activities should have been determined from the job analysis – for example, full-time or part-time. If the job is part-time a suitable working pattern, such as mornings only, should be specified.

Duties and tasks. The observation, log sheets, diaries and interviews should have shown the duties and tasks to be undertaken by the postholder. The analysis should identify which tasks are priority tasks and which are marginal activities.

Skills and competencies. The job analysis should have identified the skills and competencies required to complete the duties and tasks. Competence is the ability to consistently carry out a task to the required standards. The required skills and competencies should reflect the practical activities carried out by the postholder. There is more information on identifying, defining and assessing competence in Element 6.2 (pages 301–4).

Knowledge and understanding. This is the information that the postholder needs to know in order to carry out a job effectively – for example, knowing about the Data Protection Act and understanding its implications for the job.

Personal attributes. These are the personal qualities required of the postholder to ensure efficient and effective discharge of duties and tasks, such as the ability to remain calm when in difficult situations and the ability to work under pressure.

Figures 8.1.9–10 show an example of a job analysis.

Job title
Filing Assistant.

The title Filing Assistant was chosen to reflect the main activity of the role, and its current level of responsibility. The main activity of the postholder is manual and computerised filing. The current post is intended for a trainee; there is then scope for promotion as the job activities grow and the postholder gains a higher level of skill.

Job purpose
Maintain accurate and up-to-date customer records.

Level of responsibility, including any supervisory duties
No supervisory duties required, but responsible to the Sales Administrator.

The post in relation to the organisation's structure

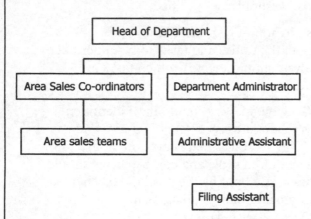

Sales Department

With appropriate experience and training, the filing assistant can progress to the role of administrative assistant and administrator. This may be from within the department or by applying for suitable vacancies in other departments.

Location
The filing assistant will be located in the administrative office in the Sales Department. The desk and office space vacated by the move of the computer programmer will be allocated to the filing assistant.

Salary/grading
According to Personnel policy on grading and salaries the post will be at Junior Administrative grade (JA1) and the salary will be on the scale £6500–£8000. The starting salary will be agreed on appointment and will depend on age, experience and qualifications.

Hours of working
Monday – Friday, 9.00 am–5.00 pm
One hour for lunch, 1.00 pm–2.00 pm

– 1 –

Figure 8.1.9 A job analysis – page 1

Duties/tasks
Priority rating
(1 = top priority, 3 = low priority)

Maintain accurate up-to-date records of customers

Enter new customers on the customer database	1
Update customer details on the customer database	1
Retrieve information from the customer database for administrative and sales staff	2
File source documents in the filing system	3

Maintain accurate up-to-date sales information

File invoices in the numerical paper-based filing system	2
Retrieve invoices on request from the numerical paper-based filing system	2
Remove out-of-date invoices every three months	3
Store out-of-date invoices in the long-term archive store	3

Provide administrative support to the sales team

Answer the telephone, pass on messages and provide routine information	1
Photocopy routine documents on request	2
Word process routine documents, letters, memos, reports, etc.	2
Deal with Incoming and outgoing departmental post	1

Skills and competencies
Skills

Essential	Keyboarding skills, good communication skills, accurate data entry skills
Desirable	Numeracy skills

Competencies

Essential	Data entry techniques, use of manual filing systems
Desirable	Operation of the photocopier for routine copying, dealing with internal telephone enquiries

Knowledge and understanding
Filing methods and systems
Computer systems
Data Protection Act

Personal attributes

Essential	Ability to work as part of a team
	Ability to work unsupervised
	Ability to work under pressure
	Logical, neat and tidy

Figure 8.1.10 A job analysis – page 2

Portfolio activity 8.1 Number 2

Collect data about the agreed job from the current postholder (or member of staff authorising development of the new post), the line manager who will be responsible for the postholder, and members of staff who will receive a service from the postholder. Use at least two different methods of data collection.

Carry out an analysis of the data and produce a written job analysis using the headings given on pages 396–7. Ensure you discuss whether Equal Opportunities legislation is satisfied (see pages 24–25). The following evidence should be collected:

• job analysis data
• written job analysis.

Note
Your employer or college should have an Equal Opportunities statement. Ask Personnel, Human Resources, the Library or the Learning Resource Centre for a copy.

Performance criteria:	8.1.1				
Knowledge and understanding:	8.1.a 8.1.i	8.1.c	8.1.d	8.1.g	8.1.h
Evidence requirements:	8.1.1–16		8.1.31–34		

Job description

The job analysis is used as the basis for the production of the two key documents that are used in the recruitment of staff – the job description and the person specification. A job description is a broad statement of the purpose, scope, duties and responsibilities of a particular job. It is particularly useful as part of the job selection process to aid interviewers and provide prospective applicants with detailed information about the vacant post. Staff involved in the selection process should have a copy, and copies should also be sent to applicants.

Some organisations may not use job descriptions as they feel that job roles are always changing and evolving and job descriptions would constantly need rewriting. Other organisations have written job descriptions that clearly identify where job roles fit into the organisation's activities. This is particularly the case in organisations that have written procedures, organisational handbooks and ISO standards (see Element 6.1, pages 286–8).

The exact content of the job description may vary depending on how it is to be used. The list of items it contains is very similar to that covered in the job analysis. The job analysis contains the results of research and the discussion of the analysis carried out to reach decisions about the job role. The job description is the final outcome of this analysis. Figure 8.1.11 shows an example of a job description.

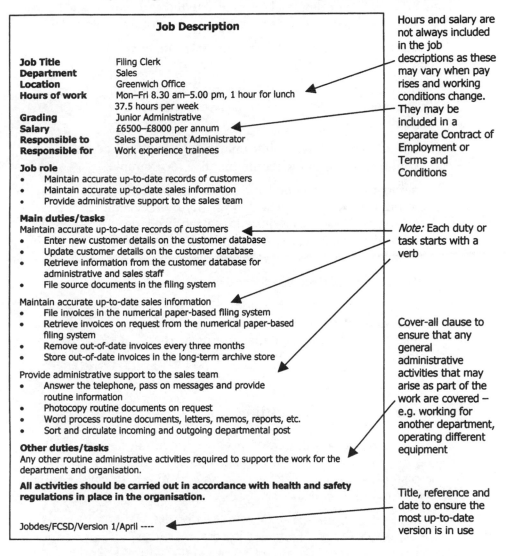

Figure 8.1.11 A job description

As well as the headings shown in the job description above, job descriptions may also contain details of:

* *responsibility for equipment* – a list of equipment to be used and any specific duties with regard to that equipment – for example:

Photocopier – routine operation of the photocopier, maintenance of photocopier stationery supplies, replacing toner cartridges, reporting faults.

- *duties and tasks listed under timescale headings* – for example, daily, weekly, monthly, quarterly and annual tasks

- *contact details* – information about internal and external contacts that need to be maintained as part of the job – for example:

    Maintain regular contact with the Sales Team to collect customer details.

    Maintain good working relationships with all customers, particularly when answering telephone enquiries.

- *particular working conditions* – information about probationary periods, induction, training requirements – for example:

    The post will initially be for a six-month probationary period. Day release is provided to Anytown college and the postholder is required to attend college and achieve an NVQ Level 2 Administration within one year.

- *any other relevant information* – for example:

    When urgent work or backlogs occur in other departments, the postholder may be required to cover work in these departments at the direction of the Sales Administrator and/or senior management staff.

Portfolio activity 8.1 **Number 3**

Using your job analysis as a basis, prepare the job description for the agreed post. Agree the job description with relevant people – for example, the postholder's line manager. The following evidence should be collected:

- job description prepared on a word processor
- witness testimony from a relevant person confirming that you have prepared the job description, agreed it with them and prepared it on time
- personal statement explaining how you prepared the job description, how you ensured it met with Equal Opportunities legislation (see pages 404–5) and how you maintained confidentiality.

Performance criteria:	8.1.2	8.1.3	8.1.4	8.1.5	
Knowledge and understanding:	8.1.a	8.1.f	8.1.g	8.1.h	8.1.i
Evidence requirements:	8.1.1	8.1.3	8.1.16–23		
	8.1.31–34				

Person specification

As a result of the job analysis you should be able to prepare a specification of the type of person who would be suitable for the post. This specification will detail the personal attributes, knowledge, qualifications and experience required in the postholder. These details may be classified as essential and/or desirable. Essential requirements are those that are necessary for the job to be carried out competently. Desirable requirements are those that would be useful. Missing areas within the desirable section may be provided by training once the postholder is in place.

The person specification will be used for the following activities.

Preparation of the job advertisement. The qualities, knowledge and experience can be listed in the job advertisement. The amount of detail provided will depend on the level and type of job. Where specialised jobs are being advertised the requirements listed may be very specific. A more general list may be provided when several jobs or more general vacancies are being advertised.

Information for applicants. More detailed lists may be provided to applicants. This will help them decide on their suitability for the post. It will also help them prepare applications that highlight the relevant requirements.

Preparation of a shortlist of applicants. The essential and desirable requirements are used to sort out the suitable applicants who will be interviewed for the post. The response to advertisements can vary considerably from a very small number to many thousands. Sorting through these can be time-consuming, so care taken at the initial stages to clearly and accurately specify the requirements should help to reduce the number of unsuitable applicants.

Basis for questioning. The areas identified in the requirements can be used by interviewers as the basis for the questions they use when interviewing. They can explore further with the candidate the relevant areas of the requirements.

Basis for selection. During the interview, the candidate may be rated by interviewers against the different requirements listed in the person specification. These ratings can then be used by the selectors to make a decision about a suitable appointment.

Figure 8.1.12 shows an example of a person specification.

Person Specification			
Job Title	Filing Clerk		
Department	Sales		
Location	Greenwich Office		

> This specification has been prepared in the form of a list so that it can be completed by selectors and interviewers

Requirements	Essential	Desirable	✓
Personal attributes	Well organised Good communication skills demonstrated by one of the following: • GCSE Grade C English • Literacy Certificate of Achievement • LCCIEB English for Business 1 • Key Skills Communications	Able to work as part of a team Able to work on own initiative Numerate, demonstrated by one of the following: • GCSE Grade C Maths • Numeracy Certificate of Achievement • Key Skills Numeracy	
Knowledge/ Qualifications	Knowledge of filing and general office procedures demonstrated by one of the following: • NVQ Level 2 Administration • RSA/OCR Certificate in • Administrative and Secretarial Procedures (CASP) • LCCIEB Diploma in Administration (First or Second Level) • Pitman Office Procedures Level 1 Keyboarding skills demonstrated by one of the following: • RSA/OCR Word/Text Processing Stage I • LCCIEB Text Production 1 • Pitman Stage I Word/Text Processing	Computer literate demonstrated by a qualification, for example: • RSA/OCR CLAIT (Computer Literacy And Information Technology) • LCCIEB Practical Computing • NVQ Level 2 Information Technology	
Experience	Previous office experience not essential	Some office experience at junior level – for example, trainee posts, work experience while at college or school	

Figure 8.1.12 A person specification

Qualifications

The specific qualifications required for a post will vary depending on the job role being advertised. For qualifications that relate to specific job roles you will need to carry out the research during the job analysis process. There is a very wide range of qualifications and they can be confusing, but the following general guidelines may be useful.

General area of competence	Vocational level of qualification	Academic level of qualification	Secretarial Administration Diplomas
Able to carry out supervised routine activities	NVQs at Level 1	GCSE grades D, E Key Skills Level 1	LCCIEB Diploma in Administration (First Level)
Able to carry out supervised activities that are more complex and with some autonomy of decision making	NVQs at Level 2 GNVQ Intermediate level	3 GCSE passes at Grade C Key Skills Level 2	OCR Certificate in Administrative and Secretarial Procedures LCCIEB Diploma in Secretarial Administration or Diploma in Business Administration (Second Level)
Able to carry out routine and complex activities without supervision and with considerable responsibility and autonomy Supervisory responsibility for routine activities and/or guidance of others	NVQs at Level 3 GNVQ Advanced level	2/3 A level passes Key Skills Level 3	OCR Diploma in Administrative and Secretarial Procedures LCCIEB Private Secretary's Diploma or Diploma in Business Administration (Third Level)
Responsible for planning, resourcing and carrying out a broad range of	NVQs at Level 4	Higher National Certificates/ Diplomas Degree qualifications	OCR Higher Diploma in Administrative Procedures

General area of competence	Vocational level of qualification	Academic level of qualification	Secretarial Administration Diplomas
complex technical or professional work activities Responsible for the work of others		Key Skills Level 4	LCCIEB Executive Secretary's Diploma (Fourth Level)
Expert professional or specialist area Senior management responsibility	NVQs at Level 5 Professional recognition – e.g. chartered status	Postgraduate degrees, Masters degrees, doctorates (PhDs). Key Skills Level 5	Master in Business Administration (MBA)

Note: Scottish qualifications are not included in this table as the levels differ from those listed and cannot be specified as rigidly.

Equal Opportunities

All activities carried out at work should comply with current laws. When dealing with people it is important to consider the requirements of the following laws.

- *Sex Discrimination Act 1975* – makes it generally unlawful for an employer to discriminate against a woman or a man either on the grounds of their sex or on the grounds of being married. When recruiting staff it is unlawful to discriminate on the grounds of sex or marriage in arrangements made for determining who should be offered employment, whether recruiting by advertising through employment agencies, job centres or careers offices.
- *Equal Pay Act 1970* – requires that employers give equal pay for men and women doing like work or work of equal value. 'Pay' covers all remuneration, including bonus payments, sick pay and pensions, and contractual benefits such as company cars. 'Lije work' means doing work of a broadly similar nature. 'Equal value' relates to situations in which jobs make equal demands on staff in terms of skill, effort, decision making and responsibility. This is why accurate grading and competence assessment is important.
- *Employment Rights Act 1996* – entitles employees to receive details of their terms and conditions of employment in writing as well as itemised pay statement.

- *Working Time Regulations* – entitles those who have been employed for at least thirteen weeks to three weeks' annual paid leave pro rata – for example, someone working two days a week would be entitled to six days' annual paid leave.
- *Employement Relations Bill 1999* – all women are entitled to a minimum of eighteen weeks's maternity leave and men and women with at least one year's service are entitled to three months' parental leave following the birth or adoption of a child. Employers must give at least one week's notice to an employee who has worked for the company for less than two years; and then at least one week for every year of service up to twelve. Employees must give at least one week's notice if they have worked for the company for one month or more (this does not increase with increased service).
- *Race Relations Act 1976* – similar to the Sex Discrimination Act 1975 and makes it generally unlawful for an employer to discriminate against applicants or employees on the grounds of their race.
- *Disability Discrimination Act 1995* – provided new rights for disabled people in the areas of employment; access to goods, facilities and services; buying or renting land or property. These laws are being implemented over a period of time – further information can be obtained from the Disability Discrimination Act Helpline (tel. 0345 622 633/644 or fax 0345 622 611).

Further information can be found by accessing the Open Government website:

http://www.open.gov.uk

It is good practice for an organisation to prepare an Equal Opportunities statement, for example:

> **This organisation is an Equal Opportunities employer. There is no discrimination on the grounds of sex, marital status, colour, race or disability. This applies to all areas of recruitment, training, promotion, dismissal and conditions of employment.**

Organisations may also be required to show that they actually monitor their employment practices to ensure no discrimination is taking place. This means checking the profile of applicants and employees of different sexes, races and disabilities to ensure they are being fairly paid and are receiving training and other opportunities equally. Some organisations may have an Equal Opportunities representative or committee who meet regularly to review policies and practices to ensure they are satisfying the legal requirements.

Cultural differences

It is important for staff to be aware of cultural differences when dealing with people in all aspects of their work – for example, job applicants, visitors, customers and colleagues. Many of our judgements about people are subjective and are made on first impressions. We look at the way people dress, their body language, tone of voice, etc., yet these can have different meanings in different cultures.

- *Dress* – dark suits or black skirts may be identified as suitable office wear and appropriate for interviews; yet other forms of dress should be equally acceptable, particularly when these are an expression of traditional cultural dress or linked to religious beliefs. Care has to be taken when issuing uniforms – the policy should be flexible in order to adapt to different cultural dress styles. For example, some religions require all females to wear trousers and these should, therefore, be available as part of the uniform.
- *Body language* – methods of greeting can vary between cultures – for example, handshakes may not be appropriate. Levels of eye contact may vary and downcast eyes may be seen as a sign of respect not indifference.
- *Tone of voice and language* – some cultures may value a quiet manner, and a member of staff who is quiet should not be judged as shy or reticent.

Cultural differences may also have implications for other work activities. For example, Christmas celebrations may not be relevant to people who are not Christians. Certain groups may also celebrate other festivals and may want to book holidays to celebrate them with their families. Canteens and food facilities should cater for a wide range of diets – for example, alcohol or coffee are not allowed by some religions and alternatives should be available.

Care should be taken throughout the recruitment process to ensure no direct or indirect discrimination takes place.

- Check advertisements to ensure they do not exclude any groups, or give any hidden messages.
- Ensure selection at all stages is made against clear, objective criteria, and that all decisions are recorded. This should include the reasons for not selecting people for interview or for final appointment.
- Ensure all the organisation's Equal Opportunities policies are clearly followed, and that careful monitoring takes place.

Confidentiality

It is very important to keep all information about jobs, grading, salaries and recruitment confidential. Care should be taken to ensure all job analysis documents are kept confidential. Job descriptions should be kept confidential until they are released for wider use – for example, when sent to job applicants. The organisation's policy on the confidentiality of pay scales and grading criteria should be checked. Some organisations have an open policy about this information, while others keep it confidential.

Treat all personnel information as confidential and do not disclose it to unauthorised people. Mark relevant documents as 'Confidential' and store the information in a folder in a locked cabinet when not in use. Use a password to protect documents prepared on a word processor. Lock disks away when not in use.

Portfolio activity 8.1 **Number 4**

Prepare a person specification for the post you are dealing with. Agree it with relevant people – for example, people receiving a service, the line manager. The following evidence should be collected:

* person specification prepared on a word processor
* witness testimony from relevant people to confirm you agreed the person specification with them and prepared it by the agreed deadline
* personal statement explaining how you prepared the person specification, how you ensured it met with Equal Opportunities legislation and how you maintained confidentiality.

Note
It is a good idea to design the person specification so that it can be used as a selection matrix to aid the shortlisting of candidates (see Figure 8.1.12 on page 402).

Performance criteria:	8.1.2	8.1.3	8.1.4	8.1.5	
Knowledge and understanding:	8.1.a	8.1.b	8.1.d	8.1.e	8.1.g
	8.1.h	8.1.i			
Evidence requirements:	8.1.1	8.1.2	8.1.3	8.1.4	8.1.16
	8.1.24–34				

Test yourself

Knowledge and understanding	Questions
a	Produce an organisation chart to show the structure of your organisation and clarify the duties of staff at different levels.
b	Name three acts of Parliament that are relevant when preparing job advertisements and list any of your organisation's rules and regulations that relate to these acts.
c	Explain the principles behind job analysis and the techniques of job grading.
d	Explain how to assess required levels of competence and desirable personal attributes for a particular job.
e	Clarify the levels of competence as related to vocational and academic qualifications for a particular job.
f	Explain what the accepted standards of achievement and proficiency at work are in relation to a particular job.
g	List and explain three ways to communicate effectively with colleagues at all levels.
h	Explain how you would devise and complete a form or document using the appropriate vocabulary, tone and style.
i	Explain how you would access, collect, select and produce information and what types of technology would be most appropriate for this purpose.

Element 8.2
CONTRIBUTE TO THE RECRUITMENT OF PERSONNEL

When the job analysis has been carried out, and the relevant documents prepared, the recruitment process can begin. The job description and person specification should be placed in a file and labelled with the job title. All further information in relation to the recruitment process should then be included in the file.

Portfolio activity 8.2 **Number 1**

Prepare a file for the post you are recruiting to and include all the relevant documents prepared as a result of activities completed in Element 8.1. The same job vacancy should be used as in Element 8.1. Prepare a separate file including information on the organisation's personnel policies – for example, the Equal Opportunities policy. Keep these files up to date as you proceed with the recruitment process. The following evidence should be collected:

- labelled file for the job vacancy including relevant documentation
- labelled file including the organisation's personnel policies and Equal Opportunities information.

Performance criteria: **8.2.1**   **8.2.2**

Recruiting methods

There are four main methods of recruiting staff.

- *Internal recruitment* – staff may be recruited from within the organisation. This can be an effective method of recruiting staff as it involves very little cost and the staff recruited should require less training because they are already familiar with the organisation's policies and procedures.
- *Reviewing informal existing contacts* – recruits may be identified from former employees, work experience students, casual callers, applicants who have been interviewed for a previous post and whose names are held on file. This is a cheap method of recruitment and has the advantage that the recruits may already be known to the company.
- *Organisation s recruitment procedure* – the organisation will put in place its formal recruitment procedure and advertise, interview and select staff. This is more expensive as it requires advertisements and staff time spent on selection and interviewing.
- *Sub-contract recruitment* – the services of an external agency may be hired to advertise and recruit staff. They may carry out the whole process – for example, advertise, interview and select; or they may advertise, screen and submit selected CVs and applications to the organisation for final selection and interview. This is usually the most expensive method of recruitment.

Advertising the vacancy

If recruitment is to be from outside the organisation then the vacancy will need to be advertised. There is a wide range of publication sources that can be used for advertising vacancies, and the choice will depend on the:

- *level of vacancy* – for example, trainee or managerial
- *type of post* – whether a specialist or general publication is required
- *cost* – cheaper sources might be used for routine posts, while more expensive sources might be used for specialist technical vacancies
- *organisation s policies* – for example, all posts might be required to be advertised internally for a period before being advertised externally
- *accounts* – the organisation may have accounts with particular publications in which all vacancies are advertised
- *local conditions* – for example, there might be a local college that provides a good source of trainee staff
- *coverage* – some vacancies might require national coverage – for example, technical specialists, professional staff.

The following table outlines the various ways in which job vacancies may be advertised:

Source	Suitable for	Cost	Advantages/disadvantages
Local press	All posts	• paid per space taken with the advertisement	• only recruits from local labour pool • not specifically targeted
National press	Professional, managerial and specialist posts	• paid per space taken with the advertisement • more expensive than local media	• recruits from national labour pool • costly • may not be specifically targeted (although some national press publications have 'specialist days' when particular vacancies are advertised)
Professional publications and journals	Professional and specialised posts – for example, *Times Educational Supplement* for teachers	• paid per space taken with advertisement. • prices will vary depending on type of journal	• recruits from specialised labour pool

Source	Suitable for	Cost	Advantages/disadvantages
Internal advertisements on noticeboards, newsletters, job lists	All posts	• no cost	• cheap • offers existing staff opportunities to apply for posts • only recruits from existing labour pool
Internet – vacancies may be advertised on company web page	All posts	• no cost if the web page has been set up with a vacancy section or noticeboard	• cheap • national/international coverage • limited accessibility
Posters and advertisements sent to local schools/ colleges/ universities	Suitable for junior and trainee posts	• no costs, apart from postage	• cheap • targeted at college students • no control of information when it has been received by college
Local job centres and careers services	All posts but may not be suitable for more specialised vacancies	• no costs	• cheap • targets particularly those people who are unemployed or positively looking for work • does not reach those already in employment
Local radio	All posts but would not be appropriate for single vacancies	• cost of preparing the advertisement, plus the cost of broadcast • depends on the length and frequency of broadcasting	• reaches a wide audience • suitable if a large number of similar staff need to be recruited – for example, staff for a new large retail store
Recruitment agencies	All posts but certain agencies may specialise in particular types of staff – for example, accountancy staff	• charges made for each member of staff recruited for customers • quite expensive	• people actively looking for work may contact an agency • may have lists of suitable people on its books • will carry out initial screening of applications • expensive

Source	Suitable for	Cost	Advantages/disadvantages
Recruitment fairs	Suitable for specialist vacancies – for example, computing personnel, or university 'milk-round' for graduate recruitment	• charge for a stand at these fairs varies, but can be relatively expensive	• targets particular technical areas or types of recruit • people are actually looking for work • expensive to hire stands, and pay for personnel to staff the stands
'Head-hunting' agencies	Suitable for high-level management or very specialised technical staff	• expensive specialist service	• Only used when key posts need to be filled

Information about the distribution of press publications and the cost of advertisements can be found in *Willings Press Guide*, which should be available in the reference section of any public library. The publications in question can also be contacted directly for detailed information. For press publications there are usually various options available, such as one-column, two-column and larger advertisements – the more space used, the higher the cost. Although large advertisements may be more expensive, some organisations believe that the quality and size of the advertisement justifies the extra cost. They may want to create a very good impression of the organisation to encourage the best candidates to apply. It is also possible that small advertisements could be missed by casual readers.

Portfolio activity 8.2 **Number 2**

Research information about appropriate publication sources for the job vacancy you wish to fill. Write a memorandum to an appropriate member of staff identifying and recommending an appropriate publication. Give information about distribution and cost and the reasons for your choice. The following evidence should be collected:

• copy of memo.

Performance criteria:	8.2.3
Knowledge and understanding:	8.2.f
Evidence requirements:	8.2.1 8.2.8 8.2.16–20

Preparing an advertisement

The advertisement for the job vacancy will need to be prepared. Not only should it appear in the right publication, but it should also be clearly and accurately worded. The media chosen and type of advertisement should be designed to do the following.

- *Generate an adequate number of replies* – there should be sufficient suitable applicants to allow some choice in selecting for interview.
- *Minimise the number of wasted applications* – too many applications will mean many disappointed candidates and additional work for the recruitment team in selection procedures and rejection letters.
- *Give a good impression of the company* – the advertisement may be read by many people, whether they apply for the job or not. It should be designed to match the company image. This may mean including logos, and choosing suitable font styles and wording. It can also include information about the organisation that will give a good impression – for example, the benefits package that the organisation offers.
- *Ensure compliance with Equal Opportunities legislation* – the advertisement should include a statement about equal opportunities, but care may also need to be taken to ensure there is no indirect discrimination. For example, use of the word 'secretary' may result in more female respondents than the word 'administrator'.
- *Provide applicants with sufficient information* – potential applicants should be able to decide whether they have the appropriate qualities/skills and whether the vacancy is worth applying for. It should also give clear information to enable applicants to make an appropriate response. For example:

  Please call Jane Headall on 01234 76345; write to Head Office, 3 Greenwich Trading Estate, Greenwich, London EC23 4YP; or e-mail hr@comcouns.co.uk for further information and an application form.

- *Provide feedback about the usefulness of different sources of publication* – the job advertisement may be given a different job reference for each publication. For example, if the reference in the advertisement is AM/23/d, then 'AM/23' may be the actual job reference and 'd' may identify the particular publication. The quality and quantity of applicant responses from each publication can then be analysed.

Figure 8.2.1 shows an example of a job advertisement.

COMPUTER COUNSELLORS

requires an

ADMINISTRATOR TO THE SALES DEPARTMENT

Salary £12,500 – £16,000 per annum
25 days annual holiday
Comprehensive benefits package including pension and free health insurance

COMPUTER COUNSELLORS is a rapidly-expanding company that provides computer solutions to business problems. We have a large number of customers in the UK and abroad. The growth in business has meant the promotion of the current postholder to Sales Department Office Manager. We now urgently need to replace this key member of staff.

The Administrator provides a key support role to our Sales Team. He/she also liaises with our customers. The successful applicant will have:

- good communication skills, with a minimum of GCSE English Language Grade C
- qualifications to NVQ Level 3 standard, for example NVQ Administration Level 3, RSA/OCR Diploma in Administrative and Secretarial Procedures or LCCIEB Diploma in Business Administration (Third level)
- good computer skills, either relevant computer experience or a minimum of RSA/OCR CLAIT, LCCIEB Practical Computing
- at least two years' administrative experience

Applicants should have recent relevant experience working as an administrator in a busy customer-oriented environment.

The post is full-time and office hours of 8.30 am – 5.00 pm are worked five days a week.

COMPUTER COUNSELLORS is an equal opportunities employer and welcomes applicants from all sections of the community.

Please apply in writing quoting reference AM/23/d and including a Curriculum Vitae to:

Miss Surindar Khan
Human Resource Manager
Oxford Technology Park
Redfern Ring Road
OXFORD
OX4 6DS

Figure 8.2.1 A job advertisement

Collecting candidate information

A range of methods can be used to collect information from the candidate. The methods to be used should be clearly stated in the job advertisements. A combination of the following methods may be used:

Letter of application. The applicant is invited to send a letter giving personal details. This should contain information about their education, experience, personal qualities and their suitability for the vacancy. Letters have the advantage that the applicant's literacy skills can be assessed. However, this may not be a true picture of these skills as they may have had help with the preparation of the letter.

Application form. An application form may be sent for the candidate to complete. This means that consistent information can be collected from every applicant. However, complicated forms may deter some applicants. Application forms should be carefully designed to ensure accurate, relevant information is collected. Many organisations have standard application forms and the Human Resources department will provide examples.

Some candidates may have a disability which makes it difficult for them to complete application forms. A statement about the acceptability of alternatives should be included with the form, for example:

> **If you have a visual or other impairment which makes it difficult for you to complete our forms, you are welcome to present the information in a typed or word-processed format instead.**

Curriculum vitae (CV). This is a summary of education, qualifications, experience, etc. prepared by the candidate. It should contain the following information.

- *Personal details* – name, date of birth, marital status, telephone number, etc.
- *Education* – details of the education received by the candidate: usually secondary education onwards.
- *Qualifications* – a list of relevant qualifications with dates, grades, boards, awarding bodies, etc.
- *Experience/employment record* – a list with dates, employer names, job titles and brief details of the job roles usually starting with the current or most recent job role.
- *Relevant personal information* – information about hobbies, voluntary activities, whether a driving licence is held, etc.
- *Referees* – two or three names of referees, usually including the current employer. Some applicants may use the phrase 'Referees provided on request', particularly when they do not want their current employer contacted at this stage.
- *Personal qualities statement* – some applicants may write a brief 'pen sketch' of their personal qualities, for example:

> **I am a well-motivated individual who enjoys a challenge. I like working in a team and get on well with people.**

As this is only a personal statement, it does not carry a lot of weight. The key purpose of a CV is to provide factual information and enable conclusions to be drawn about a candidate from that information.

What candidates leave out can be as informative as what they include. If a candidate does not include qualifications achieved at the end of secondary education, then they may be questioned about this. Also, they might be questioned about periods of time in their career history for which they cannot account.

- *Equal Opportunities monitoring form.* A form may be included to allow the analysis of applicant response from different ethnic groups, and to monitor that all groups are dealt with equally.

Providing candidates with information

If candidates are required to request an application form for a vacancy they may also be provided with further information to allow them to decide on their suitability for the post and help them prepare their application.

The following information may be provided to interested candidates.

- *Job description* – this will allow them to decide whether they are suitable for the job, and whether it is a job they want.
- *Person specification* – this will allow them to decide whether they have the appropriate skills and qualifications. It should also provide them with information about which of their strengths and weaknesses to highlight in the application process.
- *Details of rewards and working conditions* – the salary, benefits and working conditions will provide them with an idea of whether they want the job. Information about training and promotion prospects may also be included. The reward package may be particularly important when recruiting in areas of skill shortage where candidates may need to be 'tempted' to apply for jobs. Information about relocation packages and additional benefits may also be supplied.
- *Organisation information* – background information on the organisation may be supplied to give the applicant some idea of the type of activities that may be involved in a job role.
- *Local information* – where applicants are drawn from a national labour pool, local information may also be sent. This may include information on the availability and cost of local housing, schools, etc.

- *Explanation of the application process* – for example, interview dates and procedures. This should include information on when references may be taken up, for example:

  References will be taken up after interview and before final selection.

  The cost of responding to unsuccessful applicants can be considerable, and there may be a statement explaining how responses will be dealt with, for example:

  We regret that we are unable to acknowledge receipt of all applications, however, if you are shortlisted for an interview you should hear within six weeks of the closing date.

- *Equal Opportunities statement.*

The information pack should be despatched promptly to the applicant. If the information pack is self-explanatory it may be despatched with a compliments slip. Alternatively, it may be accompanied by a standard letter, or one prepared using mailmerge. Figure 8.2.2 shows an example of a standard letter of response to an applicant.

Requesting references

An alternative view of the applicant can be gained by taking up references. These are statements about an applicant provided by individuals named by the applicant. The reference may relate to their competence at work – for example, a reference from a previous employer or a college lecturer. Character references may also be requested. These may be provided by a person of 'standing' in society – for example, a doctor or police officer. References can be requested at different stages in the selection process.

- *Prior to final shortlisting and interview* – to provide information to help with the shortlisting process. This can be time-consuming as many references may need to be requested, and there may be delays in receiving the responses.
- *After shortlisting but before interview* – to provide information that could be useful for interviewers. The reference request should indicate the date of interview so that responses can be received in time.
- *After interview but before final selection* – to provide information that can be checked for consistency with the interviewees' responses. This is more cost-effective as only a few references will need to be requested. There may still be delays with responses.

COMPUTER COUNSELLORS

Oxford Technology Park, Redfern Ring Road, Oxford, OX4 6DS
Tel 01865 338927 Fax 01865 338948 hr@comcouns.co.uk

[Applicant's address]

20 December ----

Dear Applicant

Administrator to the Sales Department – Reference AM/23

Thank you for contacting us in connection with the above advertisement. I am pleased to enclose an application form, job description and information pack as requested.

Please return the following documents by 6 January ----:

• Application form completed in black ink
• Equal opportunities form

If you wish to receive an acknowledgement of receipt of your application, please complete the enclosed postcard and attach a first- or second-class postage stamp.

Shortlisted applicants will be notified by 6 February. Interviews will be held in the third week of February.

I look forward to receiving your completed application.

Yours sincerely

Miss Surindar Khan
Human Resource Manager

Encs

Figure 8.2.2 A standard letter of response to an applicant

• *After interview and final selection* – used as a final check before a contract is issued. This is the most cost-effective method as usually only one reference needs to be requested. There may still be delays with responses. This method is also often more acceptable to the candidates, as they may not want their present employer to know they are applying for another position unless they are certain they will be offered it.

The weighting given to references may vary. Employers may give good references for staff they do not want to keep, because, for example, they might otherwise have to make them redundant. Colleagues who are also friends might be used as referees and therefore might not give a true picture. Character references are also difficult to judge, as the referee is often a relation or friend of the applicant.

COMPUTER COUNSELLORS

Oxford Technology Park, Redfern Ring Road, Oxford, OX4 6DS
Tel 01865 338927   Fax 01865 338948   hr@comcouns.co.uk

10 January ----

Mr John Watson
Sales Director
Whatnot Computers
65 High Street
OXFORD
OX1 3JG

Dear Mr Watson

Reference for John Handley for post of Administrator to the Sales Department

I would be grateful if you could provide a reference for the above applicant who has given your name as a referee.

I enclose a copy of the job description and would welcome your comments on his suitability for the post. The postholder will have a key role in our Sales Department, and I would particularly appreciate your comments on his ability to work under pressure, and provide a high level of customer service.

Could you please respond by 22 February as interviews are to be held on the 26 February. I enclose a stamped-addressed envelope for your reply.

I look forward to receiving the reference and thank you for your contribution.

Yours sincerely

Miss Surindar Khan
Human Resource Manager

Encs

Figure 8.2.3 A letter requesting a reference (open format)

The reference may be requested in different formats. Figure 8.2.3 shows an example of an open format – a letter requesting a reference is sent and the format of the response is left open to the referee. The response is usually also in the form of a letter.

Figure 8.2.4 shows a more structured approach, in which a form requesting a reference is sent to the referee. The organisation may have a standard form which is used to provide references. This allows standard information to be requested – for example, punctuality, attendance, trustworthiness.

COMPUTER COUNSELLORS

Oxford Technology Park, Redfern Ring Road, Oxford, OX4 6DS
Tel 01865 338927   Fax 01865 338948   hr@comcouns.co.uk

Reference Request

Name of applicant John Handley
Title and level of job vacancy Administrator to the Sales Department
Planned date of interview 26 February ----

Your name has been provided by the applicant as a referee to support his/her application for the above post. We would be grateful if you could complete this reference form and return it as soon as possible in the reply paid envelope provided.

Referee Name	
Job Title	
Organisation	
In what capacity are you known to the applicant?	
How long have you known the applicant?	
Please comment on the applicant's suitability for the post with reference to the following:	
Punctuality	
Attendance	
Trustworthiness/honesty	
Relationships with colleagues and other contacts	
Accuracy and attention to detail	
Any other relevant information	

Signature		Date	

Figure 8.2.4 A structured reference form

Whichever method is used, details of the job are usually sent to the referee so that they can comment on the applicant's suitability for the post.

Portfolio activity 8.2 **Number 3**

1 Draft an advertisement for the job vacancy you wish to fill.

2 Prepare applicant information to be sent in response to advertising.

3 Find out about your organisation's policy for obtaining references. If the organisation does not have a policy, consult with a manager about the appropriate time and method for collecting references. Draft a letter to be sent when requesting references. The following evidence should be collected:

- job advertisement
- applicant pack
- letter requesting a reference.

Note
You can receive applications from 'real' candidates for your job vacancy, or carry out and arrange interviews by recruiting to 'vacancies' in a training office/model office in your college.

Performance criteria:	8.2.2	8.2.4	8.2.5	8.2.6	8.2.7
Knowledge and understanding:	8.2.g	8.2.n	8.2.o	8.2.r	
Evidence requirements:	8.2.1	8.2.4	8.2.10	8.2.16–20	

Selection for interview

When all the applications have been received they have to be considered carefully to identify possible candidates for shortlisting. If there are a lot of applicants, an initial sifting may be carried out to remove the most unlikely ones. The people who will carry out this sifting should be agreed at the outset of the recruitment process. The person specification should be used as a guide to help the sifting process. The person specification format shown earlier in Figure 8.1.12 (page 402) allows for comments to be written against each section, and this should be completed and attached to each application. The use of the person specification can help to eliminate prejudice and make the sifting process more objective. When the sifting process has been completed, a shortlist of applicants for interview should be prepared.

Candidates should be notified of the outcome of the shortlisting stage of the application process. Successful candidates should be informed of the interview details. An example of a letter inviting a candidate to interview is included in the section on interviews (see Figure 8.2.6, page 429). Unsuccessful candidates should also be informed, although as mentioned earlier, some organisations do not do this for all vacancies. See Figure 1.2.2, page 38 for an example of a rejection letter.

However the interview and selection process is structured, it should be remembered that it is a two-way process. Just as the organisation is making a judgement about the applicant, so the applicant will also be making a judgement about the organisation. Care should be taken to give the applicant a fair but positive view of the organisation that will attract good-calibre applicants.

The interview process

The selected shortlist of candidates will be called for interview. Before this happens, several decisions need to have been made about the interview process. The date and place of the interview need to have been decided. In addition, decisions should have been made on who will be carrying out the interviews, the type and structure of the interview, and whether any tests will be given to the candidates.

Types and structures of interview

Interviews are a standard and accepted method of selecting candidates. However, it is very difficult to eliminate bias from the interviewers. Many interview decisions are made in the first few minutes of the interview. The appearance of the candidate, the form of dress and the body language can all have a major influence on interviewers. An interviewer may then subconsciously structure the rest of the interview to achieve a desired outcome – for example, if they like the 'look' of the candidate they may ask easy questions and fail to explore more difficult issues. Some candidates may be more nervous than others, and so not project themselves to their best advantage. However, it will not necessarily be the most confident one who is the best candidate, so interviewers should do their best to help the interviewees feel at ease.

Subconscious decisions about race, gender and culture should be avoided by the interviewers – for example, they might expect female applicants to dress in a particular way, perhaps in a business suit, and any other form of dress might be regarded as 'inappropriate' despite the fact that this has no relevance to the candidate's ability to perform at work and that the clothes might be worn for religious or cultural reasons.

The quality of the interview depends on the quality of the interviewer. It is often assumed that all people can interview and no consideration is given to selecting interviewers who are skilled at asking questions and capable of making unbiased judgements. Training can be useful for helping interviewers to develop their questioning skills, and raising their awareness of personal bias. Video records of interviews are often used to help interviewers analyse their own practice.

The focus of the interview is on the candidate's ability to talk about themselves and their work. Some very capable candidates may be disadvantaged by this – for example, they could be excellent at their job, but not very good at talking about it. There is also a danger of the organisation selecting a candidate who can talk about work, but who finds it difficult to actually carry out the activities.

A range of different interview structures may be used to try to eliminate some of the problems that arise from the use of interviews.

One-to-one interview. The interview is conducted by one interviewer. This type of interview can be fairly informal and is less intimidating than others. In this atmosphere a rapport can be established between the parties that can allow for more open discussion. It is also cost-effective in staff time. The biggest disadvantage is that it can be subject to the bias of the interviewer. This type of interview may be used for routine, low-level or temporary posts.

A slightly different form of one-to-one interview structure may also be used in which different staff interview the applicant on a one-to-one basis and compare notes later. This allows staff to gain their own perceptions of an applicant.

Small group interview. Two people may interview the candidate together. This can allow a level of informality to be retained. Each interviewer can explore a different area. This structure can be particularly effective when there is a technical content to the job – one interviewer can explore the technical areas, while the other looks at more general personal characteristics.

Panel interview. The applicant may be interviewed by three or more interviewers in a panel. This type of interview can be quite formal, particularly where a large panel is used, and can be intimidating for candidates. The panel structure allows the interviewers to see the response of the applicant to a range of different questions. This type of interview should help to eliminate bias, although it can be difficult if senior managers or influential staff form part of the panel. It is also a difficult type of interview to manage – the interview may remain very structured and inflexible as agreed questions are asked; or one or two interviewers may dominate the interview dealing with a narrow range of issues.

Structured interview. This type of interview is used to try to eliminate the problems of bias and increase the objectivity of the interviewers. The structured interview has three key elements, which are:

1 questions based on the job analysis
2 standard questions used for each candidate
3 a systematic scoring procedure used to rate responses.

Presentation interview. Candidates may be asked to prepare a presentation to be given at the interview. This can then be used to assess their presentation skills, as well as their ideas on a particular topic. Issues raised in the presentation can form the basis of further questioning. However, the requirement to give a presentation can deter candidates from attending an interview and should only be used where presentation skills are relevant to the job.

Selection tests

Tests may be used as part of the selection process, and can give a more objective view of the candidate. However, they can be time-consuming and expensive to administer and need to be chosen with care. The characteristics required for a particular job should be clearly identified and the tests used as an indication of the candidate's suitability for the job. The tests should be: relevant to the job; applied fairly; free from cultural bias. The two main types of test are skills tests and psychometric tests.

A **skills test** may be, for example, a data input test for a keyboard operator. It should be remembered that candidates are very nervous at interviews and allowance should be made for this. Computer systems vary, and an opportunity for the candidate to become familiar with the system should be given before the test is administered. The test should be administered in a quiet environment where there are no distractions. This type of test is cheap to administer and can be tailored to a particular organisation and job role.

A **psychometric test** is a test that has been developed by psychologists to measure specific aptitudes or personality types. Sets of tests have been developed by different organisations – for example: the Graduate Record Examination Board (GRE); the Education Testing Service (ETS); Saville & Holdsworth (SHL). The tests have to be bought from the organisations, applied under strict conditions and checked by trained markers. They are also time-consuming to apply.

Aptitude tests have been developed that cover the following main areas.

- *Verbal reasoning and verbal ability* – candidates have to show an understanding of written passages and logically evaluate an argument.
- *Numerical reasoning and quantitative ability* – candidates have to show an understanding of tables of statistical and numerical data, and make logical deductions from the information.
- *Diagrammatic reasoning* – candidates have to recognise logical sequences in a series of diagrams or symbols.

Tests in the form of questionnaires have also been developed that can be used to identify personality characteristics in candidates – for example, the Myers-Briggs Type Indicator.

Advantages of using psychometric tests
- The people best suited to the job are identified.
- People can be placed in the job roles for which they are best suited.
- Strengths and weaknesses are measured objectively.
- The tests are fair to all candidates and eliminate bias as a result of being carefully designed and fully researched.
- Tests can be chosen so that the skills involved are relevant to the job.

Disadvantages
- Tests cannot measure some personal attitudes, such as politeness.
- People do not always perform at their best under test conditions.
- Tests cost money to buy, administer and check.
- People can practise for tests, which can bias the results.
- Tests may be chosen that are irrelevant to the job role.

Assessment centres

The use of CVs and an interview is still used by eighty per cent of organisations to select personnel, while testing has grown in importance in recent years. However, another option, used by two per cent of organisations, is to use assessment centres to select key personnel.

Assessment centres are managed by companies who offer a specialist selection service using trained assessors and a range of techniques. They will meet with the organisation to discuss the job analysis and person specification. They will then agree a strategy for selecting shortlisted candidates. The selection process for a candidate may last from half a day to two days and can consist of the following elements.

- Aptitude testing, psychological testing, written tests, in-tray activities.
- Role-play activities – for example, customer–salesman, manager–employee situations.
- Group activities – for example, problem-solving situations, planning activities.
- Presentation activities.

Assessment centres are very expensive to use, but they claim that they can provide employees who can significantly enhance a company's performance and reduce staff turnover.

Organising the interview

When the interview selection strategy has been agreed, the arrangements for the interview need to be made.

Interview arrangements

Book suitable rooms. Rooms will be required for holding the interviews in, for candidates to wait in and for the administration of any tests. The organisation's procedures for booking a room should be followed. Occasionally external venues, such as hotels, may be used for interviews and appropriate bookings should be made. The interview room should be private and have no distractions – for example, no telephones.

Arrange appropriate refreshments. Refreshments will need to be available for interviewers and possibly the interviewees. Candidates may also be put at ease if they are offered refreshments while they are waiting. If interviews are likely to go on over lunch, food should be provided for the candidates. Candidates might be offered lunch in a canteen – this can be helpful for them as they can see the organisation's facilities and staff in an informal context. It may be necessary to allocate staff to accompany them to lunch, or a special table could be reserved for their use. Alternatively, a buffet or sandwiches might be provided.

Inform interviewing staff. The availability of interviewers should be checked and dates booked well in advance. The date, time and venue should be confirmed with the interviewers.

Prepare and send interview briefing materials. A pack of information should be provided for each interviewer. This could include: interview schedule, job description, person specification; applicants' application forms/CVs/letters and any other details; interview rating/assessment form; questions to be asked; tests to be completed; organisational details; and any appropriate legal or regulatory requirements.

Prepare an interview schedule. The timing of interviews and order of candidates should be prepared. The timing of the interviews should be agreed as part of the selection strategy. The schedule of the candidates during the day will depend on the programme for the day. If candidates are to take a test, the time allocated for the test should not clash with the interview. If candidates have to come a long distance they should be given a suitable interview time. If all the candidates are travelling some distance, the interview schedule might start at a later time in the day – for example, 11.30 am – and the candidates should be scheduled in an appropriate order allowing for travelling time. To check likely travelling times, find out how long the journey would take using public transport and/or check car travelling time by calculating the mileage and assessing the journey time – computer programs such as AutoRoute will provide information on approximate travelling times. Time may also need to be allowed for hold-ups. In certain situations overnight accommodation may also need to be arranged.

Time should also be allocated in the schedule for the interviewers to discuss the candidates and take appropriate breaks.

Figure 8.2.5 shows an example of an interview schedule.

Inform security/reception. Security and reception need to know about the interviews and that visitors from outside the organisation are expected. Organise parking if it is required. Organise staff to greet applicants and escort them to waiting rooms. Tours of the building should also be arranged if they are required.

COMPUTER COUNSELLORS

Interview Schedule

Post   Administrator to the Sales Department
Reference AM/23

Date of interview 26 February 19--

Venue   Interview Room G8

Interviewers   Mr John Sharples, Sales Department
Miss Surindar Khan, Human Resource Manager
Miss Eirian Williams, Sales Department Administrator

Test procedure   20 minute warm-up and 10-minute keyboard test
Interview Room G9

Waiting room   G6

Interview – 35 minutes (allow extra 10 minutes for overrunning and/or discussion	Test – 30 minutes	
09.10	Pre-interview briefing	
09.30	Jane Wilson	10.15	Jane Wilson
10.15	Gareth McPherson	11.00	Gareth McPherson
11.00 – 11.15 Break/discussion		
11.15	Mei Ling	12.00	Mei Ling
12.00	Barry Wendover	12.45	Barry Wendover
12.45 – 2.00 Lunch and discussion		
14.00	Pamela Brown	2.45	Pamela Brown

Figure 8.2.5 An interview schedule

Inform candidates. Each of the candidates should receive a letter giving full details of the interview process and any tests they may be required to take. Information about refreshments and expenses should also be included. Candidates may also be requested to bring original certificates for checking. A computer mail-merge program or the use of standard paragraphs can make the preparation of these letters more efficient.

Figure 8.2.6 shows an example of an interview confirmation letter.

COMPUTER
COUNSELLORS

Oxford Technology Park, Redfern Ring Road, Oxford, OX4 6DS
Tel 01865 338927 Fax 01865 338948 hr@comcouns.co.uk

4 February ----

Miss Jane Wilson
36 Hubbard Gardens
Freetown
KILLINGTON
KI7 8TY

Dear Jane

Administrator to the Sales Department – Reference AM/23

I am pleased to inform you that you have been shortlisted for the above vacancy. An interview has been arranged for the morning of 26 February at 9.30 am. A short keyboarding test will precede the interview, which will be with staff from the Sales department. The test and interview should last about one and a half hours altogether. Please confirm that you will be able to attend the interview

I enclose a location map for your information. There is ample car parking in the nearby Highbury Towers car park. Expenses in the form of bus fares or refund of parking costs will be paid after the interview. Please retain your bus ticket or parking receipt.

I look forward to meeting you on the interview day.

Yours sincerely

Miss Surindar Khan
Human Resource Manager

Enc

Figure 8.2.6 An interview confirmation letter

Make arrangements for any tests. Book the room, prepare test materials and provide any required equipment.

Make arrangements for any presentations. Overhead projectors, screens, etc. may be required. You may need to inform candidates what equipment will be available for them.

Make arrangements for the disabled. Arrangements for disabled candidates or interviewers may need to be made – for example, suitable access for wheelchairs, large-print papers for tests, hearing aid or loop provision for presentations.

Prepare interview rating/assessment forms. These should be prepared to ensure standard comments or scores can be recorded during the course of the interview. These records may also be used to monitor compliance with Equal Opportunities legislation.

Interview Rating/Assessment Form

Post	Administrator to the Sales Department – Reference AM/23
Date of interview	26 February ----
Venue	Interview Room G8
Interviewers	Mr John Sharples, Sales Department
	Miss Surindar Khan, Human Resource Manager
	Miss Eirian Williams, Sales Department Administrator
Test procedure	20 minute warm-up and 10-minute keyboard test
	Interview Room G9
Name of candidate	
Name of interviewer	

Interviewer	Question area	Comments	Ratings		
			Average	Good	Excellent
Surinder Khan	General introduction				
	Education history and qualifications				
	Work experience				
Eirian Williams	Computer skills and knowledge				
	Knowledge of filing and general office procedures				
	Personal strengths and weaknesses				
John Sharples	Dealing with customers				
	Working as part of a team				
	Working on own initiative				
Overall rating	Communication skills				
	Organisation and self-presentation				

Test result

Recommendation

Reasons for non-appointment of candidate

Signed   Dated

Figure 8.2.7 An interview rating/assessment form

Figures 8.2.7 and 8.2.8 show examples of interview rating/assessment forms. The forms should be clearly and accurately completed to show that only the objective criteria stated are used in making appointments and any reasons for non-selection are clearly given. Equal opportunities monitoring may be carried out to identify why particular groups are not successful at obtaining posts and the forms can be checked to see if there are any trends that can be identified as reasons for non-appointment.

Late changes

Shortlisted candidates may respond that they no longer wish to be considered for a post, or may not turn up for interview. The schedule may need to be rearranged to accommodate this. The times of tests and interviews may be altered – for example, slightly longer might be allocated to interviews if needed, or the breaks might be taken at different times or extended. Whatever arrangements are made, everyone involved should be informed of the changes.

Alternative Style of Recording Interview Assessment					
Education and qualifications	1	2	3	4	5
Communication skills	1	2	3	4	5
Experience	1	2	3	4	5
(1 = very good, 2 = good, 3 = acceptable, 4 = poor, 5 = unacceptable)					
Note: All interviewers should sign the final section of the form					

Figure 8.2.8 An alternative interview rating/assessment form

The day of the interview

On the day of the interview the administrator should carry out the following activities.

• Prepare the interview room with water/refreshments, paper, pens, spare sets of interview schedules, applicant details and interview rating/assessment forms. Check that the seating has been suitably laid out for the style of interview.
• Prepare the candidates' waiting room, ensure comfortable seating, refreshments if required and somewhere to hang coats.

- Prepare and check the test materials and test equipment.
- Check with reception that the candidates are expected and confirm arrangements for last-minute messages.
- Prepare expenses claim forms if required, and petty cash if expenses are to be reimbursed on the day.
- Check that greeting procedures for candidates are in place.
- Confirm arrangements with interviewers for receiving messages during interviews.
- Confirm any arrangements for checking original certificates.

Portfolio activity 8.2 **Number 4**

1 Sort through all the responses to the advertisement for the job vacancy you wish to fill, rate the responses using a person specification checklist and reply to candidates unsuccessful in being shortlisted. The following evidence should be collected:

- letter of rejection after initial application
- completed person specification checklist (selection matrix)
- file with all unsuccessful applications.

2 Shortlist candidates and make all the appropriate arrangements for the interviews. The following evidence should be collected:

- letter inviting candidates to interview
- interview schedule and interviewer pack
- personal statement explaining all the arrangements you made for the interviews, and the steps you took to ensure confidentiality and security
- interview rating/assessment form
- any arrangements made for testing.

Performance criteria:	8.2.5–10				
Knowledge and understanding:	8.2.a	8.2.b	8.2.h	8.2.l	8.2.m
	8.2.n	8.2.o	8.2.p	8.2.q	8.2.s
Evidence requirements:	8.2.1	8.2.2	8.2.3	8.2.5	8.2.6
	8.2.12	8.2.13	8.2.14	8.2.16–20	

Conducting the interview

Conducting the interview is a very important aspect of the recruitment process. As an administrator you may be asked to take part in interviews.

Before the interview

It is important to make proper preparations for an interview. You should carry out the following activities.

- Ensure all practical arrangements have been carried out, as listed on pages 426–31.
- Re-read the job description.
- Read the applications and familiarise yourself with each applicant's details.
- Prepare suitable questions.

Last-minute arrangements

Arrive in plenty of time for the interview. Make sure that reception has the necessary information and that everything is ready for the convenience of candidates while they are waiting. Make sure any test arrangements are ready.

Check the interview room. Rearrange the furniture if necessary – a grouping of low chairs around a low table is more informal and can relax the candidate. Try to avoid interviews that take place across a desk as this can be off-putting for candidates. Make sure there are sufficient supplies of paper, pens and spare interview briefing materials for other members of the interviewing panel.

During the interview

The interview usually has three stages: the opening, the main interview and the closing.

The **opening** is used for putting the candidate at ease, introducing the interviewers, explaining the format of the interview.

It is important during the opening section of the interview to try to establish a rapport with the candidate. Use suitable initial opening comments or questions, such as 'Did you have a good journey?', in order to help the candidate settle down. Be considerate towards them, show that you are genuinely interested in them.

In the **main part** of the interview the interviewers collect the information they need in order to make an informed judgement on who the best candidate is. The time should be managed so that the applicant has full opportunity to answer questions in all relevant areas. The following guidelines should be followed for the main part of the interview:

- Use direct questions to determine factual information. For example, 'What subjects did you study at school?, 'What qualifications did you gain at college?'

- Control the interview – guide the candidate and the discussion along appropriate lines.
- Listen to the candidate, and ensure your body language shows you are listening – maintain eye contact and give encouraging smiles. Briefly summarise their answers and ask supplementary questions to show that you have listened. For example, 'You say that you enjoy using the computer – which software do you most enjoy using?'
- Use an appropriate language level in asking questions of the candidate. Try to avoid technical terms or jargon if these are not likely to be known by the candidate. For example, the technical level of questions about information technology would vary depending on the candidate's experience of computers and the type of job on offer.
- Use open questions to search out the applicant's real views. Allow space for the candidate to speak even if this means periods of silence – or alternatively ask further prompting questions, such as 'Why did you do this?'
- Probe more deeply into certain topics by asking questions in different ways, such as when there are apparent or real inconsistencies in the candidate's employment history or education. For example, 'Why did you leave college in October?', 'Were you not happy with the college course?', 'How did you get on with college lecturers?'
- Maintain objectivity in tone and body language; remain neutral about dress, physical appearance, regional speech, etc.
- Complete the interview rating/assessment form during the course of the interview as it is difficult to remember everything after the end of the interview.

At the end of the main part of the interview, time should be allowed for the candidate to ask questions about the organisation or the vacancy. These questions should be answered accurately and concisely. The questions may often relate to salary, further training, promotion opportunities and working conditions. The interviewer should anticipate these and have appropriate information ready. However, there may be some areas where firm commitments cannot be made at this stage – for example, on the exact salary. It might be diplomatic to say, 'The salary is in the range of £8 500 to £10 000 per annum depending on the age and experience of the candidate.' Any statements made about terms and conditions at the interview form part of the terms of the contract agreed between employer and employee, so care should be taken to make sure that all statements made are accurate.

The interview should **close** on a positive note. Thank the applicants for coming. Inform them clearly of the next stage in the process – for example, 'We will let all applicants know the outcome in writing by the end of next week.'

After the interview

Make sure that all the sections of the interview rating/assessment forms have been completed. If several people have taken part in the interviewing, time should be allocated during or immediately after the interview for discussion of the candidates. A decision should be made about which candidate to appoint. To ensure objectivity, this should relate to the responses recorded on the interview rating/assessment form.

The decision to appoint a candidate is usually based on all aspects of the application: the written application, the interview, any test scores and the references. If numbers are used to indicate a score, the scores may be added up and used as a guide to indicate the suitable candidate. However, there may be significant areas of the person specification which have been identified as crucial to the post – for example, good communication skills may be regarded as more important than experience. The person specification should be used as a clear guideline to making an appointment.

Recommendations

The final recommendations of the interview panel should be communicated to the appropriate authority. This may be a senior manager or the Personnel/Human Resources department. This recommendation may be made in the form of a memorandum, or in the form of the completed interview rating/assessment forms. Whichever method is chosen it should include the clear, objective criteria on which the selection has been based. These may be required as evidence if any appointments are challenged on Equal Opportunities grounds.

It is important to keep to any commitments made at the time of the interview. For example, it is unfair to keep applicants waiting if they have been promised a response, even if the response is that a decision is still being made.

Letters of rejection

There may be one preferred applicant who is offered the post. However, it can be a good idea to have a second choice who can then be offered the post if the first-choice candidate rejects it.

Unsuccessful candidates should be informed as soon as possible in accordance with the organisation's policy for this. Telephone calls may be made informing candidates of their failure to gain a post. This may then be followed by a letter.

The letter of rejection may vary in tone, depending on the type of organisation, the level of the post and any future actions which may arise out of the interview.

Thank them for their application and for attending the interview:

> **I would like to thank you for attending the interview for the above post.**

> **We would like to thank you for your application and for attending the interview for the vacancy as junior clerk.**

Inform them of the outcome of the interview:

> **I regret to inform you that you have not been successful.**

> **Unfortunately, on this occasion your application was unsuccessful.**

The second of these does imply that the candidate may apply again in the future. You could put this even more clearly – but only if it is true:

> **We would welcome applications from you for suitable posts in the future.**

Sometimes feedback about the interview or tests may be included:

> **We were very impressed with your application and your interview.**

> **Although you completed the keyboard test in the required time, you failed to display a suitable level of accuracy.**

A reason may be given for the lack of success:

> **The post was offered to a more experienced candidate.**

A final section could include good wishes for the future:

> **I wish you every success in your future career.**

Figure 8.2.9 shows an example of an interview rejection letter.

26 February ----

Miss Jane Wilson
36 Hubbard Gardens
Freetown
KILLINGTON
KI7 8TY

Dear Jane

Administrator to the Sales Department – Reference AM/23

I would like to thank you for attending the interview for the above post.
However, I regret to inform you that you have not been successful at interview.
The post was offered to a candidate with more experience in a sales
department.

We will keep your name and details on our file for future reference and will
inform you if any suitable vacancies arise.

I wish you every success in your future career.

Yours sincerely

Miss Surindar Khan
Human Resource Manager

Figure 8.2.9 An interview rejection letter

Making an offer

When a decision has been made, the successful applicant should
be offered the post. The organisation's policy on making offers
must be followed. Some organisations will first make an offer on
the telephone and ask the candidate whether they will accept the
offer, before making an offer in writing. Other organisations may
make all offers in writing and wait for the applicant's response.

The final offer must be made in writing, and should include the
following information.

- *Job title and reference.*

- *Conditions of service* – this may be a general statement, for example:

  The hours of work are 8.30am–5.00pm Monday–Friday, with 25 days' paid holiday per annum.

  Alternatively the conditions of service may be detailed in a separate document which is included with the letter, for example:

  The conditions of service are detailed in the enclosed document.

- *Any conditions attached to the offer* – for example, it may be subject to suitable references and/or a medical examination. If a medical examination is required, information about the arrangements should be included in the letter:

  The appointment is made subject to satisfactory medical examination. This has been arranged for 10.00am on 3 March in the Medical Centre. Please confirm that you will be able to attend the examination.

- *Arrival/joining arrangements* – for example:

  You should report to Reception at 9.30 am on Monday 1 April. Please bring your birth certificate and original examination certificates for checking on this day.

  Where candidates have to serve a period of notice in their previous employment, the actual starting date may be negotiated after the official offer has been issued.

- *Request for confirmation of acceptance* – for example:

  Please sign and return the reply slip to confirm that you have received this letter and the conditions of service document.

  Alternatively, two copies of the letter offer, contract and conditions of service may be sent and one will be signed and returned:

  Please sign the enclosed copy of this letter and return to this office as soon as possible.

Documentation on joining

It is now common practice to carefully audit claims made on CVs, application forms and at interview. One way of doing this is to take up references (see pages 417–21). Another way is to check original certificates. This may be particularly important where statutory qualifications are required – for example, check the authenticity of first-aid certificates for staff who are to be registered first-aiders. It is also important where professional qualifications are claimed – for example, medical and teaching qualifications. Other documentation may also need to be checked on joining – for example, the employee's birth certificate.

The employee should also be asked for information that relates to the salary procedures. They will need to provide their National Insurance number and Pay As You Earn (PAYE) taxation documents. If the employee was in previous employment they should be asked to bring a P45 from their previous employer.

The Accounts department is usually responsible for calculating and paying employee wages. Organisations have a legal obligation to deduct National Insurance and income tax at source and pay this to the Tax Office. These deductions are statutory deductions. Information about these deductions can be gained from the Accounts department, or from the Contributions Agency. Information can also be found by accessing the Open Government website:

http://www.open.gov.uk

and looking up the Contributions Agency or Inland Revenue in the index.

Contract of employment

The contract of employment between employee and employer can be formed in two ways: common law and statute. Under common law a contract may exist between the two parties as a result of the advertisement, interview and/or written contract provided after the interview, even if nothing has been written down. Statutory obligations are those laid down by law. There is a range of complex legislation that controls employees' working conditions. (The information included in this section is sufficient to satisfy the Higher Diploma in Administration Procedures standards. However, if you wish to find out more about employment legislation, *Croner s Guide* is a good reference.)

Employers are required to provide a written statement to all employees working more than eight hours per week, within two months of starting work. This statement should include:

- names of employer and employee
- job title and location of work

- date of starting work
- rate of pay and when it is to be paid
- general terms and conditions relating to hours, holiday pay, sick pay
- pension provisions
- periods of notice
- grievance procedures.

Confidentiality

Recruitment information is personal and should be kept confidential at all times. There are, therefore, the usual requirements for passwords, locking disks away and keeping information in folders in locked cabinets. All information about applicants is covered by the Data Protection Act (see the appendix on pages 539–45). Steps should be taken to ensure the organisation's procedures under the Data Protection Act are complied with.

Employee relations

Once an employee has joined an organisation, it is important to maintain a good relationship between the employer and the employee. One aspect of employee relations is union and staff association membership. Trade unions and staff associations are formal groups of employees who have joined together for the purpose of dealing with their employers. The level of union membership has declined over the last twenty years for the following reasons.

- *Legislation* – a series of laws were passed between 1980 and 1993 that reduced the power of trade unions. These laws included the Employment Act 1980 and the Trade Union Reform and Employment Rights Act 1993.
- *Changing employment patterns* – far more employees are now part-time, temporary or on short-term contracts and they are less likely to join a union.
- *Economic changes* – union membership was traditionally very high in the manufacturing industries. These industries have now declined and have been replaced by service industries – for example, tourism, leisure – which do not have a tradition of union activity. Service industries also employ higher levels of part-time and temporary staff.

However, there are many employees who still belong to trade unions. Their reasons for joining a union may vary but can include the following.

- *Collective representation* – the trade union can represent the views of its members and negotiate with management on their behalf – for example, to reach agreements on pay rises and working conditions.
- *Individual representation* – the trade union can represent an individual in disagreements and disputes. The union may also provide legal advice and representation for individuals involved in court cases as a result of their work. For example, the British Medical Association (BMA) represents doctors involved in court cases.
- *Political representation* – the trade union can represent the views of its members to government and lobby on issues relevant to the workforce. For example, the National Union of Teachers (NUT) lobbies government on educational issues.

Advisory, Conciliation and Arbitration Service (ACAS)

If employee relations problems do arise and disputes occur, ACAS may become involved to resolve the issue. This organisation was established by the Employment Protection Act 1975. It is an independent organisation formed to act as a third party in employee relations. This is done by offering services in the following areas.

- *Individual conciliation* – ACAS offers a conciliation service between parties involved in industrial tribunals.
- *Collective conciliation* – ACAS can be involved in trying to achieve settlements in industrial disputes.
- *Arbitration* – ACAS can arrange for final judgement or 'arbitration' to be made when all other possibilities in an industrial dispute have been exhausted.
- *Advice* – information and advice about all areas of employee relations is provided by ACAS – for example, good practice on grievance and disciplinary procedures.
- *Inquiries* – ACAS undertakes a range of inquiries into general areas of employee relations. The findings of these inquiries can then be used as the basis of good employment relations and practice.

Portfolio activity 8.2 **Number 5**

1 Carry out the interviews for the job vacancy you wish to fill. You should arrange to provide evidence of the interviews. A video recording is very useful, but you will need to gain the permission of the interviewees. Alternatively, you may be observed during the interviews. If the observer is not part of the interview process, their presence should be explained to the interviewees. When a panel interview is being used, another member of the panel could provide you with evidence in the form of a witness testimony. The following evidence should be collected:

* record of the interviews to show how you conducted them
* completed interview rating/assessment forms
* personal statement explaining how you carried out the interviews, the preparations you made, the questions you prepared and how you actually structured and carried out the interviews. Include information on how you kept all recruitment information confidential.

2 Make recommendations to the appropriate authority for an appointment as a result of the interviews. Inform all unsuccessful applicants. The following evidence should be collected:

* memorandum, report or completed interview rating/assessment forms, giving reasons for your recommendations
* personal statement explaining how you made the final selection and how you conveyed that information to the appropriate authority
* draft letter of a job offer – include reference to title of post, conditions of service, requirement for medical (if applicable), arrival/joining arrangements and request for confirmation of acceptance.

Performance criteria:	8.2.5–12				
Knowledge and understanding:	8.2.a–c	8.2.h	8.2.i	8.2.j	8.2.l
	8.2.m	8.2.n	8.2.o	8.2.p	8.2.s
	8.2.t				
Evidence requirements:	8.2.1	8.2.3	8.2.7	8.2.9	8.2.11
	8.2.15–20				

Test yourself

Knowledge and understanding	Questions
a	State three ways in which personnel and staff could be assessed and selected.
b	Explain how interviewers can ensure assessment of all applicants is fair and objective and how influencing factors could affect this assessment.
c	Why should a new employee receive a contract of employment with conditions of service and salary structures?
d	State briefly the functions of ACAS.
e	Give four sources that are commonly used to recruit personnel.
f	Name a relevant publication that your company might use to advertise a vacancy.
g	Why might a completed application form be requested instead of a letter and CV?
h	What might be included on an interviewers' assessment form and how might their completion of the form infringe on the Equal Opportunities legislation?
i	How would you ensure you communicated effectively with colleagues and applicants to establish goodwill and rapport?
j	Describe an effective questioning technique to encourage an applicant to give full information during an interview.
	Why is it important that the interviewer listens to the applicant?
k	Choose a particular position within your organisation with which you are familiar and explain the functions and procedures involved with effective performance of this position.
l	Give three psychological issues that may come up when interviewing people
	Give three cultural differences that you need to be aware of when conducting an interview.

m	State six elements that would be needed to provide a good interview environment.
n	How would you go about ensuring any documentation you draw up uses the appropriate vocabulary, tone and style, and what are the implications of badly composed communications being sent out by a company?
o	Which word processing package do you use most often, and how confident are you with this package?
p	How would you extract, analyse and compare information about applicants to make and to justify your recommendations for a post.
q	Give three factors to be taken into consideration when scheduling interviews.
r	Describe the differences between a character reference and a standard reference for competence.
s	Give three implications of the legal requirements that relate to the selection and recruitment of personnel.
t	What are the legal requirements regarding the collection, storage and dissemination of information in relation to the recruitment process?

Element 8.3

Induct new staff

When new employees have been appointed, plans have to be made for when they start work. There are practical considerations, such as providing suitable working space and the necessary supplies, stationery, etc. It is important for new employees to feel that they have a place in the organisation and that suitable arrangements have been made for their arrival. They should not be made to feel like outsiders.

Plans also need to be made for initial training of employees. The purpose of the initial training is to familiarise them with organisational information, conditions of employment, safety, work role, etc. This is called 'induction'. The aim of induction is to enable new employees to quickly become effective members of the organisation. The main objectives of induction are:

- *administration* – providing all the necessary information, such as safety information, terms of employment
- *welfare* – helping the employee to feel at home in the organisation; this may include an element of socialising, such as introducing the employee to staff, arranging for them to be accompanied to lunch, providing a mentor
- *values* – helping the employee to identify with the organisation's values – for example, commitment to customer service, quality standards.

Designing an induction programme

When designing an induction programme you should consider how these objectives can best be met. Thought should be put into what information is required, when it should be given, how it should be given and who should give it. The programme may take place over a period of time. Care should be taken not to give new employees 'information overload'.

A variety of methods and staff to deliver the programme will help the employee to remember the information. The organisation may already have a selection of training materials available which may be used for induction, such as health and safety videos.

The initial induction should provide the basic information that an employee needs in order to be able to function, and normally takes place on the first day of work. It is usually designed to cover housekeeping issues such as cloakrooms, canteen and parking facilities. Also at this time, new employees should be introduced to immediate colleagues and other relevant staff. They may also be given information to take away and read.

There may then be two or three sessions of follow-up induction to provide further training. This can cover areas like machine operation, company procedures, company products.

On an ongoing basis, a supervisor or mentor may be appointed to look after the new employee for a period of time. This person will be on hand to answer practical questions that arise during the course of work, and will also ensure the employee has a suitable workload – that is, they are not left without work, or alternatively overloaded with tasks. They may also 'keep an eye on' a new employee, to make sure they are getting on with other members of staff and are included in social activities, lunch breaks, etc.

When the induction has been completed the new employee should be informed of other training opportunities that are available within the organisation. A record of the training they have received during their employment should be kept for all staff. The induction training received should be noted on this record.

The following table summarises the induction process. Figure 8.3.1 (page 449) shows an example of an induction programme.

Information	Induction activity*	Documents etc. to be provided**
Conditions of service: • terms of employment • hours of work • leave arrangements • payment arrangements • sick-leave arrangements	• talk, briefing or presentation by a member of the Human Resources or Training department	• conditions of service • contract of employment • contract arrangements
Welfare and benefits: • profit-sharing • expenses claims • welfare arrangements • social facilities, activities, etc. • training opportunities	• talk, briefing or presentation by a member of the Human Resources or Training department	• welfare information, booklets, handouts • training policies
Company rules and policies: • equal Opportunities • grievance procedure • disciplinary procedures	• talk, briefing or presentation by a member of the Human Resources or Training department	• equal Opportunities policy • disciplinary and grievance procedures
Housekeeping: • canteen/refreshment facilities • cloakroom facilities • parking arrangements	• tour of the building	• ground plans, maps of the organisation • parking permits, etc.
Health and safety: • fire exits • fire drills • first-aid box, accident reporting • safety clothing	• tour of the building • health and safety video • talk by safety officer • completion of a health and safety questionnaire	• health and safety policies • relevant safety clothing
Trade union/staff association membership	• talk by trade union representative • introduction to relevant staff during company tour • talk, briefing or presentation by member of the Human Resources or Training department	• trade union/staff association information • application forms

Information	Induction activity*	Documents etc. to be provided**
Company information: • mission statement • organisation structure • information on company products • communication methods	• talk, briefing or presentation by a member of management, Sales department or other relevant members of staff • products may be shown on the company tour. Videos of company services or products may also be shown	• mission statement • organisation structure • information/literature about company products • organisation telephone list
Specific job training: • departmental procedures • operation of equipment • quality standards • house styles • departmental structures and staff	• tour of the building, introduction to staff • demonstrations of equipment • talk,briefing or presentation by departmental supervisor	• departmental structure • relevant procedures, quality standards • department telephone list, contact numbers • examples of the organisation's house styles
Any other issues – for example, computer familiarisation	• demonstration	• training opportunities • organisation's Data Protection Policy • computer support list

*   In a small organisation many of these activities may be undertaken by a supervisor or line manager.
** The trainee may be asked to sign a form to confirm that they have received these documents.

Portfolio activity 8.3 Number 1

This unit requires you to prepare an induction programme for a new member of staff. The person may be new to the organisation or new to a post within the organisation. This activity should be carried out as a result of real work. However, if this is not possible within your organisation, you may know of another organisation that would benefit from an information package and work undertaken for this purpose would be classified as real work.

If real work is not possible, realistic simulation can be used to generate evidence and the induction package and induction programme could be based on your own organisation/training centre, provided you have access to all the information you need.

1 Design an induction programme to cover a minimum of one day in total. This should include memos/faxes/e-mails to all involved to confirm arrangements and their involvement in

the programme. Your programme should include information on:

- objectives of the programme
- conditions of service
- Equal Opportunities
- your organisation's procedures and policies
- introduction to personnel
- staff development
- health and safety
- welfare and benefits
- names and designations of personnel involved with the programme.

The following evidence should be collected:

- copy of the induction programme
- copies of the memos confirming the arrangements.

2 Prepare an induction information package. This should include:

- your organisation's procedures and policies, including house styles
- Equal Opportunities policy statement
- welfare and benefits information
- contact numbers
- general background information about your organisation, including its mission/objectives
- an organisation chart showing lines of staff accountability and responsibility
- terms and conditions of service
- grievance and disciplinary procedures
- staff development information.

The following evidence should be collected:

- the complete information package.

Note
You should use a word-processing system and graphics/presentation package for some part of this activity. You could use a graphics presentation package to produce the organisation chart.

Performance criteria:	8.3.1	8.3.2	8.3.4	8.3.5	8.3.6
Knowledge and understanding:	8.3.a	8.3.d	8.3.f	8.3.g	8.3.h
	8.3.k	8.3.l	8.3.o–u		
Evidence requirements:	8.3.1–28				

Induction Programme – Monday 1 April

Post   Administrator to the Sales Department
Employee Mei Ling

Objectives
Provide information on:
- Conditions of service
- Equal Opportunities
- Welfare benefits
- Staff development

Familiarise employee with:
- Building and general domestic arrangements
- Company products, procedures and policies
- Sales Department team
- Organisation health and safety arrangements
- General job role
- Security arrangements and issue of security pass

Programme

9.30–10.00   Meet at Reception – Coffee and initial introduction – General domestic arrangements – Surindar Khan, Human Resource Manager

10.00–11.00 Presentation on Personnel issues – Interview Room 1 – Surindar Khan, Human Resource Manager

11.00–11.15 Questions on Personnel issues

11.15–11.30 Coffee with Oscar Wilkinson, Safety Officer – Interview Room 1

11.30–12.30 Tour of Building – location of fire exits, introduction to security staff, issue of security pass – Oscar Wilkinson, Safety officer

12.30–1.00   Health and Safety video – Oscar Wilkinson, Safety Officer

13.00–14.00 Lunch in canteen with Eirian Williams, Sales Department Administrator

14.00–14.45 Presentation about Organisation, Sales Department and Company Products – John Sharples, Sales Department Manager – Interview Room 1

14.45–15.30 Tour of Sales Department and introduction to Sales Department staff with Eirian Williams, Sales Department Administrator

15.30–15.45 Tea with Sales Department – Staff Canteen

15.45–16.45 Introduction to job role – Opportunity for questions – Eirian Williams, Sales Department Administrator

Figure 8.3.1 An induction programme

Monitoring the induction programme

The induction programme can include input from various members of staff, and take place over a period of weeks. It is important to monitor all activities to ensure they have been completed. It is also important to evaluate the effectiveness of these activities, so that changes to future programmes can be made if necessary. The monitoring may be carried out by:

- the employee signing a form to say they have received relevant documentation (see Figure 8.3.2 below)
- the supervisors recording induction activities on a checklist (see Figure 8.3.3, page 451)
- the employee completing an induction feedback form (see Figure 8.3.4, page 452).

Name of employee   Mei Ling

Title of job role   Administrator, Sales Department

Date started work   1 April ----

Please sign and date to confirm that you have received the following documentation.

Document	Date	Signature
Induction programme		
Terms and conditions of service		
Grievance and disciplinary procedures		
Welfare and benefits details		
Contact list		
Organisation's procedures, policies and house style		
Equal Opportunities statement		
Health and Safety pack		
Staff development policy		
Organisation chart		
Company background information		
Induction feedback form		

Completed form received and filed in trainee personnel file

Date

Signed
(Human Resource Department)

Figure 8.3.2 An employee documentation form

Supervisor Induction Activity Checklist

Name of employee   Mei Ling

Title of job role   Administrator, Sales Department

Date started work   1 April ----

Name of supervisor   Eirian Williams

Induction activity	Date of activity	Comments
General Health and Safety Training given	1.4.99	Shown exits, evacuation notice, first-aid kit and location of first-aider and accident report book.
Tour of the building	1.4.99	Full tour given
Introduction to team	1.4.99	All present, except Jane Ferguson - introduction to be given later
Issue of induction pack	1.4.99	Full pack issued
Filing system explained	2.4.99	Shown numerical invoice filing and alphabetical customer details filing as well as cross-referencing system
Initial photocopier training	2.4.99	Automatic document handling, single sheet, multiple copies, basic facilities covered
Initial telephone training	2.4.99	Telephone handbook given, demonstration given, observed dealing satisfactorily with an incoming call
Follow-up photocopier training	4.4.99	Advanced facilities - back-to-back, collating, book facility

Figure 8.3.3 A supervisor induction activity checklist

Name of employee				
Job title				
Date started work				

Did you receive the following during induction? (Please circle response)	If 'yes' please tick how you found them			Please make any comments about the activity
	Very helpful	Helpful	Not very helpful	
Tour of the building Yes/No				
Induction pack Yes/No				
Health and safety training Yes/No				

Signed   Date

Figure 8.3.4 An induction feedback form

Induction monitoring procedure

The monitoring and evaluation of induction should be formalised in a set procedure. This procedure should define which monitoring activities will take place, when they will take place and who will carry them out (Figure 8.3.5). The procedure may need to be approved by an appropriate member of staff or department, particularly where all procedures form part of ISO or other procedures systems (see the section on ISO procedures in Unit 5, pages 286–8).

Portfolio activity 8.3 **Number 2**

Make recommendations in writing to an appropriate member of staff for a procedure for monitoring and evaluating the induction programme. The following evidence should be collected:

- memo explaining the procedure and how monitoring and evaluation will be carried out

- copy of the procedure

- copies of documentation to be used as part of the procedure, such as examples of monitoring/evaluation forms.

Performance criteria: 8.3.3   8.3.6

Knowledge and   8.3.l   8.3.n   8.3.p   8.3.s
understanding:

Evidence requirements: 8.3.14   8.3.26–28

At the time of appointment the following activities should be completed by the Human Resources Administrator ready for employee start date:

1 Preparation of an induction programme to include information on:
- objectives of programme
- conditions of service
- Equal Opportunities
- organisation's procedures and policies
- introduction to personnel
- staff development
- Health and Safety
- welfare and benefits
- names and designations of Personnel.

A copy of this to be circulated to all staff involved before employee start date.

2 Preparation of an Induction pack to include:
- organisation's procedures policies and house styles
- Equal Opportunities policy statement
- welfare and benefits
- contact numbers
- general organisation information
- organisation chart
- terms and conditions of service
- grievance and disciplinary procedures
- staff development

The following induction monitoring documentation to be sent to relevant staff before employee start date:
- employee documentation confirmation of receipt form
- supervisor Induction activities checklist
- employee Induction Feedback form.

The induction should be completed within the first two weeks of employment, and the monitoring documentation to be returned to the Human Resources Administrator by the end of the third week of employment.

Human Resource Administrator to check that the monitoring documentation has been returned.

Human Resource Administrator to evaluate the induction feedback received and make necessary recommendations to Human Resource Manager.

Human Resource Administrator to file the monitoring documentation in the employee's training file.

Date/document title/issue number

Figure 8.3.5 An induction monitoring procedure

Motivation and reward

Employees are seen by organisations as a key resource and money is invested in them in the form of recruitment and training. However, employee retention is also important – organisations that have high employee 'turnover' can spend considerable money on further recruitment and training, as well as having the efficiency of their organisation disrupted by frequent changes to staff. It is important to keep employees motivated if they are to stay at work and give of their best.

Motivation

Motivation is the incentive or reasons for following a course of action. If you are on a college course completing an administration diploma, you will have reasons for doing it. You may want to achieve a qualification to get a better job, to earn more money, or for personal satisfaction. If you are motivated you will work hard to achieve good results.

Most people start a new job being keen and wanting to achieve, and it is important that this motivation is maintained. An understanding of motivation can help organisations plan and manage their employee resources.

There are various theories that try to explain motivation. This section looks at three of them: Maslow's theory of the hierarchy of needs; Herzberg's two-factor theory; and Vroom's expectancy theory.

According to **Maslow**, people have a range of needs – from the most basic survival needs to the need to realise their full potential. These needs are ordered in levels of priority and it is only as each level is achieved that the individual is concerned about the next level (see Figure 8.2.10, page 455).

Herzberg's two-factor theory of motivation looks at people's response to their work. He identified two key groups of factors – hygiene factors and motivating factors. The hygiene factors are negative factors: their presence is required to prevent dissatisfaction. The hygiene factors relate to the working environment – for example, pay, status, security, working conditions, fringe benefits, policies and administrative practices, interpersonal relations.

The other group of factors is identified as 'feel-good factors' or motivating factors and relate to individuals and their personal response to work. They include: achievement, responsibility, recognition, advancement and the work itself.

The key point is that the hygiene factors must be satisfied before the motivating factors can become effective. The implication for management is that first of all the basic working conditions must be right. However, when this has been achieved, work needs to be structured or 'enriched' to provide job satisfaction for the employee.

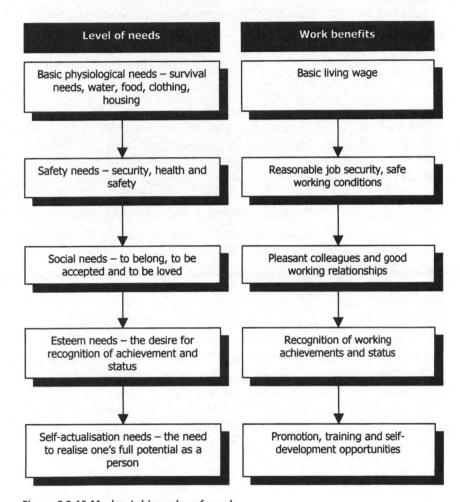

Level of needs	Work benefits
Basic physiological needs – survival needs, water, food, clothing, housing	Basic living wage
Safety needs – security, health and safety	Reasonable job security, safe working conditions
Social needs – to belong, to be accepted and to be loved	Pleasant colleagues and good working relationships
Esteem needs – the desire for recognition of achievement and status	Recognition of working achievements and status
Self-actualisation needs – the need to realise one's full potential as a person	Promotion, training and self-development opportunities

Figure 8.2.10 Maslow's hierarchy of needs

Vroom's expectancy theory is based on the idea that people act in a particular way because they expect to achieve a desired outcome. One concept of this theory is that employees at work have a performance-outcome expectancy. They believe that if they act in a particular way, they will achieve predictable outcomes – for example, if they achieve set targets, they will receive a bonus. The second concept is that different individuals will value different outcomes – for example, some individuals may be motivated by money, while others may value promotion. The implication for managers is that they need to provide predictable and valued rewards for employees who meet management requirements.

The theories are based on the assumptions that all people are the same and are motivated by similar factors. However, any workforce is made up of individuals with different individual circumstances, characters and motivators. As a supervisor or team leader, you need to be aware of the principles of motivation in order to enable you to motivate members of your team. These principles include the following.

- Ensure the basic needs of the staff are met – for example, that they have suitable arrangements for lunch breaks.
- Ensure health and safety issues are clearly dealt with.
- Ensure staff feel they belong together as a group.
- Give regular feedback – for example, recognise and praise achievement; provide support to improve standards.
- Give credit to staff for achievements. Make sure that other people – for example, management – are aware of good work.
- Recommend staff for pay rises, promotions and training opportunities where these are appropriate.

Reward

The structuring of reward packages is important if organisations are to recruit and retain employees, and also to maintain motivation. A reward is something given by employers and received by employees in return for their time, effort and satisfactory performance at work. Benefits refer to the total package of rewards – for example, pay, pension, holidays, training. Pay/salary rewards refer to the financial benefit employees receive.

The most basic form of reward is the financial benefit employees receive for their time at work. This is usually identified by its payment structure.

- *Hourly rate* – employees receive an agreed sum for each hour worked.
- *Weekly/monthly wage* – calculated as a fraction of an annual salary. Salaries may be structured on an incremental basis, that is, each year the salary increases according to a scale of payment and all employees are at some point on the scale – for example, teachers. Other structures are more flexible and salaries may rise as a result of general pay increases and personal additional increases made as a reward for merit.

- *Payment by results* – some employees have payment schemes that include payment for results. For example, employees may be paid on a piecework basis, or may receive bonuses in addition to their normal hourly rate or salary for achieving exceptional targets.

Employees may also receive further benefits. These benefits can be linked to pay or may be independent of it – for example, pensions, sick pay, savings schemes, share schemes.

Further non-payroll benefits may be given to employees – for example, company cars, free private health insurance, holidays, subsidised canteen facilities, employees' discounts, outings, social events. However, the complex PAYE tax systems may tax some of these benefits as financial benefits and the employee then pays a tax penalty. For example, company cars and free health insurance can incur a tax penalty as the tax authorities value them as 'income'.

There are also more undefinable rewards or benefits that employees and employers may identify as part of the reward packages – for example, good working conditions, job security, training opportunities, and recognition of achievement. Employees may also get other personal rewards from the work they do, such as self-esteem and job satisfaction.

Test yourself

Knowledge and understanding	Questions
a	What are an employers' legal responsibilities in relation to work practices and methods for induction of new staff?
b	What are the legal responsibilities regarding the collection, storage and dissemination of information in relation to the induction process?
c	Give three elements of Health and Safety legislation that should be covered in induction training.
d	Explain how contracts of employment, conditions of service and salary scales are structured in your organisation.

e	Explain the staff remuneration systems in your organisation and give two sources of information about statutory deductions.
f	Produce an organisation chart for your organisation and explain the main work carried out by each department.
g	With reference to a specific role, explain the function and range of duties of a new member of staff and the procedures involved in the effective performance of that particular role.
h	List the training opportunities available in your organisation.
i	Explain the roles of any trade unions and/or staff associations within your organisation.
j	With reference to one or more motivation theories, explain what is needed to motivate members of staff.
k	Explain how you would collect, collate, extract and impart information for a specific purpose.
l	How would you interpret written and verbal communications and explain given procedures in a logical sequence?
m	What are the principles of evaluation in relation to assessing the effectiveness of an induction programme?
n	Explain how you ensure you are using language and grammar effectively and why it is important to do so.
o	Why are timescales important in an induction programme?
p	Which word processing package do you usually use and how confident are you in your ability to use it?
q	Which graphics/presentation package do you usually use and how confident are you in your ability to use it?

r	Describe an instance when it would be necessary or useful to use a chart or diagram to reproduce data.
s	When would the use of guidance notes be appropriate in the reproduction of data?
t	Give two instances when the use of standard forms would help in the induction process?
u	What sort of programmes and schedules might be relevant for an induction programme?

In-tray activities

Activity 8.1

Desknote

DESKNOTE

From: Shaheen Hassan, Personnel Manager
Date: Monday, -- -- --

The departmental administrators are now responsible for the recruitment of administrative/clerical staff within their department. Outline a set of standard job analysis procedures for staff to follow before new staff are recruited. Include examples of documents to be used.

Shaheen

Activity 8.2

Minute note

MINUTE NOTE

Departmental Operating Manuals

It was agreed that each department should submit a set of documents that clearly shows the structures and functions of staff within their departments. This information should then be included in the departmental operating manual. Draft a memo to departmental administrators listing the documents they should submit, with the information that should be included in each document and samples of suitable layouts.

Activity 8.3

Memo

MEMORANDUM

To: Administrator, Personnel Department
From: Simon Clark
Date: Wednesday, -- -- --

Staff recruitment procedures

Staff are not clear about the process to be followed when recruiting a new member of staff. Prepare a detailed flow chart to clearly show the stages and documents involved in the recruitment process – from identifying a vacancy, recruiting to induction a new member of staff.

Activity 8.4

Desknote

DESKNOTE

From: *Shaheen Hassan, Personnel Manager*
Date: *Thursday, -- -- --*

At the recent recruitment standards meeting, it was agreed that types and methods of interviews were all rather ad hoc. We agreed that we need to have a clear policy on appropriate methods and types of interviews to be used when recruiting new staff. Please draft a report for discussion at the next meeting, reviewing different methods of interview. Recommendations will not be necessary at this stage.

Shaheen

Activity 8.5

E-mail message

E-mail

To: Administrator, Personnel Department
From: Shaheen Hassan, Personnel Manager
Date: Friday, -- -- --
Subject: Testing applicants

At the present time, we do not use any form of testing of job applicants and we need to consider this as part of our recruitment policy.

Please prepare an informal report for me, reviewing the different methods of testing and the advantages and disadvantages of introducing them into our recruitment procedures. Include recommendations on future actions to be taken before we finalise our policies.

9 Supervise and Develop Staff

Supervision is the act of overseeing activities. The administrator in an organisation may be responsible for overseeing administrative activities being carried out by other members of staff.

This means that the administrator is not only responsible for their own work, but also for the work of others. A good supervisor works to ensure staff meet their targets in terms of quantity and quality. The quantity may be determined by volume of work – for example, 'all files replaced' – and by the timescales set – for example, 'by the end of the day'. Quality may be determined by standards of accuracy and absence of mistakes – for example, 'accurately replaced with no misplaced files'.

Supervisory activities are regarded as the first stage of management. For example, the first level of the NVQ Management awards is NVQ Level 3 Supervisory Management. As a management activity, it is important for the supervisor to understand how the supervisory role fits in with the whole organisation's objectives.

Element 9.1
PLAN AND SUPERVISE WORK ACTIVITIES

Supervisory activity can be summarised in the following stages:

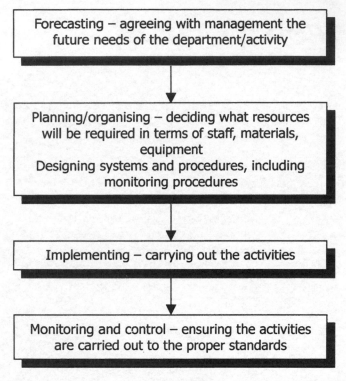

Figure 9.1.1 Stages of supervisory activity

Forecasting

The supervisor needs to be aware of the future needs of their section. (*Note:* The word section will be used to refer to the 'area of control' or 'area of activities' for which the supervisor is responsible.) The supervisor may attend meetings and discussions with a manager, line manager, planning group or work team to identify future needs. This may be for ongoing routine work – for example, maintenance of filing – or it may be for a particular project – for example, transfer of customer files from a paper-based to a computer-based system. The supervisor will need to agree the work targets and identify the impact of the activity on their section. The supervisor can then predict what resources will be required in terms of time, equipment, budget, etc. and negotiate with management for the resources required for the activity.

Planning/organising

When the targets have been clearly defined and resources agreed, the supervisor will be able to plan and organise for the activities to be carried out. Consideration of the following may be required.

- *Staff resources* – who will carry out the activities? What training may be required?
- *Materials resources* – the stationery required can be ordered.
- *Equipment resources* – the equipment required can be identified, and steps taken to ensure it is available and in good working order.
- *Systems and procedures* – the systems and procedures that will define how the activities are to be carried out should be prepared. Existing systems and procedures should be checked to see if they cover the activity; if not, new procedures will need to be prepared. This can include any recording mechanisms that may need to be put in place.
- *Timescales* – the activities can be put into a logical order and timescales set. For example, the stationery and equipment might be needed before staff can carry out the activities. Time may need to be allowed for training and for the acquisition of the required levels of skill.
- *Monitoring* – suitable methods of monitoring (see Monitoring and control, pages 478–82) should be considered and included in the planning stage. The supervisor should have a clear idea of how and when monitoring will take place during the activity.

Although it is important to have a clear plan in place, the plan needs both to be flexible and to allow for change. Staff may leave, be off sick or be promoted to another department. Equipment may break down, or may not be delivered on time. The supervisor should monitor the progress of the plan carefully, and be aware of contingency arrangements that can be made to cope with problems – for example, using temporary staff.

Action Plan

Supervisor's name	Howard Gregory	Colleague/trainee's name
Date of plan	2 August ----	Mary Hall
Location of activity		**Title of activity**
Finance Office		Filing Invoices

Aim of activity
To accurately file all routine invoices by the end of the week.

Initial training
Howard to carry out initial training on Monday 12 August 9.30–10.30 am in the Finance Office.

Initial supervision
Howard to directly monitor Mary filing an initial set of invoices approx. 10.30–12.00 Monday 12 August.

Ongoing activity
Mary to file routine invoices for rest of week, but to contact Howard if there are any problems. Howard to check with Mary at the end of each day on the progress with the invoices.

Follow-up checks
At the end of the week, Howard to agree with Mary a programme of follow-up supervision – for example, checking filing at the end of each week for a month.

Materials/equipment required
Hole punch, lever arch files, filing cabinet
Access to the photocopier

Systems and procedures
A copy of the organisation's financial filing procedures is required. This can be found in the Finance Department's organisation procedures manual held by Jane Boulder, Senior Administrator.

Supervisor's signature	*Howard Gregory*
Colleague/trainee's signature	*Mary Hall*

Figure 9.1.2 An action plan

Portfolio Note

If supervision is not part of your usual work activities, it may be possible to enlist the assistance of a work experience trainee or colleague. If your training organisation has a business centre or other model office in operation where NVQ or other vocationally-focused people are working, this will provide a suitable environment for supervisory activities.

Portfolio activity 9.1 **Number 1**

Discuss with your assessor which work activities and which individuals you will supervise. The tasks must include at least two different types of activity which must be supervised on a minimum of two occasions.

Suggestions of tasks that could be supervised as part of your usual work activities include:

- filing (required by Element 6.2)
- petty cash (linked with Element 7.2)
- computer training
- receiving and making telephone calls
- word processing (keying in business documents)
- reception work
- sending faxes
- photocopying
- postal duties
- preparing spreadsheets/databases.

Agree an action plan with your assessor and prepare your action plan, including information on resources, timescales, actions, etc. The following evidence should be collected:

- record of your meeting with your assessor to agree the action plan
- action plan.

Performance criteria:	9.1.2
Knowledge and understanding:	
Evidence requirements:	9.1.1 9.1.2

Styles of supervision

All people are different and will have different styles of supervision, ideas, strengths and weaknesses. The work of Tannenbaum and Schmidt ('How to choose a leadership pattern', *Harvard Business Review*, 1973) identified four types of management style. These management styles can be used to identify the following supervisory styles.

Autocratic. The supervisor tells an individual what to do and expects it to be done. Failure to achieve results is punished. There is no place for negotiation in this style of supervision.

Benevolent autocratic. The supervisor tells an individual what to do and expects it to be done because it is for their joint good. Achievement will be rewarded. There is some negotiation here, but it is based more on persuading the individual of the activity's benefits. The individual may need to see what benefit they gain from carrying out an activity – for example, more responsibility can be seen as recognition of ability and as training for higher-level posts.

Consultative. The supervisor asks for the individual's views on a topic and then makes a decision taking these views into account. This style involves much more negotiation and allows the individual to have a creative input into the activity.

Participative. The supervisor discusses the supervisory activity with the individual and decisions are made jointly. The supervisor then helps to plan and implement the joint decision. This style is based fully on negotiation and gives much more responsibility to the individual.

A good supervisor will try to use the consultative and participative styles as it is a good idea to involve staff at all stages of the process. This helps to give them more 'ownership' of the activities. If you listen to their views and ideas and involve them in making decisions they will feel more valued. This is an important part of motivating staff (see Motivation and Reward in Unit 8, pages 454–7). These 'consultation' discussions can also be a good way of sharing the overall objectives or 'bigger picture'. Staff are likely to perform activities better if they have some idea of the purpose and importance of the activity within the organisation's overall activities. It can also help them to understand the importance of quality requirements and the implications of errors or non-compliance.

Staff may also have good creative ideas of their own on how activities may be carried out – for example, using colour coding for files in the filing system. Listening and giving individuals responsibility for levels of decision-making can be very motivating for them and gives them a lot of job satisfaction. However, the guidelines and authority within which decision-making takes place have to be clearly understood. Where systems and procedures are agreed within formalised structures – for example, ISO 9000 requirements or audit requirements – no changes can be made without formal agreement and this may be outside of the supervisor's authority – for example, changing the structure of a customer database.

It is difficult for a supervisor to define their own management style. A supervisor may feel they have a consultative style because they ask individuals for views and comments. However, the tone of voice and body language may still be very authoritative – what they say, how they say it and the way they say it may give a very different message. For example, the supervisor might ring the individual and say, 'I need you to come and see me now to discuss the filing.' This is very different from a supervisor approaching the individual, sitting alongside them at their desk and saying, 'Is there a time during the day when it's convenient for us to have a talk about the filing?'

This is one of the reasons why some organisations use *upward* or *360-degree* appraisals, where colleagues give feedback about the performance of their line manager, supervisor or managerial staff. Supervisors are often encouraged to collect this feedback before their standard appraisal meetings.

Further information about the supervisory relationship can be found in Element 6.2 (pages 297–304).

Other factors can affect the working relationship between the supervisor and the individual. For example, if they are friends this may make it difficult for the supervisor to be critical of the individual's performance. The supervisor needs to compartmentalise any personal relationships to keep them separate from professional relationships. Keeping personal discussions out of working hours helps this. Alternatively, a new junior or work experience student may be so nervous of a supervisor that they do not like to ask for help when they need it. Try to build a relationship with them that gives them confidence to approach you when required. Using first names and taking an interest in them personally can help.

A supervisor's working practice should comply with employment legislation. All staff should be dealt with fairly and no discrimination on the grounds of sex, race or disability should take place. The supervisor should think carefully about decisions they make and why they have chosen an individual to carry out an activity. The supervisor may justify giving work to an individual because that person has shown the ability to carry out the activity; but there may be other individuals who are just as capable, but who have not received the training and are therefore not being offered similar opportunities.

Cultural differences also need to be considered – for example, dress, manner, voice. The supervisor should reflect carefully on their decisions to check the grounds on which they have made them – for example, 'She looks the part' means that a judgement has been made on the basis of the way someone looks, rather than on their ability.

Implementing

The activities listed in the plan should now be implemented. Supervision focuses on two aspects: the process and the outcome. The process relates to what has to be done, while the outcome looks at what has to be achieved. The supervisor oversees the process to ensure the outcome is achieved.

The initial stage of implementation is to brief the individual staff member who will be carrying out the activities. The briefing should allow the supervisor and individual to have clear and explicit ideas about the process and the targets. The briefing should be a two-way process, and should allow the individual to express their views and ask questions about the activity. Any arrangements for training, provision of resources and impact of the activity on other tasks should also be discussed. At the end of the discussion, the supervisor and the individual should record the outcomes, perhaps in note form in a notebook, diary, or 'to-do' list. The supervisor should check that the individual makes this record and that it is accurate.

The targets should include indications of the quality and quantity outcomes that will be required at the end of the process, for example:

> **Use a word processor to produce accurate copies of 12 letters from handwritten version by the end of the day.**

> **Accurately file all outstanding files by the end of the week.**

> **Photocopy, collate and bind 20 neat, clean copies of the staff handbook by lunchtime tomorrow.**

Assessing competence

The supervisor should have some idea of the competence of the individual – that is, their ability to carry out specific activities. Various methods can be used to assess an individual's competence.

- *Observation of the process* – you can watch them carrying out activities and make an assessment of their ability to carry out a process – for example, operate the photocopier.
- *Checking the outcome* – you can look at the finished products and make a judgement about the quality of the work – for example, the neatness and accuracy of the photocopies.
- *Checking records* – you can check recording mechanisms – for example, photocopying logs, which would give some indication of the volume of work carried out, and the ability to complete records accurately and at an appropriate time.
- *Reviewing qualifications and experience* – this can give you an idea of the ability of a member of staff. However, you may still need to check for yourself that they can carry out activities at the required standards and within your organisation's procedures.
- *Discussion* – you can talk to the individual about the activity and make a judgement from their comments and responses – for example, discussion about using the computer to complete a mailmerge.
- *Testimony from others* – other supervisors or colleagues may give you feedback about the competence of staff. They might recommend a member of staff for a particular activity, or they might identify areas where further training is required.

As well as making a judgement about an individual's current competence, you may also be making a judgement about their potential competence to carry out future activities. You know what activities they can currently carry out, and you might decide that with further training they could acquire competence in other areas – for example, a filing clerk might have shown their competence at using the computer to find out information and you might, therefore, decide that with some training they could take over responsibility for the customer database. When a decision about competence has been made, the supervisor has to make provision for any training that is required.

Providing training

The supervisor's judgement of an individual's competence, together with the initial briefing, should have allowed the supervisor and individual to agree training needs. An informal training plan should be agreed between the individual and the supervisor. This should include what training will take place, where and when. This should be recorded – for example, noted in diaries or included in schedulers.

There is a wide range of training methods and sources that are covered in Element 9.2. However, for the purposes of this element it is assumed that the training will take place 'on-the-job' and will be provided by the supervisor. The advantage of on-the-job training is that the individual is trained in the organisation's current working practice and should have a clear understanding of the implications of making a mistake. In preparing training, consideration should be given to different learning styles:

- *learning by hearing or reading* – listening to instructions and ideas, reading about an activity – for example, reading about health and safety regulations
- *learning by watching* – watching an expert carry out a demonstration of a practical activity
- *learning by doing* – the individual learns by carrying out the activity, and if necessary repeating it until the required standard has been reached.

Different individuals learn in different ways, and different activities lend themselves to different methods of training.

Methods of training

There is a range of different methods of training that can be used.

Coaching. The supervisor coaches the individual through a process in an instruction or teaching session – for example, talking the candidate through the petty cash process. These sessions should be carefully planned and the material – for example, handouts explaining the activity – prepared beforehand. A suitable place needs to be arranged for the session to take place. It may be appropriate to book a quiet room, where interruptions from telephones, staff, etc. can be eliminated.

Supervised practical activities. The supervisor gives the individual practical activities to complete under supervision. Practice activities may be used where outcomes are critical – for example, where a mistake would cause a problem, or where time constraints make it difficult to complete a real activity in training – for example, a practice petty cash activity. When the supervisor is confident that the individual can carry out the activity to the required standard, simple, real activities may be undertaken under supervision.

Demonstration. The supervisor demonstrates a particular piece of equipment, or a particular facility on the computer – for example, multiple-page copying on the photocopier or use of mailmerge. Demonstration may be followed by a supervised practical activity – for example, observing the candidate use the photocopier. Any demonstration must incorporate 'good practice' – for example, including all relevant health and safety activities.

Demonstration should include careful explanation of the activities being carried out. It is very easy to 'demonstrate' computer activities just by pressing the keys, but this means very little to the individual. The actions should be clearly explained, with the reasons, and the individual should be encouraged to take down notes – for example, 'Select the Preview icon before you print out. This will allow you to see what the printed document will look like before you print. In this way you will not waste time and paper making incorrect copies.' Notes may also be prepared beforehand for the individual to use as future reference.

The training may need to take place in stages. Little and often is better than long sessions. Long sessions become counter-productive – individuals can lose concentration and suffer from information overload.

Preparing instructions

Instructions can be prepared for training sessions and/or to provide ongoing support. Written instructions may be used for reference by the individual when they are carrying out activities. They should also help to reduce the need for the individual to interrupt the supervisor by `sking questions. The instructions need to be easy for the individual to understand and should take account of their existing knowledge – for example, when preparing instructions for complex computer activities, a certain basic knowledge of computer facilities may be assumed. It is also useful to prepare instructions that can be used by other staff carrying out the activity.

Instructions should be written in numbered format, rather than blocks of continuous text. Each point should start with the verb or action the individual has to take. The points should be logically ordered in the correct sequence. Pictures and diagrams are always very helpful. Figure 9.1.3 on page 474 shows an example of some instructions for printing documents on a colour printer.

Printing documents on the DK colour printer

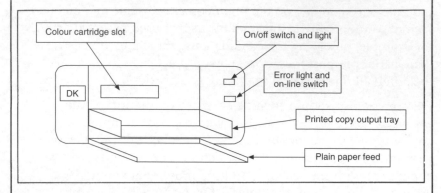

Initial checks

1   Check that the DK colour printer is switched on – the green light will appear in the on/off switch.
2   Check that there is paper in the plain paper feed tray.
Note: High-quality colour printouts should be printed on the DK colour print paper stored in the red packets in the drawer directly beneath the printer. For draft copies use ordinary printer paper.

Printing colour copies

3   Prepare the computer document in the appropriate packages, for example Word, Presentation, Excel.
4   Check the final look of the document using **Print Preview** options.
5   Select **File** from the menu bar. (Do not use the Print icon.)
6   Select **Print** from the drop-down menu.
7   Click on the selection arrow to the right of the Printer Name window.
8   Highlight and select the **DK Colourprint** printer.
9   Check that this printer is now displayed in the name window.
10 Carry out printing in the usual way.

When printing has finished

11 Close and save documents.
Note: It is important to return the print selection to the DK Laserprinter.
12 Select **File** from the menu bar. (Do not use the Print icon.)
13 Select **Print** from the drop-down menu.
14 Click on the selection arrow to the right of the Printer Name window.
15 Highlight and select the **DK Laserprinter** printer.
16 Check that this printer is now displayed in the name window.

Figure 9.1.3 Instructions for printing documents on a colour printer

Giving feedback

An important part of the supervisory role is giving feedback on performance. Positive feedback can help to motivate individuals and build their confidence. Any shortfalls in performance should be identified, but constructive feedback should be provided to give the individual the opportunity to perform at the required standard. Choose an appropriate moment to give feedback, as soon after the activity as possible. For example, if you have given a practice petty cash activity, check it and give feedback immediately it has been completed. Do not take it away, check it and give feedback days later. By that time the individual may have forgotten how they carried out the activity and the feedback may be meaningless.

Always give both positive and negative feedback. Many supervisors take good performance for granted and only comment on poor performance. Praise for good work when it is earned is always welcome and helps motivate individuals.

However, performance standards will not be improved if shortcomings are allowed to continue. As a supervisor you should point out errors and poor standards of work. This should be done sensitively. You should choose a suitable time and location to make any negative comments – do not make them in front of other colleagues or when the individual is obviously very busy or under stress. Your feedback should be clear – for example, 'There are some errors in these letters that need correcting.' The errors should be highlighted for the individual to correct. Constructive advice should also be given – for example, 'You should use the spellchecker before you print out letters.' Further training may also be provided: 'Let me show you how to use the spellchecker to identify errors.'

More formal methods of giving feedback are discussed later in this unit (pages 487–99).

Self-assessment

A balance has to be maintained between feedback, support and actually doing the job for the individual. If you highlight errors in finished documents every time, the individual may take this process for granted. An important part of supervision is to encourage the individual to assess their own performance. Make it clear that the acceptable standard is for the individual to check for their own errors. In these situations make sure you prepare action plans with very clear targets, for example: 'By the end of the week, use the word processor – including the spellchecker – to produce letters which are error-free.'

Self-assessment gives the individual more responsibility and ownership of an activity. It can be included informally as part of a feedback session. The supervisor can ask the individual how they felt about their work, what went well and what problems were encountered. More formal methods of self-assessment can be included in performance review sessions. This is covered in Element 9.2 (pages 494–7).

Compliance with legislation

At all times the supervisor must ensure the individual meets the legal requirements of the workplace. The supervisor who delegates tasks to an individual still has responsibility for these tasks, and responsibility for the actions of the individual. If a problem did arise, then the supervisor would need to show that they had taken all the appropriate actions to ensure the individual was aware of the basic legal requirements necessary. The following actions can be taken.

- *Issue appropriate company policies* – for example, health and safety and Equal Opportunities policies. These should have been issued on induction to the organisation when the employee first began work, but the supervisor can check that the individual has received them. It is also important to check that the individual has read them and understood them. The implications of the policies for the particular department can also be explained.
- *Demonstrate good practice* – the supervisor can make sure that work carried out within the department by all staff meets legal requirements. For example, the supervisor should ensure safety clothing is worn when appropriate and that equipment is handled correctly. The supervisor should also ensure the workplace itself meets all the requirements – for example, that health and safety notices are correctly placed.
- *Provide appropriate feedback* – if the supervisor observes an individual using equipment in a way that compromises health and safety – for example, leaving boxes in the gangway – the supervisor should give immediate feedback and check that the problem has been put right. On other occasions, an issue might be discussed in a general feedback session. This might be appropriate if a sensitive issue needs to be discussed – for example, if the receptionist had treated some visitors differently through making certain assumptions based on the visitors' sex or race.
- *Provide further training* – a planned programme of training can help to back up induction training and raise an individual's awareness of legal issues that arise in the workplace.
- *Keep up to date* – the supervisor should also keep up to date with the implications of legislation on the workplace.

Portfolio activity 9.1 Number 2

Arrange a meeting with the individual(s) to be supervised. Agree the targets for the supervisory activities. Include an agreement on any training that will be required, making sure that you use several different training methods. Prepare any training/support materials and provide the training. Give feedback on the training. The following evidence should be collected:

- record of targets agreed with individual
- notes of your meeting, including your training plan
- record of your meeting – for example, an assessor observation, a video or audio cassette recording
- notes, activities and support materials prepared and used during the training session
- witness testimony from the individual to say that you have carried out the training
- examples of practice activities completed by the individual, including feedback.

Note
Ensure you cover information on health and safety, legal and relevant organisational requirements in your materials prepared for the training session.

Performance criteria:	9.1.2	9.1.3	9.1.5	9.1.6	9.1.10
Knowledge and understanding:	9.1.a	9.1.b	9.1.c	9.1.d	9.1.e
	9.1.f	9.1.h	9.1.i	9.1.j	9.1.m
Evidence requirements:	9.1.1	9.1.2	9.1.3	9.1.4	9.1.11
	9.1.12				

Providing ongoing support

The individual can start to carry out the activities once they are clear about the outcomes to be achieved, and have received training for the process.

While the activities are being carried out, the supervisor should provide ongoing support. This could be in the form of written instructions or guidance notes. These may be a combination of notes prepared by the supervisor and notes prepared by the individual during training sessions. Written support may also be available in organisational procedures, handbooks and operating instructions. The individual should have copies of these, or know where to find them.

Once the individual has started the activity, they may encounter problems or have questions that they want answered. The supervisor should be available to answer these questions. If the supervisor is not going to be available, they should inform the individual and tell them what action to take if they have a problem, for example:

> **'I am going to be in a meeting this afternoon, so if you have a problem with the photocopier, then ask Jenny to help.'**

> **'Photocopy the pages and collate them using the collator. If you have a problem with the collator, put the pages in order and I will help you when I return after four o'clock.'**

> **'I am going to be in a meeting for about an hour. Prepare the mailmerge and make a note of any problems you have. I will help you with them when I return.'**

Support can also be provided by informal checking on an individual's progress – for example, by asking: 'How is the photocopying going?' The level of this support needs to be carefully judged. It should give the individual opportunities to ask questions without giving them the feeling that you are constantly checking on them and implying that you think they cannot do the job.

Monitoring and control

The supervisor needs to make a decision about the level of supervision that will be required for an individual carrying out an activity. Each situation will be different and the following factors should be considered.

* *Experience of the individual* – a work-experience student would need a much higher level of supervision than a junior who had been training with the company for a year.
* *Complexity of the activity* – simple activities will require a lower level of supervision. For example, entering numbered files into a ring binder would require less supervision than filing a range of documents in a subject filing system.
* *Criticality of the activity* – activities which are critical – that is, where a mistake could cause problems for the organisation –

require a higher level of supervision. For example, checking that invoices are correct would require a higher level of supervision than photocopying invoices as the company could lose money as a result of any errors.

The level of supervision will determine the level of monitoring and control to be employed by the supervisor. A high level of supervision implies that more rigorous monitoring and control will be used than in a lower level of supervision.

The methods and timing of monitoring may also be varied. As mentioned in the planning stage, the supervisor should determine the method and timing of monitoring at the outset.

There are various ways of monitoring individuals, including the following methods.

Observation. This may be formal, agreed with the individual and a checklist completed (see the Monitoring checklist in Element 6.2, page 299). It may also be informal, 'keeping an eye' on the activities to check that no problems are arising – for example, the individual getting angry on the telephone – or watching the body language of the individual – for example, looking perplexed at the computer screen. Careful judgement needs to be made of the level of intervention. If the individual were acting in a way that might cause damage to equipment or upset customers then immediate action should be taken. If it is a less critical problem, the individual could be given a bit of time to try to solve it for themselves.

Observation can be used to make a judgement about the individual's interpersonal skills. You can observe their telephone manner and the way they deal with customers and colleagues. However, care needs to be taken to ensure any judgements are based on objective criteria. Make notes on the incidents and activities that form the basis of your judgement – this is helpful for feedback and also as a record to ensure compliance with Equal Opportunities requirements.

Checking products. The output of the activity can be checked. For example, letters produced on a word processor could be checked before being presented for signing. Then, any errors could be identified, feedback given and corrective action taken.

Checking computer printouts. Some activities can produce printouts to show performance – for example, daily printouts of telephone response times may show how long it took to answer calls on different extensions.

Checking records. Some activities may require logs or records to be completed. These can be checked to ensure they are being completed legibly, on time and accurately – for example, petty cash records could be checked against the remaining float in the tin and the petty cash vouchers. Individuals should be encouraged to use 'to-do' lists to list daily and/or weekly tasks. These to-do lists can be checked to ensure individuals are correctly prioritising activities.

Monitoring by exception. Records can be kept of when 'exceptions' or mistakes occur – for example, errors returned for correction. These may highlight areas of concern for further monitoring, checking, etc.

Checking deadlines. Progress of work can be checked to ensure agreed completion deadlines will be met. This can give the individual the opportunity to explain any problems so that corrective action can be taken. Advice and guidance can be given to the individual to allow them to achieve the deadlines – for example, rescheduling other tasks. The individual can be asked for information on their progress, but it is always important to check out their responses carefully, for example:

> **'What progress have you made on the Sales Report?'**
>
> **'OK.'**
>
> **'Let's have a look at what you've done so far.' or**
>
> **'If you print out what you've done so far, I'll check it for you.'**

If activities are being completed for another customer check with the customer that deadlines are being met. For example, check that a manager is receiving copies of word processed documents at the end of the day.

Individual's self-assessment. The individual should be encouraged to assess their own performance and this can be used as part of the monitoring process. Formal systems for recording self-assessment may be used; these are discussed in Element 9.2 (pages 494–7).

Check up with other staff. As a supervisor you are ultimately responsible for the performance of the individual. Other managers or 'customers' of the work may come to you for progress reports. You need to be in a position to show that you are aware of the status of work being carried out by the individual. It is a good idea to check with managers and customers that work is being completed to standard and on time. This feedback can be collected and used in feedback sessions with the individual.

Sample monitoring

The supervisor needs to decide on the level of monitoring required. At times, all of an activity may need to be monitored. However, it is unrealistic for the supervisor to be checking an individual all the time and monitoring all the work they produce. The supervisor should have a sampling strategy, a plan for selecting how much and how often to check. At the beginning of an activity with an inexperienced individual, every product may be checked. As time progresses and experience is gained, it may be that while all critical items are still checked – for example, a letter in response to an important customer's complaint – only a proportion of the other activities may be checked to ensure standards are being maintained.

Sampling may also be planned to take place on regular occasions – for example, the filing might be checked once a week at a certain time. The individual may be aware of this and try to ensure the work prepared at that time is up to standard. Alternatively the sampling may be random – for example, the filing might be checked weekly but not at a preset time. If an individual knows that their work is likely to be checked at some time during the week, they are more likely to ensure standards are maintained. It can also help motivation if part of the feedback on performance includes information that the work is now up to standard and checking need not be carried out so frequently.

Improving future performance

Monitoring performance should give supervisors a clear idea of the level of an individual's performance. The supervisor may then need to take steps to improve the future performance of the individual. This could be because the individual has not yet reached the appropriate level of performance, or it might be that the supervisor wants to develop the individual to take on more complex and demanding activities. The supervisor can take the following actions to improve performance.

- *Increase the level of monitoring* – this might be needed if the shortfall in performance was of a serious nature and business problems might arise if work was not completed to the required standard.
- *Set targets that identify clear quality and quantity objectives* – the targets should be achievable but challenging for the individual. Clear timescales should also be included.
- *Organise training* – the individual may require further training to improve performance and the supervisor should identify suitable training. This is covered further in Element 9.2.

- *Organise suitable support and mentoring* – the supervisor may need to give the individual further support or arrange for a colleague to give support and mentoring.
- *Provide suitable information and resources* – the supervisor can make sure that the individual has available to them the appropriate company procedures, equipment operating instructions and any other necessary manuals. The individual should also have access to sufficient, appropriate resources to allow them to complete tasks to the appropriate standards – for example, access to appropriate hardware and software.

Reporting on performance

There may be situations when you are asked for formal written feedback on the performance of an individual. This may be required for appraisal, training, promotion or for disciplinary purposes. Any documentation you prepare should be based on objective judgements. Some organisations may have formal mechanisms for making such reports – for example, the use of appraisal forms. The mechanisms will contain specific criteria for you to follow. Alternatively you may be asked to provide information in a written report. The format of this report may vary depending on the circumstances, but a confidential memorandum would usually be appropriate. An example of a performance report is shown in Figure 9.1.4 on pages 485–6.

Portfolio activity 9.1 **Number 3**

Arrange for the individual to carry out the activities. Carry out the monitoring for accuracy and satisfactory performance and record your findings, perhaps using an observation checklist (see Element 6.2, page 299 for an example of a checklist). Satisfactory performance must take account of quality and quantity of work, ability to meet deadlines, interpersonal skills, motivation and ability to prioritise tasks. The monitoring should be completed on more than one occasion as you are required to show that you have supervised the work over a period of time and on a minimum of two occasions for at least two different types of activity.

Provide feedback to the individual, including suggestions for individuals to improve their future performance and an opportunity for them to assess their own performance. You may arrange for your assessor to observe you giving the feedback, or record it using a video or audio cassette recorder. You may also collect examples of corrected work returned to the individual and a copy of the final product.

Discuss with the individual how they can assess their own performance. Write a report on the performance of the individual you have supervised.

The following evidence should be collected:

- completed observation checklists
- monitoring plan
- personal statement explaining how you monitored the activities
- witness testimony from the individual explaining how you carried out supervision and gave feedback
- observation by your assessor of you giving feedback to individual
- record of suggestions and methods for improving future performance
- record of the individual's self-assessment
- copies of notes and any other products you used to make judgements about performance and that were used as the basis of feedback
- record of the individual's self-assessment
- report on the performance of the individual.

Performance criteria:	9.1.1 9.1.3–10
Knowledge and understanding:	9.1.a–m
Evidence requirements:	9.1.1–12

Test yourself

Knowledge and understanding	Questions
a	Explain the psychological and cultural factors that you need to take into account when supervising somebody.
b	How would you provide constructive feedback in a positive manner in order to improve future performance and increase the motivation of the person you are supervising?
c	Explain the difference between direction, demonstration and supervision. Give examples.

d	Explain how your work role might effect your relationship with a colleague, with particular reference to a supervisory role.
e	Give an example of when you might need to: • negotiate with • persuade • listen to • question a colleague. Explain how you would do each of these effectively.
f	Explain the difference between oral and non-oral communication.
	Give examples of two ways in which each of these types of communication could help you in your supervisory role.
g	Why is it important for individuals to be able and to have the opportunity to assess their own performance?
h	Explain how you would ensure you communicated effectively with people you were supervising.
i	Explain how you would: • identify • define • assess the competence of individuals.
j	When coaching an individual, how would you: • advise • instruct • provide constructive feedback?
k	How might: • employment legislation • your organisation's procedures affect a supervisor's responsibilities?
l	Give examples of three possible consequences of an individual's not complying with legal and regulatory requirements?
m	How would you compose a report on an individual's performance 1 aimed at the individual 2 aimed at your supervisor?

CONFIDENTIAL

To: Jane Alexander, Personnel Officer

From: William Oliver, Administrator, Accounts Department

Subject: Progress Report on Administrative Trainee – Jason Obed

Date: 7 April ----

Thank you for your request for a progress report on Jason. He started work in this department on 2 January after three months in the Sales Department. He has received training on the department's computer system and in petty cash procedures. He has carried out the following activities to the standards indicated:

Activity	Requires further training	Can complete activities with supervision	Can complete without supervision
Entering routine purchase orders on the computer		✓	
Entering routine sales orders on the computer		✓	
Filing invoices received in the manual filing system			✓
Completing petty cash account		✓	
Answering routine internal telephone calls			✓
Answering external telephone calls	✓		
Word processing standard letters	✓		

General feedback

Quality of work
He is accurate when keying in basic computer data. However, he requires supervision when dealing with the finance software, particularly in identifying correctly the information from the source data. He is able to wordprocess standard letters, but still makes too many errors. Further training has been arranged for this.

- 1 -

He has good numeracy skills and can carry out all basic calculations without error. His written work is neat and he completed the petty cash accounts to a good standard.

His invoice filing is accurate and he has tidied up the invoice filing system. He is also able to answer queries on the filing system.

Quantity of work
He is able to cope with the quantity of filing work. He completed all the petty cash activities. However, he is still slow when completing the computer activities.

Ability to meet deadlines
The filing was always completed on time. The petty cash was kept up to date. Again he was slow on the computer activities and deadlines in this area often slipped. However, he did report these problems.

Interpersonal skills
When he settled into the department he was able to work well with staff. He answers internal telephone calls well. However, he has sometimes had problems when dealing with external callers. The basic cause of this is his lack of knowledge of our accounts systems.

Motivation
He is willing to learn and has worked hard to understand our systems. His work with the filing system has been praised and he is now keen to demonstrate that he can master our computer systems.

Ability to prioritise tasks
On joining the department he was told that his first priority was to deal with the invoice filing and keep it up to date. He has demonstrated his ability to do this. I know that Jason is keen to use the computer and learn more of our systems – however, we have discussed this on several occasions and we have agreed that he could spend more time on the computer when the basic filing had been put in order. This he has completed and we are now spending more time on training him on our systems. His computer work is still slow and he does not always meet deadlines, but this will improve with further training and experience.

Company guidelines
At all times he has worked within the guidelines for health and safety. At the beginning of his placement he was given instruction on the Data Protection Act and our standard procedures to ensure confidentiality of information. He was given a question sheet to check his knowledge on these areas and he completed this without error. He has worked at all times on the computer within our company guidelines.

- 2 -

Figure 9.1.4 A performance report

PLAN AND CONDUCT STAFF DEVELOPMENT REVIEWS AND IDENTIFY TRAINING NEEDS

Organisations currently operate in a very competitive culture. This may be related to profits and/or service delivery standards – for example, league tables in schools. The improvement of staff performance in organisations has been identified as a key factor in improving competitive edge. Many organisations have developed appraisal systems to improve personal and organisational performance standards. Appraisal includes the review of current and previous performance with a view to improving future performance of both the individual and the organisation.

Appraisal can also be seen as a means of motivating staff. The time taken to talk to staff about their achievements and identify future plans and training needs can be seen as a way of showing them they are valued. It allows staff an opportunity to share their ideas for their own improvement and their future career plans. In this way steps can be taken to integrate individual aims with the overall aims of the organisation. However, appraisals do take time and require staff commitment. There is a danger that they can be regarded as a 'paper exercise' that is of little benefit to the individual and the organisation. If this is the case they become a very low priority and are likely to be completed without careful planning and thought.

This element looks at the development and training objectives of appraisal systems. The word 'review' is used to cover an appraisal of current performance with a view to agreeing training to improve future performance.

Objectives of appraisal

Appraisals can have two objectives – reward or development – and all staff involved in the appraisal system should be clear about its objectives. When used as part of the reward system, pay and promotion is determined as a result of the appraisal. Within a development system the organisation can identify a clear picture of the competence and skill level of each employee. This information can then be matched against forecasts for future staffing needs and any skills shortages identified. Organisation and individual training/development plans can then be prepared to meet these skills shortages.

Using one appraisal and review system to achieve both objectives can cause problems. An individual may not be willing to identify areas for improvement if they feel that admitting weaknesses will affect their ability to get a pay rise and promotion. Appraisers may also not like to identify poor performance where this can affect the financial reward for the individual.

Many organisations separate the two objectives into two different systems, although this can also cause problems as individuals may still feel that improving their performance and undertaking training should result in improved pay and promotion.

Issues that may be discussed in appraisal include:

• review of current and developing job role and job description
• review of general progress and achievement of previously agreed targets and objectives
• identification of personal strengths and weaknesses and agreement of ways to improve performance
• identification and agreement of future objectives and targets to meet the organisation's requirements
• identification and agreement of future objectives and targets to meet the individual's career plan
• identification and agreement of a future training programme.

Organising a development review

The initial discussion has so far looked at *why* development reviews are carried out. However the following questions also have to be answered: *who* will carry out the reviews; *where* will they be carried out; *when* will they be carried out – for example, every six months; *how* will they be carried out and recorded?

An organisation may have a set of procedures for carrying out development reviews which will include guidance on these issues. Procedures help to standardise the process and ensure consistency. They should also provide guidance to the people involved in the process. These procedures should be checked before any reviews take place.

Who?
Various people within an organisation can carry out reviews. For example, reviews can be carried out by a line manager, by the

Personnel department, by a nominated colleague. This will often be defined in the review procedures. However, it is usually conducted by an individual's line manager/supervisor or departmental manager.

Where?

The venue for the appraisal interview should be carefully considered. The interview should take place in a quiet room where no disturbances will take place and where the discussion will be confidential. A suitable interview room should be booked in advance. A 'Do Not Disturb' sign should be hung outside. The room should be laid out in a way that allows for open discussion – for example, interviews taking place across a desk should be avoided if possible.

When?

The frequency of reviews should be carefully planned. The organisation's policy may state how often reviews should take place – for example, annually or six-monthly. However, these are quite long periods for review and the most recent events may colour the assessment of performance. For example, the successful completion of a recent project may prejudice assessment grades favourably, while a recent error may lead to an unfavourable assessment. The use of regular interim reviews can help to overcome this problem. The outcomes of these interim reviews should be recorded, probably in a fairly simple form, and can then be summarised at the scheduled reviews.

How?

The frequency of reviews will also vary depending on the experience of the appraisee. A new member of staff may receive more frequent reviews than experienced staff. A programme of reviews may be planned as a follow-on from induction. The date for review should be agreed between the appraisee and appraiser. Any preparations – for example, issue of appraisal forms – should be made well in advance. A suitable length of time should be allowed for the interview – for example, at least an hour and a half. Appointments made for review should be treated as a priority and should not be cancelled or postponed except in exceptional circumstances. Figure 9.2.1 shows the stages in the organisation of a review.

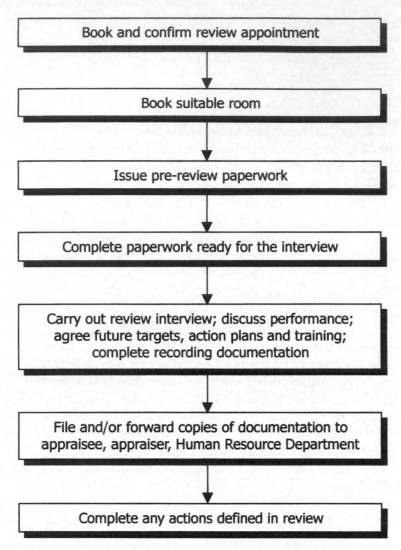

Figure 9.2.1 Stages in the organisation of a staff development review

Conducting a development review

All appropriate initial paperwork, such as appraisal forms, should be completed by the appraiser and appraisee and brought to the interview. At the beginning of the interview the appraiser should clearly explain the purpose of the interview, the format it will take and what records will be completed. Time should be given for the appraisee to give their input to the discussion. New staff may find this difficult and may need to be encouraged. The following format may be followed:

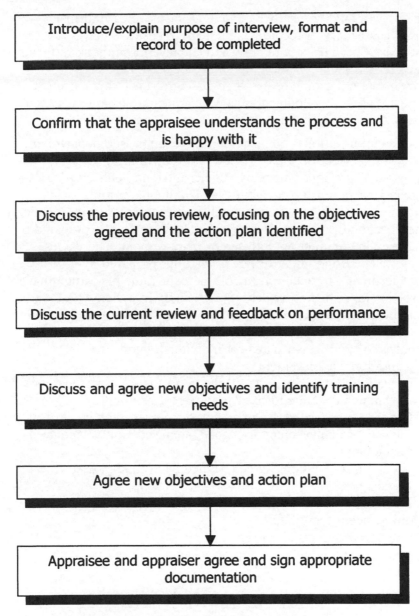

Introduce/explain purpose of interview, format and record to be completed

Confirm that the appraisee understands the process and is happy with it

Discuss the previous review, focusing on the objectives agreed and the action plan identified

Discuss the current review and feedback on performance

Discuss and agree new objectives and identify training needs

Agree new objectives and action plan

Appraisee and appraiser agree and sign appropriate documentation

Figure 9.2.2 Possible format for a staff development review

The interview should be conducted sensitively. Time should be given for the individual to respond and put their point of view. You should aim to spend less than 50 per cent of the time talking. Open questions should be used, and may be followed with questions that encourage individuals to provide evidence to support statements.

The review should be clearly recorded. Using a standard format ensures consistency of recording and helps to ensure and to show that all staff have been dealt with fairly and equally. If an organisation has agreed review documentation this should be used. If there is no documentation it should be prepared and agreed with management before it is used. Development review documentation varies between organisations, but it can include the following elements.

- Factual information – name of appraisee/appraiser, department, date of interview, period of review, dates of interim reviews.
- A record of previous objectives, actions and comments on progress.
- Analysis of performance against team value plans and organisational objectives. Team value plans are plans that identify the direction of the team's activities. They are usually prepared by the team in conjunction with senior management. The values may well be listed under different headings prepared by management – for example, a college team value plan might have a section identified as 'widening participation' – there will then be activities listed under that heading, such as 'increase the number of females recruited onto engineering courses'.
- Analysis of performance against individual, team and organisational achievement.
- Information and feedback about the performance assessed. This can include some form of grading, for example:
  - Graded numerically: 1 = excellent, 5 = unacceptable
  - Graded on achievement: exceeded, achieved, almost achieved, unacceptable.
- Plans and future actions agreed, signed by both appraisee and appraiser.
- Job description updated if necessary.
- Training needs identified.
- Promotion prospects discussed.
- Comments and input from appraisee, appraiser and possibly a third party.

The objectives set as a result of the review should be SMART:

S	Specific – for example, improve data entry into the accounting system, increase understanding of accounting systems.
M	Measurable – for example, resulting in reduced errors, improved quantity, ability to work with less supervision; obtain a qualification in accounts, attend an accounts course.
A	Achievable – previously achieved by other trainees.
R	Relevant – to the individual, department and organisation.
T	Timed – a timescale is set for achieving the objectives – for example, six months for practical skills, one year/eighteen months for qualifications.

Figures 9.2.3 and 9.2.4 show two possible review record forms.

Review Record

Name of postholder	Date		Team values
Job title	Period of review		
Reviewer name	Dates of interim review		Product knowledge
Department	Performance achieved		

Objectives set	Exceeded	Achieved	Almost achieved	Unacceptable	Comments on achievement

Objectives Individual	Knowledge/ competencies to be developed	Selected method to develop knowledge/ competencies	Target date
Team			

Comments by reviewer	Comments by postholder	Signatures
		Reviewer
		Postholder
		Date

Figure 9.2.3 A review record form

```
┌─────────────────────────────────────────────────────────────┐
│                      Review Record                            │
│                                                               │
│  Name of postholder _____    Department _____  │
│  Name of reviewer _____      Date      _____  │
│  Period of review _____                            │
│  To be completed by the manager prior to review interview     │
│  ┌─────────────────────────────────────────────────────────┐ │
│  │ A   Summary of previous (date) review including          │ │
│  │     objectives and actions                               │ │
│  │                                                          │ │
│  │                                                          │ │
│  │                                                          │ │
│  │ B   Summary of assessment of current performance         │ │
│  │                                                          │ │
│  │                                                          │ │
│  └─────────────────────────────────────────────────────────┘ │
│  To be completed jointly with the individual at the review    │
│  interview                                                    │
│  ┌─────────────────────────────────────────────────────────┐ │
│  │ C   Summary of personal assessment and development needs │ │
│  │                                                          │ │
│  └─────────────────────────────────────────────────────────┘ │
│  To be completed jointly with the individual at the feedback  │
│  review                                                       │
│  ┌─────────────────────────────────────────────────────────┐ │
│  │ D   Proposed objectives and development plan             │ │
│  │                                                          │ │
│  └─────────────────────────────────────────────────────────┘ │
│  Record of any outstanding issues or comments at the review   │
│  interview                                                    │
│  ┌─────────────────────────────────────────────────────────┐ │
│  │ E   Comments and issues arising                          │ │
│  │                                                          │ │
│  └─────────────────────────────────────────────────────────┘ │
│  Postholder's signature _____    Date  _____    │
│  Manager's signature   _____     Date  _____    │
└─────────────────────────────────────────────────────────────┘
```

Figure 9.2.4 An alternative review record form

Encouraging self-assessment

Staff may be much more positive in their attitude to self-development and improving performance if they have ownership of the process. This can be done by giving them the opportunity to regularly complete self-assessment forms and keep an ongoing personal development plan. Figures 9.2.5 and 9.2.6 show examples of self-assessment forms.

Completed self-assessment forms can form the basis for a review interview where individuals are required to identify any further development and training necessary to undertake a role.

Self-Assessment Form

Name _____   Date _____

Job title _____

List the activities you have been involved in over the last year. Pay particular attention to previously agreed objectives. Include specific examples.

List areas/activities of achievement.

List areas/activities where you have had problems.

What has been your key learning?

What improvements would you like to make in your work?

Signed _____   Date _____

Figure 9.2.5 A self-assessment form

Self-review Questionnaire

Name _____ Date _____

Department _____

Period   From _____ To _____

Training received in the last six months:

Include comments about your achievements at work over the last six months in the following areas:

Quality of work

Quantity of work

Ability to meet deadlines

Interpersonal skills

Motivation

Ability to prioritise tasks

List training you feel you need over the next six months:

Signed _____ Date _____

Figure 9.2.6 An alternative self-assessment form

Staff being appraised may also be encouraged to keep a record of their personal development. They may record their development on a log in the form of a personal development plan. This should be an ongoing record of their development needs, support given and target dates for completion. Entries can be made at any time when they identify shortfalls in their performance or identify areas they would like to develop. This can then be used as a basis for any later reviews. Staff may also be encouraged to keep a development portfolio. This portfolio should contain information about their current achievements – for example, their up-to-date CV and copies of certificates. It should also contain a record of their development – for example, copies of reviews, training plan, arrangements for training. Many young people prepare a Record of Achievement while in school or college, and this can continue to be kept up to date. Candidates on NVQ programmes or Key Skills programmes may also complete portfolios that include information about their personal development and this can be maintained. Figure 9.2.7 shows an example of a personal development plan.

PERSONAL DEVELOPMENT PLAN

What are my development needs?	What will I be doing differently as a result of development?	How will these needs be addressed?	What support is required and who from?	Target completion date	Review notes and date
16/3/---- Improve my work on the computer accounting systems	Entering data more quickly and with less supervision	1 On-the-job demonstration and training from supervisor 2 Attend a training course on computerised accounts	1 Talk to team leader and arrange demonstration and training 2 Find out about courses from local college, and training organisations	August ----	

Figure 9.2.7 A personal development plan

Collecting feedback from others

Individuals can also be encouraged to collect feedback from a third party – for example, a colleague or internal customer. Figure 9.2.8 shows an example of a feedback form for this purpose.

FEEDBACK FORM

Name of postholder _____

Name of person completing the form _____

QUESTION	CONSISTENTLY	INCONSISTENTLY	OCCASIONALLY	RARELY
Quality Does the postholder complete work to the required quality?				
Quantity Does the postholder complete the required quantity of work?				
Deadlines Does the postholder meet the deadlines for work?				
Interpersonal skills Does the postholder demonstrate a good level of interpersonal skills?				
Motivation Does the postholder demonstrate a good level of motivation?				
Prioritising Does the postholder demonstrate the ability to prioritise activities?				

Tick which of the following indicates your position:

Postholder ❏   Manager ❏

Team member ❏   Customer ❏

Figure 9.2.8 A feedback form

Portfolio activity 9.2 **Number 1**

After discussion with your assessor/supervisor, identify a suitable individual for you to review. If possible try to undertake the development reviews with the person you supervised in Element 9.1 as you will already have experienced their performance and may have already identified some of their training needs.

Investigate the systems/procedures in your organisation for carrying out development reviews and collect examples of their guidelines and paperwork. Where there is no system, prepare your own paperwork and guidelines. All paperwork should be signed and agreed by both parties and should include action planning with target dates and further review dates.

Arrange and conduct a staff development review with the individual identified. Ensure you explain clearly the purpose of the review process to the individual. Encourage and assist the individual to evaluate their own training and development needs. This could take the form of a self-evaluation form completed by the individual in advance of the review interview. Ensure the review identifies any further review dates.

You should also arrange for your assessor to assess you carrying out reviews. This should be by direct observation, or recorded on video or audio cassette.

The following evidence should be collected:

- paperwork and guidelines for conducting staff development reviews
- paperwork, memos, e-mails confirming arrangements for an individual's review
- assessor's record of assessing you conducting the review, including video or audio cassette
- copies of completed paperwork as a result of the review
- personal statement explaining how you prepared for the interview, how you carried out the interview and how you encouraged the individual to evaluate their own training and development needs
- witness testimony from the individual to confirm that you carried out the review.

Notes

1 If you are undertaking this element in a workplace where development reviews are not part of your usual activity, it may be possible for you to enlist the assistance of a work experience trainee in order to give you the opportunity to carry out this activity in a realistic way. Where this is not possible, your training organisation may have a Business Centre or other model office in operation where NVQ or other vocationally-focused people are working; this will provide a suitable environment for reviewing an individual's work performance and training needs.

2 If you follow Element 9.2 with a different individual from the one you supervised in Element 9.1, you should arrange to carry out an initial meeting where you explain your role, their role and the purpose of the activity.

Performance criteria:	9.2.1	9.2.2	9.2.3	9.2.8	9.2.9
	9.2.11	9.2.12			
Knowledge and understanding:	9.2.a–g 9.2.j–p				
Evidence requirements:	9.2.1	9.2.2	9.2.12	9.2.14	9.2.15

Training

The purpose of training is to bring an individual up to a required standard of competence. The organisation's development review process should identify areas of shortfall in an individual's competence. This may be competence within an existing job role, or may be training required to extend the individual's ability to develop their existing role, or to take on a new role within the organisation.

The outcome of the review process should be a training plan for the individual. This section looks at various sources and types of training that may be offered.

In-house training

A major source of training is available 'in-house', that is, within the organisation. This can be further subdivided into on-the-job and off-the-job training.

On-the-job training

This is a key area of training, although it is not always formally recognised. The most common form of on-the-job training is demonstration and instruction by a supervisor or other colleague. This can be identified in the training plan, with the agreement of the individuals concerned. The advantage of this method of training is that it is focused on the organisation's procedures and methods of working.

The quality of this training depends very much on the supervisors/colleagues used to deliver it. Care has to be taken to ensure bad working habits do not creep in, and that sufficient time and recognition is given to the activity. Supervisors/colleagues who are very busy may find it difficult to allocate the time to sit with an individual and carefully explain and demonstrate activities.

This type of training does not usually offer any qualifications and may also be very narrow. The individual may not gain any background knowledge and understanding related to the work-based activity.

Off-the-job training

Many organisations have in-house training facilities which provide opportunities for training 'off the job'. The advantage of off-the-job training is that training can take place in a separate place away from the pressure of the telephone and colleagues. However, there is a time cost when individuals are not engaged in their work. Many organisations have training rooms and/or resource centres and may provide off-the-job training in the following ways.

- *Self-learning materials* – training packs and materials may have been prepared to provide training to individuals within the organisation – for example, customer-service training materials. These are structured, are focused on the organisation's activities and have usually been tried and tested with staff. They offer a consistent method of training, but are not usually certificated. They also require the individual to apply a certain amount of self-discipline in spending the time studying the materials.
- *Training videos* – the organisation may have training videos – for example, health and safety videos. The individual may be asked to attend special showings, or may arrange to see the video at a suitable time. These offer a consistent standard of training, but are not usually certificated. The individual may not always remember the information shown in a video.

- *Computer-assisted learning* – training information may be available on computer – for example, software training packs. A training room may be provided with computers that have learning software loaded on them. These may deliver knowledge training, but are more usually linked to other computer activities – for example, keyboarding training. This training is not usually certificated, and may also need the individual to practise or attend regular sessions in order to achieve a level of competence. The individual may also need some basic computer skills before they can use the packages. If they do experience problems, there needs to be a support system or helpline number to provide assistance.
- *Training sessions/seminars* – the organisation may organise a programme of training sessions. These can be tailor-made for the organisation to meet specific training needs – for example, leadership training. The training may be delivered using in-house staff, or external trainers may be brought in. These training sessions are designed to meet the organisation's needs, and may be part of a certificated programme – for example, NVQs.

Certificates can be issued to individuals who have attended training and/or achieved a recognised level of competence or knowledge. In-house certificates may be issued to individuals who have attended certain training programmes. This is one way in which an organisation can recognise and reward achievement. While these certificates may be recognised as part of the organisation's achievement structure, the value of these certificates in a wider market may vary depending on the reputation of the organisation and the type of training. Externally-awarded certificates that are part of the national qualifications framework may be seen to have more value, as their level and content should be more clearly understood by employees and employers.

External training

Training can also be arranged with external agencies – for example, colleges and training organisations. The organisation may support an individual's attendance at external training by paying all or part of the fees, allowing release from work and paying expenses. The method and level of support provided will depend on the organisation's training policy, available training budgets and the relevance of the training to the organisation's aims.

External training often provides opportunities for an individual to share experiences with individuals from other organisations. This may mean that the individual can bring back new ideas and working practices to be discussed in the organisation. It can also provide a wider view, which can help individuals to understand working practices better and extend their knowledge further. External training can also provide training in areas of expertise not yet available in the organisation – for example, training linked to the introduction of new software. The individual who attends the external training may then be identified to provide the in-house training. Certification may also be available with external training.

The problems with external training are: it is often expensive; it takes staff away from the workplace; and the quality of the training may not be adequate.

The following types of training may be available from external agencies.

- *One- or two-day training seminars/workshops* – specific training programmes may be provided that are focused on a particular activity – for example, introduction to Excel, leadership skills.
- *Evening classes* – regular classes over a period of time for training in a particular subject/topic – for example, shorthand, book-keeping, word processing. These will usually offer opportunities for certification.
- *Afternoon or day classes* – individuals may be offered day-release to attend regular classes over a period of time for a particular subject/topic – for example, word processing, accounting. These will usually offer opportunities for certification.
- *Flexible workshops or courses* – these may offer opportunities for individuals to gain skills and qualifications through individual learning programmes delivered through a tutorial programme, rather than structured taught sessions as in an evening class.
- *Residential courses* – some specialist courses may take place over a period of time and include overnight accommodation – for example, a three-day management training course.
- *Distance learning* – some training organisations offer qualifications and training at a distance, that is, the individual is sent learning materials from the training organisation and completed work is returned to trainers for marking and feedback. Examples of distance learning are correspondence courses and Open University programmes. A variety of methods may be used to deliver the training – for example, television, audio tapes, videos, Internet sites, work-packs, computer programs. Occasional attendance at tutorials may be required.
- *Training organisation s own learning materials* – some training organisations develop their own programmes and may issue their own certificates on successful completion by the individual.

Sources of training information

Information on suitable training can be found from the following sources.

- *Libraries* – most libraries will have leaflets and information about training available locally.
- *Further and Higher Education colleges* – the telephone numbers and addresses of local colleges should be in the Yellow Pages. Prospectuses, leaflets and publicity information will be provided on request by the college. Particular departments may also provide information and advice about suitable courses of training and certification.
- *Internet* – many colleges and training organisations have websites, and information about their provision should be available on these.
- *Awarding bodies* – information about qualifications will be supplied by awarding bodies – for example, OCR, LCCIEB, Pitman, City and Guilds. They may also provide a list of organisations that offer the qualifications.
- *Professional bodies* – organisations that represent particular professionals will provide information on suitable qualifications and lists of training organisations that provide appropriate training courses – for example, The Institute of Administrative Management, 48 Chatsworth Parade, Pritts Wood, Orpington, Kent BR5 1EW (e-mail: iadmin@iadmin.netkonect.co.uk).
- *Local Government sources* – information about suitable local courses and training organisations can be found from the Local Education Authority (LEA), local Training and Enterprise Council (TEC) and the careers service.

Training programme

A detailed training programme can be prepared once the various sources of training have been investigated and suitable training identified. This may include short-term and long-term training arrangements. It should include:

- *dates* – on what days the training will take place
- *times* – at what time the training will take place
- *length of sessions* – how long the individual training sessions will last
- *venue* – where the training is to take place
- *training provider* – name of the individual or organisation providing the training
- *objectives* – the purpose of the training
- *level* – the level of the training to be provided

- *cover* – arrangements for covering the work of staff while they are undergoing the training
- *resources and materials* – any books, information, etc. that the trainee will need to take to the training sessions
- *costs* – the cost of the course, expenses, cost of staff cover.

Figure 9.2.9 shows an example of a training programme.

TRAINING PROGRAMME

Name of trainee   Robin Trewithin

Job role   Purchasing Department Administrative Assistant

Short-term training objective – to become familiar with the organisation's post-room procedures

---

Two-weeks' in-house training in the post room to help with the outgoing and incoming post:

Monday 19 July – Friday 23 July	8.30–10.00 and 15.30–17.00
Monday 2 August – Friday 6 August	8.30–10.00 and 15.30–17.00

Post-room training to be provided by Jane Armitage, Post-room Supervisor

Initial preparation
Robin has agreed to collect and study information on Post Office services and costs from the central Post Office.

Long-term training objective – to become more familiar with administrative procedures by completing an NVQ Level 2 Administration award

---

Attendance at Grangetown Technical College:
   September ---- to June ----   Tuesdays 13.00–17.00

Cost
Tuition, registration and certification fees	£320.00
NVQ Administration Level 2 Student Handbook	£14.50
Total	£334.50

Figure 9.2.9 A training programme

Organising training

When a training plan has been agreed with an individual, the proposed training has to be discussed and agreed with staff concerned. With in-house training, this can mean making arrangements with supervisors and colleagues. This may be done initially by personal contact, but should be followed up by a written memorandum (see Figure 9.2.10). In larger organisations the Human Resources – or Training – department may be contacted, particularly where access to in-house training programmes is required.

MEMORANDUM

To: Jane Armitage, Post-room Supervisor
From: John Lo, Administrator
Date: Thursday, -- -- --
Copies: Robin Trewithin
Susan Yendell, Training Department

Post-room training for Robin Trewithin, Purchasing Department Administrative Assistant

Thank you for agreeing to offer Robin some training on post-room procedures.

As discussed in our telephone conversation he will come to the post room every morning and afternoon for two weeks to help with the outgoing and incoming post.

The following dates and times have been agreed with him:

Monday 19 July – Friday 23 July   8.30–10.00 and
                                     3.30–5.00
Monday 2 August – Friday 6 August   8.30–10.00 and
                                     3.30–5.00

Robin has agreed to collect and study information on Post Office services and costs from the central Post Office. He should bring these with him when he comes on Monday 19 July.

Figure 9.2.10 A memorandum confirming in-house training

More formal systems of requesting training may be used where expenditure will be incurred for training. The expenditure may be for the payment of training fees and expenses. In some situations the training may also incur the additional cost of staff cover. The organisation's procedures for requesting training should be followed. This may mean completing a training request or requisition form (see Figure 9.2.11), or writing a formal memorandum to the Human Resources – or Training – department.

Training Request Form

Personal Information

Name _____ Department _____

Job role _____

Proposed Training

Course title _____

Cost _____

Dates _____

Times and length of training sessions _____

Venue _____

Training provider _____

Expenses required _____

Outline your reasons for applying for this course/training.

Identify which organisational values the course will enable you to achieve.

Departmental Approval

Head of Department signature _____

Date _____

For Human Resource Department Use Only

Date form received _____

Approved   Yes/No

Reasons for approval/non-approval

Date form returned to department _____

Figure 9.2.11 A training request form

Preparing for training

When the training has been agreed, the supervisor should ensure all the necessary preparations have been made, that is:

- the individual has any materials, books, procedures required for the training
- work will be covered while training takes place
- the individual has prioritised and completed any outstanding tasks and left ongoing work tidy
- any travelling arrangements, etc. have been made.

After the training

When the individual has received the training, the supervisor may carry out a debriefing interview and the individual should be asked to complete a training evaluation form. The debriefing interview should include the following elements.

- Review the aims for the training as agreed in the development review – for example, 'You wanted to understand more about the organisation's postal procedures. Did you find the time in the post-room helpful?'
- Check what training has taken place – for example, 'What did you do when you were in the post-room?'
- Check what learning has taken place – for example, 'Can you explain the organisation's procedures for incoming post?'
- Discuss the way in which the training has changed the individual's performance. The supervisor may give feedback on changes in performance that have already been identified – for example, 'I note that you are now preparing the outgoing post earlier in the afternoon.'
- Discuss and agree any follow-up training activities – for example, 'You explained that you now understand the post procedures and how they affect your work in the Purchasing department. As a result of your time in the post-room, please prepare a set of simple guidelines about preparing outgoing post for Purchasing department staff.'
- Prepare a further action plan, with clear targets and further review dates – for example, 'Learn to use the Purchasing department database by the end of August. On-the-job training to be supplied by Jenny Heather, Purchasing department Senior Administrator. Next training review date 1 September.'

The post-training review should be recorded – on the organisation's standard development review documentation if there is any – and future actions recorded and agreed by the reviewer and individual.

Post-training questionnaires

Individuals who receive training may also be required to complete a post-training questionnaire. This may be completed before the debriefing interview and used as a basis for discussion. There are usually two purposes for completing these questionnaires: firstly to check what training the individual has received; and secondly to collect feedback on different forms of training to see whether these may be used again in the future or may need changing. Figure 9.2.12 shows an example of a post-training questionnaire.

POST-TRAINING QUESTIONNAIRE

Personal Information

Name _____ Department _____

Job role _____

Training Received/Course Attended

Course title _____
Dates _____
Venue _____
Training provider _____

Reasons for attending this course

Feedback on Training

Briefly outline training activities undertaken.

What were the good aspects of the training undertaken?

What were the poor aspects of the training undertaken?

Would you recommend other staff attend the training course?	Yes/No
Give your reasons:	

Explain briefly how the training will help you to improve your performance.

Signature: _____ Date: _____

Figure 9.2.12 A post-training questionnaire

Reporting on training

Training activities should be accurately recorded in the individual's file and also in the departmental and/or organisational training plan. The Human Resources (Training) department may also require information and feedback on reviews and training carried out. An informal report can be prepared for a senior manager to confirm the outcomes of the development review, arrangement of the training programme and outcome of the training. Figure 9.2.13 shows an example of an individual's development review/training summary record.

DEVELOPMENT REVIEW/TRAINING SUMMARY

Personal Details

Name of individual _____ Job title _____

Department _____ Start date _____

Review date	Summary of training needs identified	Brief details of training arranged	Post-training review and feedback

Figure 9.2.13 An example of a development review/training summary record

Confidentiality

All information relating to development reviews, training, etc. should be kept confidential. Files should be kept in locked filing cabinets and any computerised records should be protected by passwords. Information discussed during development reviews should be treated confidentially and only used within the organisation's guidelines – for example, if it has been stated that reviews are independent of promotion and reward systems, this should be honoured.

Portfolio activity 9.2 **Number 2**

Following the development reviews carried out as part of portfolio activity 9.2 number 1, research sources of training for the individual and prepare a detailed training programme. The training programme must reflect research into external and in-house provision and include dates, times, length of sessions, venue(s), name of training provider(s) and costs.

Prepare requests for training and make the appropriate arrangements for training to take place.

When the training has been carried out, conduct a post-training review with the individual to evaluate the effectiveness of the training provided. Arrange for your assessor to observe/assess your performance during the review. This can be done by direct observation or by assessing a video or audio recording of the review. Report the outcome of your post-training review in writing – this could be in the form of a questionnaire for completion by the individual. The review documentation should be agreed and signed by both parties and should include an action plan with target dates and further review dates.

The following evidence should be collected:

- training plan agreed with the individual – this may be in the development review documentation for portfolio activity 9.2 number 1
- personal statement explaining how you identified and organised training
- detailed training programme prepared as a result of research into various sources of training; completed requests for training
- written confirmation of training arrangements
- record of the post-training review and documentation – this could include a report on the review/training process and evaluation
- observation report/assessment on the post-training review interview
- witness testimony from the individual confirming that you organised training and carried out a post-training review.

Performance criteria:	9.2.1–12
Knowledge and understanding:	9.2.a–i 9.2.k–n 9.2.p 9.2.q
Evidence requirements:	9.2.1–15

Test yourself

Knowledge and understanding	Questions
a	Explain what, as a supervisor, you would use to ensure you dealt effectively with: • a timid 16-year-old work experience student • an over-confident university graduate • a new member of staff who has 30 years' experience in the industry.
b	Explain how you would decide what competence, and therefore what training, a member of staff required to undertake a particular task.
c	State three ways in which you could encourage your staff to evaluate their own performance.
d	Explain how you would identify the training and development requirements of work teams and individuals and how you would forecast future requirements.
e	What effects might a lack of training have on the motivation and job satisfaction of staff and how might this effect the effectiveness of the department and the organisation?
f	Explain how you would identify, define and assess the competency and learning abilities of an individual.
g	Explain how you would establish and agree developmental objectives for and with an individual.
h	List three resources and opportunities for training and development within the field you work.
i	Explain the training methods and content of three courses available in the field in which you work.
j	Explain how you would identify the key strengths and weaknesses of an individual and how you would assess their skills and competence.

k	In order for staff to maintain effective job performance in your organisation, what functions and procedures need to be followed and what are the established standards of achievement and proficiency?
l	Explain which techniques of: • listening • questioning • summarising you would use to conduct an efficient interview with someone whom you are supervising.
m	Explain the different aspects of: • oral communication • non-verbal communication that are important in conducting development interviews.
n	Explain how you would identify the different components of a job and identify any areas of difficulty within the job role.
o	How would you explain the given procedures of a specific role in a logical sequence that will allow the person you are training to carry out the procedure effectively?
p	Give three methods you could use to establish rapport and to inspire trust when interviewing an individual.
q	State three types of adjective that should be avoided in feedback documentation to comply with requirements of Equal Opportunities.
	List the elements that you would include in review feedback documentation.

Activity 9.1

Desknote

DESKNOTE

To: *Administrative Assistant, Training department*

Date: *Monday, -- -- --*

The training programme for new administrative supervisors has been planned for the end of next month. Please prepare a handout to be given out on the introductory session. These should include information on methods of training and direction that can be used by supervisors with suitable examples to illustrate each method.

John Haines
Training Manager

Activity 9.2

Memorandum

MEMORANDUM

To: Administrative Assistant, Training department
From: Jenny Tranter, Procedures Project Manager
Date: Tuesday, -- -- --

Staff monitoring and feedback procedures

The procedures manual section on staff management is now being prepared. Could you draft suitable procedures to be used by supervisory staff to cover monitoring staff performance and giving feedback. Include examples of documents that could be used to record these activities.

Activity 9.3

Desknote

DESKNOTE

To: *Administrative Assistant, Training department*

Date: *Wednesday, -- -- --*

CONFIDENTIAL

Several staff problems have arisen with our supervisors. Staff are complaining that they are not clear what activities they should undertake, how they are progressing or that supervisors are being critical without offering any support and help.

Please write me a memorandum giving me some ideas on how we could deal with these problems.

John Haines
Training Manager

Activity 9.4

E-mail

E-mail

To:	Administrative Assistant, Training department
From:	John Haines, Training Manager
Date:	Thursday, -- -- --
Subject:	Staff development

We do not have any formal or consistent methods of conducting staff reviews. I would like to bring this up at the next staffing policy meeting. Please prepare some notes for me explaining why we should have a formal staff development policy and what information should be covered by the policy.

Activity 9.5

Meeting Note

> **MEETING NOTE**
>
> **Staffing Procedures Manual**
>
> It was agreed that the Administrative Assistant for the Training department would draft a section for the procedures manual on conducting staff development reviews, with examples of suitable recording documents.

10 Develop and Maintain Positive Working Relations with Colleagues and External Contacts

Many organisations have become very aware of the importance of 'customer focus'. By measuring standards of service they have looked at the quality of the experience received by the customer. One way of thinking about the administrative role is to think of it as providing a service to customers. The administrator can develop a 'customer-oriented' approach to their work. The customer can be defined as the person who is receiving a service provided by you, and can be internal or external to the organisation. In the case of most administrators, customers are all work colleagues and include team members, higher-level managers and those you are supervising, as well as external contacts.

In order to provide good customer service it is necessary to develop a flexible approach and use a range of problem-solving techniques. The administrator should be aware of alternative methods of completing tasks when work does not go as planned. Alternative solutions may be offered to customers. For example, if the photocopier breaks down, the administrator should be aware of other photocopying facilities available in the organisation or local area.

This unit looks at the personal behaviour of the administrator when faced with unexpected situations and demands. The administrator should be able to act in a professional manner in stressful, as well as routine, situations.

PRESENT A POSITIVE IMAGE

Stress management

It is relatively easy to maintain a professional manner when work is routine and straightforward. The real test of a good administrator is how they react when pressure builds up and unplanned events cause problems. These situations are likely to give rise to stress. There are various personal stress management techniques that can allow the administrator to remain calm, objective and clear-thinking.

Lifestyle management

Good general health reduces stress, so the administrator should try to maintain a healthy lifestyle by eating a balanced diet and getting plenty of exercise and regular sleep.

Taking regular breaks in the working day can also help to reduce personal stress levels and put work problems in perspective. It is a good idea to take a lunch break away from the office – for example, take a walk out of the office to eat sandwiches. The actual timing may be flexible, but you should plan the break into your day.

Do not drink alcohol while working. It is tempting, particularly at some conferences and events, to drink alcohol which is available for staff and guests. However, stress is much more difficult to manage if you have drunk even a small amount of alcohol. Drinking alcohol will affect your ability to remain calm, objective and level-headed. When working on residential activities, you need to remember that you are a representative of your organisation, even when you are 'off-duty'.

Managing work

The ability to delegate tasks is very important. When stress levels build up it often seems easier to take on the work yourself, rather than ask someone else to do it. Invest time during quiet periods in training staff to carry out routine tasks which can then easily be delegated when workloads build up.

Learn to 'bounce the ball back' when you are busy. Try to avoid coming away from meetings and discussions with unnecessary or inappropriate work for yourself – bounce the activity back, for example:

'I need some urgent photocopying done.'

'Janet, our administrative assistant, is not very busy at the moment. Why don't you ask her to do it for you?'

or

'I'm having problems with the printer on my computer.'

'Why don't you ring the technician, Jack Rew? He has always been very helpful when I've had printer problems.'

Care needs to be taken to avoid the impression that you always pass on work, and appear not to be helpful. You can still be helpful and look at solutions with people, but you do not always have to take on personal responsibility for delivering the solutions.

Do not be afraid to ask for help, or admit that you are having problems. Although you do not want to appear to be 'not coping', there may be times when simple suggestions and honest discussion can help to improve the working environment and reduce stress. For example, you might be finding that photocopying is taking up a lot of your time so that you are unable to carry out more complex activities. You could discuss this with a line manager and make suggestions – for example, a faster photocopier with more facilities might reduce the time it takes you to complete the work; or the allocation of photocopying duties could be reviewed and staff encouraged to use the centralised service.

You may earn more respect if you see higher-level administrative work as the planning of work and allocation of resources, rather than doing all the work yourself. For example, you might be discussing the management of an event with a senior manager. You should discuss the resources, including staff resources, that will be required for the event and you should have an idea of suitable staff who can be used to provide the necessary support.

Time-management techniques

Many stressful situations can be avoided by using appropriate techniques to manage time. Using time-management techniques, it is possible to use time more effectively – work smarter, not harder.

- *Take time to plan work carefully*. Review all activities and plan work on long-, medium- and short-term timescales. Allocate realistic time slots, allowing for contingencies. Include the use of resources in the plan to ensure that equipment, material and staff resources are available when required.

- *Make full use of planning aids*, such as to-do lists, diaries, computer schedulers, wall-charts, etc. These should be completed and kept up to date with key targets, milestones, etc.
- *Develop good working practices*. Keep notebooks with telephone names, addresses, contacts, technical terms, etc. At the end of the day ensure the desk is tidy and the 'to-do' list for the next day has been prepared. Keep stock cupboards regularly stocked. Keep pen and pencil on hand by the telephone. File papers and information daily so that time is not lost looking for papers and information. Keep information up to date and dispose of out-of-date information – for example, keep telephone lists up to date and dispose of the old ones when new ones are issued.
- *Set up and use equipment fully to save time*. For example, program commonly-used numbers into the telephone; set up standard templates, letters and mailmerge on the computer.
- *Organise your work environment* to enable you to work efficiently. Place commonly-used files in the desk drawer. Keep commonly-used reference books where they can easily be used.
- *Concentrate* on one task at a time. It is very easy in a busy office to develop a 'butterfly' approach and flit from one activity to another. This causes problems as tasks are picked up and put down and the thread is lost.
- *Allow time to take a regular break* during the day, and take it away from the office. Work is often carried out much more efficiently when it is approached with a clear mind.

Managing stressful situations

However well work is planned, stressful situations do arise. An administrator needs to remain in control in these situations. The following strategies may be used to manage stressful situations.

- Remain polite and control your voice, tone and body language to avoid giving confrontational messages. Do not raise your voice and shout. Do not use unprofessional language such as slang or swearwords. Avoid sighing and other expressions of frustration and annoyance. Avoid stamping your feet, turning your body away, shaking your head, etc.
- Try to deal with stressful situations in quiet areas where confidentiality can be maintained. For example, when dealing with a difficult customer take them into a quiet room to discuss the problem. When dealing with a difficult situation with a colleague, again deal with it in a quiet room away from other colleagues.

- Play for time. Do not react immediately to stressful situations, but try to gain a bit of time to think carefully about the situation and come up with some ideas of what you consider to be a suitable outcome. For example, if a difficult issue comes up in the course of a conversation with a colleague, arrange a meeting to discuss the issue at a later date: 'I agree we need to look at the problem with the photocopying. Could we discuss this first thing tomorrow?' This can also allow you time to collect the necessary information.

Dealing with complaints

Dealing with complaints can be stressful. You should retain a professional detachment and not take complaints or criticisms personally. Remember the following stages in dealing with a complaint.

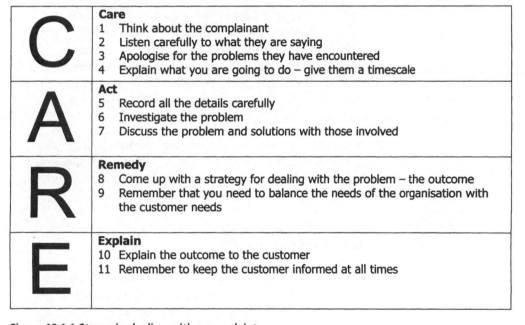

C	**Care** 1 Think about the complainant 2 Listen carefully to what they are saying 3 Apologise for the problems they have encountered 4 Explain what you are going to do – give them a timescale
A	**Act** 5 Record all the details carefully 6 Investigate the problem 7 Discuss the problem and solutions with those involved
R	**Remedy** 8 Come up with a strategy for dealing with the problem – the outcome 9 Remember that you need to balance the needs of the organisation with the customer needs
E	**Explain** 10 Explain the outcome to the customer 11 Remember to keep the customer informed at all times

Figure 10.1.1 Stages in dealing with a complaint

For example, you might need to deal with a delegate at a conference who is very annoyed with you because they have been allocated a smoking room, although they requested a non-smoking room. You know that you requested a non-smoking room from the hotel but they have not followed your instructions. However, your reaction should not be, 'Well it's not my fault – the hotel got it wrong.' Instead you should immediately apologise to the customer and express your concern: ' I do apologise for the fact that you've been allocated a smoking room. I know how unpleasant this can be for a non-smoker.'

Then you should offer an appropriate action: 'If you give me your name and room number, I'll talk to the hotel about it.' It is important to make accurate notes in these situations – it does not help if you compound errors by making further mistakes. Now think about an appropriate timescale – you may be very busy at this moment and unable to leave the conference to speak to the hotel: 'Come back and see me at lunch and I am sure we'll have been able to sort something out by then.' Next you need to move the delegate on: 'Let me take you through and get you a coffee and introduce you to our first speaker.'

When the conference is under way you can go to the hotel reception and discuss the matter. It can be helpful to have your written record of booking with you in case they say they know nothing about it. It is also a good idea to have a strategy in mind such as exchanging the room of a staff member for that of the delegate. You should also know how much business you conduct with the hotel and how much pressure you can put them under. Again it is important not to be confrontational: 'We've always been very pleased with the excellent service we've received from your hotel. However, we seem to have a problem today with …'

When you have negotiated a solution, you should inform the delegate at the agreed time. Depending on the importance of the delegate and the nature of the function you may have also arranged a 'goodwill offering' from the hotel such as fruit, flowers or wine in the room.

Professional judgement

Problems and difficulties can arise as part of the administrator's daily activities and there will be times when you have to use your professional judgement to decide what action to take. The appropriate responses and reactions can vary depending on the situation, the people involved, the nature of the organisation, etc. One way of dealing with situations is to consider them in terms of 'risk'. What will be the risk to the organisation and to your own professional reputation if no action is taken? Also, what will be the risk to the organisation of any actions you may take to deal with a situation? A professional assessment of the risk is required. The following factors may be considered.

- *Legal requirements* – at no time should you take any action that would compromise health and safety requirements. You should also ensure all actions comply with other legislation – for example, the Data Protection Act.
- *Confidentiality* – solutions and actions should not compromise the confidentiality of an organisation or situation.
- *Business values/image* – actions and solutions should be in keeping with the organisation's stated values, ethics, etc. They should also match the appropriate business image.
- *Commercial sense* – good relations with important customers and suppliers should always be maintained.

Professional judgement is often acquired with experience. However, it can be helped by having an understanding of your organisation's business activities, aims and values together with a thorough knowledge of the organisation's procedures and a clear understanding of your role, responsibility and its limitations. You also need a good working knowledge of the equipment, systems and resources for which you are responsible.

Building relationships with colleagues

All people working in an organisation are part of a team. The team works much better when good working relationships have been established. These do not always happen by accident, and care needs to be taken to ensure that good working relationships are established.

Figure 10.1.2 outlines various ways to establish and maintain good working relationships with colleagues. It takes effort to build good professional relationships, but it will pay dividends in the long term.

Enhancing relationships

Good working relationships with colleagues and external contacts should be demonstrated at all times. However, there may be opportunities to enhance these relationships. This might be seen as 'added value'. One way in which this can be achieved is by adopting the 'customer-oriented' approach already outlined at the beginning of this unit. However, other steps may be taken by organisations to enhance internal working relationships.

- *Teambuilding activities* – time may be set aside for on-site or off-site teambuilding activities. These may consist of a wide range of activities – for example, role-play, problem-solving, courses, brainstorming.

- *Social activities* – special social events may be organised to build on working relationships – for example, Christmas activities.
- *Team-based activities* – teams may be formed to focus on certain work-based activities. The teams may meet regularly to review and discuss problems, procedures, systems, etc. This helps all those involved to gain a wider understanding of the procedures and of how the procedures impact on different members of staff – for example, quality circles, where groups of staff meet regularly to review procedures and working practices and consider ways to improve the standards of service provided by the organisation.

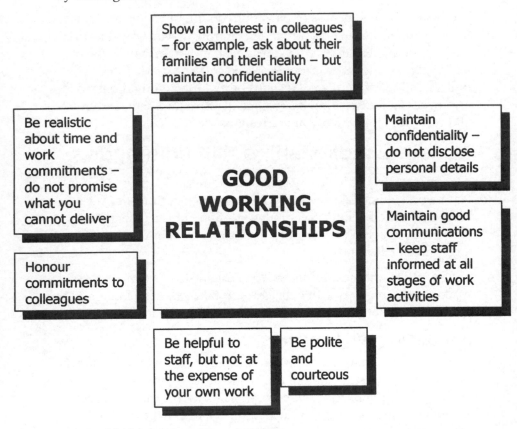

Figure 10.1.2 Establishing good working relationships

Image and standards

Your organisation's image

The 'image' or picture that people have of you and the organisation is often based on very superficial features. Judgements are made on what they see and hear. Your personal appearance, the way you behave and the presentation of documents are practical features on which judgements are made. The way you speak in meetings, your telephone manner, your choice of words and the 'tone' of documents all give messages which are perceived by listeners and readers.

Your organisation's codes and practices

Dress standards and codes of practice for appearance and behaviour are usually established within an organisation. These may be based on 'custom and practice' or they may be written. When you start work with an organisation you should follow the standards that have been set. If you are not sure about an organisation's standards, it is usually better initially to be more formal and neutral in your choice of clothes. When you have worked with an organisation for a while you may adopt a different, suitable style. In some organisations, health and safety may also be a consideration and guidelines and safety rules should always be followed. Whatever style is adopted, you should always demonstrate the highest standards of neatness and personal cleanliness. There may also be occasions when you will be required to adopt a different dress style – for example, when you represent your organisation at a public event such as a conference or promotional event. An appropriate dress style should be adopted, and if you are not sure about this you should check with a colleague. Dress standards are also discussed in Element 1.1, page 7.

Your organisation's house style

Document presentation is also important. Many organisations have a standard 'house style' which should be adopted for appropriate documents. Headed paper, letter templates, memorandum formats and other standard documentation should be used when appropriate. Documents should be presented with no errors. The presence of errors shows a lack of concern about accuracy and quality. Spellcheckers, grammar checkers and careful proofreading should eliminate errors. Dictionaries, whether on-line or of traditional style, can be used to check words.

The telephone is a key means of communication. This has raised the profile of the importance of a good telephone technique. The use of the telephone is covered in detail in Element 1.1, pages 9–21, but the following points should be observed.

- Follow your organisation's house style for greeting. Less formal styles are now often used – for example, 'Good morning, X organisation, Jane speaking.' Many telephones have different rings for internal and external calls. Listen for these and use the appropriate response.

- Listen to the caller and make careful notes of their requests.
- Be polite, courteous and efficient.
- Tone of voice can affect the caller's perception of the way their call is being received. If you are busy it is easy to give the impression that a call is an interruption and a nuisance. Sighs and banging the telephone down on the desk can also give a bad impression.
- Do not leave callers hanging on. If the call requires information which is not immediately available arrange to call back, or for the caller to call back. Give a timescale and keep to it.
- Be aware of confidentiality and security when using the telephone.

Portfolio activity 10.1

Your competence for this element should be demonstrated consistently throughout the completion of the qualification. You should, therefore, be collecting relevant evidence for this element as you are completing all the other activities. While all the evidence may not be available until you have reached the end of your programme, it is a good idea to check evidence against the performance criteria, knowledge and understanding, and evidence requirements on an ongoing basis. The following activities should be completed:

1 At the end of each month, use an evidence record/matrix sheet and track evidence you have collected for other units against the relevant performance criteria, knowledge and understanding and evidence requirements.

The following is a list of some forms of evidence you will be able to gather from undertaking the activities in other elements.

- witness testimonies from superiors and colleagues that show you have liaised with and supported colleagues and external contacts – for example, testimonies collected for Unit 3 when running an event; testimonies collected from individuals being supervised (Unit 6 or 8)
- observation assessments from superiors/colleagues/assessors; these could be supported with authenticated photographs or video/audio recordings – for example, photographs for Unit 3; video recordings of interviewing staff or carrying out a review meeting for Unit 8
- authenticated personal accounts of situations encountered and resolved – for example, witness testimonies about events

prepared for Unit 3; testimonies about handling interviews or review meetings
- examples of written documentation promoting the organisation's image to colleagues and external contacts; there should be a wide range of documentation in the portfolio that can be easily identified for this unit – for example, booking accommodation, organising events, making appointments, etc.
- work plans/schedules detailing commitments to others and testimonials stating commitments honoured – for example, schedules for organising an event (Unit 3); organising travel (Unit 4)
- work schedules/action plans showing priority tasks and target and completion dates for carrying out activities – for example, schedules for researching information (Unit 5); researching and evaluating a storage system (Unit 6)
- work schedules/action plans showing priority tasks and target and completion dates for carrying out activities – for example, schedules for researching information (Unit 5); researching and evaluating a storage system (Unit 6).

2 Regularly meet with your assessor to check your progress in this unit and make appropriate arrangements to cover any outstanding performance criteria, knowledge and understanding and evidence requirements.

Performance criteria:	10.1.1–15
Knowledge and understanding:	10.1.a–l
Evidence requirements:	10.1.1–3

Test yourself

Knowledge and understanding	Questions
a	Does your organisation have a code of practice for appearance and behaviour? If so, what does it involve? If not, what less formal standards for appearance and behaviour have you noticed?
b	How would you go about setting an example of positive behaviour for others?
c	List three important telephone techniques.

d	What are your organisation's procedures for receiving and making telephone calls?
e	Give three possible opportunities to enhance internal and external relationships.
f	List and explain three problem-solving techniques that you use on a regular basis.
g	How does health and safety legislation relate to presenting a positive image?
h	List and explain three techniques you might use to manage a stressful situation.
i	List and explain: • your work role and responsibilities • your line manager's work role and responsibilities • the work role and responsibilities of someone you supervise.
j	Give three methods of maintaining constructive working relationships: • with colleagues • with external customers.
k	Give three time-management techniques that you use on a regular basis.
l	Explain how you would assess the risk of a situation.

Element 10.2
ADVISE AND INFORM OTHERS

The final element of the book looks at advising and informing others. These activities are a routine part of the administrator's role – attending meetings, preparing and sending letters and memos, etc. all involve the administrator giving information that must be accurate, current and relevant with confidentiality maintained at all times. However, the element also contains a particular focus on health and safety, improving working conditions and the procedures to follow in recommending improvements and alerting others to changes needed.

Health and safety regulations

Health and safety requirements are covered by a range of laws and regulations. The main UK legislation covering workplace safety is the Health and Safety at Work (HASAW) Act 1974. The provisions of this Act are constantly being updated by additional regulations and codes of practice such as:

- COSHH – the Control of Substances Hazardous to Health (1988)
- RIDDOR – the Reporting of Injuries, Diseases and Dangerous Occurrences Regulations (1985)
- Electricity at Work Regulations (1989)
- Display Screen Equipment Regulations (1992)
- Fire Workplace Regulations (1997).

Information about all these aspects of the Health and Safety at Work Act are contained in the appendix (pages 539–45).

Risk assessment

The regulations require that regular inspections of the premises are undertaken to identify and assess any safety hazards. This process is called 'risk assessment'. The level of risk can be assessed by considering the outcome of an accident in terms of injury to personnel or breakdown in business activity. Once hazards have been identified and assessed, appropriate action plans can be prepared to correct them. The action plan should identify actions which would remove the hazard, reduce the risk or protect people from the risk. The action plan should be implemented and regularly monitored.

The administrator may have responsibility for carrying out regular risk assessments and reporting the findings to the Health and Safety officer or Health and Safety committee. Even if the administrator does not have formal responsibility for this activity, a requirement of the HASAW Act is that all employees have a duty of care for the safety of themselves, colleagues, visitors, etc. and should take part in any training required. Consideration for health and safety should underpin all the activities within the control of the administrator. As well as activities carried out on the organisation's premises, the administrator may also have to consider health and safety for activities carried out on other premises such as conference facilities and meeting venues.

Organisations should also have health and safety procedures that define the reporting procedures, roles and meeting structure – for example, an organisation might have a health and safety representative and hold regular health and safety meetings. Specific work projects/activities may also give administrators responsibility for the relevant health and safety considerations – for example, health and safety considerations when organising an event; or health and safety considerations in filing systems.

Health and safety risks

The major sources of risk in an organisation can be identified as fire, accident, explosion and poor working conditions. There is a range of steps that can be taken to remove hazards, reduce the risk and protect people from the risk. The following table looks at these in detail.

Risk	Possible source	Removal	Reduction	Protection
Fire	• Electrical equipment • Faulty goods • Cigarettes, matches • Inflammable liquids	• Remove faulty goods • Prohibit smoking on the premises	• Arrange regular, professional check of electrical and other equipment • Store inflammable liquids in metal cabinets away from equipment • Ensure all equipment and furniture is fireproof • Provide staff training for equipment users	• Install fire alarms, smoke alarms, sprinkler systems, etc. • Have sufficient, suitable and regularly-checked fire extinguishers on the premises • Ensure all rooms have fire notices • Ensure regular fire drills are held • Ensure fire exits are not blocked
Accident	• Slipping on wet floors • Falling over obstructions • Tripping on trailing wires • Equipment injuries including electric shock, catching hands etc.	• Arrange furniture and equipment so as to avoid trailing wires • Fit all equipment with appropriate guards • Maintain all equipment	• Provide signs to warn of wet floors • Check regularly to ensure that there are no obstructions • Provide training for all staff, particularly equipment users	• Ensure all equipment is fitted with appropriate guards • Fit electrical circuit breakers to reduce risks from electrical accidents • Provide overalls, hairnets, safety glasses etc. where appropriate

Risk	Possible source	Removal	Reduction	Protection
	• Falling off chairs, tables etc. • Lifting goods • Accidents caused by catching loose clothes, hair, etc. in equipment	regularly • Provide storage cupboards to avoid obstructions	• Provide suitable stools/steps for reaching items from shelves, etc. • Provide staff training for lifting, etc. • Provide suitable trolleys, etc. for carrying heavy items	
Explosion	• Bomb explosions, for example, terrorist and political activist action • Chemical/ electrical reactions, for example, gas explosions		• Provide bomb scanning devices for mail room • Install security controls with checks on people entering premises, closed circuit television surveillance • Provide staff training to raise awareness of suspicious mail packages, unidentified bags, etc. • Regularly check safety of gas appliances and other dangerous equipment • Store dangerous chemicals correctly	• Install bomb alarms to alert staff to bombs (these should be different to fire alarms)* • Provide staff training on bomb evacuation procedures*
Poor working conditions	• Illness and eye strain caused by poor lighting, badly-positioned VDUs	• Provide suitable adjustable chairs, tables, etc.	• Provide 'daylight' lighting • Position screens, VDUs, etc. carefully • Purchase low-glare screens	• Provide anti-glare screens for VDUs • Provide free regular eye tests for VDU operators and ensure that appropriate spectacles are worn

Risk	Possible source	Removal	Reduction	Protection
	• Headaches caused by poor lighting, screen glare, VDUs, etc. • RSI (repetitive strain injury) caused by the repeated use of a keyboard • Backache and injury caused by incorrect posture from sitting at incorrect style of chair or fixed seating		• Ensure that VDU/keyboard operators take regular breaks • Provide wrist rests and ergonomically designed keyboards and computer mice	
Personal injury as a result of violence Threats of injury	• Presence of unauthorised personnel • Angry customers • Poorly lit public and access areas, for example, car parks	• Ensure rigorous security arrangements, for example, security guards • Provide closed circuit television systems	• Provide lighting in public areas • Ensure that all staff follow security procedures • Use security screens in 'at-risk' public areas	• Train staff on security and how to cope with with stressful situations

*Bomb alarms should be a different pitch to fire alarms and staff should be aware of the difference in procedures to be followed. In a fire evacuation staff should shut windows and doors and leave immediately without removing bags/personal belongings. In a bomb evacuation windows and doors should be opened and nearby bags removed.

Limits of authority

Informing others

There are various methods of informing people of changes that may need to be made to working conditions and practices. The method chosen will depend on the nature of the problem and the organisation's procedures.

- *Verbal discussion* – issues may be raised in informal or formal meetings for routine and low-risk matters – for example, discussion of health and safety issues at a meeting to plan an event.
- *Memos/e-mails* – areas of concern may be highlighted to relevant staff – for example, health and safety representatives. Written information may be required if money will be needed – for example, a memo might be sent requesting funds for the purchase of anti-glare screens for computers.
- *Reports/presentations* – these should include information about relevant health and safety issues.
- *Forms/checklists* – performance feedback forms and monitoring/supervising checklists should include relevant information on health and safety.

Health and safety and the HDAP award

An administrator should take account of health and safety in all the activities they carry out. This can range from routine activities to special events and making travel arrangements. Health and safety requirements should be demonstrated throughout all the activities you undertake for the Higher Diploma in Administrative Procedures award. The following table shows ways in which health and safety can be demonstrated throughout the activities you are undertaking.

Unit	Element	Health and safety considerations
1 – Manage Business Communications	Plan and carry out oral and electronic business communications. Plan and carry out written business communications	• Ensure appropriate siting and check safety of electrical equipment • Ensure hygienic management of telephone head/handsets • Provide manuals and training to ensure correct usage
2 – Organise and Administer Business Meetings and Appointments	Organise and administer business meetings Chair an informal meeting Arrange and monitor appointments for self and others	• Check health and safety provisions for premises and meeting rooms • Inform delegates of health and safety requirements • Allow sufficient time for appointments to ensure safe travel

Unit	Element	Health and safety considerations
		• Consider the safety of personnel when booking venues for meetings
3 – Organise, Administer and Evaluate Business Events	Work within a team to organise and administer business events Evaluate a business event	• Check health and safety provisions for premises and event locations • Inform staff at events of safety arrangements • Include health and safety arrangements in the evaluation
4 – Organise Business Trips at Home and Abroad	Organise business trips Prepare travel documentation	• Check all health and safety considerations, for example, inoculations, health risks • Check arrangements for medical care while travelling • Check suitable insurance • Include information on health and safety in travel documentation • Include relevant health documentation
5 – Research and Present Information for a Specific Purpose	Research information for a specific purpose Present information for a specific purpose	• Include health and safety considerations in the research carried out • Include relevant information about health and safety in the the presentation
6 – Manage the Storage and Retrieval of Information	Evaluate an information storage and retrieval system Monitor and supervise an individual in the use of an information storage and retrieval system	• Include health and safety considerations in the evaluation of the information system • Ensure health and safety factors are considered when monitoring and supervising an individual, for example, include health and safety training
7 – Contribute to Financial Planning and Control Activities	Draft a budget Control a petty cash system Analyse financial information	• Include provision for health and safety training and equipment in budgets • Check suitable security arrangements are made for the security of staff who may be dealing with cash

Unit	Element	Health and safety considerations
		• Where possible, include health and safety considerations when analysing financial information, for example, checking an organisation's safety records
8 – Contribute to the Provision of Personnel	Prepare job analysis, job description and person specification Contribute to the recruitment of personnel Induct new staff	• Include health and safety factors in job analysis, job descriptions and person specifications • Check health and safety arrangements for interview rooms and interview schedules. • Include health and safety issues in interview questions • Ensure that health and safety is covered in induction and ongoing training programmes
9 – Supervise and Develop Staff	Plan and supervise work activities Plan and conduct staff development reviews and identify training needs	• Include health and safety considerations when planning work • Check health and safety guidelines are being followed when supervising work • Include health and safety in staff development reviews • Include health and safety in training needs
10 – Develop and Maintain Positive Working Relationships with Colleagues and External Contacts	Present a positive image Advise and inform others	• Check health and safety factors are covered at all times, for example, reception area, suitable clothing • Carry out health and safety check of the working environment

Portfolio activity 10.2

Your competence for this element should be demonstrated consistently throughout the completion of the qualification. You should, therefore, be collecting relevant evidence for this element as you are completing all the other activities. While all the evidence may not be available until you have reached the end of your programme, it is a good idea to check evidence against the performance criteria, knowledge and understanding, and evidence requirements on an ongoing basis. The following activities should be completed.

1 At the end of each month, use an evidence record/matrix sheet and track evidence you have collected for other units against the relevant performance criteria, knowledge and understanding and evidence requirements.

2 Arrange for your assessor to observe you carrying out relevant activities – for example, observe a meeting where you might exchange information or observe a presentation in which you are giving information to others.

3 Ask relevant members of staff/colleagues to write a witness testimony to confirm your competence for this element.

4 Write a personal statement explaining how you have carried out relevant activities for this element. You should include and reference examples of evidence that you have collected in other units.

5 If necessary, carry out a health and safety check of your working environment to cover physical environment, equipment, materials and working procedures. Advise and inform others of changes that may be required to improve working conditions and practices.

Performance criteria:	10.2.1–6
Knowledge and understanding:	10.2.a–e
Evidence requirements:	10.2.1–4

Test yourself

Knowledge and understanding	Questions
a	What aspects of health and safety legislation relate to your advising and informing others?
b	What procedures should you follow when recommending improvements in working conditions?
c	List three methods you could use to communicate effectively with: • someone you are supervising • your line manager • the managing director.
d	How are individual responsibilities and limits of authority established and defined in your organisation?
e	List three methods you could use to co-ordinate your work activities in order to achieve your work objectives.

Appendix – relevant legislation

Every effort has been made to ensure details contained in this appendix are correct at the time of writing. However, you should always check the current situation as many things can change. Decisions handed down in case law or by the European Court of Appeal could cause re-interpretation of laws.

Data protection

Data Protection Act 1984

Companies who keep information on computer about individuals – for example, employees and customers – must comply with the regulations. Individuals are protected so that they can have access to information held about them, challenge it and be compensated if it is misused in any way that causes them damage or distress through inaccuracy.

Employers using a computer data bank must state:
* what information is being stored
* why it is being stored
* how they have obtained the information
* to whom it might be disclosed.

The Act does not apply to data held for:
* national security
* payroll
* household affairs
* crime detection or prevention
* keeping of accounts
* recreational purposes
* the subsequent preparation of text (documents held in a word processor)
* the purpose of recording the 'intention' of the data user.

Additional safeguards are required if the data covers:
* racial origin
* criminal convictions
* political or religious beliefs
* physical mental or sexual health records.

The **Data Protection Registrar** should ensure that personal data is only:
* obtained and processed fairly and lawfully
* relevant, adequate and not excessive
* held for specified and lawful purposes
* held for as long as necessary
* stored in such a way so as to prevent unauthorised access, accidental loss or destruction.

Data Protection Act 1998

This gives employees access to any paper files containing their personal details. This means that information in areas such as performance appraisal or disciplinary proceedings are now open to inspection and employers may be subject to legal action for negligence or defamation should the information prove to be indiscreet.

Exemptions include:
* information relating to wage rates, redundancy negotiations or plans for promotion or demotion
* confidential references given by the employer for the purposes of education, training or employment, appointment to any office or the provision by the employee of any service.

Intellectual property

The Copyright, Designs and Patents Act 1988

This law was designed to protect an artist, author, composer, designer or creator of any type of work of art from the theft of 'their property'.

Persons requiring to use these 'properties' should pay an appropriate fee – that is, a royalty. When the law is broken, the infringement of those rights can lead to prosecution.

Protected by copyright law are:
1 literary, dramatic, musical and artistic works
2 typographical arrangements of published editions
3 films, broadcasts, sound recordings and cable programmes.

These are protected until:
1 the end of 70th year after the end of the year in which creator died
2 the end of the 25th year after the year in which the edition was published
3 the end of 70th year after the end of the year in which the work was made/released.

During these times the copyright owner has exclusive right to:
* a copy of the work
* the issue of copies to the public

- the performance, show or playing of works to the public
- the broadcast or inclusion of the work in a cable programme service
- any adaptations.

Exemptions to the above which do not constitute infringement are when the works are used for:
- private research or study
- critiques or reviews acknowledging the identity of the creator and the title of the work
- current event reports acknowledging identity of creator
- incidental inclusion – for example, a shot in a film showing a portrait hanging on a wall
- educational purposes.

When a licence is applied for the above, exemptions do not apply.

The following agencies can issue licences and in turn collect fees (royalties) for the creator in return for a percentage. The agencies include the:
- Performing Rights Society
- The Educational Recording Agency Ltd
- Video Performance Ltd
- Design and Artists Copyright Society.
- Copyright Licensing Agency
- Phonographic Performance Ltd
- Mechanical Copyright Protection Society

For:
- the reporting of parliamentary or judicial proceedings
- the proceedings of a Royal Commission or statutory enquiry
- copies of summaries (abstracts) in articles about scientific or technical subjects
- the use of some sound recordings and artistic designs

there are also exceptions to the copyright law.

Libraries and archives are subject to specific rules from the Copyright (Libraries and Archivists) (Copying of Copyright Material) Regulations 1989.

Trademarks whether words or symbols can also be protected by registration.

Equal opportunities legislation
This encompasses several Acts of Parliament that outline the requirements, the main ones being the:
- Equal Pay Acts 1970
- Race Relations Act 1976
- Disability Discrimination Act 1995
- Sex Discrimination Act 1975 and 1986
- Disabled Persons (Employment) Acts 1944, 1958 and 1986

Note: See also **Employment Legislation**.

Equal Pay Act 1970
This states that employers must pay equal amounts to men and women if they are doing the same work, or work that rates as being equivalent, or if they are doing work of equal value.

These Acts are in force to ensure that as far as possible all have an equal chance to gain employment.

Legislation for other areas – such as age discrimination is under review.

When placing advertisements for vacancies, infringement must be avoided. Racial, Sex and Disability discrimination are vulnerable areas.

Sex Discrimination Act
requires that there be no:
- **direct sex or marriage discrimination** – that is, less favourable treatment of a person on the grounds of their gender or less favourable treatment of a married person than an unmarried person of the same sex.
- **indirect sex or marriage discrimination** – that is, setting terms or conditions for employment applied equally to either sex or marital status that can only be met by a smaller proportion of either and cannot be shown to be justifiable.

Race Relations Act
This requires that there be no:
- **direct racial discrimination** – that is, less favourable treatment of a person, in the same or similar conditions, on racial grounds. Racial grounds are:
  - colour
  - nationality
  - national origin.
  - race
  - ethnic origin
- **indirect racial discrimination** – that is, applying conditions to training place or jobs that persons of certain racial groups find unacceptable or are unable to meet.

Disability Discrimination Act
This provides employers with resources to give employment to persons when their disability will not affect the job they do. This could be by the way of:
- grants to adapt the workplace or equipment for disabled people

- grants for training and provision of employment to disabled people
- industrial rehabilitation or vocational training to equip disabled people with skills to take on suitable positions.

Disabled Persons (Employment) Act
This designates certain occupations as suitable for disabled persons. Employers who give opportunity to disabled persons can claim funding to make necessary changes to workplace facilities. This could include access, toilet facilities, etc.

Employment legislation
Employment Rights Act 1996
This entitles employees to receive details of their terms and conditions of employment in writing as well as an itemised pay statement.

Working Time Regulations
This entitles those who have been employed for at least thirteen weeks to three weeks' annual paid leave pro rata – for example, someone working two days a week would be entitled to six days' annual paid leave.

Employment Relations Bill 1999
This entitles all women to a minimum of eighteen weeks' maternity leave and men and women with at least one year's service to three months' parental leave following the birth or adoption of a child.

Employers must give at least one week's notice to an employee who has worked for the company for less than two years; and then at least one week for every year of service up to twelve. Employees must give at least one week's notice if they have worked for the company for one month or more (this does not increase with increased service).

Company legislation
Companies Act 1985
A company may be registered either as a public limited company or a private limited company.

A **Public Limited Company**:
- must end its business name with plc
- must obtain a certificate of incorporation and a certificate to trade prior to trading
- must have minimum initial capital of £50 000
- must produce a set of audited accounts within seven months of the end of its financial year
- must register a memorandum of association that states it is a public limited company
- must have at least two directors and two members
- must have a qualified company secretary
- may sell shares and debentures to the public.

A **Private Limited Company**:
- must end its business name with ltd
- must obtain a certificate of incorporation prior to trading
- needs no minimum amount of capital – one member can start a private limited company with £1
- needs have only two members and one director; single-member private companies limited by shares or guarantee are allowed by the Companies Single Members Private Limited Companies Regulations 1992
- may, depending on its size and turnover, be able to avoid certain of the regulations relating to the preparation and publication of accounts
- must produce a set of audited accounts within ten months of the end of the financial year
- must not sell shares to the public

Partnership Act 1890
Under this act the duties of partners towards each other are to:
- have an equal share of the profits and bear an equal share of the losses
- be indemnified by the firm against any payment made and liability incurred in the course of the business
- pay interest to a partner who makes a payment into the firm above his or her prescribed amount
- have the opportunity to take part in the management of the business
- have no entitlement to remuneration for his or her part in the business
- agree unanimously to the introduction of a new member
- determine ordinary matters by a majority of the partners
- keep the partnership books at the place of business to which all partners should have access.

The authority of a partner depends on the type of business although normally he or she would be expected to have authority to:
- sell any goods or property belonging to the firm
- purchase goods that would normally be used into the firm's business
- receive payments from third parties on behalf of the firm
- hire staff

- engage a solicitor to act for the firm
- in a commercial partnership – to borrow money on behalf of firm and to sanction payments in and out of the firm.

Health and safety legislation

Health & Safety At Work Act 1974 (HASAWA)

This outlines the general responsibilities of employers and employees in the workplace **all** of whom have responsibilities under this Act.

Employers must 'ensure so far as is reasonably practicable the health, safety and welfare of employees'.

Employers with more than **four** employees must provide a written statement of their commitment to health and safety and details of the company's health and safety procedures. To do this employers should:
- maintain any workplace in a condition that is safe and without risks to health and to provide means of access and egress that are safe and without risks.
- undertake assessment to negate risks to health and safety in the use of handling, storing and transporting articles in the workplace
- provide and maintain equipment, machinery and appliances, also work practices that are so far as is possible without risks to health and safety
- train supervise and inform staff to use equipment and follow work practices to ensure their health and safety at work
- keep premises clean with adequate heating and ventilation
- maintain fixtures and fittings in safe condition
- provide fire extinguishers, first aid kit and accident book
- keep emergency exits clear and mark exit routes
- instruct staff in use of new equipment
- induct staff in emergency procedures and practice emergency procedures to test evacuation of premises
- regularly test emergency equipment.

This **duty of care** extends also to:
- trainees in the employers care
- those visiting the premises for legitimate reason
- those using company equipment
- those using company services or products
- those affected by work carried out on premises i.e. the general public.

Employees, while in the workplace, are responsible for:
- themselves
- trainees
- contractors' employees working at the premises
- using safety equipment available
- colleagues
- visitors
- receiving necessary training in health and safety procedures.

Employer's Liability (Compulsory Insurance) Act 1982

This Act states that employers must hold insurance to cover employees against injury in the course of their work and display a certificate confirming this on their premises. The penalties for non-compliance are:
- £2500 for employing a person when not insured
- £1000 for each day that the appropriate certificate is not displayed.

These supplement the HASAWA and shift focus of regulations to prevention by risk assessment in the work place.

Employers must:
- make reasonable assessment of risks to employees which could affect them in the course of their work
- assess risks to others
- appoint a person to manage health and safety
- set up and maintain systems
- provide employees with information about any risks
- advise employees who is responsible for health and safety matters.

Amendments

- In 1994 improvements were outlined to existing regulations to further protect health and safety of pregnant employees (including those recently confined) with regard to night work and exposure to chemicals etc.
- In 1997 requirements were added to further assess risks before employing or giving placements to young persons –**Health & Safety (Youth Persons) Regulations 1997** – the inexperience of the person makes them more vulnerable.

The risk assessment therefore must:
- consider the lack of health and safety consciousness due to inexperience and immaturity

- provide for necessary training
- judge extent of exposure to hazardous substances
- consider nature of work and layout of workplace
- evaluate workpractices and types of equipment to be used.

A **young person** is aged 16 to 18 years (under 16 years of age is a 'child'). A young person should not be required to work:

- when exposed to radiation
- in situations where they are exposed to agents that can chronically affect their health
- beyond physical capabilities
- beyond psychological capabilities
- in noisy conditions
- in extreme cold or heat that might endanger their health.

With employment of a 'child' a person with parental responsibility for the 'child' should be advised of the findings of any risk assessment carried out.

Workplace (Health, Safety and Welfare) Regulations 1992
This outlines the minimum requirements for the workplace and supersedes those set out in the Factories Act 1961 and Offices, Shops and Railway Premises Act 1963. The employer is required to:
- clean and maintain the workplace regularly
- keep equipment maintained in efficient working order and keep records of maintenance
- adequately ventilate the workplace with sufficient fresh or purified air
- keep the temperature comfortable – approximately 22°C for office workers; 16°C for light workers and 13°C for heavy workers: it should be neither too hot nor too cold for long periods
- provide adequate lighting and space for individuals
- ensure workstations allow tasks to be carried out safely
- provide suitable toilet and washing facilities, drinking water, cloakrooms and restrooms.

Manual Handling Operations Regulations 1992
These require that if hazardous manual handling of loads is unavoidable:
- the risk involved must be assessed
- procedure changed to lessen risk or suitable equipment provided to assist
- information and training in manual handling must be provided.

Provision and Use of Work Equipment Regulations 1992
These require that:
- equipment is suitable for the purpose intended
- equipment is properly maintained in working order
- staff are trained and supervised in the use of equipment
- protection is provided against identified hazards
- hazard warnings on the equipment are provided
- adequate lighting is provided
- clearly visible controls to stop and start the machinery and to isolate equipment from power source in case of accident are provided.

Noise at Work Regulations 1989
These require that:
- exposure is reduced when high levels identified
- protective equipment is provided
- 'ear protection' zones are provided when it is neither possible nor practicable to reduce noise levels – the employer is required to provide personal protective equipment if there is no viable alternative.

Personal Protective Equipment at Work (PPE) 1992
The equipment should be:
- suitable for the intended purpose to fit and protect the wearer
- maintained to remain efficient and effective
- provided with appropriate storage facility
- provided with information and instruction on use to wearer
- able to be reported on loss or defect
- provided free of charge.

Health & Safety Information for Employees Regulations 1989
All employees have a right to basic health and safety information and training. This includes the display of poster detailing the local authority with which the business is registered. It is very important to induct new staff carefully. They should be informed of:
- the company health and safety policy and procedures
- their health and safety representative
- the fire precautions and procedures (including fire drill procedures)

- the emergency exits in addition to normal exits from workplace
- accident procedures, the location of the first aid box and the accident book
- the nearest first aider (if available)
- what to do in case of illness
- the cleanliness routines
- the maintenance procedures
- the staff facilities available (restroom, toilets, cloakroom, etc.)
- any hazardous equipment and risk assessment carried out on it.
- any COSSH registered substances they may be required to handle.

Electricity at Work Regulations 1989
All electrical equipment must be safe and correctly installed and tested at regular intervals to ensure users' safety. Evidence of testing should be available.

Health and Safety (Display Screen Equipment) Regulations 1992
These require employers to ensure users of visual display units (VDUs) and other display equipment are safe by:
- providing training to raise awareness of the risks
- allowing users free eye tests and sometimes contributing to the cost of spectacles if required for VDU operation
- assessing and minimising the risks relating to the hardware, the environment and factors specific to individuals' use of the equipment
- ensuring workstations meet minimum requirements
- planning work with sufficient breaks from the equipment to avoid visual and postural fatigue.

Health & Safety (Safety Signs & Signals) Regulations – 1996
- Employees must be advised about health and safety matters via specific posters or leaflets.
- Fire exits must be clearly marked.
- Signs must be set up informing people about any hazardous area (wet floor) in the workplace.

Reporting of Injuries, Diseases and Dangerous Occurrences Regulations (RIDDOR) 1985 and 1995
The enforcing authority must be informed of:
- anyone incapacitated and unable to work for more than three days following an accident in the work place
- anyone who dies at work or one year after receiving a reportable injury as a result of that injury
- anyone who receives burns or an electric shock or loses consciousness due to an electric shock or lack of oxygen
- anyone suffering from a serious injury – a fracture (except of the hand or foot), amputation, injury to eyes or any injury that involves more than 24-hours' stay in hospital
- acute illness caused by infection caught from diseased or infected material
- chemical poisoning or gassing requiring medical treatment
- accidental collapse of building under construction or alteration
- accidental setting off of explosives
- explosion of pressurised vessels – e.g. boilers
- collapse or overturning of hoists or powered platforms
- collapse of scaffolding
- sudden escape of large quantity of flammable liquids or gas
- fire or explosion causing premises to be closed for more than 24 hours.

All incidents, however trivial, must be recorded in an **accident book** and records kept for **three years**.

Health and Safety (First Aid) Regulations 1981
These require the employer to ensure:
- all staff are aware of first-aid procedures
- someone is responsible for first aid (if more than 50 people are employed or work is hazardous, then the person should be trained and qualified in first aid)
- the location of the first aid box and the name of any first aiders is displayed
- the first aid box is of appropriate size and contents (no medication of any sort to be included).

Fire Precautions Act 1971
This requires that companies' premises are inspected and hold a Fire Certificate if:
- there are more than twenty employees on the premises at any one time (ten if above ground level)
- there are highly flammable or explosive substances stored
- there is sleeping accommodation – e.g. guest houses or hotels.

Fire Precautions (Workplace) Regulations 1997

These regulations cover some premises that escape the criteria of the Fire Precautions Act 1971. They were introduced by the European Framework and Workplace Directives. They require employers to :
- carry out fire risk assessment (could be included in general risk assessment)
- provide training for fire evacuation procedures
- provide reasonable fire fighting equipment
- maintain safety equipment (regular servicing of fire extinguishers)
- ensure there are reasonable exits available in case of fire.

Control of Substances Hazardous to Health Regulations (COSSH) 1988 and 1994

These require the employer to carry out risk assessment on hazardous substances used in the workplace. They should look at the exposure of the employee to the substance and anybody else who might be affected by it – e.g. visitors to the workplace.

During risk assessment it is necessary to establish:
- how the substance should be used
- who will be exposed to it
- how long they will be exposed to it
- how the substance could affect the body/skin
- the long- and short-term effects
- does it have an Occupational Exposure Limit (OEL) that will be exceeded
- whether the control measures are effective
- what/who is likely to be exposed if control measures fail
- what will happen if there is an accidental spillage.

Employees should have access to risk assessment carried out on the hazardous substances that they are required to handle in the course of their duties. They should also be trained to use them safely. Employees are entitled to report to the employer if they feel any substance they are using still endangers their health. Also if they wish to suggest further precautions needed for safe use. Employees are required to carry out procedures for safety laid down after risk assessment.

Public Health (Control of Disease) Act 1984 and Public Health (Infectious Diseases) Regulations 1988

These acts put responsibility on employees to decide whether or not they are suffering from an infectious or 'notifiable' disease. If so, by going to work colleagues' and clients' health could be endangered. It is also an offence to go to any public place or travel on public transport while suffering from an infectious disease. Although cases of prosecution are rare, a major outbreak traced back to one person could lead to prosecution. The notifiable diseases are:
- anthrax
- diphtheria
- infective jaundice
- lassa fever
- marburg disease
- meningococcal septicaemia
- paratyphoid fever
- relapsing fever
- whooping cough
- acute encephalitis
- dysentery
- leprosy
- lyme disease
- measles
- mumps
- plague
- rubella
- yellow fever
- cholera
- food poisoning
- leptospirosis
- malaria
- meningitis
- ophthalmia neonatorum
- rabies
- viral haemorrhagic fever

Index